D1832768

CHILD LABOUR

CHILD LABOUR
(Volume—I)

GOPAL BHARGAVA

Publications

KALPAZ PUBLICATIONS

DELHI–110052

CHILD LABOUR
(Sociology)

Rs. 1800 (Set)
Rs. 900 (Each Volume)

© Gopal Bhargava

ISBN: 81-7835-200-1 (Set)
ISBN: 81-7835-241-9 (Vol. I)

All rights reserved. No part of this book may be reproduced in any manner without written permission.

Published in 2003 in India by
Kalpaz Publications
C–30, Satyawati Nagar
Delhi–110052
E-mail: kalpaz@hotmail.com

Laser Typesetting at: Varsha Graphics, Delhi
Printed at: Mehra Offset Press, Delhi

Contents

Preface

The concept of 'child' may mean different things in different societies and at different times. In the context of child labour, a working definition of 'child' may be a person below the internationally agreed age limit of 15 years. However, different countries have different basic minimum age of employment. The economic exploitation of children has always been an area of concern in the world over. In every country, rich or poor, it is the nature of the work children do that determines whether or not they are harmed by it—not the plain fact of their working.

The number of working children is increasing from year to year. Some reasons are economic situation of their family, lack of employment opportunities for the adult member, and the preference of the employers to hire children to save on production costs. The child loses all the pleasures of life and potential of growth and development. There is worldwide awareness and laws have been enacted to prohibit children from being employed. Illegal recruitment of children still continues. There is also a great scope for exploitation and abuse of child. The social workers and activists from the trade unions are finding it difficult to help the child because of the existing legislations and other social factors. Such workers do not get proper empirically verified research data on the nature, causes and conditions of child labour, on one side, and feelings and aspirations of the children on the other.

The Minimum Age Convention, 1973 (No. 138) is a landmark achievement in the struggle against child labour. Today, a large number of both industrialised and developing countries have adopted child labour legislation that, on the whole, is progressive and reasonably close to international standards. From the outset, child labour reforms and the ILO placed top priority on controlling child labour in factories and other medium-sized or large enterprises which are often referred to as "The formal sector" At the international level, ILO is playing a leading role to eliminate child labour together with UNICEF, UNDP, UNFPA, UNESCO, WHO and World Bank.

This book gives an overview of the nature and extent of the problem of child labour and the consequences for the victims. It highlights initiatives that are yielding encouraging results in preventing this scourge, as well as in rescuing and rehabilitating bonded children. It suggests ways to expand and accelerate these initiatives by linking them more directly with national programmes and international mechanisms specifically designed to combat child labour.

Editor

1

Introduction

Child labour is a harsh reality, fostered by socio-economic and historical compulsions. It is believed that poverty, unemployment, population growth and illiteracy are the main reasons for malady and that their redress is a prerequisite for eliminating child servitude. It should be noted that the growth rate of the population is much higher among those communities in which unemployment is rampant. Similarly, there exists a correlation between illiteracy and child servitude. In the areas where there are more job opportunities for children, the dropout rate in schools is extremely high.

Many governments, especially in the developing world, lack an adequate system for obtaining accurate data on child labour. Moreover, they are reluctant to document activities which are often illegal under their domestic laws, violate international labour standards, and are perceived by many as a serious failure in their public policy. Nevertheless, the International Labour Organization has estimated the total number of child workers to be between 100-200 million.

According to the ILO, more than 95 percent of all child workers live in developing countries. As the world's most populous region, Asia accounts for more than 50 percent of child labourers. However, Africa has the highest percentage of children working, roughly one in three. In Latin America, an estimated 15 to 20 percent of all children work.

Child workers are found in a wide range of economic activities. The largest numbers work in family-based agriculture, in services (domestic servants, restaurants, and street vending), prostitution, and in small-scale manufacturing (carpets, garments, furniture, etc.). Most children work in the informal economy, which is generally not regulated by national law, rather than in the formal economy, although subcontracting in such industries as garments, shoes, and carpets often makes a distinction between formal and informal difficult to determine.

Only a very small percentage of all child workers, probably less than five percent, are employed in export industries in manufacturing and mining. And they are not commonly found in large enterprises; but rather in small and medium-sized firms and in neighborhood and home settings. Those export industries which most commonly employ children include garments, carpets, shoes, small-scale mining, gem-polishing, food-processing, leather tanning, and furniture. In some cases, government polices to promote exports of low-skilled, labour intensive products, such as garments and carpets, may have resulted in an increase in the demand and use of child labour. Without strong international pressure and corresponding international assistance, child labour is likely to continue.

Quantifying the extent of child labour in a particular export industry in a particular country can seldom be done with specificity. Complex subcontracting arrangements with layers of middlemen between the exporter and the primary production unit frequently hide or at least disguise the use of child labour. Further complicating any serious analysis is the fact that in some industries, for example in the garment and shoe industries, parts fabricated by children in one country are sent to a second country for assembly before being exported to the United States. Although these flows are no doubt significant and merit further investigation, tracing them in this study was beyond current resources and capabilities.

There is a consensus among experts that child workers are generally less demanding, more obedient, and less likely to object to their treatment or conditions of work. They can easily be taken advantage of and more often than not are. The great majority work long hours for substandard wages under unhealthful conditions. They have few if any legal rights, can be fired without recourse, and are often abused. While a few may be relatively well off compared with their peers, almost all are deprived of an adequate education and options for future work. They also may face exploitation by adult co-workers who force children to take on some of their tasks.

The reasons why children work are many and often complex. Those seeking to explain the use of child labour frequently point to traditional patterns of economic life and maintain that child labour is a time-honored and inevitable fact of life. They view poverty and survival as the driving forces and can envisage a significant reduction in child labour only in the context of industrialization and rapid economic development. Advocates for children's rights and other expert observers often challenge this analysis as too simplistic. They note that economic and social conditions vary from region to region and country to country. They argue that while poverty may be one very important contributing factor, other factors must also be taken into consideration.

Economic Self-Interest—Factory owners who overwork, underpay, and otherwise take advantage of vulnerable child workers. Public Indifference—Politicians, media, non-governmental organizations, and other opinion makers who collectively treat child labour as a non-issue. Public Policy—Inadequate resources devoted to primary education and export promotion policies that support firms and industries without regard to their impact on child labour. Government Inadequacies—Labour inspectorates that lack authority, expertise, numbers, and accountability.

Government Corruption—Government officials who not only condone but in many cases personally benefit from child labour. Societal Prejudice—Majority groups which consider child labour among less privileged groups part of the natural order. In summary, children work for a variety of reasons. Some work simply to survive. Others, in the absence of free and compulsory schooling, lack a meaningful educational alternative. Tragically too many children—those in bonded labour—work to repay debts incurred by their parents. Still others are kidnapped, or recruited by unscrupulous agents to work away from home as a source of cheap labour in many industries. Nonetheless, most apologists for child labour cite poverty as the cause. However, the amount of money earned by most child workers is generally a small contribution to the family income. Although children work because they are victims of poverty, by working instead of being educated, they tend to perpetuate the cycle of poverty. Governments, Nongovernmental Organizations, International Organizations Governmental responses to the problem of child labour vary as greatly as do the industries in which children work. Some governments enact exemplary laws abolishing or at least regulating child labour.

Others create a maze of regulatory schemes governing the employment of children fraught with loopholes and exceptions, too confusing to navigate, or with no intent they be enforced. There are governments which deny the existence of child labour and thus lack any initiatives to curtail the exploitation of child workers. There generally are no labour force statistics on economically active children under the age of 12, since almost everywhere this is illegal activity.

Too many governments contend that they lack the financial and other resources to successfully battle the exploitation of child labour. It can be said, however, that many lack the political will to enforce child labour laws, train labour inspectors, and implement health and safety regulations. Even in the area of compulsory primary education, where the relationship between the strength of the educational system and the lower levels of economic exploitation of children is commonly accepted, governments often fail. In such cases, non-governmental organizations with much fewer resources, attempt to fill the gap.

On the other hand, a number of governments are cooperating with international organizations such as UNICEF and the ILO to establish plans of action to combat child labour. In certain cases, this includes conducting national surveys on child labour, establishing more schools and non-formal education programs for children, and publicizing the hazards of child labour.

There are critics who caution that governmental agreements with international organizations to develop anti-child labour programs use this relationship to deflect attention from the child labour situation in their countries. Nevertheless, cooperative programs with international organizations as well as local labour or non-governmental organizations represent progress. The Department of Labour has also learned of projects between Labour Ministries and members of the business community to set up day care centers, schools and health facilities for child workers. The number of working children is increasing from year to year. Some reasons are economic situation of their family, lack of employment opportunities for the adult member, and the preference of the employers to hire children to save on production costs. The child loses all the pleasures of life and potentials of growth and development. There is worldwide awareness and laws have been enacted to prohibit children from being employed.

Illegal recruitment of children still continues. There is also a great scope for exploitation and abuse of child. The social workers and activists from the trade unions are finding it difficult to help the child because of the existing legislations and other social factors. Such workers do not get proper empirically verified research data on the nature, causes and conditions of child labour, on one side, and feelings and aspirations of the children on the other. A survey of the urban working children was conducted in 1984-85 by the Institute for Cultural Research and Action, Bangalore. This became the basis for drafting Child Labour Bill, 1985. Besides, the study also helped working children to acquire skills, knowledge and training so as to become productive workers. The findings of this survey along with a blueprint for elimination of child labour in the long run are presented.

Problem of child labour at the macro-level with reference to India, methodology of the study giving context to the survey, profiles of child workers and their families, employment and working conditions, wages and income, educational and career interests of the working children, the urban working children and the concerns for the working children are presented.

As children always participated in economic activities, their workplace was an extension of home and children were not given hazardous tasks. However, with the advent of industrialisation, labour now became a marketable commodity. If a family cannot afford to feed its children, that is not a problem relating to labour, but it may lead to a child being sent out, or even sold, to supplement the family income. Or it may be a cause of a child not being provided with education. That may not necessarily be rectified even if the child is not at work, but it is less likely to be rectified if the child is working every waking hour. If a child is being abused or ill-treated, it does not follow that the offender is the employer, but much of the abuse and ill-treatment of which we know is by employers.

In 1919, at its first session, the International Labour Organisation (ILO) adopted the Minimum Age Convention, providing that in industry there should be no employment of those under the age of 14. But industry, of course, touched only the fringes of the problem. There has been a subsequent total of 14 ILO conventions on the subject of child labour. The Minimum Age Convention of 1973 extended the prohibition to all child labour. It provided that no child should be in full-time employment under the age within that system of completing compulsory schooling, and in no case under the age of 15. Between 13 and 15, a child might be employed on light work, provided that it was not such as to prejudice his or her attendance at school or training. And the Convention provides that, up to the age of 18, no one is to be employed in work likely to jeopardise his or her health, safety or morals. In 1981, the UN estimated that 145 million children in the world under the age of 14 were in employment, mostly full-time. The ILO estimates that the highest rates of child labour are in Africa. But the degree of suffering among employed children is probably greater in Asia. The Bonded Labour Liberation Front of India, in 1989, convened the South-East Asia Seminar on Child Servitude. It was attended by 60 delegates from five countries in the region. Governments were not represented, but there was an ILO delegate, and a number of Human Rights workers, academics and judges. They were able to collate a great deal of evidence. What was unique is that they brought along a number of children to give their own evidence. That was no easy task. There was an element of risk both for workers and for children. The reasons which lead to child employment vary substantially with local conditions and local cultures. Where a family simply cannot afford to keep a child at home, so he or she is put out to earn. It may be at a wage, or the father may be employed, and simply take along his family to help, in order to maximise his earnings. The earnings are then paid to the father. The employer may then have no record of an individual child, a situation which has advantages in the unlikely event of an inspector asking questions. But even if no records exist, a child who tries to escape may discover that is the employer's business The child may live at home, or in accommodation provided by the employer. There are children whose families cannot afford to keep them at home, so realise whatever financial value they may have on the market. The parents may be told that the child can be adopted, where it can have a better life. Daughters may be married off as children. A bride price is paid, and the child then enters the household of the new family to do whatever work, in whatever conditions, they decide.

In many regions of Asia, poor people earn just enough to keep themselves and their families. There is nothing over to put by for emergencies. But occasions arise when a substantial sum is needed. Social conventions may require that when a child is married, the family provides a wedding feast. They may need to provide a dowry for a daughter. Even if the family is part of a community which has no status in the eyes of the more privileged majority, they need to hold up their heads within their own community. But the need to borrow money does not always arise from maintaining status. Often, there is simply not enough money or produce to keep the family through the monsoon season. Either way, a father may have to go to the local landowner, or to someone with resources and ask for a loan. And the condition may be that he must work for the creditor until the loan is repaid. Then the problems begin. The debtor has to accept whatever wage is on offer. He cannot now work his own piece of ground so effectively, and a substantial part of his remuneration is deducted to repay the debt. But the interest rate may be very high, so that frequently he is working simply to pay off the interest, leaving the debt undiminished. Often, indeed, the debt continues to increase. The debtor is probably illiterate and in any event is not given an account book, so he has to rely on what the creditor tells him. He may then have to borrow further and one of the children will be given in bond for the debt. The child, after all, is the parent's property, and the transaction is like pawning a chattel. The child works without any wages and must continue to work for the creditor until the debt is paid. But frequently, it is never paid. An unscrupulous creditor will make deductions for food or for shelter, whatever food or shelter may have been provided, or for damage or breakages, and the debt continues to grow. The debt does not cease with the death of the father, so the child may be in bondage for the remainder of its life. And if a debtor dies, leaving a debt, the debt devolves on the children, so that many children are born into bondage, a bondage which they never escape from birth until death. There are families who have been in slavery for generations because of a debt incurred by a remote ancestor. In most Asian countries debt bondage is no longer lawful. In India, in particular, a series of statutes forbids it, but the victims do not know about them. In many areas, officials are not sympathetic with the debtors.

There are those who devote themselves to enforcing the law or improving conditions, and a number of organisations now follow in the footsteps of the Bonded Labour Liberation Front, but for all we know to the contrary, there are families falling into debt-bondage as quickly as others are being released. A survey of some of the industries where bonded labour applies are described below. Most Indian handmade carpets are produced in the Mirzapur carpet industry. The industry employs some hundred thousand children, many of whom serve as bonded labourers or are simply kidnapped. The Bonded Labour Liberation Front of India discovered in 1984 that 32 children aged 6 to 14, were employed by the same loom-owner. They were brought before the Supreme Court and the judge was horrified on hearing the evidence. He ordered their release and exercising a power which is available to the Supreme Court in India, he appointed a commissioner to make a study. The case was taken up by the media and debated in the Human Rights Commission. Many more children were released, but there is still far to go. If children are not available as bonded labourers, they are frequently replaced by simply kidnapping others. The government quickly realised that there was little purpose in ordering the release of children unless they had somewhere to go, some way of earning a living, and some training. Money was set aside for this purpose, but little seems to have reached those for whom it was intended. In one instance, an eight-year-old boy was given his release certificate, plus a total of Rs. 650. His employer simply seized Rs. 500. And when his parents came to collect him, the employer demanded Rs. 1,300 which he said he had spent on the boy's training. The parents could not pay and did not know where to go for advice. The owner simply sold the boy to someone else. Enforcement is so relaxed that some loom-owners are alleged to have claimed that a child is working in unlawful debt bondage when it is not, because in that way they get their hands on some of the rehabilitation money. There is now in India a carpet manufacturing industry a Child Labour Group, which arranges for their processes to be inspected and a certificate issued that carpets are produced in accordance with good practice. Many of the larger exporters are joining. Arrangements are under way for some European importers to look for those certificates before purchasing. In India another industry which employs a substantial number of children under the bonded labour system is stone quarrying, particularly in the outskirts of Delhi. In November 1988, the Bonded Labour Liberation Front learned of 48 people, including 15 children, working as bonded labourers, all in one village. They secured their release. Their health had suffered from the dust, but it was said that the worst effects were psychological. Most of them were totally apathetic about their condition. All resistance had been drained from them. The brick kiln industry in Pakistan absorbs many bonded labourers. It has been estimated that some two million families in Pakistan are still subject to bonded labour. In 1992, the Government of Pakistan legislated against bonded labour. But the problem, as in India, remains one of enforcement. As long ago as 1988, on a complaint sponsored by the Bonded Labour Liberation Front of Pakistan, the Supreme Court held that the practice in the brick kiln industry was unconstitutional and ordered the release of the victim.

The South Asian cities provide facilities for paedophiles. Regularly, children arrive in large numbers at the main railway station, where they have been brought by kidnappers or, more usually, they have simply come to the city to find a living, waiting at the station are people known as fishermen, who take control of them and sell them on to employers looking for cheap labour. The attractive ones are sold to brothels, to satisfy the needs of paedophiles, and there they remain as slaves, often until they die of disease, or simply of exhaustion. Some years ago, a group was formed in Thailand to campaign against those practices. They formed End Child Prostitution in Asian Tourism

(ECPAT). They addressed themselves to tour operators, to airlines and to governments, hoping to persuade governments to take extraterritorial jurisdiction to try offences by European tourists in Asia. In major cities in Europe and in America, street children are organised in gangs by criminals, who send them out to pick pockets, burgle houses and generally organise them. Many of them from poverty-stricken families in Eastern Europe, particularly the gypsy population of the Balkans, are taken to other countries for this purpose. In some areas of South America, street children are going into business on their own, for example, distributing drugs There may be a gang with its own territory, and sometimes there are territorial wars between rival gangs, as in Chicago in the 1930s. But the gangs are gangs of children, and there are cases of children being murdered by other children. Children on the streets are sometimes seen as a nuisance, or worse. Their escapades evoke anger and sometimes they develop a running feud with the police. Usually, the police limit their reaction within acceptable bounds, but there is at least one example in Brazil where the police reaction went over the top. There is nothing new in campaigners seeking to draw attention to the suffering of children from poor backgrounds.

At the end of the First World War, in Europe, devastated by war, children were the first victims. The movement 'Save the Children', organised relief and campaign for more structured protection. In 1923, 'Save the Children' drafted the Declaration of Geneva. The five principles set out by the Declaration are the following: (i) The child must be have the means requisite for its normal development, both material and spiritually; (ii) The child that is hungry must be fed, the child that is sick must be nursed, the child that is backward must be helped, the delinquent child must be reclaimed and the orphan and the waif must be sheltered and succoured; (iii) The child must be the first to receive relief in times of distress; (iv) The child must be put in a position to earn a livelihood and must be protected against any form of exploitation; (v) The child must be brought up in the consciousness that its talents must be devoted to service of its fellowmen.

In 1956, the UN adopted the Supplementary Convention on the Abolition of Slavery, providing, *inter alia*, that states should abolish the practice of the delivering a child by its parents to another person with a view to the exploitation of his labour. In 1959, the UN adopted a further declaration on the rights of the child. It set out ten principles. For the first time, it addressed the question of discrimination and specifically provided that every child should enjoy all the rights set out in the declaration, without discrimination on grounds of race, colour, sex or creed. It provided that every child should be given facilities to develop physically, mentally, morally, spiritually and socially, and that the best interests of the child should he paramount. This introduced an important principle, which has subsequently been developed. The Declaration proceeded to set out particular rights, such as a health care education, protection from cruelty, recreation and appropriate treatment for the handicapped. In the 1970s, there was a discussion about a possible Convention which could identify with the obligations of governments, which would have the force of law and which at least might make provision for monitoring the efforts which governments were making to implement it.

The year 1979 was declared by the United Nations to be the International Year of the Child. In the course of the year the Polish Government proposed that they should begin work on a Convention. The UN Human Rights Commission established a working group to draft a Convention. They set themselves the objective of having the Convention approved by the General Assembly within ten years. If that appears a somewhat relaxed view of urgency, it must be seen in the context of the way in which the UN works. National delegations have to obtain instructions from their governments, and within governments, each department insists on its input. Each government has a different idea of the priorities. Some will be anxious to include a particular provision which others will find embarrassing, because of some domestic problem. There will be horse-trading, adjournments for consultation, debates and further private discussion.

In 1989, the General Assembly adopted unanimously the new Convention consisting of 54 articles. A child is defined as a human being below the age 18. Four principles are worth singling out. Firstly, the rights set out in the Convention are to apply without discrimination of any kind, in respect of race, sex, religion, ethnic or social origins, disability or other status. Thus the Convention takes in other areas of work which have been carried out on human rights. Secondly, the obligation is upon states to ensure that the rights are implemented. And the obligation applies to ever child within the jurisdiction and thus not only to the state's own citizens. Thirdly, the primary consideration should be in it has the best interests of the child. And to ensure that the child's best interests are not simply as interpreted by a provision that due weight should be given to the views of the child, of course in accordance with the age and maturity of the child. Indeed, it is specifically provided that the child should have the right freely to express its views. The fourth provision has proved not wholly uncontroversial. First, it emphasises the distinction between the interests of the child and that of the parents. Secondly, children have a right not simply to be protected but to be heard. This may impose some burden on our patience and our common sense. There were suggestions that the Convention should be called 'A Convention for the Protection of Children'. To speak of the rights of a child appears to entail that the child should be able to initiate some process for their enforcement. We protect ancient buildings, but we do not speak of their having rights. There are then a series of articles setting out substantive rights. There are articles on basic needs, food, health care, education, recreation and play. There are articles relating to protection, from child labour, drug abuse, sexual exploitation, trafficking and abduction. There are articles on civil rights, freedom of expression, freedom of thought, conscience and religion, protection of privacy, access to appropriate information and protection of justice and dignity within the penal system. There are three articles on what may be called enforcement. Article 43 establishes a Committee on the Rights of the Child, consisting of ten experts, elected by the states parties. States undertake to submit to the Committee reports on the measures taken to give effect to the rights in the Convention. The first report is to be within two years of the date when the state ratifies, and thereafter every five years. Article 49 provides that the Convention should enter into force when there have been twenty ratifications or accessions. This was achieved in September 1990. In the same month, presidents and prime ministers from 70 countries gathered at the World Summit for Children in New York, and agreed on a Plan of Action for Children, endorsed by 159 states. The intention was to undertake progressive implementation of the rights in the Convention. It declared that children should have the first call on resources And it set out targets for the year 2000, particularly relating to the elimination of certain diseases. It requires each state to prepare a National Plan of Action, including target dates and anticipated resource requirements.

In 1988, United Nations International Child's Emergency Fund (UNICEF) established the Children's Centre in Florence to advise on child rights, and to encourage initiatives by publication of information and thinkpieces. At the Human Rights Summit in Vienna in June 1993, children were high on the agenda. Stephen Lewis, the Special Representative of UNICEF's Executive Director, spoke of children as the cutting edge of human rights. We can narrow the disparities between the privileged and the underprivileged, he explained, by what he called a jump start early in people's lives. So the problems of children in Mirzapur, in Rio de Janeiro, and in Dominica are very much a topic of discussion among diplomats and politicians and lawyers. But human rights stand or fall not in conference rooms, but in streets and cellars. We cannot eliminate the problems instantly like switching off a light. People have to work at it. None the less, it concentrates the minds of governments to know that the world is asking questions. Even the most indifferent of governments likes to be loved in international circles. What is important is that the questions should keep coming. Initiatives and impetus for human rights have always come principally from the NGOs. That is not to say that governments are always hostile to Human Rights, or even totally, indifferent. Within governments there are those who care about human rights, either generally or in specific areas. But the whole scheme of international human rights enforcement is to place on governments the responsibility for ensuring that the standards are met in their respective countries, a consequence of the fact that the UN is orientated towards nation-states, and very much subject to the assertion of national sovereignty. National governments would prefer enforcing human rights themselves to having others asking questions within their boundaries. So it is not surprising that governments are less than enthusiastic to make a rod for their own backs. It was principally NGOs who made the running in relation to children's rights before, during and after the Convention process. And implementation will depend largely on the pressure which they can maintain. There is an NGO Group on the Rights of the Child, to help maintain the impetus. It is based in Geneva, at the premises of Care of Children International. It works closely with NGOs like Anti-Slavery International, maintaining pressure at the UN Sub-commission on minorities and similar international bodies.

After the 1945, the lives of children in industrialised countries improved substantially. Between 1950 and 1990, European countries achieved the fastest reduction in infant mortality ever recorded. But in the last 15 years there has been a growing number of problems relating to children. In Europe, a high proportion of children live in families with low incomes, but the figures must be adjusted to take account of redistributive taxation and social security policies. In Germany, 2.8 per cent of children can be said to be living in poverty, in France 4.6 per cent, in the UK 7.4 per cent, and in the US 20 per cent. There are further problems with families who must rely increasingly on the incomes of both parents, with consequently less time to spend caring for children, playing with them or teaching them. And this appears to be particularly true in the US and the UK. They are living with what Dr. Sylvia Ann Hewlett in her study *Child Neglect in Rich Nations* published by UNICEF, calls the cult of the workaholic. There is a disturbing body of research revealing what is possibly obvious that the more time children are left on their own, the more likely they are to develop behavioural problems, such as drug abuse. In UK, children in employment are protected by a formidable body of legal provisions, so many that Caroline Moorhead, who wrote a booklet on the subject for Anti-Slavery International, described them as a patchwork of laws, some new, some still drawing heavily on provisions passed in the last century. The Gulbenkian Foundation established the Children's Rights Development Unit in March 1992 to initiate a national agenda for monitoring and implementing the Convention, article by article, and promoting awareness of its provisions. Gulbenkian have also published a proposal by Martin Rosenbaum and Peter Newell for the appointment of a Children's Rights Commissioner along the lines of the Health Service Ombudsman and the Local Government Ombudsman. The UK duly ratified the Convention on 16 December 1991, subject to six reservations or declarations.

i) It interprets the Convention as applicable only following a live birth, so that it leaves open questions about abortion.

ii) There is some limitation on the construction of the word 'parents' to conform with UK law.

iii) The government will be bound by the provisions only so far as they are not in conflict with existing provisions on the right to remain in the UK.

iv) A child is not to be construed for all employment purposes as a person under 18. British law recognises young people as a separate category with different rights and obligations.

v) While the Convention requires that young offenders should not be detained with adults, the UK provides that they shall be subject to facilities being available, and to cases where it may be thought beneficial to detain them with adults.

vi) The right to legal representation set out in the Convention is not to apply to children's hearings in Scotland.

Causes of Child Slavery

Public opinion has a tendency to use the term "slavery" when speaking of particularly harsh and abhorrent work or working conditions of children. This dilutes the meaning of the word. In reality there exists a fundamental difference between labour and slavery: labour is an activity, slavery is a status. Labour is a visible activity, slavery is an invisible situation. The ILO committee of experts on the application of conventions and recommendations considers this question of invisibility as "a key issue in dealing with the problem of bonded labour". There are two types of invisibility. One is related to the location where children are kept or where access to child slaves is difficult. They are usually hidden, locked away in small workshops, in remote quarries, on building sites and agricultural estates, in mobile enterprises, or in domestic work where entry is often prohibited because the workplace is private property. The other type concerns the status of the child workers in relation to their employers.

The children are the property of their employer and are subject to physical and psychological violence. Fearing repression, bonded child workers generally remain silent. To keep bonded children in their service, the proprietors also need the silence of the public. They therefore usually see to it that all contact between the workers and possible investigators is limited. Such children may be given supplementary surveillance, which is at the same time part of the machinery of recruitment and control of the slaves, namely, the intermediaries. The recruiters visit the most poverty-stricken villages or slums, especially in periods of financial difficulty. A loan may be proposed to the family by attracting them with the possibility of reimbursement through the labour of one of their children. The recruiters, acting, for example, on behalf of an enterprise active in mining or forest exploitation, may offer to pay the travel expenses to the place of work, to be reimbursed later. Sometimes the children are taken away without payment of any advance, merely with the promise of feeding them and letting them acquire some skills in a particular trade. The greater the distance between the family and the place of work, the more the children will have difficulty in fleeing or being rescued by their family. Not all children in bondage are automatically taken hundreds of kilometres away from home. Many of them often live with their parents at the workplace. There are escorts who are charged with putting the children on a train or truck and ensuring that they arrive at the destination. A child in bondage is an income asset and the proprietor usually requires the uninterrupted physical presence of the child at the workplace. The more child or adult workers there are in bondage on a site, the more the surveillance of the workers will be strict and organised. The surveyors' task is to prevent attempts to escape or have communication with the outside world. It is difficult to assess the extent of child bondage because employers hide the illegal employment of children by physical restraints on their movement and other means of coercion. There are also problems of defining what constitutes bondage.

In India, the Gandhi Peace Foundation, in collaboration with the National Labour Institute, conducted a study in 1981 covering the agricultural sector in 10 out of 21 states in the country and arrived at a figure of 2.6 million bonded labourers. In the States of Orissa and Andhra Pradesh, one out of every five labourers was found to be bonded. The bonded labourers constituted eight per cent of total labourers in India. More than half (54 per cent) of the families were landless; 46 per cent were homeless and lived in the master's premises and 56 per cent were indebted to their masters. Another survey by a human rights organisation found that 3.3 per cent of Kamaiyas had been working in this way for four generations, 21.63 per cent for three generations and 28 per cent for two generations.

While trafficking in children within countries in South-east Asia has been a widespread phenomenon for some time, there is increasing evidence in recent years of children being trafficked across national borders because of the opening of frontiers and as a result of industrialisation and globalisation. Previously remote, numerous areas are now exposed to rapid social changes. This has disrupted traditional ways of life and made the population especially vulnerable to the problem of child trafficking. There exist a number of well-established trafficking routes in the Mekong sub- region. Thailand is the main receiving country where many victims are forced into prostitution and other exploitative forms of work. Most trafficking takes place over land and there are well-known gateways from each country. Cambodia and Yunnan province in China are in addition to being sending countries, also on the receiving end. Vietnamese children are being trafficked to Cambodia for prostitution and significant numbers of ethnic minorities from North Vietnam and Myanmar are trafficked under the disguise of marriage to become domestic workers, often without pay. A considerable number of them had been either forcefully abducted or tricked into going to India and subsequently sold to brothels. In addition to the economic pressure, cultural practices among certain ethnic groups also contribute to the trafficking of girls in Nepal.

In Bangladesh, the government estimates that a few thousand women and children have been victims of trafficking for labour, including prostitution, and for other purposes in South Asian and Middle Eastern countries. There have been reports of boatloads of children being halted by authorities along coastlines on their way to Central Africa. Some of these children end up in households as unpaid child labour known as "house helps", while others end up in prostitution. Children also leave their homes and cross borders into other countries to work as domestic helpers and market traders.

The international community has made the immediate suppression of child slavery one of its major priorities. The principal actors are the ILO, the United Nations and international NGOs. Some international efforts to end child slavery are:

— International legal instruments of the ILO and the United Nation's provide the legal framework for the abolition of all forms of child slavery and practices similar to slavery.

— International organisations cooperate to tackle the problem. For example, in 1992, the ILO, in collaboration with the United Nations Centre for Human Rights, organised the Asian Regional Seminar on Children in Bondage in Pakistan.

— The ILO Committee of Experts raises the issue of bonded labour—including child bondage—every year, and keeps the issue alive on the agenda of governments.

— The ILO's International Programme on the Elimination of Child Labour (IPEC) places a high priority on child bondage and supports action programmes to combat the practice in different countries.

— The United Nations Working Group on Contemporary Forms of Slavery, set up in 1974, reviews the reports and testimonies of NGOs on child bondage every year.

— International NGOs increasingly accord special attention to child labour and mobilise public opinion. Anti-Slavery International acts as coordinator for the NGO subgroup on child labour with the Committee on the rights of the child.

One of the most widely ratified International Labour Organisation (ILO) Conventions is the Forced Labour Convention, 1930, which requires ratifying states to suppress the use of forced or compulsory labour. It defines the term as "work or service which is exacted from any person under the menace of any penalty and for which the said person has not offered himself voluntarily"—other than in certain excepted circumstances, for example, the performance of military service, and emergencies such as wars, fires, earthquakes and so on. It imposes an obligation on the ratifying state to punish the exaction of forced or compulsory labour as a penal offence and to ensure that penalties are strictly enforced. Convention No. 29 is an important instrument to promote government action in countries where child bondage exists. Since it applies to everyone, whatever age, it protects children from forced or compulsory labour and is applicable to children in bondage and their exploitation in prostitution and pornography. Indeed, the committee of experts and the Conference Committee on the Application of Standards have been dealing extensively with the problem of the forced or compulsory labour of children in relation to the application of the Convention by several member states. The committee of experts has stated on several occasions that the forced labour exploitation of children is one of the worst forms of forced labour, which must be fought energetically and punished severely.

Under the ILO's Constitution, ratifying members must report to the ILO on measures taken to implement the Convention. Such information is often supplemented by reports from ILO constituents, which might forward reports from NGOs or others concerned. Moreover, reports to the United Nations Working Group on contemporary forms of slavery are also considered by the Committee of Experts. The new worst forms of Child Labour Convention, 1999, and its accompanying recommendation, provide additional and powerful weapons for the elimination of all forms of child slavery. Adopted by the International Labour Conference in 1999, the Convention applies to all children under the age of 18 and obliges member-states to act immediately against the worst forms of child labour, which include slavery and practices similar to slavery—such as the sale and trafficking of children, debt bondage and serfdom, forced or compulsory labour, including forced recruitment for armed conflicts—and the use of children in prostitution, pornography and illicit activities, in particular the production and trafficking of drugs. The Convention also requires adequate penalties and encourages member states to assist one another through international cooperation or assistance to combat the worst forms of child labour. Ratifying states are required to adopt programmes of action to eliminate the worst forms of child labour. These programmes are to include specific measures to prevent children from being exploited in forced labour and to rehabilitate and integrate them once they are removed from such exploitation. Thus, in addition to providing for a clear legal prohibition of child slavery, the new Convention is oriented towards immediate and effective action to assist the children concerned. In 1998 the International Labour Conference adopted the ILO Declaration on Fundamental Principles and Rights at work, which reaffirms the commitment of the ILO's member-states to promote fundamental labour rights, whether or not they have ratified the relevant conventions. The elimination of all forms of forced or compulsory labour and the abolition of child labour figure prominently among these rights.

Consistent with the new convention and the declaration, International Programme on the Elimination of Child Labour (IPEC) gives top priority to action which will bring an end to the worst forms of child labour, such as slavery and similar practices, the exploitation of children in prostitution, pornography and for illicit purposes. In addition, IPEC gives special attention to children who are particularly vulnerable and those who are very young and girls.

Slavery is defined as "the status or condition of a person over whom any or all of the powers attaching to the right of ownership are exercised". In 1956, a Supplementary Convention on the Abolition of Slavery applied in particular to debt bondage and serfdom. It defines debt bondage as "the status or condition arising from a pledge by a debtor of his personal services or those of a person under his control as security for a debt, if the value of those services as reasonably assessed is not applied towards the liquidation of the debt or the length and nature of those services are not respectively limited and defined". The Supplementary Convention on the Abolition of Slavery (1956) was inspired by the Universal Declaration of Human Rights, adopted in 1948, which proclaimed that "no one shall be held in slavery or servitude; slavery and the slave trade shall be prohibited in all their forms".

The International Covenant of Civil and Political Rights, adopted in 1966, echoes the assertion of the same rights. It states that "no one shall be held in slavery; slavery and the slave trade in all their forms shall be prohibited...," "no one shall be held in servitude"; and "no one shall be required to perform forced or compulsory labour".

The United Nations Convention on the rights of the child adopted in 1989, contains specific provisions against various forms of child exploitation. Article 32 of the Convention provides for the protection of the child from economic exploitation and from performing any work which is likely to be hazardous or to interfere with the child's education, or to be harmful to the child's health or physical, mental, spiritual, moral or social development. Article 34 requires the state to protect the child from all forms of sexual exploitation and sexual abuse and to take appropriate national, bilateral and multilateral measures. Article 35 imposes a similar obligation on the state concerning abduction, sale or trafficking in children. Article 36 provides for the protection of the child from all forms of exploitation prejudicial to any aspect of the child's welfare.

The constitutions of most countries contain provisions relating to fundamental rights which include injunctions that "no person shall be held in slavery, or servitude", and "no person shall be required to perform forced or compulsory labour" or to the effect that no person shall be compelled to perform work or render personal services without his or her full consent and/or without fair compensation. Some constitutions deal with forced labour under general provisions on the right to work, stipulating that everyone has the right to freedom of labour and that involuntary labour is prohibited, or that work is an obligation for every citizen but that no one may be unlawfully forced into a specific occupation.

The Constitution of India prohibits a form of forced labour known as Begar, which is "labour or service exacted by government or a person in power, without remuneration". Honduras appears to be the only country in which the Constitution itself deals specifically with children in bondage: "every child must be protected against every form of abandonment, cruelty and exploitation. No child shall be the object of any type of bondage." Penalties are provided for by law for those who violate the provision. Many countries devote a section of their labour legislation to forced or compulsory labour. Definitions are often in conformity with the ILO's Forced Labour Convention, 1930.

In about half the countries where the prohibition of forced labour is provided for in general labour legislation, there are specific penalties for the illegal exaction of work or any form of illegal constraint. Labour legislation typically declares that any person who imposes or permits the imposition of forced labour is guilty of an offence and liable to a fine of a certain amount of money and/or to imprisonment for some months or years. For example, in the Republic of Korea a person violating the provisions concerning employment of workers through violence, threats, illegal confinement or any other means of unjustifiable mental or physical restraint "shall be punished by imprisonment for not more than three years or suspension of civil rights for a period of not more than five years". Two noteworthy examples of national legislation outlawing bonded labour are the Bonded Labour System (Abolition) Act, passed in India in 1976 and the Bonded Labour System (Abolition) Act, enacted in 1992 in Pakistan. These statutes represent a real advance in the conception of the problem because they do not only prohibit the bonded labour system, but provide for the rehabilitation of liberated workers and the establishment of broad-based vigilance committees with a mandate to advise and coordinate the implementation of the provisions concerning the identification and rehabilitation of the bonded labourers.

Legislation on slavery and bondage indicates their acceptance of the international standards and sets the goal in the national context. However, these practices persist in many parts of the world, because legislation by itself, even when sincere efforts are made for its implementation, cannot wholly eliminate them. On the other hand, the battle against slavery and bondage cannot be won without legislation.

Principal obstacles to freeing bonded child workers are the hidden character of the problem and powerful vested interests to maintain the status quo. Local authorities are not keen or able to follow rules and regulations set at the national level, citing administrative apathy or complicated legal procedures. Such resistance prevails because servitude is deeply rooted in rural social and economic structure. Reinforcing the lack of political will at the highest places of authority is the apathy engulfing both the victims of servitude, who are not aware of their rights and the general public, who lack information on the human suffering taking place in their country. The few NGOs who actively combat bonded child labour face serious resource limitations and other obstacles. In some countries, these NGOs are considered by the authorities to be engaged in subversive activities. The mistrust sometimes existing between government and NGOs involved with child rights and child labour prevents cooperation between them and hampers efforts by international organisations to support NGO activities in this field.

Preventive action should take place in the legislative, economic, social protection, and educational and advocacy spheres. In countries where bonded child labour exists, legislation should be enacted to deal with the problem:

- In many cases, legislation needs to be revised and provide for precise definitions of the forms of slavery and bondage existing in the country. Slavery must appear as a crime;
- Sanctions that are tough enough to be dissuasive should be provided for;

— The question of the liquidation of existing debts and other obligations must be answered unambiguously;

— Regulations must be established to facilitate the implementation of the law, in particular to ensure rapid action from the judiciary;

— The law must envisage the possibility of special jurisdiction to be able to confront simultaneously a concentrated number of children in bondage at the same site and to safeguard the independence of the tribunals and institutions charged with executing the decisions taken;

— Laws and regulations should also be transmitted swiftly with the appropriate instructions to the local institutions and authorities charged with enforcement;

— Laws and regulations should be communicated to the victims, the offenders and society at large in a manner that is comprehensible to them, for example, in local languages and over the radio, or through meetings if the concerned population groups are illiterate; and

— Legal aid should be placed at the disposal of the child victims' parents to enable them to claim their rights, and special arrangements should be made, where required, to find the parents within a reasonable time-limit if the child is separated from them.

Poverty and social exclusion should be addressed according to the needs of the concerned population groups. Agrarian reforms which provide access to land and incomes, as well as employment-promotion measures and social protection for disadvantaged families can be effective in preventing bondage. In most cases, the bondage of a child is the consequence of an urgent temporary financial need. Providing credit opportunities other than via the employer and the region's dominant landlords, could break the vicious circle and provide an opening for the gradual lessening of dependence. Close to 10,000 institutions providing small loans have been listed in the world and many of them are modelled on the Grameen Bank approach. NGOs with the capacity to adapt appropriate micro-bank models to the local situation and introduce them to communities at risk might be one of the most promising ways of countering bonded labour.

Government and other concerned groups should be encouraged to:

- Launch research on bondage situations and facilitate analysis by organising meetings between experts of complementary disciplines;
- Diffuse information to all segments of society, provoke condemnation of bondage practices and mobilise the entire population;
- Make known to the families at risk their rights and the ways in which they are able to have them respected;
- Increase education on human rights, in particular children's rights;
- Insert in administrative personnel training programmes an introduction to the problem of child slavery and bondage;
- Launch sensitisation programmes in employers' and workers' organisations;

— Provide a specific component on child bondage in the training of labour inspectors and police officers; and

— Set up effective protection for researchers, journalists, social workers and various activists who denounce practices of bondage.

Slave owners simply cannot be treated as employers of children who must be persuaded to cooperate with programmes of action. They are guilty of a crime. A policy of deterrence must be set up and the population informed of this policy. It could include the following elements:

— Provision of sanctions strong enough to serve as both punishment and dissuasion;

— Acceleration of judicial process in regard to bonded child labour; and

— Punishment of all persons and institutions who actively participate in placing a child in bondage, not only the direct employer but equally the recruiters, escorts and surveyors.

The experience of direct action programmes concerning children in bondage, although limited, clearly presents two major lessons: firstly, without action directed towards society in general and slave owners in particular, activities targeting bonded children will have limited results and will not alone suppress the practice of bondage; secondly, support programmes must be organised taking into account that the child is in slavery and not simply at work under harsh conditions. Direct action with bonded children involves three stages: identification, release and rehabilitation.

Identification: Identification means not only physically discovering a child in slavery-type situations, but having the child recognised as such. Slave owners often deny that a state of slavery exists. Possible counter-actions include:

— launching periodic appeals to the population to denounce known cases of slavery;

— Having labour inspectors, police and social workers systematically verify whether children at work in slavery-prone areas are in bondage;

– Informing and sensitising parents so that they will testify about the slavery of their children; and

— Setting up procedures permitting children to express themselves on their situation.

Release: Firstly, the children must be physically taken out of their slave environment. This requires the parents, the child or the workmates to overcome physical barriers and thwart the surveillance of the guards in order to escape, which is often difficult. Outside intervention is therefore usually necessary but cannot be organised by an individual who has no right of entry to private property. Specific solutions could include the creation of special police units and the granting of a legally recognised intervention power to certain special authorities. Secondly, one must ensure that a child who has been freed from bondage is not recaptured by the employer. A very long period of time may elapse before the child is able to be returned to its parents. Often the child is distraught and traumatised by violence.

The slave owners may take advantage of this to regain control of the child. Temporary reception centres must be set up. Since speed of operation is a key factor, emergency procedures must be elaborated enabling the identification and the release of the child to be effected simultaneously. Thirdly, there is no real liberation until the debt which binds the child to the employer has been officially nullified. Such a decision in law assumes the participation of the two parties. As the parents of the child are often paralysed by fear of the employer and by lack of awareness of their rights, free legal aid should be put at their disposal.

Rehabilitation: Rehabilitation means supporting the return of the child to a community. It must respond to two fundamental needs of the liberated child. Firstly, the child must be guaranteed the material needs for survival. It goes without saying that if the economic situation of the family remains unchanged and if the causes which had provoked the bondage persist, the provision of a temporary allowance, for example, would have little effect. Secondly, specialised treatment is needed to repair the psychological damage suffered by the child and to assist the child's reintegration in society.

In Pakistan, a major pilot programme has been launched to prevent and eliminate child bonded labour. It is the first comprehensive programme to address child bonded labour in the country through concerted action by governmental and non-governmental organisations. The programme focuses on direct action with children and their families; strengthening government machinery responsible for law enforcement, social welfare and education at the local, provincial, and national levels; and strengthening capacities of NGOs. In addition, child bonded labour in the production of carpets will be targeted through future action programmes to eliminate child labour. The programme's strategy is to mobilise a broad alliance of governmental andnon-governmental agencies, communities, employers, parents and children in taking joint action against child bonded labour through a three- pronged approach:

— Establishing 18 Community Education and Action (CEA) centres for a selected number of children in specific economic sectors and occupations with a high incidence of child bonded labour; withdrawing a selected number of bonded children from exploitative and hazardous work, and preventing their younger siblings from entering such work, and mobilising communities to prevent child bonded labour;

— Strengthening the capacity of the Directorates of Labour and Welfare to monitor workplaces, to withdraw bonded children and to ensure that these workplaces become and remain free of child bonded labour; and

— Institutional development of other key governmental agencies and selected NGOs to provide an integrated package of support services to ex-bonded child workers, their younger siblings and their families to prevent further child bonded labour through community mobilisation.

A broad-based national task force on prevention of trafficking in children was set up under the Ministry of Women and Social Welfare in Nepal to provide guidance and policy advice for the implementation of action programmes against child trafficking. The Task Force consists of representatives of the concerned government ministries, representatives of the National Planning Commission, the police, and NGOs dealing with the issue. International organisations, such as the ILO and UNICEF, provide technical support to the Task Force.

The Ministry of Women and Social Welfare, in consultation with the National Task Force, has instructed the chairpersons of 19 District Development Committees to set up District Task Forces with themselves as the Chairpersons of the Task Forces, the Chief District Officers as the Vice-Chairpersons, and representatives from the police, social organisations, local NGOs, and District Child Welfare Boards as the members. The District Task Forces will be authorised to play an active role in coordinating district-level activities against trafficking in children and their commercial sexual exploitation; identifying the vulnerable village development committees and communities in the district and assisting in the implementation of suitable programmes in the affected areas. A consultative workshop on the development of the National Plan of Action against trafficking in children and their commercial sexual exploitation was held in Kathmandu from 22 to 24 April 1998. Sixty representatives from governmental and non-governmental organisations, employers' and workers' organisations, representatives of diplomatic missions and United Nations agencies, the police, NGOs and donor organisations participated and identified the following six areas of action to prevent trafficking:

i) policy, research and institutional development;

ii) legislation and enforcement;

iii) awareness creation, advocacy, networking and social mobilisation;

iv) health and education;

v) income and employment generation; and

vi) rescue and reintegration.

Amongst the existing release and rehabilitation programmes for children formerly in bondage, Mukti Ashram, linked to the South Asian Coalition against Child Servitude (SACCS), in a suburb of the Indian capital, New Delhi, merits particular attention. It was created in 1990 and has since rehabilitated close to 1,600 children. One of the successes of this approach is the increased number of children and youths who, after rehabilitation in their communities of origin, have become engaged in the fight against bondage. Most of the children, between the ages of six or seven were lured away or kidnapped from their native villages and taken to workplaces in industries, mines, construction sites and the agricultural sector, hundreds of miles away. The children, who often cannot understand or speak the local dialect are confined to toil day in, day out, without any wages or cash remuneration. Fifteen to 18 hours of work without adequate or proper food, abuse, beatings, isolation, and humiliation are common. The children grow up and accept slavery as their destiny. They are not allowed to change the job or go back home to join their parents or relatives.

Education, recreation, play, fun or even crying for their parents is beyond their imagination. The entire concept of Mukti Ashram has been designed to bring back their lost joy, hope and childhood. When the children are freed they are traumatised, physically sick, and completely broken in heart and soul. They have no idea of good or bad education. It is very difficult to resocialise them in families and villages. They are without any skill, initiative or enthusiasm. SACCS aims to ensure that these victims of slavery become their own liberators and leaders. This task is only possible by and adolescents in the programme. The staff running the

Ashram are freed-bonded labourers and victims of exploitation, particularly those belonging to the lowest castes in India. They have been trained and educated to meet the requirements of the Ashram. Doctors, psychologists and extension workers are given special orientation to work with these children in a participatory manner. The management hierarchy is inverted to bring about a change in the enslaved attitude of the children. For example, the Chairperson and Director are required to clean the latrines, which is normally considered as the most degrading work and normally done by untouchables. It gives a mental jolt to the children observing these unimaginable acts. The Ashram reflects the environment of a village ambience. Learning, playing, physical exercises, cooking, eating, sleeping and all routine activities are done collectively. Special cultural events, religious and traditional festivals are celebrated in a manner that they can learn the new interpretation of such events, the essence of norms and values; and, communal life. The need and advantage of democracy, the entitlement to vote and leadership aspects are taught through plays and songs. Folk culture and the use of local dialects are encouraged to give them a sense of belonging, and enable them to express themselves and gain self-confidence.

Basic literacy, social education and skills training are provided to the children for a period of three to six months. The children are stimulated, to give feedback to the staff and others. Group training and its benefits, chanting slogans, argumentation and oratory skills, initiatives and risk-taking, wall-writing, poster making, effective communication, the handling of money and problem-solving skills are among the learning activities.

The working group on contemporary forms of slavery was established as a permanent monitoring system of the application of the United Nations Conventions on slavery. It meets annually in Geneva and examines all forms of slavery throughout the world. The working group encourages the widest participation possible in its work, inviting all organisations, including NGOs, to present documents, evidence or recommendations. Governments are attentive to the information presented to the working group, whose principal strength lies in its ability to bring to the recognition of the international community situations of slavery or violations of human rights existing in a specific place, and exert pressure on those responsible. Local NGOs and community groups (such as vigilance committees) are often the best placed to be acquainted with child bondage situations. They can participate more actively in the working group by sending written evidence directly or via the NGOs which usually participate in the work of the group, or by going to Geneva to present the evidence themselves during the session of the working group.

The United Nations voluntary trust was created in 1992 and facilitates the participation of NGOs in the sessions of the working group on contemporary forms of slavery by providing support (technical, humanitarian, legal or financial) to groups or persons victimised by slavery. The United Nations committee on the rights of the child is an internationally elected body of independent experts established to examine the progress made by states parties in meeting the obligations of the convention on the rights of the child. The committee examines country reports prepared by the states on the status of their children and the measures taken by them to implement the convention. The Committee accords particular importance to child labour. To improve its assessment of the reports supplied by the governments, the committee invites NGOs to submit comments on the country reports.

In certain countries, NGO coalitions provide the committee with a counter-report on children's rights, if they consider that the government report does not actually reflect reality. In other countries, governments have invited civil society, notably through NGOs, to participate in the elaboration of the report.The NGO group for the convention on the rights of the child facilitates contact between the non-governmental community and the committee on the rights of the child. Defence for children international serves as the secretariat for the group. The NGO meetings take place in Geneva, jointly with the committee's sessions so as to take into account NGOs' views in analysing national reports. A subgroup has been established especially for child labour, for which coordination has been entrusted to anti-slavery international. All NGOs can send documentation directly to the United Nations Committee or through the NGO Group.

Several countries have addressed some aspects of the problem, for example in domestic service, in agriculture and in commercial sexual exploitation. IPEC helps countries develop comprehensive responses to the problem by adopting a series of interventions at local, national, regional and international level. In a country where the practice has been identified, practical steps can be taken to start action programmes. IPEC's focus is on assisting partner organisations at the governmental and non-governmental level to effectively prevent the problem of child trafficking so that the practice will be totally eliminated. Prevention of the problem is the key solution. Once victimised, the children suffer extreme physical, psycho- social and emotional abuse which results in lifelong and often life-threatening consequences. Simultaneously, support is extended to partner organisations to rehabilitate the child victims, not only because they need urgent help, but also because demonstration projects for the victims are a powerful tool to mobilise societies against the worst forms of child labour. A broad policy framework should include a comprehensive national policy and programme of action covering legislative reforms, effective systems to monitor the enforcement of decisions taken by the authorities, prevention, and rehabilitation and socio-economic reintegration programmes for victims through access to basic, relevant education, economic alternatives and awareness-raising among children and families. The following are examples of key components of a strategy for action against child bondage that can be carried out in different countries and regions, taking into account the context and needs in each country or region.

Formulation of a national plan of action against the bonded labour system and child bondage. This includes:

— Preparing national reports on bonded labour systems and the nature and extent of child bondage;

— Organising a national consultation on the forms of bondage, and the best ways of detecting, releasing and rehabilitating bonded labourers, including bonded children; and

— Formulating a national plan of action for the eradication of the practice and rehabilitation of the victims.

Strengthening legislation and enforcement procedures with reference to the scope and application of international conventions. This includes:

— Examining various forms of bondage relative to the existing legislation, identifying deficiencies in the coverage of legislation, reviewing the adequacy of measures in legislation for the release and rehabilitation of victims and prosecution of offenders, including the level of punishment prescribed for the offenders; and

— Reviewing enforcement, including prosecution of offenders and the strength and effectiveness of the inspectorate.

Institutional capacity-building at national and local levels. This includes:

— Establishing a national focal point to serve as a stimulus and to facilitate coordination among all partners;

— Forming a broad-based national task force which would advise on policy and programmes on bonded labour legislation and its enforcement (particularly concerning the remission/waiver of loans and release from bondage), as well as carry out surveys to identify bonded labourers and assess their indebtedness and socio-economic status with a view to their rehabilitation; awareness campaigns; orientation of governmental and non-governmental staff, and rehabilitation schemes; and

— Forming vigilance committees to assist in identifying bonded labourers, provide legal education and oversee their release and rehabilitation.

Direct action programmes to prevent, rehabilitate and re-integrate bonded children. These include action programmes to:

— Liberate children in bonded labour in specific geographical locations;

— Implementrehabilitation and socio-economic reintegration programmes not only to receive the children once liberated but also to progressively guide them into a normal social life;

— Set up a rehabilitation fund and the procedure for its operation;

— Implement savings and credit schemes for poor families who are vulnerable to resorting to child bondage; and

— Provide basic, relevant education to prevent child bondage.

Awareness-raising on the problem of bonded labourers and children in bondage among parents, employers, local communities, the general public and policy-makers. This includes:

— Collecting and assessing information on a continuing basis on children in bondage and bonded labour systems, on the law and its enforcement, and on efforts made for prevention, debt repayment and rehabilitation;

— Disseminating information and sensitising parents, the community, school teachers who are in a position of leadership in rural communities and all sectors of civil society; and

— Organising public hearings and debates on child bondage, for example, in Parliament, and during specific human rights and children's rights-related events.

Strategy for action against child trafficking and the commercial sexual exploitation of children focuses simultaneously on trafficking within countries as well as across borders. The following activities will be carried out in different countries and regions depending on the context and needs in each country or region.

1. Appraisal of the problem and existing responses; identification of national, subregional and regional strategies for action:

   — Development of national policy and programmes of action by analysing the scope and current trends in trafficking of children, reviewing the existing responses to the problem (legislation, institutional mechanisms and types of intervention at the governmental and non-governmental level), and organising consultative workshops at local and national levels;

   — Summarising the main findings, of national reports and compilation of subregional synthesis reports, leading to strategies for action at the national and sub-regional levels; and

   — Organisation of subregional consultations to discuss and adopt bilateral, subregional and regional strategies for action.

2. Implementation of comprehensive programmes against trafficking in children:

— Intensive awareness-raising campaigns among the groups at risk, their environment and society at large;

— Strengthening law enforcement, including the deve-lopment or revision of legislation where necessary and the promotion of its application through the training of law enforcement personnel and the establishment of community "watch-dog" systems;

— Undertaking investigation and rescue operations, bringing cases to prosecution and rehabilitating the victims; and

— Mobilising participation of and facilitating coordination among key actors, namely the police, non-governmental and community organisations, public prosecutors, and local and national governments.

The in-country programmes will be reinforced by action at the subregional or international level, because it is recognised that concerted action is needed in sending receiving and transit countries to stop child trafficking. Therefore the aim is to develop inter-country mechanisms to prevent the problem and to provide protection and rehabilitation to the victims.

Advocates for children's rights in the International Labour Organization, UNICEF, and various non-governmental organizations are divided as to the best strategy to address the problems of child labour. Many advocates recommend abolishing all child labour immediately; they argue that in the long run, developing countries would benefit both economically and socially from a public policy of strict enforcement of both compulsory education and minimum age laws. They maintain that many countries actually have the resources for greater investment in education but lack the necessary political will. They believe that strict enforcement of both compulsory education and child labour laws would be much easier to administer than a more differentiated system and would reduce opportunities for corruption.Other advocates for children's rights—probably a majority—believe that the immediate abolition of all child labour is unrealistic and, in many cases, contrary to the interests of the children themselves. They recommend first abolishing the most abusive forms of child labour, and, in order to avoid a situation in which a reduction of child labour in one sector of the economy will simply lead to an increase in another, governments then should strictly regulate remaining forms of child labour to provide appropriate protections and benefits for those who must work to survive. They believe that the issue of child labour, especially in the more impoverished countries of the developing world, cannot be viewed in isolation but must be addressed in the broader context of social, economic, and educational development as a whole.

Policy differences aside, advocates for children's rights agree that certain abusive forms of child labour cannot be properly regulated but must be entirely abolished. These include child prostitution, bonded labour, and hazardous working conditions. Advocates view all these as unequivocally harmful, an exploitation of children, and urge governments and the world community as a whole to take immediate corrective action. Indeed, article 3(1) of ILO Convention 138 states that no one under 18 shall be admitted to employment or work "which by its nature or the circumstances in which it is carried out is likely to jeopardise the health, safety or morals of young persons. . . ."

Children are found all over Asia working in factories and workshops where they clean and pack food, weave carpets, sew and embroider garments, glue shoes, carry molten glass, cure leather, and polish gems, to name a few. Children are also the "invisible" workers in sub-contracting systems whereby they work in homes, small village workshops, or in tiny sheds. The International Labour Organization estimates that at least half of all child workers are found in South and Southeast Asia.

Conditions in these industries range from crowded garment factories, where the doors are locked and the children work for 14 hours, to small dusty earthen huts which can seat four children to a loom, knotting carpets in a pit for hours on end. At its worst, conditions, such as in glass factories, are medieval. Temperatures are unbearably hot, glass shards line the dirt floors where children and adults walk barefoot, and children carry heavy and piping hot rods of molten glass from one station to another.

Due to the sheer enormity of its population, and the large number of labour-intensive export industries, Asia boasts perhaps the highest percentage of children working in industries which export to the United States. Simultaneously, a thriving non-governmental sector monitoring and publicizing the exploitation of child labour has developed. The combination of these factors has led to an increase in information on working children and the establishment of programs to support their health and welfare.

The International Labour Organization, in its testimony at the Department of Labour's hearings, described the complexity of child labour and issued an important challenge: "Few human rights abuses are so unanimously condemned, while being so widely practiced as child labour . . .There is no quick fix . . .Working children, all over the world, deserve better."

By gathering information about products routinely used in our daily lives that are produced by the sweat and toil of children, this report may be a vehicle to better understanding the magnitude of the problem and developing solutions to bring this continuing human tragedy to an end..International Child Labour Hearing, U.S. Department of Labour (April 12, 1994). A survey of child labour worldwide finds that children are working in considerable numbers throughout many regions of the world. Each region differs, to some degree, in the extent of child labour and the specific sectors where children may be found working.

There are also many similarities, including common areas where children's work contributes to the production of goods for export. In each region, the number of children working in industry or mining accounts for only a small percentage of total working children. In such cases, children commonly work in small-scale enterprises, home-based production, and small-scale mining operations which may be subcontracted by larger export-oriented firms and, to a lesser extent, in the larger factories of several countries. The country profiles following this section provide more specific information about the use of child labour in the manufacturing and mining of products exported to the United States. From the information collected by the International Child Labour Study. Although the International Labour Organization (ILO) estimates that there are between 100 and 200 million working children worldwide, the organization is generally the first to acknowledge that no systematic or precise survey has been conducted. Furthermore, government statistics typically do not include economically active children below a certain age.

Labour force surveys rarely cover illegal or clandestine work, home-based work, or work undertaken by refugee populations. The ILO efforts have, therefore, been turned to helping countries develop the statistical capability that hopefully will make a more reliable global estimate possible in the future. Because statistical information on child labour is uniformly poor, this report makes no attempt to assess the actual number of children working in any industry. On the other hand, where there is general agreement—or significant discrepancies—on the estimated number of children working in any particular country or industry. The real solutions to child labour undoubtedly lie in holistic sustainable development of all the countries of the world. The repercussions of the global economic and social trends have affected children most severely and it is of utmost importance that the best interests of children are placed firmly in the centre of all decisions making exercises. What is even more important is the participation of children when decisions regarding them are being carried out so that they can ensure that those decisions ensure their immediate and long-term well-being. While there is a fairly comprehensive understanding about why children work—the commitment to find lasting solutions is very inadequate.

The ILO Convention 182 is a very limited—perhaps even detrimental – response to the complex issue of child labour. An approach which is developed around 'worse case scenarios' can never lead to a long term, child centred approach to child labour. While punitive actions are required in cases of extreme violation are in place, punitive action against employers of children can only push child labour into increasingly invisible and exploitative forms of work. In most countries where programmes are being formulated on the framework of ILO 182, the rehabilitation of children is rarely thought through. Most working children express trauma after their 'release' and speak out strongly about the little or no support they receive after being removed from work. As the basic reason which led them to work remain unresolved, they return to labour. The attention on worse forms of labour deals with a 'disaster management' approach that does not take into consideration preventing marginalisation of communities and children. It does not ensure that authorities commit themselves to people centred development, which is the only way child labour can be addressed and a meaningful childhood be ensured.

It is possible to create Child Labour Free Areas with a comprehensive decentralised approach which has been developed in partnership with children and members of the local communities. In these communities, children have themselves defined 'work they can and cannot do' and their lists have been developed in connection with the various occupations children are involved in as seen within the framework of children's developmental milestones. These lists form their guidelines to declare an area child labour free. Children themselves are an integral part of the monitoring processes. While adequate resources are a must to address child labour, there is also an urgent need for realistic, child centred, innovative and sustainable strategies – from the local to the international level.

2

Shocking Scene of Child Labour

No country or region is immune from child labour, and none is shielded from the impacts of the development shocks and crises that have reverberated around the world in recent years, and indeed continue to do so. Such shocks include sharp economic or financial downturns, political and economic transition, natural disasters, armed conflict and the HIV/AIDS pandemic. Crises are often linked and countries can experience several of them simultaneously, compounding and deepening their impact. A crisis may vary in its impact depending on its type and intensity, but all crises tend to worsen poverty, to increase the numbers of people in vulnerable situations, to weaken institutions, to drain government resources available for social expenditure and to have other serious negative economic, political, social and psychological impacts.

Crises expose and exploit existing fault lines in society, and create new ones. The harshest blow inevitably falls on low-income and resource-poor groups. Most children probably comprehend little of the forces at work around them, and are unable to do much, if anything, to counter the profound effects of these on their lives. These forces can make the difference between whether a child is safe or in danger, sick or healthy, goes hungry or is fed, lives with his or her family, strangers or alone, and whether he or she works or goes to school or does both. Therefore, the existence and impact of crises are important features of the dynamic global picture of child labour today.

Economic and Financial Crises

The economic slowdown that was visible by mid-2001 and that deepened after the terrorist attacks of 11 September 2001 on the United States will have significant social repercussions worldwide. Major workforce retrenchments in developed countries have already had ripple effects on suppliers and associated enterprises around the globe. World Bank predictions suggest economic slowdown in all regions, at least in the short term. Job losses and reduced investment will exacerbate poverty, which may in turn increase child labour, if effective policy responses are not put into place to mitigate the impact. Although the relationship between economic crisis and child labour is not fully understood, experience from the recent past provides some insights. The East Asian economic and financial crisis of 1997-98 illustrates the rapidity with which downturns can occur and the consequences they can have. Child welfare in the wake of the crisis appears to have declined primarily because of:

— decreased family income as formal sector employment diminished and adult workers took employment in the informal sector;

— declining real wages as the result of inflation, which had an impact on the price of food and health care;

— a decrease in government revenue, which reduced governments' capacity to maintain social expenditures.

Yet the impact of the crisis on children seems to have been less marked than might have been expected. In general, most children continued to attend school and to receive sufficient food and health care, largely because family resources were allocated to maintain an adequate level of support. Survival mechanisms developed by the many families in the informal economy may well have cushioned the effects of the crisis. In contrast, for those in the formal sector, income dropped sharply or was lost altogether.

There were also differences across the region. The economy in Indonesia was hit the hardest, but the aggregate impact on child labour was limited. The importance attributed to education, social perceptions of child labour and the effectiveness of government schemes to counter poverty may have played an important role in maintaining school enrolment levels. The Government abolished school fees and instituted several initiatives to help poor students deal with the hidden costs of education. In 1997-98, the labour force participation of children aged 10-14 increased only 0.6 per cent, and decreased 0.7 per cent in the 15-19 age group; school attendance rates reflected this pattern.

The main impact was in fact on those children already working, apparently leading to a shift from wage labour to more hazardous informal work, and a fall in earnings or loss of work for children. And while the impact of the crisis was blunted, the earlier downward trend in child labour has not been re-established in the post-crisis period.

By contrast, the Philippines was not hit as hard by the crisis, but child labour was definitely aggravated. School enrolment, especially at secondary level, declined. At the same time, youth unemployment soared. Both children and youth were thus more vulnerable to informal, illegal and hazardous economic activities. In Thailand, the crisis had a limited negative impact on overall school enrolment, but youth unemployment rose. However, in rural areas school dropouts rates increased, possibly indicating a shift into child labour. The dropouts rate among the poor was almost double that of the non-poor during the 1998-99 school year.

Greater proportional losses by the poor in times of economic crisis have occurred in other regions as well. In severe recessions in Brazil and Chile, for example, poor children tended to be pulled out of school. But effects are not uniform across countries or socio-economic groups. As in Asia, household coping strategies appear to be heavily influenced by government policy, especially as regards social welfare and education—pointing to the particular importance of social protection for the poor to buffer the impacts of crises. Such experiences offer useful policy pointers for countries now in economic crisis, such as Argentina.

Economic and social shocks can also occur in the context of more gradual but radical transition. Both deep political change and economic restructuring have been features of many countries over the past two decades. While transition countries have had mixed experiences, thus far it would seem that the losses for children as a result of the upheavals have far outweighed the gains. Chronic poverty is an emerging issue; the most vulnerable families have been those with children, especially single-parent families, and those from socially excluded groups.

Transition has profound psychological impacts too: the dismantling of systems of state support, the loss of guaranteed employment for adults and a collapse in income and living standards have caused widespread feelings of shame, confusion and marginalization, leading to social problems such as substance abuse. In such conditions, many transition countries have seen the emergence of child labour on a previously unknown scale.

Child labour was not just ideologically unacceptable, it had no real place in centrally planned economies that operated by controlling labour mobility and by strictly regulating the job market, as well as personal freedoms. Officially, children could perform work only if it prepared them for future employment within the framework of education. To this day, Cuba states that child labour does not exist in that country. Nonetheless, even in pre-reform socialist countries, child labour existed to some extent.

With the transformation to market economies, strong new pressures have emerged on children, especially among the poor, to contribute to family income or to provide for themselves. Countries of the former USSR and those in Central and Eastern Europe have all seen, to varying degrees, an increase in poverty, family disintegration, migration and population displacement, erosion of social safety nets, deterioration in health and education services and increases in delinquency and drug use among young people. At the same time, opportunities for children to participate in the largely unregulated labour market have rapidly multiplied, especially in the expanding informal (and often illegal) economy. The interplay of these factors has led to an upsurge in child labour in all its forms. With limited or no experience in dealing with child labour, government institutions are ill-equipped to devise effective responses. Mongolia embarked on drastic economic reforms that led to a steep rise in poverty and reduced government provision for children.

Exacerbated by the decimation of livestock by a severe winter and disease in 2000, rural-urban migration has increased, including many children who now work in the informal sector as peddlers or shining shoes. Street children did not exist in any of the former socialist or pre-reform economies. Runaway children were quickly picked up by police and either returned to their families or placed in residential care. Now, as a result of poverty and migration, they can be found in urban areas in all transition countries, as elsewhere in the world. In various countries of Eastern Europe, Roma children are particularly disadvantaged.

They are disproportionately involved in hazardous labour and at high risk of poor health, delinquency and poverty. Children's involvement in agriculture has tended to increase in some transition countries. For example, in rural Viet Nam, the collapse of the collective sector combined with the introduction of a household contract system in agriculture has reinforced the need for the labour inputs of children on family farms. These may include children hired or transferred from other households, perhaps for payment only in kind. China has seen an increase in work by children on family farms, despite the enforcement of compulsory basic education laws.

Continuation of residence permits, a relic of the old system, can be a powerful factor in exacerbating poverty and social exclusion by forcing migrants, and their children, either to avoid urban centres (where they might find work) or to live there illegally, thus preventing them gaining access to whatever formal social protection might still exist. Along with social protection systems, education has been a frequent casualty of transition, adding to the child labour problem. Schools have often been starved of public funds, with teachers widely affected by nonpayment of wages.

Increased costs of textbooks and clothes, together with the opportunity of school attendance by children who could otherwise be earning, are all part of an increasing burden on overstretched family resources. In Kyrgyzstan, reduction of government educational allowances has led to a decrease in the number of public schools and overcrowded classrooms. With 55 per cent of the population living in poverty (23 per cent in extreme poverty), many children lose interest in secondary education and prefer to earn money, primarily in selling, transportation, collection or as ancillary workers.

A final factor to highlight in the context of transition and child labour is the change in values and aspirations that can accompany societal transformation. In the Lao People's Democratic Republic, increased consumerism and a desire for luxury goods has been attributed as a factor motivating adults and children alike to risk migration from rural homes to seek better income-earning opportunities in the cities. This results both in a broken social fabric in the countryside and large groups of young people living at high risk in cities. Given the rapid growth in tourism in that country, it faces the danger of being perceived as a new alternative to the more traditional destinations for sex tourists. HIV/AIDS is emerging as a key factor affecting children and the pattern of child labour across the world. As a shock to development, it probably has no equal in modern times. Children everywhere are affected by the spread of the virus-directly by its impact on themselves and their family members, and indirectly by its influence on the wider social and economic environment in which they live. At the macro level, HIV/AIDS severely undermines economic growth and productivity; when this occurs in agriculture, there is the accompanying threat to food security. The age and gender composition of entire nations is drastically altered, putting a heavier burden of the dependent population (including children) on the dwindling, most productive age groups. While the ways in which the pandemic affects child labour are as yet under-researched, it is clear that this pandemic is having profound direct and indirect impacts. In turn, child labour fuels, in part, the spread of the disease through the commercial and other sexual exploitation of children. The social inequalities that foster the spread of HIV/AIDS mirror in many ways those that perpetuate child labour.

There are already an estimated 13 million AIDS orphans under the age of 15. This number is expected to increase dramatically in the years to come. Orphanhood as an outcome of HIV/AIDS exposes children to increased risks of discrimination, and ill health and lost opportunities for education and training. During the 1990s, AIDS orphans tended to remain in the care of the extended family. However, evidence from countries such as Uganda, Zambia and Zimbabwe shows these systems are breaking down under stress and that there is an increase in the number of child-headed households and further impoverishment of families where fostered orphans live, which also affects the other children living in those households.

HIV/AIDS has a direct impact on children's participation in the work-force. Prolonged periods of illness and eventual death in the family cause dramatic cuts in income and loss of assets. Even before one or both of their parents die of AIDS-related illnesses, children, especially girls, are likely to have to take on a heavier workload within the household, including domestic chores and caring for siblings and sick adults. This can compromise their schooling and their health. Both boys and girls may be obliged to seek income-earning opportunities to make up for the lost adult income and to help pay medical expenses.

Children are also likely to be called upon to compensate for the loss of women's labour in farming tasks. Increased migration as a consequence of HIV/AIDS, by both boys and girls, from rural settings to urban areas swells the ranks of children in the urban informal economy. The presence of children on the street and their need for money, food, shelter and companionship all increase their chances of being drawn into casual sexual relationships or into commercial sexual exploitation. This, in turn, increases the risk of their becoming infected with HIV and thus the circle from being affected to becoming infected is completed.

HIV/AIDS is driving a flow of ever-younger girls into commercial sexual exploitation, often because of long-standing myths about sexually transmitted diseases. Girls from the mountain areas of Viet Nam, for example, are said to be in demand in Cambodia because they are perceived to decrease the risk of contracting HIV/AIDS or other sexually transmitted diseases.

HIV/AIDS impacts indirectly on child labour through education by affecting both pupil and teacher populations. Research from Zambia provides the most thorough assessment so far of the educational disadvantages of AIDS orphans, who are more likely to be out of school than children orphaned for other reasons. Even if children from households with one or more adults affected by HIV/AIDS are not withdrawn totally from school so that they may work, their classroom attendance may be sporadic. In Uganda, for example, breaks in school attendance have lasted from five weeks to a term and a half; the most common reasons are lack of money to pay school fees and the need for children to help at home with the care of HIV/AIDS patients.

Schooling for all children is severely affected by the impact of the pandemic on teachers in countries with high infection rates. In 1998 in Zambia, for instance, deaths of teachers equalled two-thirds the number of graduates from teacher training colleges, and the ratio was increasing. Deaths from AIDS-related illnesses deprive schools of their most needed asset. However, teacher absences, because of their own or relatives' illnesses associated with HIV/AIDS, also result in classroom disruptions and lower quality education, and potentially contribute to higher student dropouts and repetition rates. These translate into children's reluctance to attend school and parents' doubts about the usefulness of pursuing their children's education, which increases the chance that they will become child labourers and reduces the future supply of skilled workers, including teachers.

Alongside these various impacts of HIV/AIDS on child labour are the devastating emotional and psychological effects on children of seeing parents, friends, relatives and teachers succumb to the disease, and the fabric of their communities being torn apart. This cannot but lead to a heightened sense of vulnerability to exploitation and discrimination in its many forms, placing children at greater risk of child labour.

Natural Disasters and Child Labour

Crises also come in the form of natural disasters—both from the disaster itself and from the economic and other shocks that follow. Hurricanes, floods and earthquakes have devastating and immediate direct human and financial costs. They also bring in their wake far-reaching shocks to development, such as destruction of infrastructure, disruption of essential services, production losses (including food), plummeting income, unemployment, population movements, economic stagnation and price increases. It is no coincidence that natural disaster and poverty seem to go hand in hand. Repeated disasters lead to chronic poverty; funds and resources are almost permanently diverted to relief rather than invested in development. And poverty breeds conditions in which the effects of disaster can be most catastrophic. Both adults and children feel the effects of natural disasters, but the intimate social world of children.

3

Reforms in Child Labour

In 1930s, U.S. welfare and income support programs have played an important role in providing benefits to children. Unlike programs directly targeted to children, however, welfare programs are designed to produce economic and employment impacts on adults, so that any effects on children would be indirect. When Aid to Dependent Children was established in the 1930s, its principal goal was to promote the welfare of children. Under the assumptions of the day, that meant assuring not only that basic physical needs were met (orphanages could do that), but that children could be cared for by their mothers. Since then, children have been major beneficiaries of U.S. welfare programs for low-income families.

In 1995, for example, approximately two-thirds of recipients in the Aid to Families with Dependent Children (AFDC) program were children-many under age three. Children's health and development is still an implicit goal of welfare programs, and policymakers often assert that program changes will produce benefits for children. For example, one common argument is that employed parents provide positive models of productive, self-sufficient citizenship.

At the same time, critics have worried that policy changes made in the Personal Responsibility and Work Opportunity Reconciliation Act of 1996 will diminish families' ability to provide both material and personal resources to their children. Current federal welfare policy embodied in the new program, Temporary Assistance for Needy Families (TANF), was designed to address the following three major goals:

1) to increase paid employment among parent recipients;
2) to reduce "welfare dependence" -that is, to reduce the number of families receiving welfare over a long period of time; and
3) to influence family structure by encouraging marriage and two-parent families, reducing the incidence of out-of-wedlock child-bearing, and requiring that both parents provide for the child.

The framers of welfare reform legislation did not make poverty reduction a goal, but in recognition that merely trading welfare for work often does not improve a family's economic situation, states were given the option to include various financial incentives to encourage recipients to work.

The 1990s also brought major changes in policies designed to help working poor families outside the welfare system, contributing to increased employment and other outcomes observed since welfare reform. For example, the maximum earned income tax credit (EITC) benefit for a family with two children increased from $1,511 in 1993 to $3,888 in 2000. Similarly, both child care assistance and health insurance for children have been extended to more non-welfare working poor families. These changes are designed to reward employment, but unlike TANF, they also are explicitly intended to reduce poverty among working families with children.

Goals for Child Development

Economic and employment policies define their goals for children somewhat differently than do policies focused on early childhood education, which are intended to improve children's lot directly. Welfare and income support policies are based in economic thinking, whereas many child policies are rooted in child development, education, and related fields. The following analysis explores the issues, tensions, and common threads in these different approaches to defining goals for children and suggests a more inclusive set of goals that may be useful in considering existing research and provoking new questions. Because most welfare policies entail spending public funds, economic considerations are understandably important in evaluating all policies affecting children.

The economic perspective has led to the idea that public spending on children is an investment in their future economic productivity. For example, early interventions are evaluated by their long-term effects on adult educational attainment, employment, and income. Although costs and benefits are legitimate issues, there is a danger in requiring that all investments in children be justified by demonstrable "profits" to society in the form of later economic productivity. It puts an enormous burden on any policy to require that it show economic benefits 10 to 20 years later.

In contrast, those who specialize in child development regard quality of life during childhood as a legitimate goal in its own right, even though they also stress Children's achievement of developmental aims as preparation for later life. In the United Kingdom and parts of Europe, scholars are bringing a human rights perspective into policy discussions, framing the discourse around children's rights as embodied in the United Nations' Convention on the Rights of the Child.

Several issues underlie these discussions about what outcomes for children should be sought in welfare policies. First, tension stems from the difference between considering a child's worth in the present and a child's worth as a future adult. To what extent should a child's well-being be valued for its own sake? To what extent should policies for children be judged by their contribution to the adult that child may become? One way of crystallizing this issue is to ask: How much public investment would be worthwhile to care for a terminally ill child who would not live beyond age 12? Second, debate continues about whether public spending on children should be justified on the basis of moral or human rights, or on the basis of present and future productivity. To what extent do children have the right to certain types of protection or benefits from society? To what extent should public resources be concentrated on outcomes for children that are associated with short-term or long-term productivity? Should assistance to poor families be justified, for example, by demonstrating that it enhances children's well-being by reducing their exposure to violence or low-quality schools? Or should it be justified as a means of increasing the probability that children will become economically productive citizens? Third, differences exist among those who emphasize prevention of harm and those who emphasize positive development. The youth development movement, for example, stresses the difference between programs designed to enhance skills and those aimed at preventing problems, arguing that prevention is not sufficient. Should welfare policies for parents make positive contributions to children's well-being? Or is it sufficient to do no harm?

Some maintain that child well-being should be defined solely by the child's characteristics, whereas others believe the context in which the child lives should also be considered. In models and research investigating policy effects on children, the "child outcomes" are the child's behaviours and attributes, such as school achievement, social skills, behavioural problems, and health status. Developmental psychologists and policy researchers alike think of the child as the locus of development. But others have begun to focus more on the contexts provided to children.

For example, among the rights listed in the United Nations' Convention on the Rights of the Child is an obligation of the state to provide assistance to parents, such as income supports, child care services, children's health care services, and education. A consortium of state policymakers recently brought together to select a common set of indicators to evaluate welfare reform also focused on contexts, nominating outcomes that included many aspects of children's environments, such as reduced child poverty and adequate housing. Such indicators reflect the view that a policy's effects on the home environment, for example, are as relevant as effects on a child's school performance.

These contrasting perspectives illustrate the multiple and sometimes contradictory criteria and objectives for public policies affecting children. The most reasonable approach to assessing the impact of welfare and income support policies on children would keep various objectives in balance: emphasizing a child's present well-being as well as his or her future as an adult; considering a child's well-being as well as his or her productivity; expecting policies to promote positive development as well as prevent harm; and defining child outcomes to include healthy contexts as well as skills and behaviours.

Following are the Goals for Healthy Child Development:

— Health and physical comfort, including shelter, nourishment, freedom from pain and abuse, and medical care.

— Family or adults who care, are reasonably constant and reliable, and who provide love and encouragement. Consistency of care givers and settings.

— Development of intellectual and other capabilities to their fullest, such as language skill; school achievement; and skill in athletics, music, or art.

— Emotional well-being and mental health, including self-worth, sense of personal control, and freedom from depression and anxiety.

— Skills in relating to others, both adults and peers, including, for example, assertiveness without violence, sociability, cooperation, understanding others' perspectives, complying with adult expectations, and leadership.

— Responsibility and morality, including the ability to guide one's own behaviour and act in accord with societal standards of right and wrong.

— In adulthood, ability to support self and family, be a good parent, contribute to society, be mentally and physically healthy, and not commit crimes or abuse substances.

Welfare reform and efforts to support working poor families are designed to change the economic and personal behaviour of parents. Any effects on children occur indirectly, most likely through an impact on parents' employment, family resources, use of early education and child care, and other family circumstances. Welfare and income support policies are designed to influence parents' employment (especially maternal employment), income and material resources, and family structure. Changes in employment, resources, and family structure are likely in turn to influence children's physical and material environment, family environment, and child care, school, neighbourhood, and community environments.

Environmental contexts and child characteristics are both potentially important, albeit indirect, outcomes of public policy directed at families. Environmental contexts that support a decent quality of life can be justified on that basis alone, but they are also important because they can affect children's physical, intellectual, and socioemotional development. Random-assignment experiments, which randomly assign some participants to the program and others to a control group have established the causal influences in some instances-that is, whether the context affects the child, the child affects the context, or both are caused by other factors. But it is also recognized that children often play a role in both selecting and responding to available contexts, and they in turn are influenced by their experiences. Thus, most current child development theories maintain that effects on children and context are bidirectional-that is, they are mutual and intertwined.

There are three key elements contribute to a healthy physical and material environment for children:

1) an adequate standard of living (particularly sufficient food, clothing, and housing);
2) health care services, including prevention and treatment (such as immunization); and
3) safety from injury, violence, and environmental hazards.

In contrast, the physical and material environments that poor children experience are often characterized by hardship, hunger, homelessness, exposure to toxins and other dangerous substances, exposure to violence and other hazards to physical safety, and inadequate preventive health care. When families and communities do not have-or do not provide-the necessary preventive resources, children are at greater risk of injuries, failure to thrive, mortality, untreated medical and dental conditions, and health problems such as asthma. Policies that improve family income or provide assistance with food, housing, and child care increase families' material resources. Income is often used as a proxy for material resources, but it is not a direct index of the material goods and services available to children.

Although intensive qualitative interviews with mothers living in poverty show that most families budget money in ways that will benefit children, families vary in how much of their income they spend on children. By middle childhood, and certainly in adolescence, children's perceptions of their family's economic strain or material hardship can be an important influence on their sense of well-being.

Parenting and the quality of the home environment play an extremely important role in children's lives. For healthy development, children need adult family members and other adults who are mentally healthy, responsible, constant, and reliable to provide them with love and encouragement. The parent-child relationship should be characterized by warmth, open communication, and firm (but not harsh) discipline. And children benefit when both parents assume responsibility for their emotional and financial support. Welfare and income support policies that change parents' employment status, family resources, and family structure could affect children's home environments by changing parents' time at home, parents' personal sense of well-being, and the relationships among family members.

Experimental evidence has shown that the quality of the home environment can be improved by interventions that teach mothers about child rearing, but no evidence documents the effects of interventions less directly focused on child rearing. In the very large amount of research relating parenting and the home environment to children's cognitive and intellectual development, some consistent patterns have emerged. First, although children who develop strong intellectual skills also tend to demonstrate positive social and emotional behaviour, the home and family characteristics associated with intellectual versus social development are somewhat different. For infants and preschool children, the cognitive and social environment provided in the home predicts children's language development, intelligence, school readiness, and school achievement in reading and math, even when controlling for numerous other family and demographic characteristics.

Maternal intellectual ability also is a strong predictor of children's academic performance, a finding that suggests both genetic and environmental contributions to a child's performance.

Children's social behaviour and emotional well-being are more strongly related to the quality of parent-child interactions, and less strongly to income and cognitive environment. Maternal depression is associated with behavioural problems much more consistently than with problems in cognitive or intellectual functioning, probably because of its effects on parenting practices.

Children and youth who demonstrate positive social behaviour and low levels of psychological distress perceive their relations with parents positively, and they tend to have mothers who are warm and who avoid harsh punishment. Young people who engage in deviant and delinquent behaviour tend to have parents who provide low levels of supervision, monitoring, and control.

Virtually all of this literature is subject to some methodological problems that should be of concern in evaluating policy effects. First, links between parent and child characteristics are probably due, at least in part, to genetic similarities. Second, children's behaviour elicits and influences parenting and parent well-being as well as responds to it, so the association of parent and child behaviours probably indicates bidirectional causation.

For example, in one recent series of studies, better "outcomes" were found among adolescents whose parents monitor their whereabouts. Investigators argue persuasively that these outcomes are not due to parents' vigilant supervision, but instead are due largely to the fact that better-adjusted adolescents volunteer such information about their whereabouts. Finally, in many of the studies evaluating welfare policies, children's social behaviour is measured by maternal report only, so the measure reflects the mother's reaction to the child as well as the child's behaviour.

Child care, schools, out-of-school activities, mass media, social supports, and neighbourhoods are sources of formative experiences for children in general. Such resources may be especially important for children with a single, employed parent. Research suggests that healthy development can be promoted by child care that is reliable, safe, and of high quality; by education and out-of-school activities appropriate to a child's ability and culture; and by neighbourhood and communities that are safe and that have resources for serving children.

From the time children are infants through their school-age and teen years, the environments they experience while their parents work can play an important role in their development. Federal, state, and local programs provide child care assistance to low-income families, especially those moving from welfare to work, in a variety of ways, including subsidies and resource and referral services. Research suggests that the impact of these policies depends on the age of the child, and the quality, type, and stability of care.

Even very young children are now spending a large amount of time in child care. Current welfare policy permits states to require parents' participation in work-related activities when children are infants, leading to concerns that a mother's time away from her infant will interfere with early development of a positive mother-child relationship and a secure attachment. Some evidence suggests that mothers who return to work very early in their infants' lives (before about three months of age) or whose infants have extensive early child care are less sensitive to their children than are their counterparts.

Maternal sensitivity is associated with the development of secure attachments for infants, but there is little evidence that time with a child per se affects the development of secure attachment.

An abundance of evidence shows that high-quality child care—care that provides intellectual stimulation, social involvement of adults with children, and language interactions-can have a positive influence on Children's intellectual development, particularly among children in low-income families. Longitudinal, correlational studies consistently show a relationship between high quality of care and small but significant gains in children's cognitive and language development, even with controls for demographic characteristics and parenting behaviour. These results could be due to unobserved characteristics that differentiate families who choose high-and low-quality care, and that some of the results do not endure into later childhood and adolescence. Nevertheless, experimental studies show that high-quality programs for low-income infants and pre-schoolers lead to short-term and, in some cases, long-term improvements in school performance.

Preschool children who receive care in formal center-based settings show better cognitive and language development on average than do those cared for by relatives or nonrelatives in home-based settings. Similarly, somewhat older children, especially those living in low-income areas, who participate in formal after-school programs have been shown to perform better in school compared with those in other types of after-school arrangements. Between about third and fifth grade, many children phase out of formal child care programs and spend less and less time under the direct supervision of their parents.

During this transition, organized youth activities offer opportunities to build skills and interact with peers with at least some adult supervision. Youths who participate in structured activities approved by adults have better school performance and less deviant behaviour than do those who spend after-school time in unsupervised activities with peers, especially in low-income families and neighbourhoods.

Stability of care appears to be more consistently related to social and emotional well-being than is quality or type of care. Low-income children who experience unstable child care-frequent changes and multiple arrangements-tend to have more behavioural problems than do those with more stable child care.

Changing child care arrangements may be a sign of instability in other facets of family life, including housing, parental employment, and family composition-a pattern that has been described as "turbulence." Also, counting evidence suggests that children who enter care early or spend many hours in care throughout the preschool years may have more behavioural problems than do those who spend more time in the care of parents.

As children get older, they have increasing control over where they spend their time, whom they associate with, and what activities they experience. Thus, the links between their out-of-school environments and any positive development probably reflects bidirectional influences-that is, youths who are more attached to school and nondeviant peers select more positive activities, which in turn reinforce positive behaviour. An important developmental "outcome" may be the choices that young people make about how and with whom they spend their time.

The effects of neighbourhoods and communities are considerably smaller than family influences, children's development nevertheless is influenced by where they live. Young children and adolescents who live in middle-class neighbourhoods perform better in school than do children from comparable families living in less affluent neighbourhoods, even with controls for individual family characteristics. Safety and school quality are neighbourhood features with important potential consequences for children's development. Results from the Boston site of "Move to Opportunity," a random-assignment experiment in which families were given vouchers to move from public housing to low-poverty neighbourhoods, suggest benefits for children.

Children and youths in the experimental groups had lower levels of behavioural problems (boys only), fewer asthma attacks and injuries, and were less often the victims of violence than were the children in the control group. Parents reported less gunfire and less drug activity in the neighbourhood. No measures of cognitive or academic performance were reported, but in an earlier quasi-experiment (the Gautreaux Project) in which families moved from inner-city public housing to suburban communities, positive effects on children's school performance were found.

In sum, the evidence linking environmental contexts to child development, especially among low-income families, is quite strong. Children who are deprived of adequate physical and material resources, who lack attention from a warm and loving family, or who spend lengthy hours in low-quality child care settings tend to show negative intellectual and behavioural outcomes. Thus, policies that work to ameliorate these conditions are likely to have a positive impact on children's development.

In 1996, major welfare policy strategies include work requirements, time limits on welfare receipt, sanctions for failing to participate in work-related activities, casework, financial incentives such as increased income disregards, which allow recipients to earn more before losing benefits, quotas and incentives for states, and transitional Medicaid and child care assistance. States can and do use federal dollars and their own funds for a wide range of other strategies. And, of course, the EITC, the largest federal antipoverty program, provides a strong work incentive for low-income families. Because single mothers are much more likely to be poor than are single fathers or married parents, these policies are especially likely to increase maternal employment in single-mother families.

Although there is little disagreement that families fare better when the father is employed, researchers have long debated the effects on children when a mother is employed. The effects of maternal employment on children in low-income families probably depend on whether overall family resources increase, characteristics of the job(s) (benefits, stimulation, schedule), characteristics of the child (age, sex, temperament), characteristics of the mother (health, mental health, attitudes and beliefs), and available support (family, child care, community programs). If maternal employment increases material resources, its effects on children are likely to be positive. Data indicate, however, that trading welfare assistance for employment earnings does not always change family income, and resources may decline when the costs of employment, such as transportation, child care, payroll taxes, and clothing, are considered.

Mandatory employment in conjunction with time limits could result in reduced disposable income in some families. Some types of employment might increase parents' skills (human capital) or contacts with adults (social capital), which in turn could have positive effects on the home environment. Proponents of welfare reform emphasize the value of parental modelling; children who see parents going to a job regularly and bringing home a paycheck will accept employment as the norm of adult life. Parents' work lives can serve as a model for their children, but both positive and negative messages could be conveyed.

Mothers who have a positive attitude about combining work with family are more satisfied and report less role strain than those who believe they should be at home with their children. When parents' jobs are routine and repetitious or have very low wages, their children may infer that work is dull and boring. Parents' employment reduces the time they have available for child care and activities with the child. Young children are in someone else's care when mothers are at work, and the quality of that care is likely to mediate effects of parental employment. But many school-age children and youths are in "self-care" while their mothers work. Although parents often monitor their children by telephone and through neighbours, children without direct supervision are vulnerable to antisocial peers or, if they stay home, to many hours in front of the television set.

Self-care in late childhood and early adolescence does not appear to pose risks for middle-class children, but, for those who live in poverty and in dangerous neighbourhoods, the odds of behavioural problems increase when young adolescents are unsupervised. In fact, parents appear to recognize the differential risk; middle-class and white children are more likely than poor and minority children to be in self-care.

The effects of maternal employment vary with a child's age, but potential harmful effects do not necessarily decline as children get older. In fact, researchers have found that maternal employment during the adolescent years is associated with adolescent delinquency, lowered educational attainment, and low adolescent well-being. One reason may be that, unlike younger children, adolescents with employed mothers are generally not in supervised alternative settings.

Maternal employment can also affect children's responsibilities and family routines. Policymakers often assert that employment will provide a structure for family schedules of getting up, having meals, and going to bed. If a parent has a regular work schedule, this result might occur, but many low-income jobs have irregular and unconventional hours, and many parents work more than one job. In addition, studies suggest that unconventional and extended work hours may result in children assuming more responsibility for household tasks or caring for siblings, rather than spending more time in child care. Such a shift in responsibility could lead to either positive or negative consequences for children.

Most of the literature on low-income families suggests that children's cognitive and social development is more positive in families with employed mothers than in those with unemployed mothers. But it appears that much if not all of this difference is a function of preexisting differences in demographic attributes, skills, personality, and child-rearing practices between employed and unemployed mothers rather than being a product of employment.

In a large sample of mothers and infants, employed mothers provided a higher-quality home environment than unemployed mothers did, but these differences were entirely accounted for by maternal characteristics. Parents with more skills, and better psychological and physical health, are probably more likely to find and maintain paid employment. Parents with those same qualities are also more likely to provide better environments for their children.

Children might benefit if the job pays decent wages and provides some opportunity for social or cognitive stimulation; if children are in good-quality child care, youth programs, or neighbourhoods that support positive development; if the mother does not feel excessive role strain, depression, or conflict about her dual roles; and if family economic or social resources are improved. Children might suffer, however, when these conditions do not pertain. Moreover, the consequences of a mother not being employed may be more negative under welfare reform because the time limits on receiving welfare threaten seriously reduced income and because people may be discouraged by their failure to meet society's expectation that they support their families.

Welfare policies that include wage supplements, income disregards (which allow recipients to earn more before losing benefits), and subsidies for necessary expenses such as child care increase overall family income and resources. If income disregards or other subsidies are part of states' new welfare programs under TANF, however, they end when a recipient reaches a time limit or leaves welfare for any reason.

Programs outside the welfare system, such as the EITC, improve family resources with no time limit as long as the parent is employed. Although there is considerable debate about the influence of income per se on children's cognitive and social development, to the extent that increased resources improve a family's material circumstances, the quality of the home and child care environments, opportunities for children to participate in beneficial activities, and the neighbourhood in which a family lives, results for children are positive. Family income during the preschool years appears to be particularly important in predicting cognitive and educational attainment, probably because income affects the quality of the home and child care environments.

The home is an important source of intellectual stimulation before children enter formal schooling, and analyses show that the degree of cognitive and social stimulation at home varies with family income. Higher-income families also are more likely than low-income families to use center-based care or higher-quality home-based care for pre-schoolers.

Income guarantees led to slightly better school achievement for elementary-school- age children (but not for high school students) and to better nutrition for a very disadvantaged rural sample. Income supports also led to a higher probability of separation and divorce for couples experiencing high levels of conflict, but not for those with low levels of conflict. Environmental contexts were not assessed, but families in the experiment did buy homes or improve the quality of their rental units more often than controls did, probably leading to better neighbourhood conditions for their families.

Poverty and income loss affect the socioemotional climate of the home, which in turn influences children's psychological well-being and behaviour. Studies of poor families and families that experienced large reductions in income indicate that the effects on children are mediated primarily by parents' psychological distress, which may be reflected in practices such as low warmth and frequent use of harsh punishment. Policy researchers not only debate how much good might come from raising poor families' income, some argue that welfare income has harmful effects.

Comparisons of families receiving welfare with comparable poor families not receiving welfare show that long-term welfare recipients provide lower-quality home environments than do other poor families. Although many studies show little or no relation of welfare receipt to children's cognitive and social development when differences in demographic and family characteristics are taken into account, some studies have shown that welfare predicts higher rates of grade retention, lower academic achievement, and lower completed schooling among children. By contrast, adolescents in welfare families placed more importance on school than did those in poor, non-welfare families. It is clearly important for policymakers to understand why and how families receiving welfare differ from other poor families, and why welfare income may not confer the same benefits as other income. But it is very difficult to find samples with truly comparable material resources and parental characteristics.

People receiving welfare by definition have almost no assets, whereas other people with low incomes may have more resources of various kinds. Also, unlike other income supports (such as the EITC), welfare carries a stigma that may affect the way others treat parents and children, as well as the way they think about themselves. The poor are not immune from the value placed on work in U.S. society and from the strong implication of failure for those who receive public assistance. Children as young as second grade express negative stereotypes about poor children's behaviour and motivations. In addition, entry into and out of welfare is often associated with other transitions and changes, such as job loss or entry, parents separating or acquiring new partners, and changes in child care.

Such changes affect parents' and children's well-being, parenting, and the family environment. Mothers report high levels of behavioral problems among children in families who have made a transition either into or out of welfare, compared with families whose status has not changed. To understand how policies that affect family material resources also affect child development, studies are needed to examine how a family's overall resources are perceived and deployed, and how these behaviours affect the contexts experienced by children. Experimental studies that randomly assign participants to different types of programs are extremely important; otherwise it is difficult to isolate which differences are a result of policies and which are due to personal characteristics.

Some of the major goals of the federal welfare reform law of 1996 were to discourage women, particularly adolescents, from having children outside of marriage; to encourage people with children to marry; and to promote paternal financial responsibility for children. The strategies intended to advance these goals include incentives to states to reduce their out-of-wedlock child-bearing rates without increasing abortions; family caps; a requirement that adolescent welfare recipients attend school and live with a parent or responsible adult; and a requirement that applicants for cash assistance identify the father of the child, and cooperate with efforts to collect child support.

Young women who delay child-bearing receive more education and have fewer children than those who give birth early, but poor school achievement can be a motivation for pregnancy as well as a consequence. Although preexisting differences between unwed teen mothers and other young women account for most of the differences between them, some of the negative effects on their children can be attributed to early child-bearing and single parenthood. Young and single mothers provide home environments that are, on average, less stimulating and supportive than do older and married mothers.

In an investigation of mothers ranging in age from their late teens to their forties, older mothers spent more time with their infants, were more sensitive and stimulating to them, and provided higher-quality home environments than did younger mothers, even after controlling for demographic and marital status. Single mothers also were less sensitive and provided lower-quality home environments than did married mothers, but these differences were largely accounted for by differences in age, ethnicity, and maternal education. In a sample of children ages 4 to 16, those with single mothers spent more time watching television on weekends, but also spent more time in school or preschool on weekdays than did children of married mothers.

Policies designed to promote paternal responsibility for children, through either marriage or child support, are motivated in part by the high risk of poverty for single-mother families, but many observers also consider father involvement important for children's socialization and well-being. Child support reform began in the mid-1970s, but by 1990, only 6 of every 10 eligible mothers had child support awards, and the rate was much lower for those with children born out of wedlock than for those who had been divorced. Of mothers with awards, about 25% did not receive any payments. A recent demonstration program, Parents' Fair Share, was designed to spur low-income fathers to provide for their children. The program increased employ-ment and formal child support payments, but in some cases, informal supports to children were reduced. Moreover, paternal involvement was found to be a double-edged sword. Slight increases in fathers' efforts to be active parents led to increased disagreements with mothers

Although much is known about how family structure, maternal age, and child support relate to children's development, some major questions remain about how welfare and income support policies designed to change fertility patterns, family formation, and decisions about marriage might affect children. First, do policy variations have any effect on decisions about fertility and marriage, particularly for adolescents? In the United States, the availability of AFDC may have provided an incentive for adolescent child-bearing. In contrast, Sweden's family leave and other policies provide incentives to begin work before having children, and the teen birthrate is low compared with that of older women.

Sweden is one of the few countries where the probability of having a child is higher for more-educated than for less-educated women, controlling for other background variables. Second, if adults were induced to marry before having children, would benefits accrue for their children? Children in two-parent stable families generally show more positive development than do those in never-married, divorced, and remarried families, but these differences may be due to preexisting differences in parents' individual characteristics or the degree of conflict between adults who remain married and those who do not. Both domestic violence and physical abuse of children occur in a large number of low-income families.

For example, in one large sample of welfare recipients, some 28% had been abused by an intimate partner in the previous year. Most research on divorce shows that family conflict, including domestic violence, before and after a divorce is a major predictor of children's emotional and behavioral problems.

Even for couples who do not engage in high conflict, one cannot infer that inducing parents to marry or to stay married would provide conditions comparable to those in families where parents choose marriage without inducement. In addition, children do not appear to be better off when their mother marries someone other than their father, even though family income is, on average, substantially greater.

In a longitudinal analysis of children ages 5 to 10, those from blended families did not perform better on intellectual tests than did those in single-mother families. Similarly, children in step-parent and single-mother families have similar rates of dropping out of school and adolescent pregnancy. In sum, the available literature offers provocative hypotheses, but results are limited in several respects.

Virtually all of the findings are correlational, so selection effects and unobserved confounding variables make it difficult to establish causal explanations. In addition, much of the information predates 1996, so parents' decisions about employment and fertility were made in a different policy context than the current one. Policies that attempt to improve parents' employment, resources, and family structure probably affect children's development, but the effects can be either positive or negative.

Child Welfare System

The challenge for United nation's welfare system is to determine how best to help children in families that do not have the support of both parents and that do not have enough income. About half the children born in the 1980s will spend some time in a single-parent family before age 18. More than one-third will spend some of their childhood living in poverty.

The federal welfare reform law, the Personal Responsibility and Work Opportunity Reconciliation Act of 1996, sought to reduce the number of children growing up in poor, single-parent families by promoting marriage and requiring mothers to move from welfare to work. The 1996 law essentially transformed U.S. welfare programs into employment programs. Riding the wave of a strong economy, these new programs successfully moved many mothers from welfare to work, and improved many children's lives as a result-many, but not all. Even in very prosperous times, some families were unable to overcome their barriers to employment, and many families who found employment still needed additional supports to help make ends meet. As the economy weakens, the need for supports is likely to grow.

Reauthorization of the federal welfare reform law offers a critical opportunity to re-examine the goals of reform. If the ultimate goal of promoting work and marriage is not just to end families' dependence on government benefits, but also to improve disadvantaged children's chances for success in life, then more attention must be paid to structuring programs for low-income families in ways that promote positive child development and wellbeing. This is important not only for the children themselves, but for all of society, as we all pay the costs of educational failure, increased crime and violence, and reduced worker productivity-costs that inevitably result when children fail to get the nurturing and supports they need to achieve their potential.

Passage of the federal welfare reform law in 1996 brought many changes to the broad array of programs serving low-income children and their families. Prior to reform, all children in poor families that met state eligibility criteria were entitled to assistance under the Aid to Families with Dependent Children (AFDC) program, although many states set the threshold so low that only the poorest families qualified. The federal government reimbursed states for at least half the cost of providing this assistance, with no cap on expenditures. AFDC receipt also assured ready access to other benefits, such as Medicaid and food stamps.

Families who participated in AFDC-related work programs were provided with child care assistance, but these programs were often underfunded and involved only a fraction of eligible families. Most mothers receiving AFDC payments stayed home and cared for their children themselves. Program structures, priorities, and funding streams all changed dramatically with passage of the 1996 law.

The AFDC program was replaced with a block grant to the states called Temporary Assistance for Needy Families (TANF). Funding levels for TANF were based on states' historical expenditures under AFDC. Families' entitlement to assistance ended, and the links between cash assistance and other benefits and services were severed.

Instead, the law gave states increased flexibility to design their own welfare programs and support services for low-income families. At the same time, the law's focus, as indicated by its title, was to increase parental responsibility and work, and a major theme was to move families off welfare and into employment. Thus, families receiving TANF cash assistance had to meet several important new rules, such as more stringent work requirements, sanctions for noncompliance, and time limits. The law also increased funding for child care to facilitate mothers' employment, and strengthened the child support enforcement program to help ensure that fathers would contribute to the support of their children. Two other key themes in the 1996 law were promoting marriage and reducing out-of-wedlock births.

Provisions of the law that addressed these goals focused primarily on allowing more liberal eligibility criteria for two-parent families and imposing more stringent requirements on unmarried minor teen parents. The law also called on the U.S. Department of Health and Human Services to establish a strategy for preventing out-of-wedlock teen pregnancies, and provided new funding for abstinence education and bonuses for states with the highest reductions in out-of-wedlock births.

The law changed benefits and services for low-income children in other ways as well. For example, it restructured two significant funding streams for prevention of child maltreatment and services to reunify families split apart by child abuse or neglect, potentially reducing the total amount of funding for such programs. The law also modified the definition of childhood disability, restricting children's eligibility for assistance from the Supplemental Security Income (SSI) program. An estimated 100,000 children lost their eligibility under the new definition in 1996, and another 70,000 adolescents lost benefits when eligibility redeterminations were conducted between 1997 and 2000.

The law restricted legal immigrants' eligibility for many services and benefits, including cash assistance, food stamps, and Medicaid. Some restrictions on legal immigrants have since been lifted, but most remain ineligible for food stamps, and those entering the country after passage of the law are ineligible for nearly all federal benefits for five years. The changes that resulted from the 1996 law could affect poor children in many ways, both directly and indirectly. For the most part, however, the underlying premise of the law was that children would benefit from seeing their parents leave welfare and go to work.

In fact, many lawmakers expected the promotion of job preparation, work, and marriage to improve parenting practices and child wellbeing, as well as reduce dependence on government benefits. It appears, however, that the links between reform efforts, improved parenting, and positive child outcomes are not as simple or straightforward as envisioned.

Overall, low-income families have fared well since reform, both economically and structurally. Poverty rates have declined, and fewer children are being raised in single-mother households. The primary goal of the 1996 law was to end families' dependence on government benefits, and efforts to address this goal have been very successful. Bolstered by the strong economy of the 1990s and policies that help "make work pay," such as the earned income tax credit (EITC) and expanded health insurance programs for low-income children, many families moved off welfare and into jobs.

In August 1996, 4.4 million families were receiving cash assistance. As of September 2000, the number of families receiving cash assistance had declined by half, to just 2.2 million. The dire predictions made by some critics when the law was passed-that the number of homeless and destitute families would skyrocket, and that there would be a massive migration of children from welfare to foster care-have not materialized. Yet even in a strong economy, many families who left welfare were struggling, and many remaining on the rolls faced serious barriers to employment. What can be gleaned from the research about how low-income children are faring since welfare reform in terms of their economic wellbeing, family structure, and daily life experiences is summarized below.

Welfare reform policies clearly have helped many poor families take advantage of economic opportunities over the past five years and move successfully from welfare to work. More than half the families no longer receiving cash assistance are working, and the combination of earnings and other work supports has boosted the incomes of most single-mother families. Poverty rates declined from 14% in 1996 to 11% in 2000, and child poverty rates also have fallen, from 21% to 16%.

Recent findings from evaluations of welfare-to-work demonstration programs point to the importance of increasing family economic resources to improve children's outcomes. Although these demonstrations were implemented before reform, they included many features similar to those enacted in the 1996 law, such as work requirements, time limits, and financial incentives to work. Results show that, for the most part, families' participation in these programs had no widespread impacts on children.

When impacts were found, some were positive and some were negative, but most were weak. Even when programs resulted in more positive impacts, the children in these families still lagged behind national norms for positive child development. Nevertheless, some patterns have emerged that reinforce the theory that increasing families' employment and income is good for children.

Children in families participating in programs that increased employment and income tended to do better in school and have fewer behavioural problems than children in families not participating in the programs. Positive impacts were found most often among school-age children. Programs with the most positive impacts on children were those that increased families' employment and income through earnings supplements without a mandatory work requirement, such as in an early version of the Minnesota Family Investment Program.

In addition to having positive impacts on children, programs that increased both employment and income through incentives without a mandatory work requirement also had small but significant impacts on the parenting practices of mothers who participated. Compared with nonparticipant mothers and those required to work 30 hours a week, long-term recipient mothers participating in these programs had lower levels of depression and harsh parenting. These mothers were also more likely to marry if single, more likely to stay married if married, and less likely to experience domestic violence. According to Chase-Lansdale and Pittman, the critical factor leading to these positive impacts appears to be that the mothers could work less than full time and still benefit from income gains compared with mothers not participating.

When programs helped families gain jobs but did not increase their income, the evaluations of the pre-reform welfare-to-work demonstrations found few impacts on children. The impacts that did occur were mixed. Children in participant families tended to score higher on assessments of their cognitive skills, but also to receive more reports of behavioural problems, compared with children in families not participating in the programs. When programs resulted in families making no economic progress or experiencing a setback, the effects on children tended to be negative across all types of outcome measures.

Thus, when families move from welfare to work without an increase in income, the impacts on children are less likely to be positive. Unfortunately, this is likely to be the case for many families leaving welfare since reform. Many families leaving welfare for work enter low-paying jobs with no employer-provided benefits, and about 40% of families that have left welfare are not working. Economic resources have declined among many of the poorest families due to the loss of benefits such as welfare and food stamps.

Census Bureau data show that between 1995 and 1997, total annual resources for the poorest 10% of single-mother families declined by $814, on average, from $5,687 to $4,873; among the next poorest 10%, resources declined by $319, from $11,584 to $11,265. The decline in economic resources among poor families is especially sobering because it occurred during a period of sustained economic growth. Following the attack on the World Trade Centre on September 11, 2001, jobs have been disappearing rapidly in manufacturing, services, and transportation-especially low-wage jobs, the types of jobs that welfare recipients would likely fill. During October and November 2001, more than one million jobs were lost, and according to the U.S. Bureau of Labour Statistics, the increase in the jobless rate has been particularly severe for blue-collar workers. Thus, until the economy rebounds, many more poor families are likely to experience declines in their economic resources.

Family structures for low-income children appear to be changing for the better, although any link to welfare reform policies is dubious. Between 1995 and 2000, the percentage of children living with both married parents continued to decline among families above 200% of poverty level, but the percentage remained unchanged, at about 50%, among children in families below 200% of poverty. In addition, the percentage of low-income children living with a single mother declined slightly, from 34% to 33%, whereas the percentage living with a mother and a cohabiting male increased from 5% to 6%. Also, teen births have continued to decline over the past decade.

Between 1990 and 1997, the teen birth rate decreased from 60 to 52 per 1,000 women ages 15 to 19. To the extent that fewer children are being raised by teen parents and single parents, child wellbeing is likely to have improved. Both adolescent and single parenting are associated with lower educational and occupational attainment by mothers and higher developmental risks for children. Young and single mothers are at high risk of poverty and generally provide less stimulating and supportive home environments than those provided by older and married mothers.

Although experimental evaluations have found few impacts on young children's development linked to single parenting, other studies of older children have found that adolescents with single mothers are at greater risk of dropping out of school than are adolescents living with both biological parents. However, the data suggest that many single mothers are not rearing their children alone. 41% of all nonmarital births in the early 1990s occurred to cohabiting couples. In what McLanahan and Carlson refer to as "fragile families," many unmarried parents are working together to raise their children, either by sharing a household or maintaining frequent contact. Such father involvement is important-both financially and emotionally-to children's development.

Single-parent families, especially those with no male present, are much more likely to be poor, and the children are more likely to suffer adverse effects on their development and wellbeing. In 1998, for example, the poverty rate for female-headed families with children was 39%, compared with 8% for male-present families with children. In addition, positive father involvement, particularly by fathers who live with their children, has been linked to less frequent behavioural and emotional problems among children and adolescents, including delinquency, substance use, anxiety, and depression.

Moreover, a recent analysis of several studies found that increased father involvement-such as father-child closeness and authoritative parenting-was associated with significant gains in children's academic achievement and reductions in behavioural problems. Thus, evidence of increased involvement of males in single-mother households might be a positive indicator for child well-being-with three important caveats. First, it is the presence of fathers, not unrelated males, that is linked to positive effects on children.

For example, studies have found that children's school performance and behaviour generally do not improve if their mother marries someone other than the biological father, even though family income is, on average, substantially greater. Second, many low-income families are coping with conflict and domestic violence. In one large study of welfare recipients, for example, 28% reported having been abused by an intimate partner in the previous year. To have positive impacts on children, increased male presence must not bring increased family conflict or domestic violence. Finally, cohabiting couples' relationships are more vulnerable than those of married couples, and if the relationship ends, father-child contact is more likely to diminish.

The movement of mothers from welfare to work has brought significant changes to the daily lives of many children. As increasing numbers of low-income mothers move into jobs, young children are spending more hours in nonmaternal care, and older children are likely to be spending more time unsupervised. At the same time, many low-income children live in families who are receiving welfare, yet are not participating in a welfare-to-work program.

For some, the situation is temporary, but for others, the reasons for lack of participation are likely to persist for some time. In other cases, children's families are not working, but they are not receiving welfare or other benefits due to such reasons as loss of eligibility, sanctions, or time limits. Little information exists on how children in these families are faring.

Welfare policies designed primarily to change the economic and personal behavior of parents can impact the nature and quality of the environments where children spend their time, at home, at school, and in the community. Changes in children's environments in turn can affect their development. Considerable evidence documents the links between each of these factors, but the connections are complex. Policies that require low-income mothers to work could have a number of different impacts-either positive or negative-on children's environments and thus their development and well-being. Therefore, where and how low-income children spend their time while their mothers work warrants greater attention.

Low-income families' access to subsidies is a key factor in their decisions about where their children spend time during work hours. As a result of changes to child care programs stemming from the 1996 welfare reform law, total federal and state funding for child care for welfare and working poor families has increased dramatically, from $2.8 billion in 1995 to $8.0 billion in 2000. Federal and state spending on pre-schools and after-school programs has also grown. The movement of mothers from welfare to work, together with this increased funding for child care, has changed the daily environments of many low-income children.

Infants and toddlers need safe, high-quality child care if they are to benefit from their mothers moving from welfare to work. Under reform, states are encouraged to require single parents on welfare to seek work when they have a child as young as one year old, and can require single parents of even younger children to participate in welfare-to-work programs. As a result, 16 states now have work requirements for single parents with children under age one. In 11 states, parents with children as young as 12 weeks old are required to participate in work activities. Survey data gathered in 1997 indicate that among families with children under age three, low-income working mothers rely mostly on the other parent or a relative for care, whereas a greater percentage of higher-income families rely on formal center-based care, a family child care home, or a nanny.

The research literature is mixed about whether requiring mothers of young children to work has positive or negative effects on the children. On the one hand, some evidence suggests that when a family's income increases, young children benefit, especially young children living in families below poverty level. Moreover, some studies suggest that younger children's enrolment in full-time, high-quality child care can be beneficial, especially for children in low-income families.

On the other hand, other studies indicate that parent-child interaction may be harmed when infants spend extended lengths of time in child care. What seems to emerge from these studies is that while increased income is likely to have positive impacts on young children, the effects of nonmaternal child care can be either good or bad depending on the quality of care, the number of hours in care, and the quality of maternal care provided in the home as the alternative. Evaluations of pre-reform welfare demonstrations found few impacts on the youngest children studied, suggesting that infants and toddlers may not be affected by their families' participation in welfare-to-work programs as much as expected. The data are limited, however. Further research concerning the impacts of different types of care on young children is needed.

Pre-schoolers, especially those from low-income families, appear to benefit from high-quality child care centers-that is, child care characterized by caregivers who are sensitive, responsive, and talk frequently with the children, and a setting that is well-stocked with a breadth of learning and play materials. Low-income children ages three to five who were placed in high-quality centers did better on school readiness scores than children in home-based settings. It has been estimated that at least one million preschool-age children moved into new child care settings between 1996 and 1998 following changes under welfare reform.

Studies indicate that the majority of welfare families rely on informal arrangements when they begin to participate in work activities, yet, families moving off welfare and into more stable, full-time employment are more likely to choose centers and family child care homes over less formal care providers, such as relatives or neighbours.

Total hours of care, stability of care, and type of care all can affect children's development, but the quality of care appears to have by far the greatest influence. For example, some evidence indicates that preschool children spending long hours in care may be more aggressive, assertive, and defiant than children spending less time in care. Studies also show, however, that children who benefit from high-quality daily interactions in their child care settings tend to display better cognitive and language development, school readiness, and early school achievement, compared with children in settings with less engaged caregivers.

Although the effects of child care are modest overall compared to the stronger influence of the home environment, high-quality care has been found to be especially effective in improving outcomes for children growing up in poverty or facing other family-based risks.

More low-income school-age children could benefit from participation in structured after-school activities. Although the number of programs is increasing, many low-income school-age children still are likely to be left in self-care while their mothers work. As a result of greater availability of child care subsidies tied to welfare reform, as well as other initiatives to create more and better after-school programs for youth, an increasing number of low-income school-age children are attending structured programs after school while their mothers work.

For example, in 2001, nearly $850 million in federal funding was provided for the 21st Century Community Learning Centers initiative, a program designed to provide expanded learning opportunities for school-age children in a safe, drug-free, supervised environment. Tens of thousands of other after-school programs are offered by schools, youth organizations, religious groups, and local governments throughout the country.

Moreover, studies suggest that school-age children can benefit from time spent in structured after-school activities, as opposed to self-care. In one study, for example, low-income first and third graders who spent more time in self-care were less socially competent and received lower academic grades in sixth grade, compared with low-income children who spent less time on their own. After-school activities can provide children with opportunities to explore new skill areas, discover their talents, and build self-esteem. After-school programs also can serve as a safe haven in neighbourhoods where crime rates are high and the time after school can expose children to deviant peers, illegal activities, and violence.

Although data are limited, there is some evidence that in families with mothers moving from welfare to work, an increasing number of school-age children may be left home alone. Pre-reform data indicate that working poor families were more than twice as likely to leave their school-age children in self-care than were non-working poor families.

Adolescents Potential effects on adolescent children received virtually no attention during the debates leading to welfare reform. The tacit assumption seemed to be that adolescents would be affected less than younger children by what their parents might be required to do. However, evaluations of Pre-reform welfare-to-work demonstration programs generally found negative impacts for this age group, even in programs that increased families' employment and income, and that had positive impacts on younger children. For example, in the Minnesota Family Investment Program, a higher percentage of mothers rated their adolescent children's school performance below average compared with ratings of adolescent children by control group mothers.

In Canada's Self-Sufficiency Project, mothers enrolled in the program reported that their children had more school behavioural problems, and adolescents themselves reported more smoking and drinking. And in the Florida Family Transition Program, adolescent children in the program group were more likely than those in the control group to have been suspended from school or to have been rated lower on school achievement.

The reasons for these negative impacts are unclear. Possible explanations range from an erosion in parenting quality and monitoring to an increase in adolescent responsibilities within the household. However, these findings reflect only three studies. Additional data for this age group from other evaluations are due to be released in early 2002, which may help to clarify how teens are being affected by reform.

Families not participating in welfare-to-work activities account for over two-thirds of the welfare caseload, on average, nationwide. Some of these families are subject to work requirements and are not participating. But more than half the caseload comprises two major categories of families not subject to work requirements: families with adults who are exempt from requirements for "good cause," and families with no adult recipients in the household, referred to as "child-only" cases.

Because neither of these types of families is required to participate in welfare-to-work programs, they receive little attention from program administrators or researchers, and as a result, not much is known about how the children in these families are faring.

Among the two million adults on welfare nationwide during fiscal year 1999 (on average, per month), 28% were not required to participate in either work or education activities. Most were exempt for "good cause," such as having poor health or a disability, caring for a household member with a disability, being advanced in age, being the victim of domestic violence, not being able to find suitable child care, or caring for a young child. Use of exemptions varies widely among states.

For example, Arizona and Vermont exempted more than 75% of their adult recipients from work requirements in 1999, whereas Nebraska and Oregon exempted fewer than 20%. Exemptions can protect vulnerable families from sanctions and time limits, but they also may remove any sense of urgency about providing families with the services they need to overcome their problems. When families are struggling with barriers that affect family functioning as well as employability, the risk to children can be great. In households coping with serious problems such as substance abuse and maternal depression, some children are resilient and do fine, in general, however, children in such households are at increased risk for harmful consequences.

The majority of children in the foster care system are from families on welfare. Studies have found that the screening tools used by welfare offices to identify serious family problems, and the services provided to address these problems, are inadequate. Moreover, though many families are exempted only temporarily, others may remain so indefinitely, awaiting services that are in short supply. Aside from the fact that children in these families continue to receive benefits, little is known about their wellbeing.

In 1999, about 770,000 families (29% of the total case-load) were "child-only" cases, down from a peak of 978,000 cases in 1996. Because these families receive cash payments only for the child, not the adults in the household, they are not subject to work requirements or time limits.

Child-only cases are created when adults are ineligible to receive benefits, such as when children are not living with their parents and the caretaker adults are ineligible, when parents receive SSI benefits, or when citizen children are living with non-citizen parents. Some researchers have suggested that child-only cases may require intensive interventions to address families' problems, but these cases generally are not being screened to identify such needs. As with children in families with exemptions, little is known about the wellbeing of children in families receiving child-only benefits.

Studies show that poor households are not earning enough to explain the steep drop in cash assistance and other supports. Many children still live in poverty, but without welfare and other benefits that they likely would have received prior to passage of the 1996 law. Although little is known about the wellbeing of children in these poor families, it is unlikely they are faring better as a result of welfare reform. Reasons for families becoming disconnected from benefits vary, ranging from burdensome administrative procedures to loss of eligibility and the impact of sanctions and time limits.

For example, some families have been discouraged from seeking benefits, or they abandoned the effort in the face of the complex administrative procedures for enrolling and maintaining eligibility. In his commentary, Guerra describes the difficult circumstances many poor families face, and the precariousness of their daily lives. Time-consuming, bureaucratic procedures to obtain benefits simply add to the demands on these families, causing many to be disconnected from the services and supports they may be eligible to receive and may need to cope with their problems.

Other families are disconnected from benefits because changes to the welfare reform law made them ineligible. In particular, certain groups of legal immigrants are no longer deemed "qualified" to receive benefits. Some states have established state-funded substitute programs for immigrants, but these programs have not filled the gap left from the loss of federal assistance, and participation rates remain low. Also, many U.S. citizen children of immigrant parents do not access benefits they are eligible to receive. Food stamp participation among such children fell by 74% between

1994 and 1998, compared with a 24% decline among other families with children.

Still other families lost benefits because they exhausted their time limits or failed to comply with program requirements. Data from the U.S. Department of Health and Human Services indicate that in 1999, about 156,000 families left welfare due to sanctions. Greenberg and colleagues note that families whose cases are closed due to sanctions are likely to have low education levels, little or no work history, and more serious employment barriers. Little is known about the development and well-being of children in poor families disconnected from benefits. But, as Primus notes in his commentary, many families who leave welfare without finding a job are floundering.

Indeed, evidence of hardship has been found in surveys of families who have left welfare. For example, two waves of families leaving welfare were interviewed in the National Survey of America's Families, one group in 1997 and another in 1999. About half the respondents in both groups said they have had to cut the size of meals or skip them because they did not have enough food in the past year. About 40% said they were unable to pay the mortgage, rent, or utility bills at some point in the past year. In sum, fewer children are living in poverty; however, those children who are living in poverty are less likely to be receiving the benefits they would have prior to reform.

Many poor families are disconnected not just from welfare, but also from other supports they need to help make ends meet. At the same time, low-income children are more likely now to be living in a home with a male present. If that male is the father and not violent, a child is likely to benefit, but more information is needed to understand who the cohabiting males are and how they interact with these children. Finally, as more low-income mothers move into the workforce, their children are spending more time in nonmaternal or self-care. Time spent in structured programs can be positive, but the quality of the program is key. Among families still receiving welfare, most are not involved in work activities and little is known about how their children are faring.

Welfare programs and other supports focus primarily on moving mothers from welfare to work. This may be a good first step, but it does not guarantee positive outcomes for children. Reauthorization of the federal welfare reform law offers a critical opportunity to re-examine the purpose and goals of the law in terms of providing an effective safety net for low-income families and their children.

Before the economic downturn took hold in the fall of 2001, a nationwide poll found that more than half of those surveyed viewed poverty as a big problem. Of those aware of the new welfare law, 61% thought it was working well, mostly because it requires people to work. At the same time, respondents voiced strong support for providing more assistance to help families trying to move off welfare into work. Large majorities of those surveyed said they supported expanding job training programs and public employment; improving public schools in low-income areas; increasing the minimum wage and tax credits for low-income workers; and expanding subsidized day care, medical care, and housing.

Especially now, as the economy slows, having strong supports in place for the families of low-wage workers and the unemployed is crucial. What we have learned about how low-income children are faring in this new social policy landscape can point to ways the safety net could be strengthened to offer the greatest promise for improving children's chances to succeed in school and in life. Three key strategies address what is most important for low-income children: helping families achieve an adequate standard of living, helping them provide stable and supportive homes, and helping them access quality child care and after-school programs and activities.

A family's economic resources influence child well-being, because they are necessary to meet children's basic needs for food and shelter. In addition, a family's economic resources influence the quality of environments children experience at home, in child care, at school, and in the community.

Children in families with adequate resources tend to be healthier and to do better in school; they are less likely to be involved in criminal behavior and are more likely to graduate from high school and to earn higher incomes as adults. Welfare-to-work programs that increase family income as well as employment have been shown to have the potential to improve children's academic progress and, to a lesser extent, their behavior. For example, subsidy programs that increase economic resources in low-income working families by as little as $1,200 to $4,000 per year have been shown to have positive impacts on the development of preschool and elementary-school-age children.

Important steps needed to help low-income working families attain adequate resources include stronger efforts to connect them to support services and to help them find better jobs and move up career ladders to higher wages.

Government supports such as the EITC (which refunds a portion of earnings to low-income taxpayers), food stamps, health insurance, and subsidized health care and child care are essential to maintaining sufficient economic resources for families earning low wages. Studies show that participation in the EITC is generally strong, with about 85% of eligible families receiving the credit. But the same is not true of other programs intended to help make work pay.

Many families who have left welfare are not using other, nontax supports to augment their earnings. For example, one study found that 57% of families leaving welfare were not receiving food stamps even though they were eligible. Half the families with incomes below 50% of poverty were not receiving food stamps. Similar trends have been noted in Medicaid coverage and receipt of child care subsidies.

In the Urban Institute study of families leaving welfare between 1997 and 1999, only 22% reported receiving government help in paying for child care after three months. When families are not receiving welfare, they may be unaware of their eligibility for food stamps, Medicaid, child care assistance, and other supports. Differences in income, assets, citizenship, and recertification standards create confusion and errors in determining the eligibility of families seeking benefits across various programs. In addition, services are often provided at times and in locations that make access difficult for low-income working families. Without extensive outreach and advocacy to address such problems, available benefits may never reach many eligible families. Programs adopted following the 1996 law should be judged by their ability to restore and increase participation among the working poor.

Getting a job and moving off welfare does not assure that a family will have adequate economic resources. Even when working full time at a minimum wage job and receiving all available supports, families do not have adequate resources. For example, the Urban Institute study of welfare leavers found that median monthly wages were $1,093 in 1999.

According to studies in eight states, the average monthly earnings of former recipients during the first three months after leaving welfare were even less, generally ranging from about $733 to $900. Some studies have found that at least half of families leaving welfare have fewer economic resources than they would have had if they had stayed on welfare. Many, in fact, end up returning to the rolls. In the Urban Institute study, for example, 29% of families leaving welfare between 1995 and 1997 returned to welfare, as did 22% of those leaving welfare between 1997 and 1999. After mothers find work, they need supports to help them keep their jobs and increase their earnings. As of October 1999, states were providing case management for at least some recipients who had found jobs or who no longer received cash assistance.

Generally states provide post-employment support services such as transportation aid, help in purchasing work clothes or tools, and payment of work-related fees. It is unclear whether these efforts have actually helped increase steady work, however. Some evaluations have found that they have no impact on how long families keep jobs or how much they earn. Sixteen states had policies to support employer-based education and training services to promote job advancement. But most of these efforts served only a small number of families. Alternatively, some states were addressing the issue of job advancement by increasing access to post secondary education or training that would enable unemployed parents to find better jobs.

The current welfare system rewards states for moving families off the rolls, but not for ensuring that those families gain steady employment and earn an adequate income. To encourage states to develop better approaches to helping families keep their jobs and increase their earnings, an expansion of welfare's goals is needed.

In particular, a greater emphasis on education and training is warranted. Many families currently receiving welfare could benefit from further education. In 1999, more than 40% of adults on welfare had less than a high school education.

Prior to reform, welfare programs had education components that focused on helping recipients enhance their basic skills, but this approach demonstrated little success in moving families into higher-paying jobs. Largely as a result of these findings, the 1996 law placed restrictions on education and training as a work activity, and on the length of time families could receive assistance. Under current rules, not more than 30% of recipients being counted toward a state's work participation rate can be participating in educational activities for no more than 12 months, including teen parents still completing high school.

Research suggests, however, that when combined with other activities such as job search or work itself, education can play an important role in helping families find better jobs. Further, training for low-income parents who are between jobs is a wise investment, especially during times of high unemployment. In addition to improving a family's future earning potential, maternal educational progress appears to be linked to positive child outcomes.

Preexisting differences in mothers' attributes, skills, and personalities likely influence both educational attainment and economic progress. Nevertheless, in Zaslow and colleagues' synthesis of findings from evaluations of Pre-reform welfare-to-work demonstrations, maternal educational progress tracked more closely with favourable child outcomes than did economic progress-that is, increased educational attainment more consistently resulted in positive child outcomes than did increased family employment and income. Perhaps seeing a parent go to school provides an even better role model for children than seeing a parent go to work. Taken together, these findings suggest that welfare programs could promote more positive outcomes for children by enabling mothers to increase their education while receiving temporary cash assistance within established time limits.

Although having adequate economic resources is important, a nurturing and secure home environment, including the love and support of both biological parents, remains the most critical influence on young children's adjustment and wellbeing, even for children who spend substantial time in child care and encouragement of adult family members and other adults who are mentally healthy, responsible, constant, and reliable is extremely important to children's healthy development.

Many states are using welfare funds to implement initiatives targeted directly at improving parenting, such as providing home visits to new parents or requiring certain welfare recipients to attend parenting classes. Although parenting behaviours are complex and difficult to change, welfare programs can help strengthen family functioning and the home environment in various ways depending on a family's circumstances. Different approaches are required depending on whether a family is moving from welfare to work, or is struggling with barriers to employment. In many situations, greater involvement of fathers can be a key strategy for strengthening families and promoting children's well-being both financially and emotionally.

In families with a mother moving from welfare to work, parenting practices and the home environment could be affected by a change in family resources, family relationships, parents' time at home, and parents' personal sense of well-being. According to Chase-Lansdale and Pittman, the limited available literature on this topic indicates that, compared with unemployed single mothers, single mothers who choose to work may provide a more cohesive, stimulating, and organized family environment, and may do more to promote the value of education. But other studies have found that mothers who were required to participate in welfare-to-work programs experienced higher levels of depression and stress than those who were not required to participate.

Many low-income families live on the edge, both economically and functionally. According to data from the National Survey of America's Families in 1997 and in 1999, about three-quarters of adults on welfare had at least one potential barrier to employment, including very poor mental or physical health, limited education, minimal work experience, or family responsibilities that limit their ability to work, such as caring for an infant or a disabled child.

When families are struggling with serious barriers—such as substance abuse, maternal depression, and domestic violence—the problems not only present challenges in getting and keeping jobs, they also detract from parents' ability to provide stable and supportive homes for their children. Estimates of the percentage of welfare recipients with substance abuse problems range from 16% to 37%. About 22% to 28% are estimated to be suffering from very poor mental health, and 10% to 31% to be coping with domestic violence.

Some of these families are exempt from work requirements, whereas others are not, since states' policies on exemptions vary widely. But simply providing welfare and exempting families from work and time limit requirements will not enable most families to overcome their problems, enter the workforce, and provide stable and supportive homes for their children. The underlying conditions contributing to a family's precarious situation must be addressed. Often these underlying conditions are rooted in the mothers' own childhoods.

Many low-income mothers have grown up in families that did not provide good models of positive family functioning. They may have experienced sexual and physical abuse. Among participants in a New Jersey welfare-to-work program, for example, 20% report having been sexually molested as children. Other studies indicate that the proportion of teen mothers with histories of sexual and physical abuse may be as high as

68%. Thus, it should not be surprising that a large proportion of mothers on welfare have scars from the past that contribute to their difficulties in coping with their complex lives, and may lead them to substance abuse or involvement in high-conflict relationships.

In 1997, Congress enacted the Welfare-to-Work program to support state and local efforts to help the most disadvantaged welfare recipients (as well as noncustodial parents) address specific problems affecting their employment prospects and move into the labour force. Some states have begun implementing programs to address families' barriers to employment, but most serve only a small percentage of those needing help and little information is available on program outcomes and effectiveness. Most caseworkers have limited training or skills to identify families with barriers. To deal more effectively with families struggling with serious difficulties, a restructuring of services may be needed.

Families coping with mental illness or learning disabilities, for example, should be treated and monitored by the mental health system or the developmental disabilities system, not by welfare or employment programs. This does not mean that such families should not be encouraged to move from welfare to work, only that specialized systems are better equipped to provide the supports that can enable these families to find appropriate work situations. Such systems are also better able to help these families connect with long-term parenting supports that may continue to be needed even after their economic situation improves.

A large number of low-income children grow up in homes with no father. In 2000, nearly half of all families living in poverty were headed by a female with no husband present. Although many unmarried parents work together to raise their children by cohabiting or maintaining frequent contact, father involvement for most low-income families in this situation is not stable and tends to decline over time. Yet research in the last decade has pointed to the range of contributions fathers can make in their children's lives, both financially and emotionally.

Welfare programs and other support services could be restructured in various ways to promote greater inclusion and involvement of low-income fathers in their children's lives. For example, most unmarried couples are closely connected to each other and invested in their new family when a baby is born.

Thus, a window of opportunity exists around the time of birth to strengthen the connections between fathers and their children. In a study of approximately 3,700 children born to unmarried parents across the country in 2000, 99% of the new fathers who were interviewed expressed a desire to be involved in raising their children, and 93% of mothers said they wanted the father to be involved. Targeting fatherhood programs to unmarried fathers at the time of a child's birth appears to offer the greatest promise of successful involvement.

In addition, the chances for positive father involvement would improve if a broader range of TANF services were targeted to two-parent families and noncustodial parents, as noted in the commentary by Primus. For example, programs that provide employment opportunities for fathers help increase their ability to pay child support and also make them more appealing as marriage partners.

More successful programs that teach men to be good fathers and reduce family violence are also needed. Finally, reducing the marriage penalties in programs aimed at helping low-income families-including welfare, food stamps, and Medicaid, as well as state and federal EITCs-has been noted as an important societal signal and support for marriage. The way these programs are currently structured, benefits generally decrease as household income increases. Because marriage results in one combined household income, a couple could lose thousands of dollars a year in benefits compared with what they would be eligible to receive if they each remained single.

Improving the child support system is also important, not only for increasing collections, but also for promoting more positive father involvement. Child support can significantly augment the wages of single-parent families. One study found that child support provided 14% of the income for families with incomes below 150% of poverty who were not on welfare, and 35% of the income among all families receiving some child support. Other research found that $1,000 in child support was associated with higher grades and fewer school problems among children, and that child support income was associated with a larger gain in children's well-being than an identical amount of income from other sources.

The positive effects of child support income are likely due to the fact that fathers who pay child support also tend to be more involved with their children. Unfortunately, most poor children eligible for child support do not receive it. Child support is collected for only 44% of families who have left welfare and 25% of families on welfare. In large part, low collection rates are due to a lack of support orders. Unless an order is established, it cannot be enforced. Among families receiving welfare in 2000, fewer than half had a support order established. Increased efforts to establish support orders among low-income families is an important first step to increasing collections.

Low collection rates also stem from the fact that many fathers of poor children are themselves poor and have limited ability to pay. Several demonstration projects were undertaken in the 1980s and 1990s to improve fathers' employment and earnings, but without much success. More recently, nearly $2 billion in grants were awarded in 1998 and 1999 through the Welfare-to-Work program to help move noncustodial parents (and other hard-to-serve populations) into unsubsidized jobs. As mentioned earlier, little information is available on the effectiveness of these programs, but an evaluation is under way.

Beyond having few resources, fathers of children in welfare families generally have little incentive to pay child support because, for the most part, it goes to repay welfare expenditures and not to increase family income. Only a small amount, if any, is "passed through" to the family. However, a demonstration project in Wisconsin allowed all support to be passed through to TANF families, and the project appears to have had positive results. Noncustodial fathers participating in the program were more likely to establish paternity and pay support to their families, and family conflict around child support was reduced.

High-Quality Child Care

Welfare reform brought with it a clear mandate that low-income single mothers should work. An equally clear mandate is needed that while their mothers are at work, low-income children should have access to high-quality child care and after-school options in their neighbourhoods. Providing quality environments for children not only enables mothers to work, but it is also an opportunity to enhance children's development and well-being.

Studies show that poor children are especially likely to benefit from positive experiences in child care and after-school programs. The increases in funding for child care since welfare reform have helped many low-income families afford higher-quality options for their children. However, high-quality child care and after-school options for low-income families are often still constrained, both in terms of cost and supply. Despite funding increases, state studies show child care subsidies are used by less than one-quarter of all eligible families. Data compiled by the U.S. Department of Health and Human Services indicate that nationwide, of the 14.7 million children eligible to receive subsidies in 1999, only 1.8, or 12%, received them. This percentage does not include families participating in Head Start or other state-funded preschool or child care programs, but subsidy utilization rates, especially among working poor families, are still low.

Although eligible for assistance, working poor families tend to have less access to subsidies than families on or just leaving welfare, and the availability of high-quality programs in low-income communities is uneven. Fuller and colleagues identify several barriers to use of subsidies and high-quality care, including state eligibility criteria, copayment policies, reimbursement rates, burdensome administrative processes, and lack of high-quality centers in many low-income neighbourhoods.

Though not eligible for child care subsidies, teens also benefit from participation in structured activities after school. Several studies have shown that participation in targeted prevention programs can reduce high-risk behaviours among teenagers. For example, in four consecutive annual evaluations, participants in the Teen Outreach Program, sponsored by the Association of Junior Leagues International, were shown to be less likely than their nonparticipant peers to have experienced either pregnancy or school failure. An evaluation of another youth development program, the Quantum Opportunities Program, also found significant positive effects on economically disadvantaged high school youths.

A recent evaluation of the Children's Aid Society model found similar results. In light of the initial negative impacts found on teens whose mothers participate in welfare-to-work programs, additional investment in programs for low-income youth may be warranted.

As low-income mothers move into the workforce and their children spend more time unsupervised or in child care and after-school programs, those experiences have an increasingly important influence on children's development and wellbeing. Low-income children of all ages could benefit from increased access to high-quality child care and after-school programs and activities.

The evidence is clear that moving mothers into jobs is a good first step, but further efforts are needed to promote better outcomes for children.

Working poor families need to stay connected to supports, including job advancement and continuing education and training, to ensure that children have adequate resources. An adequate income is important to meeting children's basic needs and enabling families to provide healthier learning environments for children both inside and outside the home. Welfare and other income support programs need to continue to provide services and supports to families after they find jobs to help them increase their earnings and escape poverty. Welfare programs should also allow single mothers to work more flexible, part-time hours and pursue more education and training. Not only would this enhance a family's earning potential, but maternal educational advancement also appears to foster positive impacts on children's school performance and behavior. Such a strategy makes sense in the current economy, as finding and keeping low-wage jobs becomes increasingly difficult.

Many families are neither working nor participating in welfare-to-work programs for a variety of reasons, and more families are likely to join their numbers as the economy slows. Welfare programs need to develop better strategies for identifying families with serious barriers to employment and healthy family functioning, and to explore new ways of helping these families, such as by integrating services with mental health and developmental disabilities systems.

Welfare and other income support programs also need to encourage greater father involvement by engaging fathers soon after a child's birth, and by adopting more evenhanded policies providing access to services and benefits. Fathers, as well as mothers, need programs to help them find jobs and advance in their careers, and to help them address their barriers to employment and positive family functioning.

And third, children and teens need high-quality child care and after-school activities in their neighbourhoods to ensure that the time they spend while their mothers are at work plays a positive role in their lives. For low-income children especially, such programs can provide safe havens and a range of opportunities to enhance their development. Welfare programs need to work with child care agencies to expand access to child care subsidies for working poor families, and to expand the supply of high-quality options for children of all ages in low-income communities.

For the nation's welfare programs to improve the lives of low-income children, child well-being needs to be a top priority. This analysis has highlighted some of the ways that current welfare programs could be restructured to help promote healthier child development among low-income families. As the economy weakens and more families are forced to go on welfare, more funds will be needed for cash assistance and less will be available for some of the services described here as beneficial to children, such as programs to help families address barriers to positive family functioning as well as employment; programs to promote father involvement; and programs to improve the quality of child care, enrichment activities, and programs for teens.

The present level of funding for welfare and other support programs needs to be maintained, at a minimum-and increased, if possible-to ensure that the progress made since reform in restructuring programs to help families move from welfare to work is not lost, and that a strong safety net for poor families is in place. The goal of welfare programs should be to reduce poverty among families with children.

4

Challenges of Measuring Child Labour

If action to abolish child labour is to be effective, it must be based on a thorough understanding of the size and shape of the problem. As a complex social and economic phenomenon, child labour has always presented challenges for conventional research methods. With world attention now focused on the worst forms of child labour, it is all the more essential to have good quality information available on which to base policy and programme design. A major difficulty lies in counting and researching the many children working in the informal economy, in private homes, in family enterprises and in illegal and hidden activities. For a long time, the lack of reliable methods of measurement and the absence of statistics on child labour were serious impediments to its effective abolition. The situation has improved considerably in recent years, but there is still some way to go.

The ILO has made considerable strides over the years in assisting member States and other partners to collect and disseminate information about child labour, using innovative research methods. Since 1979, when a large number of country studies were commissioned for the International Year of the Child, there has been an ongoing programme of child labour research providing new insights through counting, describing and analysing the work of children in a variety of economic settings. This work was given a boost in 1998 with the launch of the Statistical Information and Monitoring Programme on Child Labour (SIMPOC) within IPEC. ILO constituents, other international organizations, NGOs, academics, activists and others have all contributed to the rapidly expanding knowledge base about child labour.

Child labourers in the world today

The ILO estimated that in 1995 some 250 million children between the ages of 5 and 14 were working (i.e. "economically active") in the developing world; at least 120 million of these children were working full time. This undoubtedly helped to raise public awareness of the scale of the problem and to promote action against it. These estimates were based on the data available at that time, primarily from replies to special questionnaires sent to national statistical offices and some experimental child labour surveys, along with published labour force and population statistics. While neither estimate corresponded to the global number of "child labourers" (according to the provisions of Convention No. 138), they nonetheless gave a clear indication of the magnitude of the problem to be tackled. The time is now ripe to update and refine the estimates, and to make an attempt - in full recognition of data and methodological constraints—to assess the number of children involved in the often hidden worst forms of labour. New estimates by the ILO now provide us with an updated, more complete picture of the child labour problem across the world.

A single estimate of economically active children does not capture the various kinds and intensities of work in which children are involved. Estimates were therefore made of the number of children (aged under 18) engaged in the following categories of economic activity, for the year 2000:

— children engaged in any type of economic activity, including for short periods of time, and in light work;

— children engaged in all types of child labour to be abolished;

— children engaged in hazardous work which, because of its nature or the number of hours worked, jeopardizes their health, safety or morals; and

— children engaged in the unconditional worst forms of child labour.

The numbers of children involved in these different categories of economic activity, according to age group. Various statistical data, including national SIMPOC surveys of child labour and other household and community surveys such as the surveys conducted under the World Bank's Living Standards Measurement Study (LSMS), were used to estimate the numbers of children engaged in all types of economic activity, in all types of child labour to be abolished and in hazardous work. Statistical techniques were applied to allow extrapolation from national data sets. For the worst forms of child labour, global estimates were based on an assessment and aggregation of existing national and regional estimates for each worst form. The global estimates for the year 2000 are:

— Of an estimated 211 million children aged 5-14 engaged in some form of economic activity, 186 million children are engaged in child labour to be abolished (including in its worst forms).

— Of an estimated 141 million children aged 15-17 engaged in economic activity, 59 million children are engaged in child labour.

A detailed breakdown of the aggregate figure, by economic category of activity and by the age group of the children involved. The global estimates of economically active children and those involved in child labour or in hazardous work are broken down into the numbers of girls and boys involved. Girls and boys are equally involved in economic activity up to the age of 14, but above this age, the proportion of boys increases. Boys' involvement in child labour is higher than that of girls in both age groups, and particularly among older children in hazardous work.

Available estimates of children's involvement in the unconditional worst forms of child labour indicate a global total of at least 8.4 million girls and boys of all ages. The majority of these (two-thirds of the total) is thought to be trapped in forms of forced and bonded labour. Approximately one-fifth, nearly two million children, are believed to be exploited through prostitution and pornography. Estimates by economic or regional grouping are possible only at the level of economically active children.

Table 1
Percentage of girls in economic activity, child labour hazardous work

	5-14 ys	*15-17 ys*	*Total*
Economically active children of which:	50	47	49
Child labours of which	49	42	48
Children in hazardous work	47	42	45

Table 2
Estimated number of children involved in the unconditional worst forms of child labour

Type of worst form of child labour	*Global number of children (in millions)*
Forced and bonded labour	5.7
Forced recruitment into armed conflict	0.3
Prostitution and pornography	1.8
Other illicit activities	0.6
Trafficked children	(1.2)
Total	**8.4**

If we subtract the numbers of economically active children in the developed and transition economies from the global estimate of 211 million, we arrive at a figure of 206 million for the developing economies. It might then be tempting to make a comparison between the 1995 and the 2000 global estimates—and thereby conclude that the number of economically active children (5-14 years) in the developing economies has decreased from 250 million to 206 million, and that the situation must therefore be improving in many countries. It is undeniable that the

2000 estimate for economically active children is less than the 1995 estimate. However, because very different methods and data sources were used for the two computations, the conclusions that can be drawn from a straight comparison. Two basic propositions (not mutually exclusive) are possible:

1) The difference between the estimates reflects the different and improved methods and data used to compute the 2000 estimate.
2) The difference reflects an actual decline in the number of working children across the world.

It is not possible to know which of the above propositions carries most weight in explaining the difference between the 1995 and 2000 estimates. However, the size of the difference between them (44 million or a decrease of almost 20 per cent) might suggest that indeed there has been a global reduction in the number of children working over this five-year period, giving some grounds for cautious optimism that the measures being taken to combat child labour, considered in Part II of this Report, are having an effect. The main value of the new estimates lies in the insight they give us into the dimensions of the child labour to be abolished.

They show us clearly that, while some progress may have been made, there is no room for complacency. Although it is not the purpose of the Global Report to provide a detailed analysis, some of the main conclusions that emerge from an initial look at the new estimates can be highlighted.

— *Child labour persists on a very large scale:* Although numerous young people are engaged in work that is consistent with their full development, many more are being harmed by child labour. The estimates indicate that there are some 186 million child labourers aged 5-14, and 59 million aged 15-17 worldwide; on average, one child in every six aged 5-17 can be classed as a child labourer.

— The extent of the worst forms of child labour, particularly hazardous work, appears to be more serious than was previously thought. More than two-thirds of the total number of child labourers, i.e. one in eight children across the world, or a total of nearly 180 million children, are exploited in the worst forms of work.

— It is especially alarming that almost two-thirds (or 111 million) of the children who are engaged in hazardous work are less than 15 years old, and so should be immediately withdrawn from this work. This still leaves some 59 million young workers between 15 and 17 years old who are exposed to hazards at work, and who urgently need either immediate protection from the dangers they face or to be withdrawn totally from such work.

— There are still major problems of data availability and reliability for the unconditional worst forms of child labour. While the estimates represent a best attempt, with the methods and data currently available, to quantify children's exploitation under the unconditional worst forms of child labour, the ILO is keenly aware of their limitations. Further research, using new methods, is urgently needed. There will always, however, be severe limits to the accurate measurement of these essentially clandestine activities.

— With regard to the gender dimensions of the global estimates, at all ages, boys have a slightly higher level of involvement in child labour than girls and the proportion of boys involved increases with age. Boys represent around 60 per cent of the children aged 12 years and over in hazardous work.

— The estimates according to economic or regional groupings for economically active children (as a proxy for child labour) indicate where the problem is most serious. The Asia-Pacific region harbours the largest absolute number of working children (5-14 years), some 127 million or 60 per cent of the total, followed by sub-Saharan Africa with 23 per cent of the total. However, the intensity of the problem is highest in sub-Saharan Africa, where 29 per cent of all children under 15 are at work, compared to 19 per cent in Asia and the Pacific. Children are also economically active in transition and developed countries, although in much smaller absolute numbers and proportions.

— The human dimension of these aggregate statistics is difficult to comprehend and convey. In a very real sense, a single child subjected to child labour, especially to its worst forms, is one too many. But the estimates show that child labour remains a problem on a massive scale. We have surely reached a moment in history where the absolute number of child labourers, and the proportion of a country's children who are subject to child labour, particularly to its worst forms, should become key indicators of economic and social development.

Numbers of child labourers alone paint only part of the picture. While it is important to know how many children globally are involved in different types of labour, to help them we need to know where they are, what their work involves and how it is affecting them. Contrary to popular opinion, child labour is not confined to developing or poor countries: it is found in all countries, to a greater or lesser extent. The ILO's new estimates indicate that nearly 3 per cent of children in the 10-14-year age group in developed countries are economically active, as are just over 4 per cent of children in transition countries. In the review of annual reports under the follow-up to the ILO Declaration for 2002, at least five governments of developed countries acknowledged the suspected existence of one or more of the worst forms of child labour in their country. It is clear that economic growth does not automatically lead to the disappearance of child labour, as is too often assumed. However, the problem is most critical in developing countries.

Popular perceptions of where children work can easily be distorted by uneven coverage in the media and other sources of public information. For example, much attention has been paid in literature and advocacy to the involvement of children in export-oriented manufacturing, and in international activities such as sex tourism. Yet it is estimated that only 5 per cent of child labourers work in formal-economy, export-related jobs, and commercial sexual exploitation of children is dominated by local rather than by foreign customers.

It is also important to remember that, far from being static, children's involvement in the labour market is constantly changing. Individual children move in and out of school and work, and between different types and intensifies of work depending, for example, on the season, the immediate cash needs of the family, and where income opportunities are perceived to exist. At the macro-level, the market for child labour is constantly evolving, in the context of globalization, and demographic and attitudinal change. Experience teaches us that child labour is a very stubborn problem: its abolition in one economic sector may be accompanied by its re-emergence in another, and nowhere has it been completely abolished.

The following review of the main types of work undertaken by children around the world today helps us to understand better the 'who, what and where' behind the principle of the effective abolition of child labour. It does not pretend to be a comprehensive overview of child labour in the world today.

The review starts by looking at children's participation in legitimate sectors of economic activity, in which the activity per se is not illegal, but the type of work or the conditions in which it is performed by children, and the age of those children, may mean that they are victims of child labour or even of its worst forms because of the hazards to which they are exposed. The review then looks at the forms of child labour that, by their very nature, constitute worst forms.

Surveys in developing countries tell us that the vast majority (70 per cent) of children who work (i.e. are economically active), are engaged in agriculture, fishing, hunting and forestry. Less than 9 per cent are involved in manufacturing, and the same number in wholesale and retail trade, restaurants and hotels. This is followed by community, social and personal services, including domestic work (6.5 per cent) and transport, storage and communication (4 per cent). Around 3 per cent of children are involved in construction, mining and quarrying combined.

For example, exactly what types of activity are being undertaken by children in these different sectors? How many and which boys and girls are at risk of physical or other harm through their work, and what kinds of harm? Is work in mining (regarded as a hazardous sector) necessarily more damaging than that in agriculture? How many children are working full time or combining their economic activity with schooling, and how many have had their education suffer because of their work? What are the gender and age differences in participation in different types of work? Are there differences along lines of ethnicity, race, class or other social group? Only when we can examine these details will we be able really to understand the dynamic forces behind the child labour that we are trying to abolish, and how to go about achieving that goal.

The informal economy is a burgeoning field of economic activity to be found throughout the developing world as well as in transition and in some developed countries. It encompasses the expanding and increasingly diverse group of workers and enterprises in both rural and urban areas operating informally ... they share one important characteristic: they are not recognized or protected under the legal and regulatory frameworks ... Informal workers and entrepreneurs are characterized by a high degree of vulnerability. The informal economy is where by far the most child labourers are found. It cuts across all economic sectors and may be closely linked to formal sector production. In agriculture, for instance, highly organised commercial plantations may contract out some production to small-scale family farms. In manufacturing, the factory of a multinational or a national enterprise may use parts or materials sourced from small workshops or through contractors from families working at home. Most small and micro-enterprises are characterized by an informal work setting, unsafe conditions, cheap (and sometimes unpaid) labour, including that of children, and relatively low productivity and returns on investment.

Where activities such as mining, fishing, and home-based production and assembly work are unregulated, untaxed and do not involve recognized employment relationships, children can be considered as working in the informal economy. The preponderance of child labour in the informal economy beyond the reach of most formal institutions in countries at all levels of income, 36 represents one of the principal challenges to its effective abolition. Many other aspects of the lives of poor people are informal, in addition to their economic activity, thus compounding their overall poverty and vulnerability.

They may have no land or property rights, be unregistered as citizens and have no access to formal social protection, legal recourse or financial and other services. Households headed by women or children are the most insecure of all. Although informal safety nets exist, they are often far from adequate, and they are less reliable in urban areas compared to rural areas. Urban households tend to share fewer assets with others, making them more dependent on jobs for income. In such conditions, the risks of children being pulled into income-earning activities are all too obvious.

The agriculture sector contains 'the bulk of the world's poor, working long hours for meagre returns and under

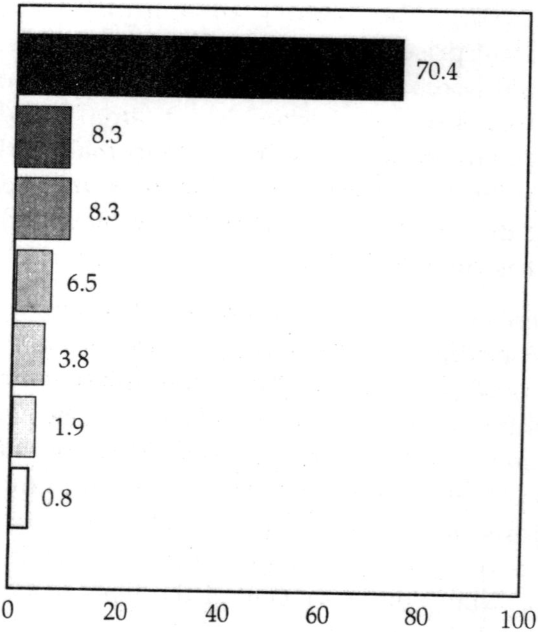

- Agriculture, hunting, forestry and fishing
- Manufacturing
- Wholesale and retail trade, restaurants and hotels
- Community social and personal service
- Transport, storage and communication
- Construction
- Mining and quarrying

Fig.1: Sectoral distribution of working children

hazardous and difficult conditions'. Exercise of the rights to freedom of association and collective bargaining is denied many adult agricultural workers around the world. Work performed by children varies widely—from short periods of light work after school to long hours of arduous work that may involve dangerous chemicals and work processes, both in subsistence-oriented and commercial production. While children's involvement in agriculture may indeed be a normal and useful part of their socialisation in many countries, imparting skills for the future, the reality of such work is often harsh.

Evidence from India suggests that the combination of poor nutrition and agricultural work in childhood results in stunting, which then impairs earning ability later in life. 40 In the Philippines, family-based vegetable farming has been shown to be a hazardous occupation for children, by virtue of exposure to infection from soil and water, the use of heavy watering cans and the lack of protective clothing. Processing of agricultural products can also pose hazards. Peeling, cutting and grading cashew nuts, for example, exposes children to cuts, skin irritation and fatigue, and pain from sitting or standing for long periods.

Gender roles are important in determining what work children do in agriculture. Both girls and boys generally contribute to the work of adult women, yet may be assigned different tasks requiring different levels of effort. In rural Bangladesh, girls begin work at a younger age and, because of their domestic tasks, work longer hours than boys. The number of boys and girls in a family and their birth order is also a factor. Among the rural Tonga of Zimbabwe, for instance, both boys and girls help women with household tasks. Many agricultural tasks are classed as women's work but, if women do not have daughters, they can rely on their sons, until the latter turn 10, for help in the fields. Children's work in agriculture too often goes hand in hand with debt bondage, one of the worst forms of child labour.

The very poorest families, without land or with too little of it to meet subsistence needs, can quickly become entrapped by debt to their landlord or to a third party. Parents or guardians may have little choice but to bond their children into agricultural or domestic labour to repay the debt. Child labour often assumes serious proportions in commercial agriculture, associated with global markets for cocoa, coffee, cotton, rubber, sisal and tea, and other commodities.

Children may represent a substantial portion of the commercial agricultural workforce. Studies in Brazil, Kenya and Mexico have shown that children under 15 make up between 25 and 30 per cent of the total labour force in production of various commodities. Recently, the spotlight has turned to child (and forced) labour in cocoa production in West Africa. In Central America, too, large numbers of children work on plantations. Rapid Assessments (RA) carried out by IPEC have shown striking similarities among children who undertake agricultural work on plantations:

— parents have low levels of educational attainment;

— most children attend school, but work at weekends or during school vacations;

— children's wages are included in those of the working parent(s); and

— children do not like the work but are resigned to helping out with household expenses and/or school fees.

Children's involvement in agriculture has also increased dramatically in certain transition countries with the break-up of collective farms into private, family-held smallholdings—increasing the need for the unpaid labour inputs of household members. In the Russian Federation, however, there are indications that children now work less in agriculture than they did during the Soviet period, as the forced involvement of children in crop-harvesting on collective farms, organized through schools, has been curtailed.

In many developed countries agriculture is also the sector in which most children work. Family farms are a common exemption from minimum age legislation. In the United States, 'children of any age may be employed by their parents or persons standing in place of their parents at any time and in any occupation on a farm owned or operated by their parents or persons standing in place of their parents', with the implication that these children may engage in activities that they would not be allowed to undertake in other circumstances.

Seven per cent of all farm workers (approximately 126,000) are between the ages of 14 and 17. However, the risk of accident and injury in modern agricultural production is high. In the United States, this sector has the highest number of occupational fatalities for youths under 18, accounting for 42.7 per cent of all fatalities in that age range. Fishing is a particularly hazardous occupation, even for adults. In the small-scale sector, which accounts for over half the world's seafood catch and millions of small fishing craft, health and safety problems are endemic for all age groups. The contribution of children is most widespread in small-scale fishing where it can be critical for the profitability of the enterprise. In El Salvador, children work in small-scale, family-based or private enterprises in which boys and girls harvest shellfish, and girls also market the product. For both sexes, this work begins well before the age of 10.

Some child labour in fishing occurs outside the family or traditional sector. For example, muro-ami fishing (named after the net used) in the Philippines takes place on large vessels, and the profits are reaped by the group that monopolizes the business. Children are engaged as swimmers and divers for catching reef fish—extremely dangerous work. In southern Thailand, children work as fish sorters, factory workers and as crew on fishing boats. They carry out a wide range of tasks on board, and may be away at sea for several months at a time. In central Java, work undertaken by children in fishing includes handling and repairing nets, diving, draining boats and cooking.

Clear gender roles 84. As in agriculture, gender issues are important in fishing. A strong connection in general between fishing and cultural perceptions of masculinity, as well as income that looks high to boys, encourages them to go to sea as early as they can. As a good deal of fishing takes place at night, these boys make poor daytime pupils, and high school dropout rates are a feature of fishing communities. Girls and women are engaged in marketing as well as fish processing, which can cause cuts and skin damage.

Although the informal economy is sometimes described as invisible, children working on the streets of cities across the world are probably the most visible face of child labour. Their activities are diverse—vending food and small consumer goods, shining shoes, washing windscreens, repairing tyres, scavenging and ragpicking, begging, portering, and numerous others. They face hazards both from the work itself and more importantly from the environment, such as traffic, exhaust fumes, exposure to the elements, insecurity, harassment and violence.

Work in the urban informal economy also includes work in small businesses and workshops providing carpentry, car repair, food preparation or other services to urban dwellers. Children may be part of family or other informal enterprises and networks, or they may be self-employed. Actual street work is often associated with socially excluded (especially ethnic) groups.

Increased numbers of street children can be a reflection of upheavals and crises. A 24-country study by the Council of Europe found a higher number of street children in all European countries after the collapse of the communist system. Children and youth migrated to the West searching for work in the face of sudden poverty and loss of state social protection at home.

A similar story applies in Jakarta, Indonesia, in the wake of the Asian crisis, and indeed in many other countries affected by crisis. Street work has gender dimensions too, tending to involve more boys than girls, although more girls are involved in prostitution. Surveys of children working on the street in Moscow and St. Petersburg, Russian Federation, found that about 75 per cent are boys and 25 per cent girls. In most developing countries, the proportion of boys among street children is even higher.

Child labour in manufacturing

Children in supply chains 88. While far from being the sector employing the greatest number of children, manufacturing for export has had the highest profile in relation to child labour, for example, in carpet-weaving, soccer-ball stitching and clothing production. Typically, however, children are involved at the end of supply chains producing largely for the domestic market, in home-based, informal work to assemble parts or finish products in a wide range of industries. These range from textiles, clothing and footwear, to production of fireworks and matches in many countries around the world.

The explosion that killed children who were making fireworks during their school lunch hour in China in 2000 showed just how dangerous such work can be. Some production processes, such as leather tanning and brassware production, are particularly hazardous because of the toxic products used. In glassmaking, children risk burns and cuts and are exposed to hazardous dust and lead. Incense stick production in India and Pakistan causes upper respiratory tract problems. Because this work is mostly carried out by girls, it is they who are especially at risk. Often the conditions under which production occurs make the work even more dangerous because of the lack of proper engineering, work organization and protective equipment. Low profit margins do not encourage investment in improvements.

Home-based work involving subcontracting appears to be increasing in many countries. A comparative study in Asia (covering India, Indonesia, Pakistan, the Philippines and Thailand) found that production had shifted from factories to homes for products ranging from carpets to leather goods to hybrid seeds. This reduced labour costs for employers, with the work being carried out by women and children, especially girls. In some cases, older children were working between 20 and 30 hours a week, and reported suffering back and muscle pain from the cramped working conditions. Developed countries can also have child labour in manufacturing. Portugal, having encountered significant numbers of children in the textile, clothing and footwear industries, has placed control of the problem high on the Government's agenda. In southern Italy, children are reported to work in small industrial/manufacturing workshops in unsafe conditions, for well below the equivalent adult wage. Of Spain's estimated 200,000 under-14-year-old workers, many work in small subcontracting businesses, in particular in the footwear industry.

In the hotel, catering and tourism industry, children carry out a variety of jobs, from bellboys and maids to dishwashers, beach attendants, hawkers and golf caddies; worldwide in this industry, 10-15 per cent of workers (between 13 and 19 million) are under 18 years of age. While much of the work of young people in the sector is legitimate, there are indications of considerable abuse. Low pay is the normal experience of young employees in hotels and catering.

Many children work in the informal economy which surrounds and supports the formal tourist industry. Active recruitment and trafficking agents may pull children to work in the sector, although poverty and the lure of consumerism are key push factors. Children's work in tourism may have a spillover effect into prostitution—exposing children to the risk of sexual exploitation because of the element of "personal service" involved and the stark discrepancy in income between workers and clients. In Acapulco, Mexico, children aged 7-12, employed by beach restaurants to bring in customers, are paid exclusively by commission on the customers' drinks. Studies of India's Dhaba boys reveal that those working in small hotels receive such meagre daily wages that they have to take out loans from their employers. The terms of repayment and interest can lead to debt bondage. In Kenya, children's work related to tourism includes selling crafts, food and other items, entertainment, beach work and prostitution.

Most children are involved in a combination of jobs; many work at night when they can gain the most money from entertaining tourists. Children's wages are often very low, but their employers expect them to find their own ways to earn more money, such as through tips or by taking on more work. Economic exploitation leaves young workers in an extremely vulnerable situation, exposing them to other forms of exploitation, including commercial sex.

There are large numbers of children in domestic service but they are among the most invisible child labourers and are therefore difficult to survey and analyse. There are clear links between children in domestic service and trafficking, both within and between countries. Child domestics are often ignored by policy-makers and excluded from the coverage of legislation; indeed, even adults in this sector are often hidden from view in private households and denied legislative protection, let alone guarantees of the right to organize. A number of countries have reported under the follow-up to the Declaration that their labour laws exclude domestic work in private households altogether.

Child domestic work is a problem across the world, affecting rich as well as poor countries.

While most child domestic workers are between 12 and 17 years of age, some are as young as 5 or 6. The majority are girls, but boys are involved too; in Kathmandu, Nepal, more than half the child domestics are boys. Child domestics, often isolated and far from their families, are under the total control of their employer and are often deprived of emotional support, good nutrition and education, and work long hours for meagre payment in kind. They can be victims of physical, emotional and sometimes sexual abuse. In addition, the mantle of foster care or informal adoption can be thrown over a relationship that ends up being pure child exploitation.

In other cases, there may not be a great wealth difference between employer and employee; even urban slum-dwelling families may have a young female servant, perhaps a distant relative from the countryside. The domestic, unpaid labour of young girls may enable adult women to take up new opportunities in the paid labour market.

The problem is a sizeable one. The Government of Haiti reports that some 250,000 children of disadvantaged parents are in domestic service (known as "restavek", or "stay with"). A substantial proportion of the child population of a country can be involved. In Brazil, Colombia and Ecuador, 20 per cent of all girls between the ages of 10 and 14 are engaged as domestics, and in rural areas the percentages are even higher. Official statistics normally capture, if at all, only child domestics who are working in the homes of other people. Yet, where school-age children are systematically kept at home by parents or other adults to undertake long hours of domestic work instead of going to school, this too can amount to unacceptable child labour.

Child labour in construction

These sectors pose the most obvious hazards for children, although they probably involve the smallest number of child labourers. Children of construction workers, particularly when they live on-site, are at risk of child labour in several ways. They may not be in any one place for long enough to attend school regularly, they may take up casual work with parents as an alternative to idleness or play, and they may, by virtue of their location, be exposed to the hazards of construction.

In developed countries, work in construction poses hazards to young workers. In New Zealand, one study revealed that construction has the second-highest injury rate for adolescents, at more than one per four full-time equivalent workers. In Italy, a recent survey by the labour federation, Confederazione Generale Italiana del Lavoro (CGIL), estimated that, of the 400,000 children aged 11-14 at work, 10 per cent were in construction.

In different countries of Africa, Latin America and Asia, children work alongside their parents, or independently, in underground mines, opencast mines and quarries. They also carry out support functions such as collecting, sorting and transporting aggregate, or cooking and cleaning in remote mining enclaves. The hazards of such work are multiple: from cave-ins to long-term damage from carrying heavy loads and exposure to dust or chemicals, and they vary according to the substance mined and the way the work is organized.

Children as young as 6 or 7 years old are breaking up rocks, and washing, sieving and carrying ore. Nine-year-olds work underground setting explosives and carrying loads. An IPEC survey in Madagascar found that 53 per cent of the children in small-scale mines and quarries were aged 12 or younger. In Guatemala and the United Republic of Tanzania, as in other countries, children work alongside their parents crushing rock to make gravel for the construction industry.

And while the children may work just as hard as the adults, they are paid much less, if at all. Mining sometimes involves debt bondage (as with gold in Peru), and it may coincide with the bankrolling of armed conflict (as with diamond mining in Sierra Leone). While much of the mining that involves child labour is small scale, the hazards it poses are not. In a closely related field of production, children are directly employed in brick-making in many countries, often in connection with bonded labour (as in South Asia) or family production quotas (as in some countries in Latin America).

Thus far, we have considered child labour in legitimate economic sectors, where national law determines whether or not a particular activity is permissible for children of different ages. The unconditional worst forms of child labour are those which, under any circumstances, are in contravention of international law. While increased research is certainly leading to a better understanding of these forms of child labour, we still face a huge problem of data availability and quality. The evidence is patchy and incomplete, and thus the dynamic global picture remains partial—a sketch rather than a sharp image. The next Global Report on child labour four years from now will provide an opportunity to see how much the gaps in our current understanding have been filled. Forms of child slavery such as sale and trafficking, debt bondage, serfdom and forced or compulsory labour The various forms of child slavery that are outlawed under Convention No. 182 (and other international instruments) can occur across different economic sectors and types of activity. For example, we have seen already how debt bondage occurs in agriculture and in brick-making, and how children are trafficked into domestic service.

The labour practice under which an otherwise harmless economic activity occurs may transform this activity into a worst form of child labour. It is thus important to understand that the worst forms of child labour can come about as a result of the type of work undertaken or the labour practice used to exact the child's work, or a combination of the type of work and the labour practice. Debt bondage, regardless of whether parents have contracted a debt that is to be paid off by their own labour or by pledging the services of their children, places children ultimately at the mercy of the landowner, contractor or moneylender, where they suffer from both economic hardship and educational deprivation.

The main difference between adult and child bonded labour is that children have not themselves contracted the debt - it was done on their behalf by adults. The link between child labour and the intergenerational perpetuation of poverty could hardly be clearer. Bonded child labour flourishes in different parts of the globe; not only in South Asia with which it is most commonly linked, but also in Latin America, Africa and South-East Asia.

Debt bondage is increasingly linked with trafficking of children for labour exploitation. Rural poverty, coupled with population growth and rapid urbanization, leads some parents to place their children with agents, not only in exchange for money but also in the hope that the child will receive education or training at the point of destination. In other cases, children themselves make the decision to leave their home.

The child victims, who may end up in commercial sexual exploitation, domestic work or sweatshops, may never know the amount of the debt they are working to pay off or the terms of repayment. The subjection of children to forced labour through trafficking has age and gender dimensions: the younger the child, the less likely he or she is to be able to escape a forced labour situation. Boys and girls may be forced into different types of activity, for instance, girls predominate in commercial sexual exploitation and domestic work, and boys in forced recruitment for armed conflict and for camel jockeying in the Middle East, although there is considerable overlap. The routes and mechanisms for trafficking are increasingly well understood, 74 but the numbers of children involved remain vague. It is thought that child trafficking has become a billion-dollar-a-year business, with an estimated 1.2 million children falling victim annually. It is a truly global problem connecting all countries and regions of the world in a complex network of illicit movements of human beings.

Sources, destinations and routes for trafficking are constantly evolving in the face of global changes in supply, demand and the regulatory environment. In West and Central Africa, most trafficking is family-based, related to traditional systems of fostering that have now become exploitative. Trafficking of young children for exploitation in agriculture and domestic service has only relatively recently been recognized as a problem in sub-Saharan Africa, for example, while in South-East Asia, trafficking for prostitution is a long-standing source of concern. Countries in Western Europe and North America now openly acknowledge that they are destinations for trafficked men, women and children from around the world and for a variety of purposes. Transition countries are witnessing a huge upsurge in the problem.

The Republic of Moldova, Romania and Ukraine are major source coun brought to Bosnia and Herzegovina, Kosovo or Albania where they are sold to local gangs to be trafficked to Western Europe for prostitution. Other transition countries, such as Kyrgyzstan and Mongolia, have also become targets of sophisticated international trafficking rings that channel girls through the Russian Federation to Western Europe and through China to Japan and Australia.

Forced recruitment of children

The experiences of children forced to participate in armed conflict, particularly in Africa, led the International Labour Conference to include this practice as one of the worst forms of child labour. Although 'child soldiers' comprise only a small proportion of the child population of any country in conflict, the trauma they endure is extreme. As a government loses effective control over parts of its territory (e.g. as in Colombia), its scope of action against children's involvement in armed conflict diminishes. The number of children under the age of 18 who have been coerced or induced, either by the State or by non-state military groups, to take up arms as child soldiers or to serve as porters, messengers, cooks and sex slaves is generally thought to be in the range of 300,000,[78] with 120,000 of those in Africa alone. These children are reported to be as young as 8 years old.

The part played by girls in armed conflict is important and often misunderstood. Although often portrayed only in the context of forced provision of sexual services to adult soldiers, girls have multiple roles, including that of front-line fighters. Children recruited as soldiers in times of armed conflict and as child labourers in peacetime originate from the same groups:

— children separated from their families or with disrupted family backgrounds (e.g. orphans, unaccompanied children, single-parent families, child-headed households);

— economically and socially disadvantaged children (e.g. the rural and urban poor, those without access to education, vocational training and a reasonable standard of living); and

— other marginalised groups (e.g. street children, certain minorities, refugees and the internally displaced).

Examples of forced recruitment of children and adolescents abound: in the northern part of Bosnia and Herzegovina in 1996, children aged 16-18 were caught up in forced labour brigades digging trenches, moving supplies, evacuating dead and wounded combatants, acting as human shields, harvesting crops, cutting firewood and working in factories without pay. It is notable that most were from socially excluded groups among the Muslim, Croat and Roma communities. Low-intensity, long-term conflict means that children are more likely to become combatants as educational opportunities and infrastructure are progressively destroyed. Changing labour markets may also play a role. In Sierra Leone, for example, during the 1980s, the diamond-mining industry reverted to small-scale, local entrepreneurs, who kept profits high by paying young people low wages. Educational investment in mining areas was also low. It was therefore easy for the Revolutionary United Front (RUF) to target disaffected youth for recruitment.

Some were forcibly abducted to work as soldiers but others joined because of incentives such as informal education, better wages and access to drugs. Not all children are physically coerced into becoming combatants; soldiering may tragically appear to be the best economic option available for marginalized, vulnerable groups of children. In addition, children, particularly adolescents, may be lured into armed conflict by the ideology associated with it, be it religious expression, the struggle for self-determination or other social causes.

This worst form of child labour illustrates, in the most dramatic way possible, how the powerlessness of children renders them vulnerable to exploitation by adults. For many children, being drugged, abducted, abused and/or sold by their parents or other relatives can lead them down the path to exploitation through prostitution, production of pornography and pornographic performances. However, it is not always so easy to draw the line between children involved in commercial sexual exploitation and those who, because of their situation, are prone to sexual exploitation and abuse by adults. Children may be persuaded or threatened into having sex with adults who have power over them. Sexual abuse of children by male teachers in the closed school environment has been widely reported in sub-Saharan Africa.

The terrible consequences of sexual exploitation for children, both emotional and physical (as a result of sexually transmitted diseases, HIV infection, unwanted pregnancy and abortion, physical violence and abuse by clients) are liable to lead to loss of self-esteem, mental and physical illness, infertility, behavioural problems, substance abuse and death.

Prostitution and the sale and trafficking of children, particularly of girls, was the worst form of child labour most often cited as 'known or suspected to exist' in reports submitted under the 2002 follow-up to the Declaration by countries at all levels of development. While estimates of the numbers involved go into the hundreds of thousands in some countries, the true extent of the problem is unknown. Where data do exist, they are often not disaggregated by sex or age. Sociocultural factors driving children's, often girls', involvement in commercial sexual exploitation include lack of education and economic opportunity, the relatively high earnings perceived to be on offer, a cultural obligation for children to support their parents by earning money in whatever way they can and disintegration of the family. As in many other transition countries, prostitution of children in the Russian Federation (12-15 per cent of prostitutes in Moscow are estimated to be under 18, with higher percentages in smaller cities) is often related to internal or external migration. In a number of developed countries, a high representation of children of indigenous groups or of foreigners in such activities has been noted (e.g. Canada, the United States).

Demand, of course, also plays an important part in determining the shape of the problem as it affects children. The presence of military troops or of large public works projects may act as pull factors. Tourist centres create high demand for prostitution. Client preferences for young children, particularly in the context of HIV/AIDS, inevitably get translated into an increased supply. Clients in the sex tourism trade are both male and female, as are the children they exploit. For example, beach boys in Gambia and in Jamaica cater to the female tourist trade.

Commercial sexual exploitation of boys is reported to be increasing. A recent IPEC Rapid Assessment in El Salvador found that one-third of the sexually exploited children aged between 14 and 17 were boys. Although in most countries, boys represent 10-20 per cent of the children involved, there are some countries, such as Pakistan and Sri Lanka, where boys are in the majority. While both boys and girls may experience sexual exploitation differently, and boys may be less subject to physical coercion, neither experience is any less intolerable than the other.

5

Children and Prostitution

In spite of international commitment to the eradication of all practices associated with the sexual exploitation of and sale and traffic in children, there is little comprehensive data on the extent, mechanisms or root causes. Research has thus far been largely exploratory, to a great extent using data generated from secondary sources, most frequently from journalism and non governmental organisations, whether these have a campaigning or welfare orientation. There is an urgent need for more systematic and global knowledge of the nature and incidence of the problem, including an understanding of the cultural, social and economic contexts in which it arises and flourishes and the development of typologies and categories that can be of use not only in developing appropriate conceptual frameworks and methods of research but also eventually in policy formulation and programme development by national and international bodies. It is also clear that there is a critical need to develop operational definitions that will capture the phenomena involved in the commercial sexual exploitation of children, so that they can be measured, monitored and combatted.

Structure of the research

Let us discuss about the research took place at the request of UNICEF Headquarters, New York. The research about 'Children in Especially Difficult Circumstances Section' as a background document for the Congress against the Commercial Sexual Exploitation of Children, held in Stockholm 25-31 August, 1996. Researchers were based at the Centre for Family Research, University of Cambridge, which is a Key Institution of Childwatch International, an international network of child research institutes and researchers.

The researchers were thus able to take advantage of an existing structure of monthly child research seminars and the expertise of a number of children's rights, child labour and child sexual exploitation researchers working in the university as well as of the Childwatch International Indicators for Children's Rights Project, which is also based at the Centre for Family Research;

It is worth mentioning that those present at the Consultation have expertise in various aspects of the social sciences including studies of women, children, gender and prostitution, as well as direct research experience in (inter alia) Nepal, UK, India, West Africa, South Africa, East Africa, Latin America and the Caribbean, Thailand, Vietnam, Papua New Guinea, Netherlands, Sri Lanka, Norway, Poland and Egypt. Papers from the Consultation were also shared with Andrew Bainham, Dr Jo Boyden, Dr Charlie Davison, Dr Michael Edwards, Richard Fentiman, Dr Angie Hart,

Edda Ivan-Smith, Dr Ziba Mir-Husseini, Dr Martin Richards and Philip Van Haeke.

This edition of the review includes materials developed during three days of workshops immediatley preceding the Congress Against the Commercial Sexual Exploitation of children, in which the team members were joined by Mark Connolly of UNICEF Headquarters, New York, Children in Especially Difficult Circumstances Section.The researchers are thus grateful for the invaluable support and guidance of a number of individuals given when investigating, structuring and writing this review. Nevertheless, as authors they bear responsibility both for the opinions expressed and for any errors or omissions.

Objectives and scope

The objectives of the research were to:

— Map the discourse of the commercial sexual exploitation of children, showing the main ideas in operation and the main organisational and geographical contexts in which they arise;

— Map the data showing what data are available, their strengths and weaknesses, together with a critique of methods and assumptions;

— Describe the context of the production and reproduction of knowledge in this field;

— Discuss the implications of the current state of discourses and data and their potential for future work, particularly in the area of measurement.

In order to develop the most useful and systematic research typologies and methods, the literature review team considered in the first instance the widest possible range of reported occurrences of the sexual exploitation of and sale and traffic in children for sexual purposes. These included:

— prostitution

— pornography

— marriage broking

— sex tourism

— cultural practices such as devadasi

— adoption and fostering of older children

— sexual abuse in institutional settings

— sexual abuse of domestic servants

Literature from appropriate sources in major European languages was searched using both electronic and manual data bases. Some literature was not located and other material was located but could not be accessed in the time available. One major set of literature that was not addressed in detail was the official discourse of governments, inter-governmental organisations and of the Congress Against the Commercial Sexual Exploitation of Children itself. Further major lacunae in the research process were materials from Francophone countries and information about Islamic nations.

Structure of the review

In the first instance, data were collected and examined on a regional basis. The team members met regularly to review progress and consider the conceptual and theoretical issues raised by material collected and read. Monthly team seminars, attended by members of the peer review group, developed specific themes addressing definitional and methodological issues. At the mid-term Consultation, the research team specifically requested advice on:

Identifying phenomena and defining concepts. This was not to say that it was intended to develop 'concepts for all time' but rather to find operational concepts that might be used for the purposes of research and measurement.

Deepening their critical review of the literature. Although new references were welcomed, the team had discovered that, in general, data are too weak in this field to justify further literature searches. On the contrary, it was felt necessary to pinpoint the reasons why these data are so poor and also to consider the manner in which they are produced.

Ideas about the most productive routes to follow in order to clear a path for work to measure and monitor the commercial sexual exploitation of children. In this respect, the expert group was asked for advice about the most useful concepts to define, the background literature most appropriate for this purpose and the most productive areas to research in more depth.

This current review is structured on the basis of the lively discussion that took place at the Consultation. The most important single factor in the structure is the fact that the original approach, which had been to review literature on a regional basis, was abandoned in favour of using the United Nations Convention on the Rights of the Child as a universal conceptual framework that can be applied to all regions, bearing in mind the requirement to be cognisant of and sensitive to cultural differences.

The review thus consists of two parts. In the first, after a consideration of the problems raised by taking a regional perspective, the relevant articles of the Convention on the Rights of the Child are explored with respect to some of the phenomena to which they refer, the concepts that capture these phenomena, the data that will be required to measure them and the potential for constructing a system of indicators for monitoring not only the current situation with respect to the commercial sexual exploitation of children, but also the impact of interventions aimed to prevent and eradicate it, as well as to rehabilitate those children who have been and are involved.

The second part of the review consists of an annotated bibliography, organised on a regional basis, with brief introductory essays overviewing the main themes encountered in each region, cultural aspects and some consideration of the type and quality of data represented. The works included in the bibliography represent those most pertinent to the themes of this review, but do not give a comprehensive account of the totality of literature consulted.

Perhaps the most significant aspect of the review is the relative lack of coverage of the topic of pornography. On the advice of the experts at the Consultation the research team decided to concentrate their efforts for this background document for the Congress Against the Commercial Sexual Exploitation of Children on the topic of children and prostitution. This decision was taken for purely practical time considerations. However, the choice of title, 'Children and Prostitution' was not arbitrary. This was chosen in order to aid conceptualisation of the entire topic, avoiding the narrower scope of terms such as child prostitute and child sex worker as well as the problems of using phrases such as 'commercial sexual exploitation' in certain cultural contexts, particularly in Africa.

The definitions with which the research team began were those common in international human rights circles. They were not necessarily regarded as the most pertinent within the scope of this study and, as the text will show, considerable adaptation occurred in the course of conceptualising a new framework that is not bound to regional discourses. Nevertheless, the following definitions were used as a guide for the purpose of data collection:

'Child' was used as defined by the United Nations Convention on the Rights of the Child, Article 1 as "every human being below the age of 18 years unless, under the law applicable to the child, majority is attained earlier".

With respect to child prostitution and pornography the point of departure was taken from Vitit Muntarbhorn, then United Nations Special Rapporteur on the Sale of Children, at the 48th Session of the United Nations Human Rights Commission, 1992:

> Child Prostitution refers to the sexual exploitation of a child for remuneration in cash or in kind, usually but not always organized by an intermediary (parent, family member, procurer, teacher, etc.)"

The term child pornography refers to the visual or audio depiction of a child for the sexual gratification of the user, and involves the production, distribution and/or use of such material."

It should be noted that, whereas this definition of 'The Child' has been adopted by the United Nations General Assembly as integral to the Convention on the Rights of the Child, the definitions given by the former Special Rapporteur on Sale of Children are simply part of his first report to the UN Human Rights Commission -- they are thus not official UN definitions.

For the purpose of data collection, 'commercial sexual exploitation' was distinguished from sexual abuse, by the fact that some pecuniary advantage is achieved by some party to sexual activity. Pecuniary advantage is understood in the wider sense that includes cash and kind so long as there is some means of accounting in monetary terms. Sexual activity is not limited to penetrative sex, or even to genital sexual activities. Moreover, as stated above, and in common with the definitions of child and child prostitution, the conceptual and theoretical work carried out for the review resulted in considerable modification of this definition.

Current Literature and its Consequences

The research began with a review of available literature, organised on a regional basis. This had two justifications. In the first place, there appears to be no universal structure of ideas informing discussions on the commercial sexual exploitation of children, which is dispersed among a variety of agencies with a number of disparate objectives and activities varying from law and advocacy to welfare, and even arguments in favour of paedophilia. In the second place, it was clear that certain aspects dominate the discourse in specific regions of the world. The research thus began with a twofold purpose, examining existing discourses for what they might provide in the way of well argued, internally-consistent structures of ideas. In this respect, it has to be made clear from the outset that by 'discourse' we mean clearly distinguishable sets of ideas, publications, speeches and other social products that inform and construct the way people think and act.

Any discourse on child commercial sexual exploitation will be related to other discourses—on childhood, sexuality, exploitation and prostitution, for example. It will produce and reproduce these ideas in ways that tend to reinforce current structures of power and hierarchy. The first task for this review, therefore, was to examine not simply the evidence about the commercial sexual exploitation of children but, more importantly, how it is being produced, reproduced and presented.

The regional approach

South East Asia, particularly Thailand and the Philippines, is the key to any discussion of the commercial sexual exploitation of children because it was the situation in this area in the past two decades that raised public awareness of the commercial sexual exploitation of children and mobilised public opinion against 'child sex tourists'. The discourse derived from these two countries has set the parameters and tone of the debate. The issues debated with respect to Thailand and the Philippines have become key to the global discussion of child prostitution to the extent that it is impossible to talk about commercial sexual exploitation without reference to them. Thailand and the Philippines have provided much of the mythology and iconography of the commercial sexual exploitation of children so that it is important to look at these two countries in detail in order to understand the origins and the boundaries of the issue.

The role of non-governmental organisations (NGOs), in particular End Child Prostitution in Asian Tourism (ECPAT), in raising awareness cannot be underestimated. It is they who first brought the issue to public attention, set the agenda and have continued to dominate the debate. Although the countries for which they mainly campaign are Thailand and the Philippines, they are also concerned with Sri Lanka, Taiwan and Korea. Their work is widely disseminated through both the Western media and national English language press.

These NGOs also publish articles widely in the popular press and ECPAT is responsible for two influential books, The Child and the Tourist and The Rape of the Innocent, popular paperbacks designed to appeal to a non-specialist audience. Drawing on ECPAT's success, other groups now campaign against child prostitution but ECPAT remains a central information source. It is rare to find an article on child sexual exploitation in a Western newspaper that does not make reference to ECPAT.

The content of this information follows predictable formulae. A typical example would be a case study of a very young girl forced or tricked into a brothel where she is obliged to service 20 customers a night for very low remuneration. In the story she will be rescued by a welfare agency and sent back to her village, only to discover that she has contracted HIV and will shortly die. It will be stated or implied that it is demand from

Western men that causes her to become a prostitute. Aspects of degradation and abuse are repeatedly emphasised, as is the youth of the girl. The language used is often emotive. For example, one report describes 'the lifeless body of an eight year old child, left in a Saigon hotel room after a night of sexual abuse', while a campaigner told the press 'I still remember vividly the tears in the eyes of the child rescued from a Bangkok brothel who told me how she begged a customer not to harm her, only to have her pleas mercilessly rejected'.

In the current campaigning literature, both within South East Asia and in the West, the image of child commercial sexual exploitation is of small children being sought out and exploited by Western tourists. Much press coverage now is concerned with finding and punishing these men (and it is assumed that all sex tourists are male in this geographical region, even though there are reports of female sex tourists in other areas).

Yet around the slums of the port of Klong Toey in Bangkok, men who cannot not afford a 'real' (meaning fully grown) woman will find a young girl a reasonable substitute because she is cheaper and easier to control. While this is an aspect of child prostitution that many campaigning groups in Asia would prefer to ignore, it is likely that the majority of young prostitutes are not found in the bars of Bangkok or Manila but in the brothels in the rural areas or the back streets of cities.

In many local brothels in Thailand and the Philippines, younger women are said to be prized for their innocence and freshness, while girls even younger are prized for their cheapness (Ennew, 1986; Black, 1994). Even among the better-off Thai men, there is a marked preference for younger girls. A 1994 survey conducted among students, office workers, and residents of a slum area, to assess the impact of HIV on children found that the most desirable age for prostitutes is under 18: 'Many males felt that child prostitutes between 15 and 18 were more desirable than adults, but that it was wrong to sleep with younger ones'.

In other parts of South East Asia, although the discourse is not as influential on the world stage, the issue is also often constructed on the basis of the idea of the foreign male exploiter. There is less information on Vietnam, Cambodia and China but these three countries share the language of 'social evil', which is behaviour or ideas that are contrary to and damaging for national culture. Child prostitution, like AIDS, is described as a problem imported from other cultures, not always the West, or considered in terms of trafficking so that Vietnamese girls, for example, are forced across the border to Cambodia or China without any acknowledgement of indigenous prostitution.

China however, adds another component to the picture. Chinese girls are said to be the victims of traffickers, especially young girls from the Yunan region but Chinese men, rather than foreigners, are often blamed for the problem. It is also repeatedly claimed that Chinese men will pay to have penetrative sex with a virgin because this is believed to be a cure for AIDS. This is a common assertion in the literature worldwide, even though there is no ethnographic evidence to prove it. In Vietnam and Cambodia in particular, anti-Chinese feeling leads to the repetition of this notion.

In addition to the accounts of NGOs and journalists, a relatively small amount of information is produced by anthropologists and sociologists who have worked on limited research projects. The resulting articles and books are concerned with the cultural background, particularly religion and societal norms that can be predisposing factors in encouraging or discouraging children to become prostitutes.

In this respect a major issue is the apparent religious sanction given to prostitution by Buddhist values, which stress models of duty and sacrifice for children especially for girls. One argument is that by supporting her family through prostitution a girl gains merit rather than bringing shame on herself and her family, a justification that is frequently manipulated in some areas of the literature. However, these texts are usually published in the academic Western press, with a relatively small circulation among other academics.

One problem in the NGO literature is that the academic literature seems to be largely ignored or unknown. In addition, within the mainstream, campaigning literature, certain categories become blurred. Thus it is a feature of the reporting that:

- child prostitutes are often by implication only girls;
- pre-pubertal and post-pubertal children are often included in the numbers given for child prostitutes along with young women over the age of 18 years;
- numbers given for Western tourist clients are confused with numbers of Western tourists as a whole, with no account given of local clients;
- within the undifferentiated category of child prostitute, the origins of child prostitutes are hidden, obscuring aspects of origin, such as ethnic or socio-economic factors.

A second major geographical focus is South Asia—India, Nepal, Sri Lanka and, to a lesser extent, Bangladesh and Pakistan. This has three components, the girl child, religious prostitution and trafficking for sexual purposes. The idea of the girl child arose largely through Indian attempts to assign a special space in social philosophy and policy to girls. 1990 was named The Year of the Girl Child by the South Asian Association for Regional Cooperation (SAARC) and the UNICEF India Office. Two main themes of the year were prevention of child marriages and rehabilitation of child prostitutes. One Indian woman's comment on the material published in the Year of the Girl Child shows the reproductive nature of the information purveyed in the resulting 'spurt of publications':

> Many of the papers are clones of earlier ones. The self perpetuations occur through citations being made circular, until a body of knowledge is assumed to have been created. The sum and substance of much of this writing concern the low status of the girl, her limited opportunities for education and the gender bias in the home. The television screen has also sensitized people to the plight of the girl child as a drudge.

This was not the intention of 'girl child' campaigners such as Sheela Barse, who makes it clear that she is opposed to the 'feminist method of carving out the female persons' group out of the human race and examining it in isolation, on the presumption that females are always wronged'. Barse states that it is more important to establish that girlhood cannot be the entire province either of womanhood in the women's rights movement, or of childhood in the children's rights movement.

Nevertheless, the notion of the 'girl child' has been reified, as if there is something essential about all female children regardless of wealth or ethnicity, something that makes them more vulnerable than boys in general. This focuses on vulnerability to sexual violation, early marriage, unplanned teenage pregnancy and is a new manifestation of the old control over women's sexuality and fertility. It masquerades as concern for their vulnerability but actually implies that females cannot control their own sexuality, which should consequently be under male control. This is reflected in three approaches to development aid programming for girls:

— The link between female education and child survival;

— The emphasis on the employment of girls as prostitutes, which is a minor exploiter of girls compared to agriculture, domestic service and manufacture;

The immense silence about the specificity of certain kinds of exploitation that are exclusive to boys.

In India and in Nepal the 'girl child' discourse focuses on religious prostitution (of which devadasi is the best known form) and trafficking in children, while in Bangladesh, the rape of pre-pubertal girls hired as domestic servants is an important theme. In Pakistan, Baluchistan and the North West Frontier provinces of India, much of the literature on the girl child is legal. A further concern is the fate of the daughters of prostitutes who on account of social opprobrium are said to be forced into prostitution.

Religious prostitution is practised in various parts of India and Nepal. Devadasi cults are found in Southern

India and also practised in other parts of the country such as Uttar Pradesh and Orissa. They derive customary sanction from oppressive upper-caste temple traditions. Pre-pubertal girls, aged between five and nine years, from poor, low-caste homes, are dedicated by an initiation rite to the deity in the local temple during full moon. After a girl is married to the deity by the tali rite, she is branded with a hot iron on both shoulders and her breast.

She is then employed by the temple priest. Sometimes, even before menarche, she is auctioned for her virginity; the deflowering ceremony known as udilumbuvadu becomes the privilege of the highest bidder. The market value of a girl falls after she attains puberty, when she is said to have no recourse other than prostitution. Yellama is represented as the principal goddess who is worshipped but, as recent research has shown, the practice of devadasi is prevalent in many other temple towns and other deities such as Meenakshi, Jaganath and Hanuman are also propitiated. Religious prostitution is known by different names such as venkatasani, jogini, nailis, muralis and theradiyan.

In Nepal, particularly the western parts, religious prostitution known as badini and jhuma is also practised. Although little is known about these practices, they do not seem to vary significantly from devadasi. However, the main sexual exploitation issue in Nepal is the traffic with India, the open border between the two countries making it difficult to monitor. It is also stated that, because of corruption, official assistance is given to the sale and the trafficking of young girl. In most accounts Bombay is given as the main destination. The international trade routes most frequently mentioned are from Nepal and Bangladesh to India, and from India and Pakistan to the Middle-Eastern countries.

In sharp contrast to the emphasis on the 'girl child' in the rest of South Asia, in Sri Lanka the discourse revolves around boys and sex tourism. ECPAT and other advocacy organisations have influenced the discourse here, claiming that male western paedophiles are targeting Sri Lanka because of the availability of boys. For instance, it is argued that, despite the civil war, the number of tourists who visited Sri Lanka increased from 102,000 in 1989 to 169, 000 in 1996, although of course this does not necessarily mean that all tourists are male, let alone sex tourists.

According to the literature, the South West coast, Negombo and Hikkawuda are the main destination points. They are close to the beach and some hotels assist paedophiles in procuring boys mostly aged between six and 15 years, although most boy prostitutes in Sri Lanka appear tend to work independently of either brothels or pimps. Although there is evidence of sex tourism in Sri Lanka, the picture is not clear because of the tendency to reproduce information. One case in point is the frequent reference to the role of Spartacus guides, which provide male homosexual tourists with up to date information about the availability of sexual contacts in most countries, and were notorious in the 1980s, particularly with respect to both Sri Lanka and the Philippines, for giving locations where boy prostitutes could be encountered. Despite the fact that the magazine no longer explicitly refers to children, and the then publisher of Spartacus has died, the magazine's role in the sex tourism business is constantly reiterated in popular literature on the commercial sexual exploitation of Sri Lankan boys as if no changes had occurred.

A third major geographical region with a characteristic discourse that influences global debates might be designated the Anglophone West and consists the United States, Canada, Australia and Western Europe. From the late nineteenth to early twentieth century there was considerable public concern about the 'White Slave Trade'.

Many aspects of this earlier discourse are clearly visible in current debates. Nevertheless, modern concern about what is always referred to in the academic literature as 'juvenile' rather than 'child' prostitution resurfaced in the late 1960s alongside the issue of runaway children. Journalists were quick to use labels like baby-pros or, with respect to pornography, 'kiddie porn'. Then, the concern was for children who joined the 'hippie' culture of America's big cities, in particular San Francisco and New York. Britain and Canada, where many of the same social problems as America were reported, but a few years later, experienced similar concerns in the early to mid 1970s.

The earliest indications of a juvenile prostitution 'problem' can be found in the mass media, but academics were also involved from the very beginning. In addition, since the late 1960s there have been a number of moral panics about child abuse in North America and Western Europe. Thus interest in juvenile prostitution has come in waves, eclipsed at times, by concerns about 'battered children' or more recently 'satanic' or 'ritual' abuse. Thus, there have been few long term studies of juvenile prostitutes, but rather a flurry of papers and articles at times when interest in the issue is high. Currently, concern is focused on young male prostitutes, because they are seen as vectors for the spread of HIV and research into their lives is conducted along bio-medical models that are concerned with certain areas of behaviour and particular attitudes. Both academics and journalists have remained interested in the issue of delinquency and deviancy psychology, which it is assumed many young prostitutes share but, again, this is linked to bio-medical models with particular perspectives and limited range.

Western journalists have a major role in disseminating information about the commercial sexual exploitation of children. Articles on young male prostitutes, often referred to as 'rent boys' in the English language press, as well as young female prostitutes, remain an occasional feature of many newspapers and women's magazines and are presented as campaigning or investigative journalism, while revealing prurient details designed to shock and sensationalise. Popular books written on the issue of child prostitution and pornography are mostly written by journalists with a stated mission to reveal the truth. Playlands and Child Pornography, two influential books on the subject were both written by journalists and one of the most famous books, H: Autobiography of a Child Prostitute and Heroin Addict, was written in collaboration with journalists from the German newspaper, Stern.

Due to the ease of access and a history of journalistic interest, the material is very heavily urban based, with San Francisco, New York, London, Birmingham, Melbourne,Amsterdam and Berlin over-represented. Other cities with known groups of child prostitutes, such as Dallas, Washington DC, Sydney, and in the United Kingdom, Brighton and Cardiff, are not discussed in nearly the same detail. In the USA especially, there are certain centres of expertise on child prostitution such as Huckleberry House in San Francisco and Covenant House in New York, with long campaigning and advocacy histories, so that it can be easier to gain access to both children and experts in the 'treatment' of abused children through these types of organisation. In Canada, particular emphasis has been placed on Ontario, not because of the higher concentration of juvenile prostitutes there, but because the Queen's University Social Program Evaluation Group has taken particular interest in the problems facing homeless and prostitute youth.

In the USA, the source of a good deal of the literature is part of the university sector that specialises in 'objective' non-judgmental studies of AIDS awareness and/or delinquent psychology. In the USA much emphasis is placed on the 'runaway' phenomenon, first noted in the 1960s and now closely tied to the prostitution discourse. The current prostitution problem continues to be seen as having its roots in the alternative culture movements of the late 1960s, with a special emphasis on the hippie communities in San Francisco. It is claimed that many children ran way to join these communes but, on leaving them, found themselves unable to make any money other than through prostitution.

In Canada, the emphasis has been on AIDS prevention and protecting children for their own good and that of society. It is notable that the Canadian literature concentrates on Canadians of European descent. Native Canadians are seldom mentioned, despite the fact that they tend to show higher-than-average rates of what are regarded as predisposing factors such as coming from broken homes with a history of drug or alcohol use, or having been placed in state institutional care. Yet in the rest of the literature, the multiple problems that lead children into prostitution are emphasised. This in direct contrast to United States research, where race or ethnicity are especially important markers. No study of juvenile prostitutes in the USA is complete without a breakdown of prostitutes' racial backgrounds and a discussion of what this might mean.

In the United Kingdom, the stress is on boy prostitutes. 'Rent boys' have become a staple of the British media and even the more serious academic studies, have tended to concentrate more on boys than on girls, despite the smaller numbers of boy prostitutes. The West Midland Police, which covers Birmingham where there is a major red light district, commissioned a report on young male prostitutes and came up with a report based on a sample group of less than 20. While the police have concentrated on boy prostitutes, the advocacy groups discuss young children of both sexes, highlighting the problems they experience when they leave institutional care and the lack of support they are given.

NGOs such as the Children's Society in the United Kingdom have published papers and articles suggesting that it is both lack of institutional care and the brutalising effect that many children's homes have on their inmates that contribute to their recourse to prostitution when they are discharged or escape.

A further contributory factor stressed in Western literature is the role of broken homes. Many of the juveniles surveyed have suffered sexual and physical abuse within the family and many are runaways from abusive situations. In Britain, the emphasis is placed more on children who have been in state institutional care rather than those from abusive families, yet the literature remains framed within the discourse on dysfunctional families.

Throughout almost all the books and articles on the subject in the West, runs the theme that these children are outside society, and that reasons have to be found for their deviancy. Their life histories are presented in terms of theories of deviancy. There is a notable absence of views of the children themselves or, when literature does include their opinions, this is often countered by an authorial voice giving reasons why they are wrong.

The particular emphasis on boy prostitutes is related to a concern with the mental health of sexually exploited children in general. In the case of boys, there is considerable discussion about whether these boys are homosexual or 'really' heterosexuals whose commercial sexual activities are focused on financial gain. One concern frequently expressed is that heterosexual boys with homosexual clients may become gay by being prostitutes, resulting in a good deal of discussion about exactly what boys will let there partners do to them and whether they take an 'active' or 'passive' role in sexual activities.

A parallel debate is entirely absent in the literature on female prostitution. Nor is there any information about young men who have female clients. The only similar discussion in literature on female prostitution is whether or not girl prostitutes can become good mothers. The underlying implication is that, whether they are boys or girls, juvenile prostitutes will not have learned appropriate gender roles.

Literature on the poor psychological health of young sex workers also seems to take for granted they suffer from low self-esteem, suicidal tendencies and the inability to form relationships, generally without exploring scientifically the causal relationships involved. The assumption is that low self-esteem results from prostitution, rather than that some juveniles become prostitutes because their self-esteem is low. One dissenting voice can be heard in the published words of a woman sex worker.

Many texts stress degrading aspects of child prostitution, including being forced into being prostitutes, raped by pimps, terrorised by gang members and becoming dependent on drugs. There is constant reference to the apparently inevitable links between prostitution and heroin use. Yet there is little information about the long-term effects in adulthood because there is no systematic research on the results of prostitution in childhood, simply the impression from reiterated assumptions that juvenile prostitutes end up either dead or living worthless and useless lives. Some accounts of the lives of boy prostitutes suggest that the average length of time as a prostitute is between two and seven years but longitudinal studies seem not to be carried out.

A further concern for those writing about young girl prostitutes is the part played by males who live off their earnings, with far more attention paid to this than to the role of female adult exploiters. Pimps are almost always portrayed as vicious and evil psychopaths, and the fact that many girls speak fondly of their 'protectors' is explained as co-dependency. Even though not all prostitutes work for pimps and some men living with prostitutes are part time prostitutes themselves, the overwhelming impression given of pimps is that they are older, manipulative men. The assumption that all girl prostitutes must be controlled in this way is, of course, a reflection of overall societal assumptions about the vulnerability of women and the need to police their sexuality.

These three discourses, from South East and South Asia and the West represent the majority of studies on the commercial sexual exploitation of children. In each case the discourse on children and prostitution is constructed within structures of ideas about society, childhood, gender and sexuality. In South East Asia the literature on children and prostitution tends to dominate current discussion of childhood. There is no developed literature on children and the social phenomenon of childhood, but a long tradition of constructing gender and sexuality on the basis of an image of passive, childlike women as well as defining cultural norms in opposition to external or foreign evils.

The current debates about female children in South Asia, subsumed in the incorrect, essentialist notion of the 'girl child' have been providing a trenchant feminist critique of the unequal status of women in society. This stresses the more vulnerable aspects of female sexuality and thus not only emphasises the oppressive aspects of tradition, through concentrating on the image of girl children as temple prostitutes, but also pivots on the notion of women and girls as objects, as in trafficking.

Western discourses on the commercial sexual exploitation of children, on the other hand, are more individualistic and thus concentrate on the deviant behaviour and mental health of individual cases, as well as a concern with the causal relationship between deviant, abusive families and prostitution, showing overall societal concerns only in with respect to the proper assimilation of gender roles. In contrast, the literature on child sexual exploitation in Africa and in Latin America is far less developed and cohesive. In both areas, the literature on childhood has different emphases.

In so far as they exist at all, child studies in Africa, focus on child health and construct the idea of children as victims, without any particular focus on commercial sexual exploitation of children. Indeed, it is often claimed that this term cannot be applied in most African contexts because the distinction between sexual abuse, sexual exploitation and commercial sexual exploitation can not be clearly drawn, not only in analytical terms within studies, but also within cultural understandings.

Africa's diversity makes the definition of childhood in itself a research issue. The African social science community, includes very few specialists on children's issues outside traditional concerns with health, education and psychology. The main themes in academic research on children in Africa carried out by Western researchers have traditionally been socialisation and initiation or puberty rites. In the nexus between academia and programme makers, a good deal of more recent research has concentrated on medical anthropology, with an interest in traditional health practices in child care and nutrition.

African social science researchers with an interest in child studies now tend to focus on the broad area of child abuse, although, as will be argued below the definition has a particularly African texture. A further major interest in all circles, in research largely dominated by Western researchers, is HIV/AIDS. In the African context this concerns children rather more than it does in other regions of the world, partly because the pattern of infection has long been recognised to be heterosexual, thus affecting children through vertical transmission; partly because of the existence of a relatively large number of 'AIDS orphans', principally in East Africa. A number of mostly Western psychologists have also been studying children affected by armed conflict, concentrating on aspects of traumatisation and victimisation.

The considerable upheavals due to wars, conflicts, natural and man-made disasters, together with mounting impoverishment among African populations, increasingly affect African children. Yet very few socio economic studies of these effects have taken place. Research on children appears to be fragmented and there are few outlets for publication of research on children's issues. Two recent annotated bibliographies of studies of African children and childhood provide no references to published work on sexual abuse, much less on commercial sexual exploitation of children.

Within this context, the topic of the sexual exploitation of children is part of an overall emphasis on children as victims, fitting within the concerns of a relatively-well developed discourse on child abuse and neglect. This latter is largely the outcome of the activities of ANPPCAN, the African member of the International Society for the Prevention of Child Abuse and Neglect. Based in Nairobi and with national chapters in many African countries (largely Anglophone), ANPPCAN has been active in promoting research in this area as well as advocacy for children's protection rights.

It has to be said, however, that the concept of 'abuse' used by ANPPCAN, and entering the African literature, is not structured in the same way as used in the general

Western literature, which can lead to confusion between researchers from different regions. The presentation given by an ANPPCAN functionary in Nairobi cited by Dallape makes this very clear. Child abuse is seen as a feature of other social phenomena or situations, rather than as a phenomenon in its own right:

'The following are the areas where child abuse is commonly evidenced:

— Child labour

— Children in prison

— Handicapped children

— Battering of children

— Children under psychological stress

— Abandoned children

— Children in war situations.

Sexual abuse and/or exploitation are mentioned under child labour, prisons, psychological stress and abandonment in this list. The problems this presents for arriving at even an operational definition for sexual exploitation are clear. This is possibly why, in another ANPPCAN publication, a study of child agricultural labourers (male) and prostitutes (female) makes it clear that by 'prostitute' is meant any unmarried girl who has sexual intercourse.

The field of sexual abuse in Africa cannot be separated from the literature of largely-Northern, feminist campaigners against female excision and infibulation. This is likewise implicated in the anthropological literature on initiation. Although campaigners sometimes like to include these debates within the general field of sexual exploitation of children, this is conceptual nonsense. It does not advance the purposes of advocacy to obscure issues by merging disparate concerns with different root causes.

The study of child sexual exploitation in Africa cannot be separated conceptually from constructions of sexuality and sexual morality. It is notable that the literature shows a particularly marked distinction not only between the behaviours expected of boys and girls, but also the expressed attitudes towards sexual morality of both groups. A further focus of study in this area is the migration nexus, together with the contrasts drawn between rural morality and town morality, and between generations. This is also situated within the overall massive population movements within the continent in the face of natural disaster, war and impoverishment.

Nevertheless, although there is considerable anecdotal evidence of child sexual exploitation resulting from these types of situation in which children are rendered particularly vulnerable to the misuse of adult power, hard facts and properly-conducted research are difficult to come by. In terms of academic discourse, or even within NGO and IGO literature, the topic of child sexual exploitation in Sub-Saharan Africa, consists of an almost total vacuum, in which dispersed and disconnected items of journalistic and project-oriented text are floating aimlessly. The vast majority of the latter material is unpublished.

Although there is a considerable body of literature on children in Latin America it is dominated by the discourse on so called 'street children'. It is worth noting that the Latin American model of street children has tended to dominate work in this area in all developing countries, largely because the ideas (but not the texts) have been disseminated by Western aid agencies. Children who live on the street often engage in sexual relationships, with each other and in the course of prostitution, which may be occasional or virtually full time for both boys and girls. Thus the literature on the commercial sexual exploitation of children often seems to be merged with that on street children.

The street children discourse in Brazil and Colombia in particular is characterised by ambivalence. Street children are worthy of pity if young, and feared if older adolescents. In either case they are often stigmatised and the literature, frequently dominated by writers from outside the region, is often lurid and lacking in any kind of academic rigour.

The HIV/AIDS complex has largely overwhelmed the literature on sexuality since the late 1980s, together with a specific interest in street girls in Brazil, due partly to the influence of two charismatic female project directors. The literature on this issue is on the one hand largely tied to project publicity and on the other to medical discourses.

More recently, psychologists in several Latin American countries have shown an interest in studying child sexual abuse, which now constitutes a proper field of study and is resulting in some interesting publications. In general, but to a less hysterical extent, Latin America is going through the same kind of discovery of child sexual abuse that occurred in the USA and Europe in the late 1980s.

Prostitution itself is enmeshed in a series of ideas about men and women. These include the idea that men's sexual appetites are uncontrollable and have to be satisfied by women who enjoy sex (prostitutes) rather than by 'good women' (mothers, daughters, wives) who do not enjoy sex. This is related to ideas of honour and family. A man's honour is tied up in the chastity or purity of the females in his family, wives, sisters and daughters. In its most macho form, masculinity entails protecting the honour of the women in your own family while proving your virility by manifestations of virility.

This means that female prostitutes perform an important role with respect to families. Both journalism and research tend to reproduce the same historical accounts that justify the existence of prostitution as a necessary social evil that protects the purity of mothers, daughters and wives and thus ensures the continuing existence of the family. However, it should be noted that this role is exclusive to female prostitutes, many of whom, according to most accounts, begin this work around the age of 15 years. As the majority of street children are boys, the prostitution in which they are engaged belongs within an entirely different complex of social ideas, which does not seem to have been researched in depth. The overwhelming majority of studies of children and prostitution in Latin America is concerned with female children.

There are two resounding absences within the literature on the commercial sexual exploitation of children on the world scene: Eastern Europe and Arab/ Islamic countries. However these absences occur for different reasons. Such literature as does exist in Islamic societies is dominated by legal considerations, which is to a certain extent replacing a culture of denial. Whereas in the past the tendency was to comment that child abuse and exploitation is forbidden by the Koran and therefore does not take place, there now seems to be evidence of considerable reflection on children's issues in general and exploitation and abuse in particular. This remains within religious paradigms, but is adding considerably to understanding of the attitudes of Islam to both children and sexuality.

In so far as any link might be said to exist between the literature on child sexual exploitation in Arab countries and Eastern Europe and the former Soviet Union is the dominance of lurid journalism on the topic of trafficking in girls and women. There is an established link in sex trafficking between Arabs and South Asian countries such as India and Bangladesh. One estimate suggests that 200,000 girls from Bangladesh were taken against their will to work in Arab brothels. However the data are anecdotal.

With the sudden economic and social changes of 1989 families in all the former socialist countries of Eastern Europe and the former Soviet Union have been faced with the collapse of welfare systems and the burden of child support has largely shifted to families, many of which are undergoing severe hardship. Children have been particularly badly affected and accounts by journalists suggest that there has been a sharp increase in child sex exploitation. The evidence is extremely patchy and usually sensational, telling for example of the longest in the world situated between Berlin and Prague called the 'Highway of Cheap Love' managed by the 'Chechen Boys,' where 'kids are sold like a kilo of bread'.

The press view of the commercial sexual exploitation of children worldwide AMSTERDAM, Mar 26 (IPS)— Beneath New York's endlessly high buildings, in the glare of the neon lights and fancy storefronts which carve that city's image, is a hauntingly sombre reality: thousands of children selling their bodies to survive.

Halfway across the globe, in Kenya, a police raid in a Nairobi hotel in January found West African and Japanese men frolicking with nine girls aged between 12 and 16. In Sierra Leone, a nation ravaged by conflict, few tourists come to visit these days. Those who do find themselves being solicited by legions of young victims of civil war and poverty willing to provide sex for the price of a meal.

Economic need and the insatiable appetite of a new breed of tourists are pushing downwards the age of participants in the flesh trade. No longer is sex an 'attraction' promoted through subtle messages: it has moved up front, and children play a conspicuous role.

The single most important factor uniting the literature on the commercial sexual exploitation of children is the way in which information is managed. There are few examples of rigorous research or of data presented within a comprehensible cultural context. Rare examples of good research practice do exist, such as the study of girl prostitutes in Costa Rica carried out by Tatiana Treguear and Carmen Carro in which both methodology and method are laid bare and it is possible to judge the quality of the data by the way they are presented, and the exploration of cultural understandings of child abuse in Zimbabwe, carried out by a team of researchers working with participatory methods. But these are exceptions. In general terms, the available global discourse on this theme is characterised by a poor understanding and use of quantitative information, lack of attention to research techniques, the reproduction of myths and unsubstantiated facts, as well as the use of assumptions and campaigning imperatives in place of established bodies of theory. If, as is frequently stated, children indeed deserve the best we (adults) have to give, they are not receiving their just deserts in a field in which they are particularly vulnerable. Or, as has been said with respect to the discourse on street children and its effects, it is not acceptable that international organisations, policy makers, social institutions and individuals who feel entitled to intervene in the lives of children with problems, do so on the basis of obviously unclear and arbitrary knowledge about the reality of these children's lives.

Perhaps the most serious of these aspects is the way in which numerical data are manipulated and reproduced. International interest in children gained momentum in the United National International Year of the Child and was given further impetus through the adoption and entering into force of the United Nations Convention on the Rights of the Child yet, in the space of nearly two decades, little has changed in terms of the way research is carried out and used by child welfare and advocacy organisations, despite considerable advances in theories of childhood and methods of researching children's issues within the academic community.

What this amounts to is that the numbers provided for all groups of children in need of special care and protection have tended to remain the same, based on guestimates rather than research. Whereas guestimates have their place in the early stages of research, provided that they are based on sound reasoning, the role they should play is that of baseline hypotheses, to be proved or disproved so that the true scale of a problem can be understood and children protected using programmes grounded in a real understanding of their situation. In the case of child sexual exploitation, however, guestimates have become fact, partly because they have become inscribed in rhetorical discourses aimed to raise awareness.

The objective appears to be to heighten public and policy interest in the issue by stressing the scale of the problem. Yet this is neither ethically acceptable nor logical. In the first place, as stated as far back as 1983 by the United Nations Special Rapporteur on the Suppression of the Traffic in Persons and the Exploitation of the Prostitution of Others, 'The important point is not the scale of the problem but its degree of seriousness as a violation of the fundamental rights of the human person'. In the second place, the normal practice within the literature of providing a raw number, such as 'There are 1 million sexually abused children in Asia', does not actually provide an idea of scale. To do this would require some knowledge of source, time, relative location and proportion.

A correct statement of scale would be something like 'According to estimates made by A on the basis of B type of calculation, in 1996 there are 1 million sexually abused children (under 18 years of age) in Asia. This is C% more than the calculation made on the same basis in 1994, D% more than estimated by the same method in Africa in the same year, and represents E% of the total population of Asian children in this age group.' Scale can only be understood in these terms. Moreover it is a poor excuse for adult society to claim that, after nearly two decades and with information technology that can provide minute details of weather, money markets and economic cycles for every country in the world, to claim that guestimates are the only data available. Some relevant data do exist and more could be collected. We have the technology. But agencies 'who feel entitled to intervene in the lives of children' fail to use it.

The current situation on the quantification of the commercial sexual exploitation of children is characterised not only by widely differing figures but also by very different definitions. Data on children are frequently hidden within and confused with data on adults. One problem is caused by the different age groupings used. In many studies the juvenile population is defined as under 21, rather than 18, years. Combined with the vague bases for guestimation, this makes it difficult to judge the scale of commercial sexual exploitation of children even within a single national context. In the case of the USA, for example, one study provides an extraordinarily broad estimate of between 100,000 and 300,000 of young prostitutes (cited elsewhere as 'child prostitutes') on the basis of a sample of people aged 14 to 34, with a mean age of 22 years.

Another study, of the USA, suggested that there are 2,400,000 child prostitutes and estimated a total of 100,000,000 sexually abused children in the world, but did not distinguish adequately between the categories of child prostitute and sexually abused children. Gibsonainyette and colleagues estimated that the number of prostitutes under the age of 18 in the USA in the 1980s and also stated that there had been a 242% increase in underage prostitution between 1967 and 1976. Campagna and Poffenberger claimed in the same year that 1.2 million children were being sexually exploited in the

USA but did not define sexual exploitation. Combining these figures results in a highly confusing picture.

Even greater difficulties become apparent in attempts to disaggregate data on child prostitutes by ethnicity. Most studies give percentages of whites, Asians, Afro-Caribbeans and so forth but with no commentary and little additional information. The reader is not told what is meant by the category 'White'. Does this include Hispanics or not? Are Chinese and other East Asians placed in a different category to South Asians or are they all simply classed as Asian? If the reader is told that, for example, 60% of a sample of prostitutes are 'Non-white' this might imply (especially in a journalistic account) that Caucasians are under-represented.

Yet, if the 60% were disaggregated one might discover that 15% were Afro-Caribbeans, 15% South East Asian, 15% Latino and 15% South Asian, which would mean that Caucasians were over represented in comparison with other designated 'racial' groupings. Blurred categories provide perfect fodder for stigmatisation, particularly if the discourse involved focuses on ethnicity without taking into account other markers of social status and bases of exploitation, such as age, gender and socio-economic class.

Numbers are an important part of any campaign because they endow it with urgency and a overwhelming sense of importance. Campaigns, journalism and academic literature tend to use the same unreliable statistics, either without reference to the source or citing one of the texts that have attained credibility. A case in point is Narvesen, The Sexual Exploitation of Children in Developing Countries, which claims that there are one million sexually exploited children in Asia, although other texts take this to mean one million prostitutes. It is normal for the highest figures to be given. They are always 'increasing', usually at an 'alarming' rate, reaching 'epidemic' proportions. Yet no reason is given for this except for the 'fact' that customers are turning to ever younger prostitutes because they believe them to be AIDS free. There is no evidence either way for this claim, but it has been endlessly repeated until it has become a 'fact'. This reproduction of inauthentic or innacurate information is a characteristic of the literature on the commercial sexual exploitation of children. Even before the AIDS pandemic, the literature on child prostitution from all parts of the world repeated, without evidence, that child prostitutes were sought after because they were believed to be free of sexually transmitted diseases (STDs), including the apparently worldwide belief that penetrative sex with a virgin is a cure.

Other commonly repeated myths include female customers injecting boys' penises (sometimes with an unspecified substance, sometimes with a variety of named but unlikely liquids) in order to produce or maintain erections. The evidence for these myths is may simply not be provided, or given as a citation to another text that itself provides no evidence, or take the form of hearsay evidence, the unverified statement of someone who knows somebody who knows these things are true.

Many of these myths are employed in order to demonise the clients of child prostitutes, as if the violation of children's rights involved were not sufficient condemnation. At other times myths are used as distancing devices as part of the construction of the client as outside the society in question, a foreigner, or a tourist. Unresolved question raised by this literature review include how to explain the conditions of production of these myths. What explains the prevalence of particular myths and figures and the dominance of oral over written discourse in this area?

Although the language of women's rights and children's rights is sometimes used, child prostitutes are seen as a symptom of the wider problem of foreign (often Western) influence, as in the use of the term 'social evils' in countries such as Vietnam. Although legislation to combat social evils came into force in Vietnam in February 1996, even the Ministry of Social Affairs, which is responsible for implementation, does not have an official definition of the term, which is used as a blanket phrase to mean all that is contrary and harmful to Vietnamese culture, yet associated with gambling, theft and prostitution, none of which are exclusive to non-Vietnamese. As in other 'sex tourism' countries, this mechanism parallels the distancing mechanism in the West that places the emphasis on 'stranger danger', so that sexual abuse within the family is played down in favour of fear of child rape by unknown, asocial men. As Jean La Fontaine states in her seminal study of child sexual abuse in the United Kingdom.

If people do think of the possibility of sexual assaults on children they see them as a risk from casual encounters in the street. The belief in the natural relationship between parent and child is the basis for the firm conviction that if danger threatens any child, it can only come from 'outside' the family. When the damage inflicted is sexual, the offending person must be an unknown, a shadowy and frightening stranger, not anyone with whom one has daily contact, let alone someone who is part of the familiar circle of family and friends....Newspapers report the rarer and more dramatic cases of children who disappear and in doing so reinforce the general idea that strangers carry a risk to children involving acts of the greatest perversion, serious damage and even death.

Similarly, the image of the foreign tourist has been constructed as both a sexual threat to children and the root cause of child prostitution in certain countries. Other writers have described the situation of young prostitutes within the overall social and economic contexts of their lives, which contextualises the life choices and survival strategies that children use.

There is some first hand information from Cambodia that examines child prostitution in terms of local clients and a video made by the Cambodian's Women's Association video examines the role of local men. While acknowledging that certain foreigners, in particular members of the United Nations Transitional Force in Cambodia, were clients, the organisation sees this primarily as an issue of exploitation of the girls involved and is less interested in the nationality of the abusers. In Cambodia, the role of Vietnamese child prostitutes is given special attention as Vietnamese prostitutes are reported to make up over 50% of the prostitute population. Working illegally and not speaking the local language makes these children vulnerable to abuse.

The concentration on child prostitutes who service foreign clients raises the concern that other child prostitutes catering for local customers are being neither counted nor provided for within current policies and programmes. The concern with sex tourism may well be obscuring a large part of the child prostitute population, just as focus on street children forces attention away from the far larger numbers of deprived and marginalised children living and working in urban and rural areas. By presenting information in the way they do, many organisations committed to the eradication of the commercial sexual exploitation of children make it appear that child prostitution to has a single root cause and a single solution—foreigners, the external enemy.

This means that questions about national structural causes of poverty and marginalisation need not be asked. The approach taken by Treguear and Carro in their study of girl prostitutes in Costa Rica is thus all the more refreshing. Even though Costa Rica is a major tourist destination and gender relations are implicated, they lay the blame for child prostitution on structured, economic and political violence against the poor, who are defined not simply in terms of lack of access to employment, goods and services, but also more specifically through their lack of access to power.

Actions Against Sexual Exploitation of Children

One of the main conclusions of the literature review is that children's rights, as provided in the Convention on the Rights of the Child, can be used as the framework for both understanding and measuring the commercial sexual exploitation of children in the broadest possible context. The relevant articles of the Convention should not be limited to Article 34 or even to other articles relating to protection from abuse and exploitation. If eradication of sexual exploitation is the aim, then the maximum force of articles should be brought into action, in order to ensure that eradication campaigns do not consist merely of declarations of intent, legislation, prosecutions, rescue operations and rehabilitation of victims. Protection of children from sexual exploitation requires making use of all relevant articles.

Although attempts to monitor the Convention on the Rights of the Child began with the idea of developing an article-by-article list of indicators, this has now been abandoned by most workers in this field, in favour of constructing systems of linked indicators, based on clusters of related articles. One way of clustering the articles of the Convention to produce a nationwide monitoring system is already under construction in Vietnam and Nicaragua, as part of the Childwatch International Indicators for Children's Rights project.

However, in the context of particularly intractable and urgent problems, such as the sexual exploitation of children, articles could be bunched or focused, in order to provide a framework for monitoring a specific issue. The fundamental articles in this figure appear in the shaded portions. These are basic to understanding not only the commercial sexual exploitation of children, but also the contexts in which it takes place. For this reason Article 34 is not the first to appear in this figure. It is preceded by articles relating to the definition of childhood, children's identity and dignity, the very aspects that are violated when sexual exploitation takes place, indeed the reasons why all 'protection' articles are necessary.

The unshaded portion of the figure contains a groups of articles that are linked to the fundamental articles in various ways, mostly related to provision. The eradication of sexual exploitation cannot take place without monitoring the impact of service provision of many kinds, including special programmes of prevention and rehabilitation.

Putting such a framework into operation first entails attention to a critical aspect of indicator development, the definition of operational concepts. It is impossible to measure a phenomenon, unless you know what it is. Thus, before rushing to count the numbers of children engaged in any activity, it is vital to spend some time thinking about the ideas involved. For this reason, the right-hand side of the figure contains lists of ideas that have to be defined so that the phenomena involved can be measured. The beauty of such a scheme is that, although the framework is universal, the definition of ideas can be culturally appropriate without violating the basic principles of the Convention.

Although it is often claimed that measuring the commercial sexual exploitation is impossible, we would argue that this is an effect of the lack of conceptualisation in the discourse as a whole. Up to this point in time, the main purpose of information gathering on this topic has been advocacy and awareness raising. In view of the fact that 133 nations were represented at the Congress Against the Commercial Sexual Exploitation of Children, each making a declaration that acknowledged the existece of a problem in their country, it can be argued that the advocates have met with considerable success.

Now is the moment for a new, more accurate form of data collection, that will provide information of sufficient accuracy to develop programmes of prevention, protection, elimination and rehabilitation. Thus the time is ripe for measurement and monitoring. The process of measurement depends less on techniques than on prior work to identify the phenomena involved, and capture their essential features in operational definitions—not definitions for all time but ideas that can be grasped and expressed in measurable terms.

The method of deriving operational definitions is:

— map ideas in current use;
— compare with the Convention;
— compare with national realities;
— decide on a pragmatic, measurable concept.

Nevertheless, as an example of the way in which such debates might proceed, the next part of this text will consider briefly and non-exhaustively some of the aspects necessary to defining two fundamental ideas:

— What the chronological definition childhood means with respect to sexuality and sexual activities;
— The dignity of children.
— The sexual age of a child

The Committee on the Rights of the Child make clear, although a child is defined by the Convention as a human being under the age of 18 years, this cannot encompass all the milestones of childhood, which take into consideration such aspects as criminal responsibility and minimum age for work. It is the nature of childhood to be a development towards maturity, as explicitly mentioned in Article 12, for example. Sexual maturity is perhaps the most notable milestone of childhood after learning to walk and speak. It is marked by rites of passage both formal and informal throughout the world. Yet the timing of these rites is by no means universal.

One of the earliest considerations of the research for this literature review was the influence of the onset of puberty on the commercial sexual exploitation of children, particularly with the idea of constructing a classificatory matrix to understand better the market for child sexuality.

It could be argued that the timing of puberty determines the beginning of sexual development, and the start of sexual behaviour, marked by psychological and physiological changes. But a biological determinist model cannot be accepted. Sexual behaviour does not emerge as inevitable result of biological changes and bodily development is also influenced by the social context of childhood and by a child's experiences. Although the appearance of secondary sexual characteristics, and changes such as the onset of menstruation may 'mean' that children are reproductively mature in a physical sense, most social groups require further social proof of reproductive responsibility, such as the skills or means to support the next generation. In addition, children experience the world as boys and girls and are viewed and treated by others according to their gender. In a sense they grow up in different worlds, so one cannot properly speak of child sexuality, but rather of the development of sexuality (both in the sense of sexual activity and sexual identity) in boys and in girls.

The expectations of boys and girls in different societies may entail differential ages for entry into adult reproductive maturity. Thus, for example, where women and children are largely economically dependent on men, a girl's passage to womanhood may take place far earlier, at a chronological age fairly close to the average age of menarche for her social group. Boys, on the other hand, may have to wait far beyond physical maturity to become recognised as men who can build their own house and support their own wife and children. In many African societies this is explicitly recognised through a system of age sets.

This basic asymmetry in the social world of boys and girls finds religious sanction in attitudes towards menarche. For instance, in Hinduism, the advent of puberty indicates procreative power or sakti for girls, because blood is in itself seen as the immediate source of health and vitality. In addition, it is connected with unbridled sexual energy. It is believed that women accumulate so much blood (energy) that it needs to be drained regularly or it is believed that even five men cannot hold one woman down. These beliefs also inform the Buddhist tradition. Girls have to learn reticence, undergo privation and practise self sacrifice as they grow into adults. Hinduism marks the onset of menstruation by a rite of passage consisting of an elaborate ritual of worship. A girl then also has to conform to new forms of dressing, which include the covering of breasts, application of herbs and restrictions in her movements. outside the family home.

The blood of a virgin, and her general 'heated' state, on account of her purity, is regarded as more dangerous because the force of her blood has not been harmonised with the physis of a male to 'cool it down'. Thus on account of gender differences and cultural expectations, puberty marks a distinct stage in the life-cycle of a girl who is now regarded, whatever her sexual feelings or desires may be, as a woman whose body is full: a body with special procreative and sexual powers that needed to be controlled. For boys, on the other hand, the process of development is far less clearly focused and is not remarked upon.

All these considerations, which have their parallels in every society, complicate the notion of puberty and make it a shifting notion that is less than useful for defining the age of sexual maturity, despite almost universal acknowledgement of the physical changes it brings. It would of course be simpler to decide on an arbitrary age below which sexual activities are regarded as unacceptable. However, it would be difficult to arrive at a universally acceptable age and current national legislations varies enormously in this respect. In any case, the grounds for unacceptability might be different, based on moral, physical, psychological or economic factors. What is clear is that the decisions involved are taken by adults who decide at which age sexual activity ceases to be harmful. In the West, this is related to a tendency to distinguish between younger children as victims of sexual activity, while older children's sexual activities are likely to be viewed as delinquent.

Although this kind of pattern could be (and in many cases is) imposed on other societies in the name of children's rights, it is this kind of action that impedes implementation. Definitional rules that do not make sense tend to be ignored. One path worth pursuing in the search for the sexual age of children was taken by a research group in Zimbabwe. In focus group discussions with groups of youth, adults and child welfare professionals in urban and rural settings, the researchers focused discussions on the age at which children become mature, particularly sexually, and whether they are able to make their own decisions and are able to act. This approach not only takes into account current debates about informed consent (in many areas of life including sexual activities) it also underlines the value of clustering articles to produce a framework for thought and action with respect to rights. It shows that it is difficult to define sexual maturity without taking into account power and maturity. The results of the discussions are interesting:

— Rural communities rate children as maturing at earlier ages than urban;

— Professionals and youth rate children as maturing earlier than adults;

— Physical maturity is seen to happen earlier than mental maturity in urban areas, and later than mental maturity in rural areas. Rural people generally rate children as becoming mentally mature at much earlier ages than in urban areas;

— Rural groups rate children as able to decide to have sex at much earlier ages than urban people (about five years difference), and youth in both urban and rural areas identify that children are able to decide to have sex at earlier ages than other groups.

— The adult groups in urban areas felt girls matured later than boys, but in rural areas the opposite applied. In urban areas signs of maturity were given as the ability to communicate, take on challenges outside the home, be independent, discriminate good from bad and make responsible decisions. In rural areas, similar signs were used, although there was also a strong aspect of the individual's ability to contribute to household work, farming and other tasks.

The researchers concluded that:

> 'The definition of a "child" is thus a combination of a series of physical, mental, sexual and emotional attributes, in which the family and social environment play a role. the ages given by the groups for moving from childhood to adulthood range from 10 to 24. With respect to sexual issues, the law sets 16 as the age for ability of a child to knowingly give consent to sex: while rural groups generally agree with this age. urban groups felt that 17-22 (or an average of 18) was a more appropriate age'.

Among the first considerations to be taken into account in finding operational concepts to begin the process of measuring and monitoring the commercial sexual exploitation of children are ideas of dignity and innocence, which are implicit in all discourses, but seldom examined. Without making these ideas explicit, and culturally relevant, the enterprise of combatting child sexual exploitation will continue to founder on the quicksands of repetition and the reproduction of exhausted, biased assumptions. Because the Convention on the Rights of the Child is the most detailed and comprehensive of all of the existing international human rights instruments it has raised particular issues with respect to the application of universal standards. Thus cultural relativism has now become a particularly important issue within human rights debates, no more so than in the area of the sexual exploitation and abuse of children. It can be claimed that:

> At a certain level, the debate over the nature of the relationship between international or 'universal' rights standards and different cultural perspectives can never be resolved.

But perspectives on children and childhood are the very basis of culture, because children are always in the process of developing into adults, which means they call into question, by their very existence, what it is to be a human being in terms of any social group. This also reflects on other fundamental aspects of social life, such as sexuality. Thus the exploration of cultural meanings must be the basis of any research, advocacy or monitoring of the commercial sexual exploitation of children. To say this is not to fall into the trap of cultural relativity, which could preclude action and advocacy on behalf of children whose lives are difficult:

> Just as culture is not a factor which should be excluded from the human rights equation, so too it must not be accorded the status of a metanorm which trumps rights.

The abuse, exploitation or commercial use of children's sexuality is a fundamental of their dignity as human beings. The Convention on the Rights of the Child refers to dignity seven times and it has been claimed that it is 'a concept that permeates the document'. Nevertheless, it is not defined. A former Special Rapporteur to the United Nations on Sale and Traffic points out that 'in the first article of the Universal Declaration of Human Rights, the word 'dignity' comes before rights'. This means that human dignity is the foundation and justification of all the rights defined later in the Declaration.

With respect to pornography he suggests that images published should 'take account of all aspects of the fundamental principle of respect for human dignity and which safeguards in particular the dignity of women and the innocence of children'. This raises the question of whether the dignity of children might perhaps be different from that of adults, and rest in their innocence. There is no social science discourse on innocence, but there is a considerable body of literature on purity, which is worth exploring in this respect, much of it related to the ideas of honour and shame that appear in many of the regional discourses on child sexual exploitation.

The literature from Latin America was referred to earlier, but the distinction between honour and shame is also important in most other parts of the world, although taking on a different texture in different cultures. Most anthropological writings agree that cultural notions of honour and shame both critically influence, and are informed by, the constructions of sexuality and sexual morality. They often act as the fundamental axis of evaluation. Moreover, such notions are conceptually inseparable from understanding child sex exploitation. Whatever the extent of its significance in each culture, the honour/shame nexus regulates both inter-sex and intra-sex relations and is tied to power.

Honour/shame, purity/innocence are mediating concepts by which people and situations are to be judged; and they also provide the terms of reference for determining the acceptable levels of behaviour in other aspects of society. Clearly, traditional beliefs influence notions of honour, shame and purity in most cultures. Further, there is an important correlation between purity and aspects of physical development, such as puberty. This furthers an understanding of puberty in epistemological terms. There is nothing specifically sexual about the concept of 'purity' and yet it is consistently used to refer to sexuality and is inextricably linked with the concept of chastity.

Yet defining purity is problematic; does sexual purity mean virginity? Or does it mean keeping to socially sanctioned expressions of sexuality, such as marital fidelity? Does it in fact have nothing to do with sexual purity but is linked to other factors such as menarche? To be pure, especially when talking about either women or children, often means to be sexually untouched but it has further connotations also in that it also means sexually ignorant and passive. Both women and children are supposed to be sexually pure but it takes different forms for both of them and often has very contradictory meanings.

Where morality is derived from Christian tradition, the emphasis on purity is very strong and in these contexts, to be a 'good' woman means being a chaste or pure one. The emphasis on virginity for women is strong as are the generally negative connotations of sexuality. St Paul, for example, saw celibacy as a better and purer option than marriage and viewed sex as something to be avoided or if that did not work, to be channelled into marriage.

Orthodox Catholicism equates spiritual purity with intactness. The Virgin Mary, for example, is believed to have given birth without breaking her hymen, therefore she remained virgo intacta, even though she was a mother. While this is obviously impossible to emulate, Catholic women are expected to divorce sexuality from reproduction. Even though the only excuse for sexual behaviour is that it may lead to pregnancy, pure women are not supposed to be sexual or enjoy sexual activity.

This view is not limited to the West or to the Christian tradition. In Thailand, the same division is apparent. Pure women are mothers, impure women are prostitutes. A mother is not supposed to enjoy sex, or to initiate it or to experiment. Men go to prostitutes because they are expected to be the exact opposite of this, sex with them is for enjoyment, not reproduction.

Pure women, in these instances, are women who have sexual knowledge that is kept tightly within the socially sanctioned bonds of marriage. They are not sexually untouched but they are sexually restrained and remain sexually ignorant of any man other than their husbands.

However, there are contrary currents to this as well in that while women are urged to be sexually faithful, they are often mistrusted and viewed as highly sexual beings whose purity or honour must be kept by their men folk. Their sexuality is so strong and uncontrollable that it has to be constantly watched and guarded, first by fathers and brothers and then by husbands. This also links into the view that women cannot be trusted sexually and that their power is so irresistible that men must be protected form it.

Whether or not this takes the form of certain types of Islamic society, whereby a woman must remain covered so she is not a threat to men and does not tempt them, or even in certain situations in the West, where a woman is said to 'lead a man on' because of what she wears, women are seen as highly sexualized, dangerous beings who use their sexuality, knowingly or not, for male destruction. Women can never be pure because they are always sexual and always destructive. In many ways, the sexuality of girls is viewed with the same ambivalence as that of women.

On the one hand, girls are expected to be innocent and virginal, having no experience or knowledge of sex yet they are also thought to be sexually knowing. In the West, girl children of around puberty are treated with considerable ambivalence. Some are presented as still children, innocent and therefore to be kept ignorant and there is often tremendous fuss over issues such as teaching 12 year olds about sex education. However, there is also the view of girls as natural seductresses—the Lolitas or sexy school girls who know exactly how to entrap and seduce older men. The current 'super models' capture this uncertainty well, they are getting younger and younger and more and more child like yet they are also presented as sexual. There is still considerable opposition to Freud's notion that children are naturally sexual and that civilisation represses them but it is fairly clear, even to those who dislike Freud and consider many of his propositions seriously flawed, that children are capable of sexual feelings and that sexual purity in children in the sense that it is something they know nothing about, is a myth. Again, this leads on to further debates about the nature of sexuality and the arguments about what children understand about their sexual feelings and whether they label them as sexual but the notion of the sexual child is still one many people are very unhappy with. There is considerable emphasis in this society on stopping children displaying any sexual behaviour in public; girls are sanctioned for sitting improperly so that they may display their underwear and both boys and girls are told off if they touch their genitals publicly.

Another link between women and girl's sexuality is that of passivity. Both are considered to be passive, waiting for a man to 'discover', develop and deflower them. It is still expected that girls will be taught about sex by an older man. Purity in this case is strongly linked to being passive and waiting. The only instance in which as woman can be active is if she is fighting to preserve her purity. Under Islamic law, for example, a woman who kills while trying to prevent herself being raped is treated leniently while if she is raped the penalties on her are harsh and she is punished for impurity.

The biggest difference however between the sexual purity expected of women and girls however, is the emphasis on sexual ignorance as opposed to sexual restriction. Girls are supposed to be ignorant of sex, untouched and virginal. The distinction between adults and children is their supposed lack of sexual knowledge and it is this that gives them their innocence. Innocence for children also means ignorance and knowledge of their bodies or its functions is considered bad.

Whether or not this is the same as purity is debatable. There has undoubtedly been a conflation of purity, innocence and virginity but this is problematic. For example, if we take pure to mean sexually pure, then its opposite is sexually impure which is not exact. Sexual impurity does not simply mean not virginal—it means breaking sexual restrictions and has heavy negative implications. A woman who has had sex is not necessarily sexually impure as long as she has remained with her husband only. However, she may not be seen as sexually pure either if she has had sexual knowledge—which category does she fit into?

The sexuality of boys is much less problematic as ideas of purity are much less relevant. Boys' sexuality is far more integrated into their personality and sexual experience is acceptable. Despite attempts to separate any discussions of women's and children's sexuality, the history of both has meant that they have consistently been placed in the same category. As women have become sexually liberated, children have taken the place of women as the innocent in need of protection. It is hard to generalise about purity and innocence because of the huge cross cultural variations and the need for detailed studies of individual societies' purification beliefs. However, the links between notions of purity in women and children and the fact that this concept can be discussed with much greater ease then men or boy's purity does tend to suggest that purity is a powerful concept which women and girls have to deal with in many environments in a way males do not. Purity is central to many beliefs about children yet it is rarely discussed or defined. It is taken as a given of childhood in the same way as a term like innocence is and is so fundamental, especially to Western societies, that it is rarely questioned.

Children's purity and their innocence are directly tied to their ignorance and powerlessness and all are seen as essential components of childhood. It is an area where there is little research or debate yet from the point of view of measuring and monitoring the sexual exploitation of children it is important to arrive at acceptable definitions.

The process of measuring and monitoring children's rights requires definitional work in order to identify the data that will be needed to capture the phenomena involved and meaningfully measure the concepts derived. The data themselves must be children-centred and disaggregated in order to distinguish the groups of children who are most at risk of having their rights violated or not achieved. Data that are gathered to serve the needs of institutions, or organised around adult centred units such as households are not adequate, nor are global national data that provide a single indicator for the entire national child population. It goes without saying that the kind of data that have been produced in general in the discourses on the sexual exploitation of children are not appropriate.

6

Global Response to Child Labour

The world's indignation about the many injustices faced by its children is now being translated into action, on an ever-larger scale, to rid communities, sectors and countries of child labour. Long-term policies can create an environment in which recourse to child labour simply makes no sense for employers, for families or for children. Short-term, targeted initiatives to withdraw children from labour and to provide them with viable alternatives are needed if today's child labourers are to benefit.

The ILO and its partners are now able to draw upon a growing body of experience in policies and programmes that work and can be adapted and applied to different situations. Research on child labour provides the indispensable bridge between the child labour problem. Building understanding of child labour and taking action to abolish it must go hand in hand. Convincing data can be used both to reinforce advocacy against child labour and to promote the political will to correct it. Thorough, accurate baseline analysis of the child labour situation leads to the design of effective policies and programmes, thus saving time and money and enhancing sustainability. Rigorous monitoring and evaluation enable projects to stay on track with their objectives and draw attention to the lessons to be learned.

Child labour is a complex socio-economic phenomenon and hence presents many research challenges. For many years, the lack of good information and statistical data on child labour stood in the way of finding effective ways to tackle the problem. While many promising new approaches to child labour research have emerged in recent years, with the spotlight now on its worst forms, even more innovative methods are urgently needed.

Research innovations contributed by the ILO over the past two decades include advances in measuring household and women's work, informal sector studies and the use of ethnographic techniques and time-use studies, all of labour. Throughout the 1990s, the ILO worked to improve methods for gathering quantitative data on child labour. IPEC's Statistical Information and Monitoring Programme on Child Labour (SIMPOC) now provides technical and financial support to countries to carry out child labour surveys, set up national data banks and disseminate information. The data, which are disaggregated by sex, serve as essential tools in identifying the incidence, scope and causes of child labour, providing information for awareness raising and monitoring trends and evaluating the impact of interventions.

By the end of 2001, 52 countries had requested SIMPOC assistance, 11 surveys had been completed and 26 more were under way. SIMPOC has also developed a set of indicators on child labour to assist in programme development, impact monitoring and country comparisons. These indicators help to track the magnitude, distribution and consequences of child labour.

In response to demand for policy research and analysis, IPEC has recently investigated the economics of child labour and its elimination, the impact of financial crises on child labour, the effectiveness of social-labelling programmes, and the links between HIV/AIDS and child labour in southern Africa.

By working together, agencies can capitalize on each other's strengths. For example, the ILO and UNICEF have jointly developed a Rapid Assessment (RA) methodology, which combines a wide range of data-gathering techniques, as a timely and cost-effective research approach. This is being used to provide information on hard-to-reach groups of children such as those in prostitution, trafficked children, domestic workers and children in other worst forms. By the end of 2001, 38 RAs had been completed in 23 countries, focusing on different worst forms of child labour.

In addition to generating information for programme design, important methodological lessons emerging from the RAs include the value of studying situations where child labour is not used as well as those where it is, and of talking to children who do not work as well as to those who do; the need for additional surveys to produce baseline data against which progress can be measured; and the need to focus on children and not solely on a particular sector where there are worst forms of child labour, because children may simply move from one sector to another.

The ILO and the World Health Organization (WHO) are also collaborating with a child labour task force working in the WHO Collaborating Centres in Occupational Health to support the development of an operational definition of hazardous child labour.

Despite increased knowledge of child labour, important gaps in understanding it remain. For example, more needs to be known about the interplay between micro-level decision-making by families (e.g. choosing between work and school) and macro-level decision-making by enterprises and governments. There are certain groups of children about whom relatively little is known, including child domestic workers, children affected by armed conflict (not only child combatants), children in prostitution and children involved in illicit activities such as drug trafficking.

Hard evidence about the short- and long-term effects on children of different working conditions and environments is relatively scarce, although there are some exceptions. While it is helpful to begin with lists of occupations and working conditions that place children at risk, this does not necessarily resolve some pressing questions, such as "How does one decide whether one kind of work is more detrimental to children than another? How much physical risk equates with how much psychosocial jeopardy? How would short- and long-term effects be compared?"

The Hazard Rating Matrix (HRM) is one simple tool, developed in the Philippines that can be used to help assess the hazards involved in work which might, at first sight, not appear harmful to children, such as vegetable cultivation on a family plot.

There is a clear research role in this area for the ILO and WHO, in collaboration with the public health community as a whole. The health assessment carried out by the WHO Regional Office for the Americas/Pan American Health Organization, in collaboration with IPEC, on children working in fishing, on sugar-cane plantations and in garbage dumps in El Salvador represents the beginning of a new model for this kind of research. The ILOs' InFocus Programme on Safety and Health at Work and the Environment has a solid foundation on which to build more in-depth knowledge of the hazards that children face at work.

Better information on schooling is also needed. Sex-, age- and location-disaggregated data on dropout and repetition rates, absenteeism and failure to transfer from primary to secondary education, when linked to data on number of hours, type and intensity of children's work outside school, would help build an understanding of the linkages between child labour and school performance.

One important recent advance for child labour research is the widespread acceptance that children are important partners in generating valid information about their lives. This means that, although adults' perceptions are not devalued, the adults themselves are no longer considered to be the sole authorities on children's lives. As children cannot always verbally express themselves well, researchers have to find alternative methods to elicit information, for example, through role plays, drawings and group discussions. Such methods are being incorporated into IPEC's Rapid Assessments.

Monitoring Child Labour

A holistic approach to research about children takes into account all dimensions of their lives - work, school, home, service provision, community life, relationships with adults or other children - and how these elements interact. A wide range of disciplines can contribute, including demography, economics and statistics, epidemiology, geography, law, nutrition, psychology, public health and social anthropology. Ideally, research should study children over time, so as to shed light on the changing nature of their work, school and home lives, which cannot be captured in a snapshot of what children are doing at a single point in time.

The term "monitoring" is used in a variety of ways with respect to child labour: monitoring a country's compliance with labour standards (addressed by ILO supervisory mechanisms and thus not covered here), monitoring specific projects to ensure they have the desired impact (programme monitoring and evaluation or PME) and monitoring child labour in a locality or occupational sector to verify that children are being removed from hazardous or inappropriate work and to track what happens to them afterwards (child labour monitoring or CLM).

Systems for PME have been strengthened considerably in recent years. Sound monitoring and evaluation mean that project performance can be continually improved by incorporating the lessons learned, both positive and negative.

CLM is a major, relatively new, area of work, which is attracting considerable interest among international donors, consumers and ILO constituents alike. CLM enables an overall, rather than a project-specific, assessment to be made of the extent to which action against child labour is having a positive impact. There are three main subcategories of CLM:

- Workplace monitoring to determine whether children are present, whether their work is hazardous or not (and what minimum ages should be respected), their conditions of work and possible improvements in their situation (e.g. removal of children from the workplace, removal of hazards, reduction in working hours, provision of protective equipment or removal of other bad practices). Such monitoring is most often done by labour inspectors, employers through self-monitoring, trade unions, independent monitors or NGOs.
- Social protection monitoring to determine what support services former or current child labourers receive (such as formal or non-formal education, vocational training, health care, counselling or other rehabilitation services, and income generation assistance/microfinance services for their families) and the impact of this support. Social protection monitoring can be undertaken by the community, NGOs, children, parents and families, teachers or various local government welfare or other agencies.
- Monitoring by communities to determine whether children working in the home, in traditional subsistence agriculture, fishing or other family-based occupations and in the informal economy receive decent treatment and are engaged in activities that are appropriate to their age and that do not interfere with their education and development.

A new IPEC project aims to develop and test materials and build capacity in government labour inspectorates and in employers' and workers' organizations to undertake and sustain comprehensive child labour monitoring or verification, covering not only the formal sector but the informal and rural sectors as well. These systems will have a twofold aim: to verify that children are withdrawn from child labour, especially from its worst forms, and to ensure that the situation of these children, once withdrawn, really is better than before.

In order to meet these many pressing information needs, research capacity at all levels, from national government to communities, must be strengthened. There should be an exchange of knowledge between national, regional and international agencies. Research results and methods must be properly documented and evaluated, and user-friendly training materials developed. The different agencies involved in collecting data about children need to be better coordinated, so that the information they gather can be compared, pooled and used to greatest effect.

The best way of learning is often through practical experience. For example, labour inspectors in Indonesia, the Philippines, the United Republic of Tanzania and Turkey have been trained through participation in field research. The IPEC time-bound programmes include capacity building of national institutions in:

- training in interview techniques for difficult topics;
- interviewing children;
- data processing and development of databases;
- special techniques for researching illegal activities and hazardous work;

— addressing gender issues in surveys and analyses;

— strategies for integrating child labour surveys into routine national data collection;

— harmonizing age groups in different data sets to improve comparability and ensuring the inclusion of young children in surveys;

— monitoring and evaluation, and impact assessment techniques.

Solid research, monitoring and evaluation, undertaken through partnerships of different stakeholders, are essential if interventions to combat child labour are to be tailored to children's, families' and communities' needs and circumstances. Thus, although research may sometimes appear to be an additional cost to an already overstretched budget, experience shows it to be a sound investment as it increases the effectiveness of interventions.

International Action to Support National Partners

Child labour is part of a wider social reality at local, national and international levels. Only through understanding and action at all these levels, in mutually reinforcing ways, can its effective abolition be achieved.

The international labour standards of the ILO, reinforced by the ILO Declaration on Fundamental Principles and Rights at Work and its Follow-up, provide the Organization with the framework for action to combat child labour.

Promoting child labour standards and supervising their application in those countries that had ratified the relevant Conventions was, for many years, the predominant ILO approach to the problem. Reflecting this work, the legislation of most countries now prohibits certain types of work for persons not having attained a minimum age. Country reports submitted under ILO supervisory procedures in the case of ratification of the relevant Conventions contain ample information in this regard. Information with regard to countries that have not ratified the fundamental Conventions can be found in reports submitted annually under the follow-up to the Declaration.

With the advent of an approach to child labour in the late 1980s based on technical cooperation, some people were afraid that action for the application of minimum age standards might somehow be weakened and that ILO work in this area would become less effective.

There has been, over the course of the 1990s, a dramatically increasing readiness on the part of governments to acknowledge that a child labour problem exists and to undertake positive action to combat it, often with the support of IPEC.

The feared spectre of negative reactions from trading partners, consumers, trade unions and others has receded in the light of the realization that, in reality, a willingness by individual countries to address child labour is perceived very positively by the global community at large. Far from slowing down, ratifications of Convention No. 138 have accelerated. Experience with child labour therefore confirms that there is no inherent conflict between technical cooperation and normative action - the two approaches are complementary.

International labour standards show the importance of the abolition of child labour in countries' overall development strategies and offer guidance on the elements of a comprehensive policy to achieve this. The Minimum Age Recommendation, 1973, that accompanies Convention No. 138 envisages development as an inclusive, gradual process requiring the "progressive extension of the interrelated measures necessary" such as "firm national commitment to full employment, ... the progressive extension of other economic and social measures to alleviate poverty wherever it exists and to ensure family living standards and income which are such as to make it unnecessary to have recourse to the economic activity of children, ... the development and progressive extension of adequate facilities for education and vocational orientation and training ...". Building on this, the ILO takes an approach that is as comprehensive as possible in its technical assistance strategy for the elimination of child labour.

The campaign for universal ratification of Convention No. 182 has given the general fight against child labour a new urgency and scope, by focusing world attention on its worst forms. Its implementation will contribute to the abolition of all forms of child labour - the Declaration's third category of principles and rights - and indeed to respect for all the fundamental principles.

International Programme on the Elimination of Child Labour (IPEC)

IPEC was launched as a major ILO technical cooperation programme on child labour in 1992, building on an earlier interdepartmental project. Before this, systematic project work to eliminate child labour barely existed at the global level. Reform of national policies and legislation had been proceeding slowly and, despite enormous efforts on the part of many different actors, there was little coherence, much duplication and many valuable experiences were not shared.

Since then, the situation has much improved and IPEC has expanded exponentially. In its early days, IPEC worked in six countries with financial support from a single donor government, Germany. By December 2001, it was operational in 75 countries, had 26 donors (countries and organizations) and managed a portfolio of active and planned projects in excess of US$200 million. Annual expenditure on technical cooperation projects reached over US$33 million in 2001.

The number and range of IPEC's partners have also expanded over the years, and now include government agencies, employers' and workers' organizations, private businesses, community-based organizations, NGOs, the media, parliamentarians, the judiciary, religious groups and, of course, children and their families. Almost 150 NGOs across the world have been working with IPEC through action programmes. It is, by a long stretch, the biggest single operational programme of the ILO.

IPEC's approach to the elimination of child labour has evolved over the past ten years as a result of the experience it has gained and the changing needs of its partners for assistance. The programme now incorporates the different categories of ILO work against child labour, including research and statistics, technical cooperation, advisory services and advocacy, as well as its own unit for monitoring and evaluation, therefore providing member States with comprehensive support to combat child labour.

IPEC has supported governments and partner organizations to develop and implement innovative and experimental activities since its inception. Once a Memorandum of Understanding has been signed between the government and the ILO, a phased approach to action is followed, including determining the nature and extent of child labour, devising national policies and protective legislation, setting up mechanisms to provide in-country ownership and operation of national programmes of action (under the guidance of a national steering committee involving ILO constituents and other agencies concerned), and creating awareness in communities and workplaces.

The country programme approach has been instrumental in mobilizing broad support for the fight against child labour and enhancing capacity in national institutions. But its effectiveness in making a large-scale impact on child labour has often been hampered by the small size and scope of the individual action programmes scattered across the national territory and frequently subcontracted out to local implementing agencies, which themselves suffer from capacity constraints.

Since 1997, IPEC projects have increased in scope, tending to cover larger geographical areas or whole economic sectors, through comprehensive programmes with correspondingly higher budgets. Work has progressed on development of new approaches to workplace monitoring and to social protection, in its broadest sense, for child labourers and their families. These programmes have resulted in the direct withdrawal of many thousands of children from work, while endeavouring to keep workplaces free of child labour and ensuring that former child labourers and their families are provided with viable alternative livelihoods.

Experience is also accumulating with comprehensive projects aimed at combating child labour on a national or regional scale. Such projects have multiple components, including child labour surveys and awareness raising alongside the three central pillars of the IPEC approach - prevention of child labour, the withdrawal of children from child labour and their rehabilitation

Several major cross-border regional projects have recently been launched to address trafficking in children (the Greater Mekong subregion), child domestic workers (Central America), small-scale mining (Latin America), commercial sexual exploitation (Latin America), commercial agriculture (East Africa) and horticulture (Latin America). A comprehensive state-based approach to the elimination of child labour is under way in Andhra Pradesh, India, and this aims to generate a replicable model for other Indian states to take up.

Thus, the essentially experimental approaches tried and tested by IPEC through the 1990s are increasingly being brought to scale through larger, integrated programmes. The latest step in this evolution is the time-bound programme (TBP), which has been developed in response to requests from ILO member States for assistance in putting into practice the provisions of Convention No. 182.

Child labour is increasingly being taken up as an issue in other ILO programmes that have the expertise to bring to bear on the problem. The ILO Bureau for Employers' Activities and the ILO Bureau for Workers' Activities conduct and support activities against child labour by the ILO social partners.

The ILO Declaration provides a framework under which child labour can be addressed as part of broader initiatives that encompass all four fundamental principles and rights at work. In Bolivia, for example, a project focusing on the cashew nut sector in the Department of Beni includes the elimination of child labour and discrimination against women as crosscutting themes.

With the involvement of IPEC, the project aims to strengthen the bargaining power of the workers involved in this sector with a view to improving their conditions of work. A slightly different approach has been taken in Benin, Burkina Faso, Niger and Togo, where projects undertaken under the In Focus Programme on Promoting the Declaration have begun by conducting national studies to identify the obstacles that these countries face in giving full effect to all four categories of fundamental principles and rights at work. This places the analysis of child labour in relation to a broader context, thereby also encouraging interministerial cooperation at the national level.

Unfortunately, neither economic reforms nor conventional development models have yielded the promised outcomes for large sections of the population in the developing world. The average income today in the richest 20 countries is 37 times that in the poorest 20 - a gap that has doubled in the past 40 years.

But a worldwide commitment now exists to attack poverty. The United Nations Millennium Summit, held in New York in September 2000, put in place the Millennium Development Goals (MDG). Progress towards achievement of each one of these goals, and, in particular, the goals to halve, between 1990 and 2015, the proportion of people living in extreme poverty and to ensure universal primary education by 2015, will provide a backdrop against which the effective abolition of child labour can itself be realized.

Poverty reduction on the massive scale required is an unprecedented challenge to the global community. In September 1999, the World Bank Group and the International Monetary Fund (IMF) determined that nationally owned, poverty reduction strategies should provide the basis for all their concessional lending and for debt relief under the enhanced Heavily Indebted Poor Countries (HIPC) Initiative. Poverty Reduction Strategy Papers (PRSP) are now being developed by country authorities for submission to the Boards of directors of the World Bank and the IMF. To date, more than 40 countries have prepared either Interim PRSPs (I-PRSPs) or full PRSPs.

Recognizing the brevity of childhood, the World Bank suggests that policies on child labour should include "faster-acting measures" than those customarily adopted in poverty reduction programmes. It is also critical that support be provided for poor people to manage risk and shock, as this reduces their vulnerability and allows them to take advantage of higher-risk, higher-return economic opportunities.

The United Nations Development Assistance Framework (UNDAF) provides another vehicle through which the ILO and its partners seek to ensure that child labour is firmly on the development agenda. The presence of an ILO office in the country, and therefore of IPEC, clearly facilitates constructive engagement in country-based development planning. For example, the UNDAF is currently being updated for Zimbabwe.

The ILO, through its regional Multidisciplinary Advisory Team for Southern Africa (ILO/SAMAT), based in Harare, is represented in the steering committee for this process. ILO/SAMAT is participating actively in different aspects of the process, with the result that the recently completed Common Country Assessment (CCA) devotes a section to the worst forms of child labour; activities and responsible agencies for the issues identified will be included in the revised UNDAF. The United Nations Country Team Thematic Group on Human Rights and Governance is active in child labour and children's rights issues.

International action for children's rights

Awareness of children's rights and commitment to their implementation grew during the 1990s, in parallel with the swelling concern for poverty reduction. The World Summit for Children in 1990 resulted in the development of national plans of action targeting nine out of ten of the world's children. Many of the Summit's goals, particularly those on health, education and gender equality, prefigured the Millennium Development Goals. For the follow-up United Nations General Assembly Special Session on Children in May 2002, the ILO, with the support of the social partners, is seeking to ensure that the outcome document clearly reflects the global commitment to the elimination of all child labour, with the use of the minimum age for employment or work as the yardstick.

In May 2000, two optional protocols to the CRC were adopted. The Optional Protocol to the Convention on the Rights of the Child on the sale of children, child prostitution and child pornography entered into force on 18 January 2002. It emphasizes the need "to strengthen international cooperation by multilateral, regional and bilateral arrangements for the prevention, detection, investigation, prosecution and punishment of those responsible for acts involving the sale of children, child prostitution, child pornography, and child sex tourism".

The Optional Protocol to the Convention on the Rights of the Child on the involvement of children in armed conflict entered into force on 12 February 2002. It requires ratifying States to "take all feasible measures to ensure that members of their armed forces who have not attained the age of 18 years do not take a direct part in hostilities" and establishes a ban on compulsory recruitment below 18 years.

It calls upon ratifying States "to cooperate in the implementation of the present Protocol, ... including through technical co-operation and financial assistance" for rehabilitation and social re-integration of former child soldiers.

Cooperation between the various international organizations concerned with children, poverty and development has intensified in recent years. The structural causes of child labour, such as poverty, inequality, and deficient education, health and child protection systems, fall within the mandates of different agencies. Thus, the core mandate of the ILO in this field is complemented by those of UNICEF, the World Bank, WHO, UNDP, UNESCO and others, each of which has expertise and programme experience to bring to bear on solving the problem.

By working together, synergies between agencies can be exploited. The ILO and UNICEF drew up an agreement in 1996 to strengthen existing co-operation, confirming the complementary and mutually supportive roles of the two agencies in the progressive elimination of child labour and protection of working children.

This agreement provides a framework for cooperative action to ensure coherent positions on policy and practice in child labour, to convene joint regional and subregional workshops on research for purposes of disseminating and exchanging experiences and to continue with technical cooperation and follow-up activities. In operational terms, the ILO and UNICEF implement joint programmes in Bangladesh, Brazil, Nepal, Pakistan, the United Republic of Tanzania, and collaborate in many other countries.

Developing New Strategies for Understanding Children's Work and Its Impact is an important new interagency project coordinated from the UNICEF Innocenti Research Centre in Florence, Italy.

Launched in December 2000, this joint initiative of the ILO, UNICEF and the World Bank aims to improve child labour research, data collection and analysis, to enhance local and national capacity for research and to improve the evaluation of interventions. It is assessing existing information so as to identify major gaps and ways of filling them. Indicators are being developed to chart the dimensions of child labour and to relate them to income, gender, health condition and education.

Another example is the cooperation between the ILO, UNICEF, UNESCO and Education International in a project to mobilize teachers, educators and their organizations to combat child labour. This collaboration produced two outputs: an information kit for teachers, and a report, which assembled country experiences and assessed the extent to which education systems respond to the challenge of child labour, the obstacles faced and successful strategies to overcome them.

The ILO collaborates closely with United Nations organizations concerned with human rights and children's rights, such as the Commission on Human Rights, the Working Group on Slavery of the Sub-Commission on Prevention of Discrimination and Protection of Minorities and the CRC. The CRC has expressed its intention to reinforce its cooperation with the ILO on child labour, especially with respect to the trafficking of children.

The call for universal, free and compulsory basic education is a central pillar in both poverty reduction and children's rights goals. But despite many countries' efforts to promote universal primary education and especially access for girls, progress has been disappointingly slow. Current trends in enrolment in sub-Saharan Africa, South Asia and the Arab States, which are home to 95 per cent of out-of-school children, give profound cause for concern. All States were enjoined, at the Dakar World Education Forum in 2000, to develop or strengthen national plans of action by 2002 at the latest and to integrate these into a wider development framework to address the chronic under-financing of basic education. Bilateral and multilateral funding agencies were urged to mobilize new financial resources, preferably in the forms of grants and concessional assistance. Countries qualifying under the World Bank's HIPC Initiative are now expected to increase expenditure on education with the funds at their disposal.

The first meeting of the High-Level Group on Education for All, in October 2001, reasserted that "no countries seriously committed to education for all will be thwarted in their achievement of this goal by a lack of resources", and called for greater coordination of efforts, partnerships with civil society and increased and more efficient funding of basic education. Only through this, supported by a more concerted campaign at the global level, can the target of universal primary education by 2015, which is so critical to the abolition of child labour, be met.

The international community has recently recognized the challenge of creating employment for the world's 1.2 billion young men and women who will enter the working-age population during the next decade. This is reflected in the Millennium Development Goal to develop "strategies for decent and productive work for youth". The ILO has the lead role in helping to achieve the employment goals set by the World Summit for Social Development in 1995.

Promoting productive employment for youth is closely linked to the abolition of child labour in two main ways. First, the general prospect of future unemployment or underemployment discourages children and their parents from investing in education and skills training, thus helping to perpetuate child labour among younger children. Second, the lack of decent work opportunities for young people leaving school and entering the labour market for the first time means they may fall prey to unprotected, hazardous work, thus themselves becoming child labourers.

To address the challenge, the United Nations Secretary-General, with the support of the ILO and the World Bank, has convened a High-Level Policy Network on Youth Employment. A high-level panel met for the first time in July 2001. Its recommendations included forming a global alliance for youth employment, with particular attention to a youth employment dimension integrated into comprehensive employment strategies, institutional support for youth employment policies, investment in education and training, bridging the gap between the informal and the mainstream economies, and ensuring a social floor for young people by improving their working conditions, promoting their rights and recognizing their voice and representation at work. The ILO is taking a lead role in the follow-up, through its In Focus Programme on Skills, Knowledge and Employability.

The social partners are also responding to the challenge. The International Confederation of Free Trade Unions (ICFTU), has established a Global Youth Programme. The Employers' group, following on from a survey conducted by the International Organisation of Employers (IOE), proposed a resolution on youth employment to the 86th Session of the International Labour Conference in 1998, where it was adopted with unanimous support. The ILO has recently produced a report: Meeting the youth employment challenge: A guide for employers, a collaborative effort between the In Focus Programme on Skills, Knowledge and Employability and the ILO Bureau for Employers' Activities. This is designed to help employers and their organizations to initiate and expand action to promote productive employment for youth.

Types of child labour that involve cross-border activities demand coordinated action at the international level. Tourism for the commercial sexual exploitation of children is a case in point. In this field, a number of promising initiatives have been taken, including the establishment of a broad-based Task Force to Protect

Children from Sexual Exploitation in Tourism, and its online service, the Child Prostitution and Tourism Watch, involving employers' and workers' organizations.

Bilateral agreements between source and destination countries of "sex tourists" can allow for exchange of information, harmonization of laws and judicial procedures, police cooperation and the ensured safety and welfare of child witnesses. For example, two such agreements have been concluded between the Government of the Philippines and the Governments of Australia and the United Kingdom.

The need for such international collaboration in the context of the commercial sexual exploitation of children was recognized in the Yokohama Global Commitment 2001, which emphasized the importance of close networking among key actors at the international, interregional, regional/subregional, bilateral, national and local levels.

Significant international action is also being taken to combat trafficking of children, for example in the Greater Mekong subregion, South Asia and West and Central Africa. A bilateral agreement concluded between Côte d'Ivoire and Mali to fight cross-border trafficking, provides for joint preparation of national plans of action for prevention, control, repatriation and rehabilitation.

The United Nations Protocol to Prevent, Suppress and Punish Trafficking in Persons, Especially Women and Children, Supplementing the United Nations Convention Against Transnational Organized Crime, adopted on 15 November 2000, gives new impetus to international efforts to reduce trafficking in children for purposes of their labour.

Cooperation to combat child labour also happens more generally at the regional level. The Subregional Plan for the Eradication of Child Labour was launched by the ILO and MERCOSUR in December 2001. Each MERCOSUR member country has established a National Commission for the Eradication of Child Labour and an action plan. The three-year MERCOSUR Plan, in which Chile is also participating, includes the following:

— generation of statistics on child labour (with SIMPOC support);

— improvement of labour inspection;

— linkages between social safety nets and the trade union movement;

— adaptation and application of legislation to give effect to Convention-Nos. 138 and 182;

— promotion of social programmes to keep children in school;

— development of programmes on the worst forms of child labour, with emphasis on commercial sexual exploitation, domestic work and manufacturing.

Another example of regional cooperation is the work of the Southern African Development Community (SADC), led by its Employment and Labour Sector, to promote coordinated action among its member States and the social partners to combat child labour.

7

Actions Against Child Labour

The International Labour Organization (ILO), from its inception, has made child labour one of its central concerns. ILO work on child labour over the decades has mainly taken its cue from the phrase "protection of children" in the Preamble to its Constitution. The ILO's prime tool in pursuing the abolition of child labour has always been, and remains to this day, the labour standards that embody the concept of a minimum age to enter into employment. This approach responds to two concerns: to protect children from work that interferes with their full development and to pursue economic efficiency through well-functioning adult labour markets.

Early minimum age standards were linked to schooling. The Minimum Age Convention, 1973, which built on the ten instruments adopted before the Second World War, expresses this tradition by stating that the minimum age for entry into employment should not be less than the age of completion of compulsory schooling. By establishing such a link, the aim is to ensure that children's human capital is developed to its fullest potential, benefiting children themselves, their families and communities and society as a whole by the increased contribution they can, when grown, make to economic growth and social development.

Soon after the World Summit for Social Development, held in Copenhagen in March 1995, had squarely identified the elimination of child labour as a key to sustainable social development and poverty reduction, the ILO Governing Body approved, in 1996, the development of a new ILO instrument on the subject.

The aim of such an instrument was to consolidate the growing consensus, fuelled in part by the ILO's own increasing work under its International Programme on the Elimination of Child Labour (IPEC), that certain forms of child labour demanded urgent, immediate action for their prohibition and elimination.

Preparatory work began in earnest for a new Convention and Recommendation; and ideas for such instruments were subsequently discussed within the ILO and at other international meetings in Amsterdam and Oslo the following year.

In 1998, the adoption by the 86th Session of the International Labour Conference of the ILO Declaration on Fundamental Principles and Rights at Work and its Follow-up reconfirmed the effective abolition of child labour as one of the principles concerning the fundamental rights to be respected by all ILO member States, even if they had not ratified the fundamental Conventions.

At that same session of the Conference, debate began on the proposed new child labour instruments and, as witnessed by the Global March Against Child

Labour, children themselves decried their treatment at work. The unanimous adoption of the Worst Forms of Child Labour Convention, 1999, and its accompanying Recommendation, marked yet another milestone in the movement against child labour.

The momentum has since continued. The speed of ratification of Convention No. 182 is unparalleled in the history of the ILO. With these ratifications have come many more ratifications of Convention No. 138, which had reached a total of 116 by the same date. Meanwhile, IPEC's expansion has accelerated; it now represents a coalition of almost 100 countries, including 26 donor governments and organizations and more than 70 countries with active programmes to combat child labour.

The 89th Session of the International Labour Conference in 2001 saw the launch of the latest development in IPEC—the first three time bound programmes on the worst forms of child labour. New data revealing the extent of the worst forms of child labour confirm the priority that such programmes merit. These and other milestones along the way reflect the serious commitment and hard work of many groups and individuals within the ILO and outside it. Such efforts form part of the dynamic global picture to be presented in this Report.

However, let us first consider the meaning of the term child labour, the effective abolition of which is called for in the ILO Declaration. While the principles of the ILO Declaration do not equate with the more detailed provisions of the fundamental Conventions of the ILO, there is a definite link between the two. Conventions Nos. 138 and 182 establish the boundaries of the work by children that is targeted for effective abolition. The term child labour does not encompass all work performed by children under the age of 18. Millions of young people legitimately undertake work, paid or unpaid, that is appropriate for their age and level of maturity. By so doing, they learn to take responsibility, they gain skills and add to their families' and their own wellbeing and income, and they contribute to their countries' economies.

Child labour does not include activities such as helping out, after school is over and schoolwork has been done, with light household or garden chores, childcare or other light work. To claim otherwise only trivializes the genuine deprivation of childhood faced by the millions of children involved in the child labour that must be effectively abolished. Child labour slated for abolition falls into the following three categories:

1) Labour that is performed by a child who is under the minimum age specified for that kind of work (as defined by national legislation, in accordance with accepted international standards), and that is thus likely to impede the child's education and full development.

2) Labour that jeopardizes the physical, mental or moral well-being of a child, either because of its nature or because of the conditions in which it is carried out, known as hazardous work.

3) The unconditional worst forms of child labour, which are internationally defined as slavery, trafficking, debt bondage and other forms of forced labour, forced recruitment of children for use in armed conflict, prostitution and pornography, and illicit activities.

Under the Declaration, the elimination of all these forms of child labour has become the shared goal of every one of the ILO's 175 member States. It is also an objective of the Organization as a whole, which has pledged, in the same instrument, to assist its Members to realize the principle of the effective abolition of child labour. This is the focus of IPEC. The prohibition of child labour applies to a wide range of economic and non-economic activities; policy responses must be designed accordingly.

To take an extreme example, the measures to rescue a 7-year-old being used as a "mule" in the drugs trade will have little in common with those to prevent a school-going teenager undertaking some additional, but unlawful, hours of work in an office job.

The interaction between the type of work and the age of the child involved that defines the boundaries of child labour for effective abolition. Let us turn first to the concept of minimum age for admission to employment or work.

With the aim of abolishing child labour, national legislation should fix a minimum age or ages at which children can enter into different kinds of work. Within limits, these ages may vary according to national social and economic circumstances.

The general minimum age for admission to employment should not be less than the age of completion of compulsory schooling and should not be less than 15 years; but 16 years is the general minimum age to which countries should aspire.

Developing countries may make exceptions to this and may apply a minimum age of 14 years. Light work that is compatible with a child's schooling may be allowed from age 12. Children who engage in work when they have not yet attained the minimum age specified for it are classed as child labourers.

The adoption of Convention No. 182 helped to focus the spotlight on the urgency of action to eliminate, as a priority, the worst forms of child labour, which it defines as:

(a) all forms of slavery or practices similar to slavery, such as the sale and trafficking of children, debt bondage and serfdom and forced or compulsory labour, including forced or compulsory recruitment of children for use in armed conflict;

(b) the use, procuring or offering of a child for prostitution, for the production of pornography or for pornographic performances;

(c) the use, procuring or offering of a child for illicit activities, in particular for the production and trafficking of drugs as defined in the relevant international treaties;

(d) work which, by its nature or the circumstances in which it is carried out, is likely to harm the health, safety or morals of children (Article 3). A distinction can be drawn between two categories of the worst forms of child labour:

— the "unconditional" worst forms of child labour, referred to in Article 3(a)-(c) of Convention No. 182 above, that are so fundamentally at odds with children's basic human rights that they are absolutely prohibited for all persons under the age of 18;

— hazardous work, as defined by national legislation, that may be conducted in legitimate sectors of economic activity but that is nonetheless damaging to the child worker.

These worst forms of child labour entail violations of children's rights that demand immediate action for their prohibition. For example, as current and former child labourers recently reported to IPEC, they were "sometimes beaten by their employers and exposed to physical injuries at work, denied wages, forced to work long hours and sexually abused". However, such forms of exploitation of children also highlight the necessity of effective poverty reduction measures and long-term, sustained economic growth for their prevention. It is abundantly clear that the poverty conundrum at the very heart of this problem—where poverty breeds the worst forms of child labour and the worst forms of child labour breed poverty—must be tackled head on.

The concept of the worst forms of child labour helps to focus attention on children, as well as on the work they perform. These forms of child labour are not only the most intrinsically harmful, they are also the ones that are performed by the most vulnerable children. The boundaries of hazardous work are therefore not always easy to draw, especially when the harm being done to children is not obvious in the short term. Hazardous work had already been singled out in Convention No. 138 as requiring a minimum age for admission of 18 years or older (Article 3(1)). Its identification as a worst form of child labour adds impetus to the drive to eliminate it.

Work may harm a child through the task itself, the tools used, the hours or conditions of work, or any other factor that affects his or her physical, mental, emotional, psychological, moral or spiritual development. Health and safety hazards for workers under the age of 18 are greater than those for adults. Because of their process of growth and development, children are more susceptible to occupational hazards; and exposure to dust, chemicals and other substances, as well as physical strain, can cause irreversible damage to their growing bodies.

Chronic physical strain on growing bones and joints causes stunting, spinal injury and other lifelong deformation. Moreover, tasks that are harmless for well-built, well-fed children may harm those who are malnourished. Even seemingly light work can be dangerous for children who are exhausted at the end of a long working day.

Lack of maturity and experience may lead children to take or accept risks that their older colleagues would know to avoid, and machinery and tools designed with adults in mind are unlikely to be adapted to the physical and mental capacities of younger workers. There may be other, less obvious but nonetheless debilitating effects on children of work that, at first sight, appears innocuous, such as heatstroke incurred through long hours herding animals or exposure to agrochemicals through vegetable cultivation. The physiological damage from exposure to different substances and work processes is relatively well known for adult workers, but more needs to be learned about the short- and long-term effects of different types of work on girls and boys of various ages and health status. Such understanding is needed in order to decide what types of work to prohibit for children under the age of 18 and to plan for appropriate rehabilitation of children who are withdrawn from hazardous work.

More detailed scientific evidence may well reveal there to be more hazardous forms of work for children than was initially believed, in all countries, whatever their levels of development. The rates of occupational injury and death reveal the consequences of the hazards faced by workers under the age of 18. Statistics are patchy but evidence can be found in studies in developed countries, which have examined hospital records and awards under workers compensation schemes.

In the United States, the rate of injury per hour worked appears to be almost twice as high for children and adolescents as it is for adults. Rates of work-related deaths of young workers during 1992-98 in the United States were highest in agriculture, forestry and fishing, followed by retail trade and construction.

A survey of children aged 13-17 in Denmark, Finland, Norway and Sweden in 1997-98, revealed injury rates ranging from 3 to 19 per cent for children working before or after school. In Denmark, the accident rate among children working in agriculture is reportedly higher than it is in other sectors.

A number of developed countries have referred to statistics of occupational injuries and deaths of workers under the age of 18 in their annual reports under the follow-up to the Declaration, including Australia, New Zealand and the United States. The ILO itself has conducted surveys on work-related injuries and illnesses sustained by children.

A study in 1997 in selected developing countries revealed the following average rates of illness and injury among working children by economic sector: 25.6 per cent in construction (34.8 per cent for girls), 18.1 per cent in transport, storage and communication, 15.9 per cent in mining and quarrying (20.8 per cent for girls) and 12.2 per cent in agriculture (15.5 per cent for girls).

In all these sectors, with the exception of transport, rates were significantly higher for girls than they were for boys. While information on this subject is not sufficient, what we do have clearly indicates that children and adolescents are highly susceptible to illness, injury and even death through hazardous work in developing, transition and developed countries alike.

Perceptions of children have evolved over time: children are now viewed less as passive objects of adult concern and more as human beings with rights of their own. It is of course true that concepts about children and childhood, including what is allowed and expected of children of different ages, maturity and gender, vary widely across and within countries and cultures; there is no "universal" child. In industrialised countries, for example, some teenagers are not expected even to look after themselves, while in many poor countries, quite young children shoulder considerable responsibility within the house-hold.

Indeed, as we will see later in this report, in those parts of the world most affected by HIV/AIDS, alarming numbers of children are becoming de facto heads of households, taking full responsibility for the wellbeing of their younger siblings. Yet there has been, over recent years, an undoubted convergence of thinking about children, marked by the adoption in 1989 of the United Nations Convention on the Rights of the Child (CRC), now almost universally ratified. Amongst many other rights, it recognizes "the right of the child to be protected from economic exploitation and from performing any work that is likely to be hazardous or to interfere with the child's education", and it endorses the ILO concept of a minimum age. The CRC also defines a child as every human being below the age of eighteen years and sets the seal on children's right to participate and to have their views taken into account in matters that affect them.

An essential feature of ILO technical cooperation is tripartite action involving governments and employers' and workers' organizations. The ILO social partners are uniquely placed to convey people's concerns at and about work to their governments. Furthermore, active participation by the social partners in policy development and practical action against child labour has proved to be crucial at the regional, national and international levels. An important number of IPEC's action programmes call for the participation of employers' and workers' organizations in their implementation.

When employers' and workers' organizations, together with individual companies or corporations and other stakeholders, become involved in the fight to eliminate child labour, then success is all the more likely. More coherent and effective policies and plans can be developed and implemented through tripartite and "tripartite-plus" structures and agreements based on constructive social dialogue at industry, national and international levels.

The recently adopted Protocol for the growing and processing of cocoa beans is a prime example of how major players in industry can join forces with human rights, workers' and other organizations to seek to put an end to the worst forms of child labour and forced labour across a whole sector.

In 1999, an agreement was reached between the International Tobacco Growers' Association (ITGA) and the International Union of Food, Agricultural, Hotel, Restaurant, Catering, Tobacco and Allied Workers' Associations (IUF) to fight child labour in the tobacco industry through a joint programme of research, information exchange and action. The agreement recognized the link between child labour and the prevalence of HIV/AIDS in the poor rural communities where tobacco is grown. This agreement was followed, in 2000, by the establishment of a partnership with a major private sector company to tackle child labour.

Informal tripartite agreement was also reached recently, in the context of an ILO-sponsored workshop, in the gemstone industry to work together to ensure the elimination of all child labour from that industry, with "verifiable, time-bound targets" set by tripartite bodies in each country. The workshop recommendations highlighted that removal from child labour should not worsen the situation of the children or have an adverse effect on family income, and emphasized the importance of a credible monitoring system.

Tripartite sectoral meetings organized by the ILO provide opportunities for governments and the social partners to address the abolition of child labour along with other sectoral concerns. Sectoral meetings that have considered child labour issues in 2000-01 include those on agriculture, fishing, footwear, leather, textiles and clothing, construction, and hotels and tourism.

Collective bargaining is another way for trade unions and employers to come together to combat child labour. One example of this is the agreement signed between the National Union of Plantation and

Agricultural Workers (NUPAW) and the Kakira Sugar Works in Uganda, which includes a clause stating that no child under the age of 18 shall be employed by the company.

Another example is the work of the National Confederation of Workers in Agriculture (CONTAG) in Brazil, which conducts training courses for trade union leaders on how to incorporate clauses on children's rights, including child labour, into their collective bargaining agreements. A review of existing clauses on child labour found that they focused on the prohibition of the employment of children under the age of 14. Certain agreements included educational provisions for children of workers.

At the international level, the International Union of Food, Agricultural, Hotel, Restaurant, Catering, Tobacco and Allied Workers' Associations (IUF) has developed a model collective agreement aimed at combating prostitution in tourism to assist affiliates in addressing this issue through collective bargaining.

The model elaborates nine points for negotiation with employers. Codes of conduct have also been developed by trade unions and by employers for particular sectors. The ICFTU and the Global Union Federations (GUF, formerly the International Trade Secretariats) have produced a basic model code that has been adapted by some GUF to reflect sector-specific considerations.

Employers and their .representative organizations have a key role to play in combating child labour, through mobilizing themselves and their members across the world to join the fight against it. Although a minority of employers, particularly in the informal economy, may contribute to the problem by offering children work, all employers can equally be part of the solution.

A firm commitment to this cause was declared in 1996 in the resolution adopted by the General Council of the International Organisation of Employers (IOE) calling on "employers everywhere" to raise awareness of the human, economic and social costs of child labour and to develop action plans to put its policies into effect. The resolution specified a range of practical measures to be undertaken by employers to address child labour. Many of the important initiatives since undertaken by national employers' federations are described in the Employers' handbook on child labour: A guide for taking action.

In addition to the human dimension of the problem, most employers are acutely aware of the detrimental impact of child labour on human resources development, economic growth and ultimately on the ability of national economies and enterprises to compete globally. As stated in the IOE Handbook: "The mere accusation that a company is using child labour in its operations, either directly or indirectly, can lead to an immediate blow to its reputation and the threat of consumer boycotts." And such pressure can initially result in unfortunate consequences for the very children that are supposed to be helped.

There is a wide range of potential roles for employers and their organizations in combating child labour. The more headline-grabbing initiatives at the corporate level include the adoption of voluntary codes of conduct by companies involved in international export markets, as well as various social labelling, certification and other market-based approaches associated with the "socially responsible business" movement.

An ILO survey of around 215 private sector codes in 1998 found that just under half addressed child labour; among these, the majority used "self-defined" prohibition, sometimes but not always specifying a minimum age for employment, usually of 14 or 15 years; fewer than 10 per cent of these codes referred to Convention No. 138.

One key issue in all approaches is the need to devise and implement effective, transparent monitoring and/or enforcement mechanisms (whether strong government labour inspection, independent monitoring or other systems) to ensure that production chains are truly free of child labour. Another is to ensure that, before such measures are instituted, appropriate social protection mechanisms are in place for the children and families affected.

At country level, employers' organizations have been involved in:

— influencing the development of national policies on child labour;

— identifying child labour in specific industries or tasks;

— implementing basic educational and vocational training programmes;

— human resources development and skills enhancement;

— supporting alternative means of income generation for parents of child labourers;

— finding ways to improve children's working conditions as a transitional measure, outside the worst forms of child labour.

Specific examples of action by employers at country level are awareness-raising activities in Ghana, Nepal and the

Philippines, and sector-specific work in India (bangle-making, stainless-steel production, bidi-making, hotels and small automobile garages and workshops), Kenya (commercial coffee, rice and sugar plantations) and Peru (brick-kilns, garbage recycling and vending). Programmes to remove and rehabilitate child labourers are under way in Central America (coffee industry, targeting 20,000 children, more than most such programmes) and Pakistan (child domestic workers and soccer-ball stitchers) with the active support and participation of employers.

In Turkey, employers' organizations are responding to the challenge of child labourers (90 per cent are boys) employed in small-scale enterprises in which pay is low, hours are long and conditions not appropriate for their age and development needs. The Confederation of Turkish Tradesmen and Handi-crafts (TESK) has established and funded a system of workplace inspection and consultation groups with initial support from IPEC. There are now 4,500 workplace inspection and consultation groups. Working adolescents have been directed into the government vocational training scheme and working conditions have also improved. Periodic medical screening of working children has improved both child and employer understanding of occupational safety and health. The Turkish Confederation of Employer Associations (TISK) has concentrated its efforts on small and medium-sized enterprises in the metal industry, encouraging employers to register working children in formal apprenticeship programmes and to improve safety.

The wide array of possible approaches for employers and corporations to adopt points to a need for systematic, rigorous and independent assessment and documentation of how effective each one is, and for the elaboration of guidelines on their potential advantages and pitfalls in different situations.

Employers are an extremely heterogeneous group, ranging from multinational corporations to micro-enterprises, and the measures appropriate to each category of employer, and even within categories, will be similarly diverse. Given the predominance of child labour in informal and hidden parts of the economy and at the end of long supply chains, the most effective approaches involve an alliance of partners working together at different levels.

The ILO Bureau for Employers' Activities (ACT/EMP) assists employers' organizations in member States with information, advice and assistance regarding child labour, often in collaboration with IPEC. ACT/EMP is carrying out a project in Colombia, Costa Rica, Ghana, Guatemala, Peru, Senegal, Uganda and Zimbabwe to enhance the participation of employers' organizations in national efforts to eliminate child labour. It aims to establish child labour units in each national employers' organization, to improve understanding of the characteristics and consequences of child labour among employers and to involve employers in advocating the elimination of child labour as a priority of national policy.

Action involving the private sector also occurs at the international level. The Global Compact is a voluntary initiative launched by the United Nations Secretary General in 1999 that challenges the business community to work with the United Nations to uphold nine human rights, labour and environmental principles, including all four ILO fundamental principles and rights at work. The

International Finance Corporation (IFC) has issued explicit guidelines prohibiting the use of forced or harmful child labour in the private sector projects it finances, making reference to the provisions of Convention No. 138. Provisions aimed at avoiding child labour are increasingly being introduced into the guidelines of international agencies for procurement of goods and services.

Government departments are following suit. The United States General Accounting Office (GAO) released, in January 2002, the report Defense management: Industry practices can help military exchanges better assure that their goods are not made by child or forced labor that recommends a framework to ensure that its private label exchange merchandise is not produced by child or forced labour in the supplying factories located abroad.

Workers' organizations have been active in the child labour field through direct project interventions, documentation, research and advocacy. Most of the GUF and many national trade union organizations have policies on child labour that formalize their commitment to work towards its abolition. The GUF have carried out studies on child labour in different sectors, for example, the International Federation of Building and Woodworkers (IFBWW) on brickkilns in Malawi, the International Textile, Garment, and Leather Workers' Federation (ITGLWF) on the textile sector in Asia, and the Universal Alliance of Diamond Workers (UADW) on the involvement of child labour in the gemstone industry in India, Sri Lanka and Thailand.

National trade unions have also undertaken surveys of child labour in specific sectors. The Kenya Union of

Domestic, Hotels, Educational Institutions, Hospitals and Allied Workers (KUDHEIHA), for example, participated in a study of child labour in tourism in the coastal region, with support from the IUF and the ILO Bureau for Workers' Activities (ACTRAV).

The Conservation, Hotels, Domestic and Allied Workers' Union (CHODAWU) in the United Republic of Tanzania has been active, with IUF, ACTRAV and IPEC support, in combating child labour through research, awareness raising, prevention and withdrawal. An IUF/ ILO-sponsored seminar in 1998 involving representatives of CHODAWU and KUDHEIHA focused on child domestic workers; it resulted in the production of the trade union manual Child labour in domestic service: Methods and strategies for policy development and action plans. Trade unions have undertaken awareness-raising campaigns, including production of materials such as videos, manuals, leaflets, posters and T-shirts. For example, Public Services International (PSI) has developed a handbook, campaign materials and guidelines on how the public sector can ensure that child labour is not used in the goods and services that it procures.

The World Confederation of Labour (WCL) actively campaigns through its members for ratification and implementation of Convention No. 182. In March 2001, the ICFTU launched its Global Unions Campaign: Get involved to stop child labour, which includes the involvement of youth structures and committees representing the 15-18 year age group. The ICFTU has also worked with the Global March Against Child Labour in a range of advocacy and information activities. ICFTU youth campaigns recognize that as young people usually make up the majority of the population in developing countries, this is an important group to target in the development of strong national trade union movements.

Trade union influence can be increased when several unions join forces. For example, in India five national trade union centres and four teachers' organizations are working towards the elimination of child labour by regularly meeting to share experiences and information. Such cooperation is also evident in Nepal, Sri Lanka and Thailand.

Teachers' unions have a special role to play, given the centrality of education in any effective strategy to abolish child labour. Yet, as long as teachers' status, training and wages are inadequate —which is the case in so many places across the world — they will be sorely ill-equipped to fulfil their role in helping to keep children in school and out of work. The ICFTU has emphasized that action to ensure education for all must include support for teachers' rights to organize and to bargain collectively, and the removal of discriminatory barriers that exclude certain groups from the profession. Education International adopted a resolution on child labour in 1998 and has developed a toolkit for teachers on child labour issues. Teachers can help to keep children in school by providing good quality, relevant education, but to do this they need good training, material and curricula. They are uniquely placed to raise awareness of the consequences of child labour at community level, and can also help monitor child labour incidence.

Unions can also lobby government regarding legislation. In Paraguay, the Paraguayan Education Workers' Trade Union (OTEP) contributed to moderating those articles of a draft Labour Code that would have favoured child labour.

In Brazil, the National Confederation of Education Workers (CNTE) campaigns for children by conducting research and disseminating information on education and child labour, fighting for appropriate public policies and resource allocation for schools as well as for proper pay, status and training for teachers and social educators. Other recent examples of teachers' organizations working in innovative ways against child labour, with the support of IPEC, are in Bangladesh, Egypt, Kenya, Nepal, Peru, the Philippines and the United Republic of Tanzania.

Trade unions of media professionals also have an important role to play in combating child labour through responsible media coverage. The International Federation of Journalists (IFJ) has produced draft guidelines and principles for reporting on issues involving children; these were published at the Second World Congress against Commercial Sexual Exploitation of Children held in Yokohama in December 2001.

Child labour is one of the priority areas for technical cooperation for ACTRAV, which currently runs two worldwide projects dealing with child labour: Developing national and international trade union strategies to combat child labour, and Action against child labour through education and training. The objective of these projects is to strengthen the ability of trade union organizations to develop policy and action plans to combat child labour.

Workshops and activities have been carried out in cooperation with the GUFs and national trade unions and federations. The projects are operational in Africa, Asia, Latin America and the Middle East in around 50 countries and territories.

ACTRAV also supports the GUF to press the international financial institutions to pursue policies that are consistent with the ILO fundamental principles and rights at work and ratified ILO Conventions, including those on child labour. A series of booklets, Trade unions and child labour, has been developed by ACTRAV and disseminated widely to assist trade unions in their activities relating to child labour.

Many other partners also have an important contribution to make in the fight against child labour: children and their families, international and national nongovernmental organizations, communitybased organizations, the media, universities and religious groups, to name but a few. Given the limited reach of formal institutions, including employers' and workers' organizations, into the informal economy, broadbased partnerships that capitalize on the comparative advantage of each partner must be forged.

The NGO role can take on particular importance in situations where freedom of association and expression is difficult and where the extent and severity of child labour is either unknown or concealed. NGOs can also help vulnerable and marginalized groups, including child labourers, have their voices heard by government and other decisionmakers at local, national and even international levels.

NGOs working in the field of child labour vary in size and scale from international through to local NGOs whose scope of operations may be limited to a single group of children in one town. NGOs can be broadly subdivided into those with a greater interest in advocacy and those with a greater interest in welfare and protection. After the CRC was adopted, international

NGOs began to reconsider their work with children to bring about a change from an essentially welfare-based, adult-focused, charitable approach to a more children-centred, rights-based approach.

NGOs often have a comparative advantage in piloting and evaluating alternative strategies and interventions at community level. They have also played a vital role in advocacy for the elimination of child labour by publishing materials in local languages and running training workshops for staff of local partners.

NGOs are active in advocacy and participatory research at local level in order to understand and change community attitudes to child labour. Considerable experience exists in ways to develop community ownership and longterm sustainability. This includes experience in promoting the involvement of children in decisionmaking.

As the ILO has found in Latin America, local NGOs can be well placed to build on the trust that exists at community level when setting up microfinance and microinsurance schemes aimed to encourage parents to withdraw their children from work and to send them to school.

Thus, IPEC projects frequently include NGOs as partners, along with employers' and workers' organizations and governments. On the basis of a decade of experience in IPEC, many important lessons have emerged and these are being reflected in the design of new programmes and the development of existing ones.

IPEC examined experience in child labour programmes in seven countries in order to identify good practice examples. The study confirmed that action is needed to create the conditions necessary for action on child labour, to build the capacity of major actors, and to assist working children directly and prevent new child labour.

Building national ownership of programmes among a broad alliance of government and civil society organizations is crucial for effectiveness and longterm sustainability, but takes time. A comprehensive approach is needed, combining many different elements in a multipronged attack on child labour, through education and training, awareness raising to change attitudes, legal reform and enforcement, income generation and employment creation for adults, and appropriate social protection systems, with strong involvement of communities and children at all stages in the process.

Investment in prevention of child labour is the most costeffective approach in the long run. But, while longerterm alternatives and prevention strategies are taking effect, it is imperative to act immediately to eliminate the worst forms of child labour, removing specific dangers and prohibiting children from engaging in dangerous activities.

Information is a vital tool in planning effective programmes, but capacity needs to be built for its collection, analysis and dissemination. Action research is difficult and can even be dangerous in the case of worst forms. In addition, there may be many more worst forms than at first envisaged.

Hazards are often overlooked because the harm done to children may at first be invisible, as with cognitive and psychological damage. Expert assessment of the actual risks to working children can be a powerful tool for motivating change among children, parents and policymakers alike. Policymakers can focus more easily on hazardous forms of labour, and this focus provides an entry point to deal with all child labour, and also adult labour, conditions.

Rehabilitation and reintegration of victims of the worst forms of child labour is difficult and costly. Costeffective models that can be adapted and replicated more widely need to be established and documented. Communitybased solutions offer the most promise, yet there are some cases in which families and communities may not be willing or able to welcome children back. Realistic alternatives for children who are withdrawn from work must be identified before this withdrawal commences.

Many national partner institutions lack capacity in programme design, delivery and monitoring. Capacity building can take place at the same time as action there is no better way of learning than through practical experience. IPEC's role should increasingly be in building this capacity, providing advice, sharing experience and good practice, and acting as a catalyst and facilitator for the abolition of child labour. IPEC's own success cannot therefore be judged only in terms of the numbers of children and families directly benefiting from programme interventions. The development of the capacity of national partners to deal effectively with child labour is equally important and, in the longrun, the only sustainable solution to child labour.

Labour inspectors have a critical role to play in keeping workplaces free of child labour and in educating employers and community members. But they cannot adequately cover all child labour situations. Innovative mechanisms, involving a range of stakeholders, are required to monitor the informal economy. Such shared responsibility results in greater sustainability.

A nonexhaustive typology of child labour interventions, classified by the level at which they occur (children, family, social partners and civil society organizations, government) and by the category of intervention (education and training, social protection and welfare, rescue and rehabilitation, working conditions, monitoring and enforcement, advocacy and social mobilization). All projects and programmes involve a combination of interventions, at different levels. The table illustrates the diversity of measures that can be applied, adapted and combined in different ways.

Advocacy and social mobilization at all levels are crucial components of any effective effort to abolish child labour. More information than ever before is available, as are means at our disposal for communicating it from traditional print, through the spoken word, to the electronic in all its forms and each must be used to its best advantage. Information must be put to work to raise awareness among politicians, the public and parents, to motivate adult workers, employers and trade unions to protect children from exploitation, and to mobilize all sectors of society, including children, to put an end to child labour.

The struggle against child labour is first and foremost a matter of changing attitudes. Once people at all levels are convinced that no one gains through child labour, action to abolish it is bound to encounter much less resistance and receive much greater active support. People must be convinced not only that child labour should be abolished but also that it can be abolished.

The ILO campaign for universal ratification of Convention No. 182, launched in June 1999, has been an example of highly successful mobilization of public opinion on a global scale against the worst forms of child labour. This campaign has involved many different partners and has targeted wider audiences than the ILO constituents, including parliamentarians, intergovernmental and nongovernmental organizations, national and international media.

Many different communication technologies, campaign materials and approaches are used, including some addressed specifically to children. Campaign activities have been conducted at many highprofile international and regional events, including the African Cup of Nations in Mali in January 2002 with the Red Card to Child Labour campaign. IPEC supports campaign activities at country level with local partners. Information materials that take on board the prevailing cultural perceptions of child labour are produced in local languages on the basis of information gathered through national surveys.

Many other organizations have also taken up the cause of universal ratification of Convention No. 182 with zeal, reflecting the strong international consensus that it embodies. For example, both the ICFTU and the WCL are carrying out campaigns promoting ratification of Convention No. 182 in the context of the overall abolition of child labour. Cooperation with networks such as the Global March Against Child Labour and the SubGroup on Child Labour of the NGO Group for the Convention on the Rights of the Child (which has its own campaign to promote ratification of Convention No. 182) further enhances impact at all levels.

While the ILO campaign currently focuses on encouraging ratification of Convention No. 182, it also aims to raise awareness of child labour more generally and to mobilize society for implementation of the Convention. UNICEF is also promoting ratification through its country programmes.

Strategies for social mobilization at a national level must be tailored to the various target groups. Experience shows that, inter alia, the following approaches are effective:

— creating a social alliance of institutions; bringing together the various institutional players on a joint platform to give them greater power to influence policy and ensure that adequate resources are mobilized;

— awareness raising among the general public, using all forms of media from radio and TV to street theatre and exhibitions, with the participation of children and youth as well as that of prominent personalities;

— obtaining public commitments by policymakers and opinion leaders;

— empowerment of communities at risk of and affected by child labour.

Communitybased organizations are often best placed to ensure that programmes to combat child labour are realistic and adapted to the local context. In Nepal, for example, community surveillance groups are active in preventing the trafficking of children by identifying, monitoring and supporting "at risk" families and children.

The mass media have a critical role to play in communicating information about child labour. The information they convey can have a significant influence on public policy and programming, as well as on the priorities of donors. Images and stories of street children, for example, have tended to direct money into projects targeted at this group, at the expense of other groups who may indeed be larger or in greater need of help. Sensationalist treatment of exploited children in the press is contrary to children's rights and may even endanger children and the people who work with them.

Various initiatives are under way to ensure that child labourers get a fair and balanced hearing in the media. An NGO called The PressWise Trust, working together with the International Federation of Journalists and UNICEF, offers training to journalists to help them respect the rights of children when dealing with the commercial sexual exploitation of children, and encourages them to establish their own codes of conduct to regulate coverage of child abuse.

The use of radio, TV and the press is at the top of the list for awareness raising according to a sevencountry study by IPEC. One of the most effective examples encountered was a TV series on the lives of working children shown on a popular children's show in the Philippines, which was later reproduced on video and shown in schools. In the United Republic of Tanzania, the Department of Information Services established, with support from IPEC, a partnership with leading newspapers, radio stations and TV channels. Each partner publishes articles or broadcasts programmes on child labour at least once a month. They visit project sites in order to give solutionoriented messages concerning child labour.

The journalists concerned meet regularly to review publications and take steps to improve the quality of information. Media initiatives such as videos, children's books and cartoons form a key part of IPEC activity in Latin America. The Government of Germany reports a project it has initiated, with Terre des Hommes and the European Commission, which has produced a brief information film on the fight against child sex tourism. 55 The film is screened on the international flights of various airline companies, and has also been widely shown on German public and private television stations.

Current and former child labourers can themselves be the most powerful advocates for change.

Countries have adopted, often with IPEC support, a range of approaches to ensure that children withdrawn from child labour, those who remain working in the short term, as well as those at risk of being drawn into labour, are provided with and able to derive the maximum benefit from education.

School readiness programmes — for very young children — provide an excellent opportunity to spread the word to parents and communities about developmental needs, rights and the importance of education. Children whose early childhood experiences are positive perform better in school, and they are less likely to drop out and be drawn into child labour. Such programmes can also help detect special needs of children.

Children-friendly schools can provide a safe learning environment, equitable access, and also recognition of children's rights and responsibilities. Participation of children, families and communities is key to the philosophy. For example, in India, the M.

Venkatarangaiah Foundation in Andhra Pradesh, uses a multifaceted approach strategy to prevent early dropout and involvement in child labour, by motivating parents, easing enrolment problems and bridging the gap between home and school.

The programme involves government teachers' groups, local community elders, employers/landlords involved in bonded labour and locally elected representatives. As a result of the systematic extension of this programme, 85 villages have been made child labour free in the past decade.

Flexible timetables and other forms of flexibility in education can also help to accommodate the needs of working children and their families, as a transitional measure.

In Mexico, for example, the national Agricultural Day Labourers' Programme of the Secretariat of Social Development addresses the needs of children of migrant workers, who often work together with their families and may live away from their home areas for months at a time, thus missing school. The programme allows children to enrol in a school in one state and attend in another. The Government is also undertaking a nonformal education (NFE) programme for urban child labourers, aimed at using community and family strengths to ensure that working children and adolescents stay at school. A model was designed, targeting 90 per cent of the children working in streets and public places. It is currently operational in 35 towns with the aim to achieve national coverage by 2002. The Government also offers academic and training grants.

Different forms of NFE have been widely tried and tested. NFE is crucial in smoothing the transition from work to school for child labourers who are not ready or able to make the move straight from the workplace to formal school.

NFE programmes that combine basic education with practical life and work skills are responsive to the needs of former child labourers, enabling them to reenter the labour market later in better jobs.

NFE is not normally an alternative to the staterun formal system, but rather a stepping stone to mainstreaming children into formal schools as and when they are ready. IPEC's general guideline is that children under 10 years old should go directly to mainstream education systems, those aged 11-12 should leave NFE within 12 months and enter the formal system, and for older children NFE can lead either to mainstreaming, or to vocational training, higher education or employment.

The ILO has found that economic incentives, if they are implemented as part of a comprehensive approach that includes improved educational quality, awareness raising and community involvement, can encourage parents to send children to school, and thus help to reduce child labour. The food-for-education programmes are one of many schemes that provide compensation in return for school attendance.

Other mechanisms include school meals, family food supplements, school vouchers, cash stipends, skills and vocational training that bring in some income, microcredit loans and scholarships. For example, bolsa escola is a family stipend/school scholarship initiative that has been taken up on a national scale in Brazil and is now being extended to the least developed countries in Africa. It provides a minimum monthly salary to poor families that agree to keep all their 7-14-year-olds enrolled in and recording 90-percent attendance in school.

Unemployed adult family members have to be enrolled in the national employment system. At the same time, a School Savings Programme was implemented as an additional incentive. The school dropout rate was reduced to a minimal level. Such schemes can alleviate poverty in the short term as well as increase a family's assets in the long term. And the cost need not be prohibitive: in Brazil, it was 1 per cent of the Federal District's annual budget.

Education programmes can form part of the response to a crisis, thus preventing the children affected being drawn into child labour.

Highquality education means that teachers must be trained and confident in childrencentred teaching approaches and methods, and skilled in classroom management and in evaluating learning.

Teacher training is a feature of the TimeBound Programme in the United Republic of Tanzania, where less than 50 per cent of primary school teachers have a Grade A certificate (even lower for female teachers) and the better teachers are concentrated in urban areas.

Apprenticeship and vocational training also have a crucial role to play in preparing young people for decent work and preventing child labour. Traditional apprenticeship systems can be upgraded by, for example, providing access to capital and credit, work premises, craft associations and technological improvements. Skills upgrading of trainers, through intensive evening courses, can be an effective means of improving informal apprenticeships, as has been demonstrated in the United Republic of Tanzania.

Vocational training schemes could be much improved by better market research to determine not only what skills are in demand now, but also what skills will be in demand in the next five to ten years when these young people will be attempting to support their own families. Better followup programmes need to be put in place to support trainees once they graduate.

For former child labourers who have missed out on formal schooling, broader forms of vocational training that provide basic education, life skills (including jobseeking and work habits) and a range of transferable skills, rather than a single skill, may be the most effective.

IPEC programmes now frequently include a vocational training component for older children. For example, a project in North West Frontier Province in Pakistan has enabled the Directorate of Manpower and Training to deliver six to ten months' prevocational and vocational training in car repair, tailoring and domestic wiring to around 100 boys and 200 girls; an evaluation in mid-2001 showed the children's interest to be high. Models are needed of how such training can be provided at a reasonable cost and on a large scale.

Systems of social protection provided by the State or non-state agencies must be carefully designed and implemented to complement rather than to undermine existing forms of resource transfer through family, community, kin or religious group. As can be seen, informal social protection can have powerful benefits in terms of strengthening social capital, social cohesion and governance.

Families need income security and social benefits, such as health insurance, in order to survive in the short term and plan for the long term, and particularly to be able to view investment in schooling as a viable option for their children. Microinsurance schemes, organized by civil society groups at the local level can be linked into larger structures, such as banks and credit schemes; the State can help by providing startup funds, matching workers' contributions and developing a supportive legislative and regulatory framework. Selfhelp groups can provide assistance through cooperatives, mutual benefit societies and burial societies that are usually financed by beneficiary contributions.

The ILO STEP (Strategies and Tools against social Exclusion and Poverty) programme, together with IPEC, is providing services that enable community- based groups to develop their own social protection schemes. For example, in the United Republic of Tanzania, STEP has a joint project with the United Nations Population Fund (UNFPA) to increase access to quality health care through microinsurance schemes. In Bangladesh, similar work is under way with the Grameen Bank and the Bangladesh Rural Advancement Committee; this project also addresses employment creation for poor rural women.

Integrated approaches offer the best way forward. The ILO is working towards a wider vision of social security for all workers, which will include housing and food security, child education benefits, medical care, family benefits, and support in times of sickness, unemployment, invalidity, old age and death. This broader view addresses many of the shocks to family income that are known to result in child labour.

The HIV/AIDS pandemic presents a huge challenge for social protection; appropriate ways of supporting children are needed so that they do not become victims of child labour.

Development of economic alternatives for adult family members is another key component in a broad vision of social protection to combat child labour. Small enterprise development and productivity improvement can help increase family income and hence reduce the need for children to work. There is a vast amount of experience in this field, which must be reflected in the design of new project interventions. For example, ways must be found to ensure that small businesses set up using microfinance facilities do not inadvertently increase demand for child labour, either directly by drawing them into the production process, or indirectly by increasing the need for a child to undertake household chores when his/her mother is away working.

In Bangladesh and the United Republic of Tanzania, the ILO Gender Promotion Programme (GENPROM), in collaboration with IPEC, is examining the relationship between women's employment and child labour to see how an increase in the former can most effectively lead to a reduction in the latter. Microfinance must be integrated with other community empowerment interventions. Ways are needed to combine financial with nonfinancial services in a sustainable way, and in line with good practice in the provision of such services, which increasingly looks to "marketled" rather than "welfare" approaches, including for the poorest client groups. The impact of loan repayment on the availability of family resources to pay for children's education and care must also be carefully considered.

The InFocus Programme on Boosting Employment through Small Enterprise Development (SEED) undertakes activities to help parents engaged in incomegenerating activities to withdraw their children from labour, and to support small and microenterprises to improve working conditions and productivity, and phase out their use of child labour. In El Salvador, the parents of children who work in firework manufacture and on garbage dumps are given access to credit, provided that they withdraw their children from work and send them to school. The credit agency monitors this and its overheads are paid out of the interest generated on the loans. Assistance is provided to parents to find employment and vocational training.

SEED highlights the important role that generation of quality jobs for adults in small and microenterprises can play in creating sustainable alternatives to child labour. There are many ILO tools already available to support such work—including Start and Improve Your Business, Grassroots Management Training, and Women's Entrepreneurship Development. Useful tools have also been produced to enhance productivity in small enterprises (Improve your Working Environment and Business and Work Improvements in Small Enterprises), which can also contribute to creation and maintenance of childlabour-free workplaces. Such tools can be adapted for use in different situations; followup with trainees is essential to support them and to see the impact of the training, including whether, indeed, children have benefited as a result.

Children in the worst forms of child labour need urgent action for rescue and rehabilitation. Measures used to withdraw children from hazardous work and other worst forms range from persuasion (through dialogue with parents, children, employers or law enforcement authorities) to more radical "rescue" operations. Experience shows that communitybased, integrated solutions tailored to the specific needs of each target group, with close community participation, are the most effective.

Alongside action to rescue child victims of the worst forms of labour, a holistic approach is needed that attacks underlying family poverty through longterm solutions, including access to land, housing and economic opportunities. Although cultural perceptions of longstanding practices can limit success initially, even these can be overcome by painstaking work.

In Nepal, children who were bonded labourers under the kamaiya system prevalent in the western part of the country were targeted in an IPEC programme that built a broad alliance between government, employers, workers and NGOs. It combined legislative reform, enforcement mechanisms, policy development, direct support, alternative economic opportunities and unionization of adult workers.

Working children were mainstreamed into formal schools and their families provided with microfinancing through credit/savings groups. Parents were persuaded to remove their children from bonded labour, through villagebased awareness raising.

Following the decree by the Government of Nepal in July 2000, making the kamaiya system illegal, a joint Declaration-IPEC project was launched. It continues to support local partners in a wide variety of ways, to ensure that former adult and child bonded labourers do not fall back into exploitative labour relationships but secure sustainable alternative livelihoods and that children benefit from educational and other support.

In the carpetweaving industry in Pakistan, the Bunyad Literacy Community Council (BLCC) in Punjab, with the Pakistan Carpet Manufacturers' and Exporters' Association (PCMEA), set up the training and education for carpetweaving children as a communitybased rehabilitation and prevention programme, which encouraged awareness and participation of community members in a range of project activities aimed at improving the situation of child carpetweavers, including counselling, nonformal education, recreation, health and safety services.

Having gradually gained acceptance in the community, social workers were able to advise families on a whole range of work and child-development-related issues. "Social workers meet family problems head on, motivate the children and their parents, encourage children not to drop out from classes and help raise awareness of the entire community on the consequences of child labour." Such sector or industryspecific initiatives make sense where there is a concentration of children in certain hazardous types of work, although care must be taken to ensure that action in one sector does not simply push children into another, possibly worse, form of work.

Considerable experience has been gained in working with street children. In Namibia, the Ministry of Health and Social Services is running a programme that aims to take homeless children off the street by placing them in shelters until they can enter vocational training or other appropriate facilities. Their parents or guardians are offered incomegenerating assistance. In Haiti, the Government Action Plan provides for the social rehabilitation of street children using functional literacy programmes and canteens providing one hot meal per day. The plan also emphasizes the reorganization and extension of the social welfare system in favour of the most vulnerable groups.

IPEC-GENPROM strategies to combat trafficking in the Greater Mekong subregion include direct assistance, counselling, repatriation and family reintegration, advocacy, capacity building and the enhancement and enforcement of legislation at country level and through bilateral and subregional agreements.

The project takes care to ensure that activities are locally relevant. Interventions are designed by local implementing agencies in consultation with target families. Income-generating schemes designed to prevent trafficking are based on analyses of local market needs and informal education materials are grounded in local cultural understanding. The project has sought to avoid top-down planning, even in countries where this might be expected by the government, through the use of participatory approaches.

Particularly sensitive approaches are needed for children who have been sexually exploited. In Nepal, IPEC has developed an approach to the rehabilitation of children and adolescents rescued from commercial sexual exploitation. Children who are kept in remand homes and police custody after being rescued must be protected from further abuse, and ways found to spare them the trauma of court appearances. Therapy and counselling must be child centred and nonjudgemental. Training should contribute to selfesteem and provide marketable skills that will effectively counter the lure of income available through prostitution.

IPEC's thematic evaluation on trafficking and commercial sexual exploitation of children pointed to lessons learned from work in this area, including the need to intervene in the source areas to interrupt the flow of child labourers, to build coalitions with law enforcement agencies to change attitudes that seek to punish victims rather than violators, and to target awareness raising at specific groups, such as the police in border areas or men in areas where prostitution is concentrated.

The evaluation also highlighted approaches that have not been successful, for example, prevention programmes that do not simultaneously tackle demand for prostitution, programmes that do not include health aspects (disease prevention, health education and birth control), running institutional homes and lengthy psychotherapy for victims, and projects focusing on traditional forms of prostitution such as in streets, bars and brothels, while ignoring other forms that proliferate elsewhere.

Increasing experience exists with prevention and rescue of child domestic workers, despite the difficulties of access to this group. For example, in rural areas of the United Republic of Tanzania certain povertystricken areas are wellknown sources of child domestic workers. The Conservation, Hotels, Domestic and Allied Workers' Union undertook an integrated package of activities with IPEC support. The project began with awareness raising and social mobilization in five villages, through radio broadcasts, community seminars, newspaper articles and brochures in Kiswahili, as well as public meetings on child labour. Child labour committees were formed and trained on how to address child labour in the community, formulate bylaws and carry out censuses.

A revolving fund was established for very poor households so that they could begin small-scale businesses, for which they were provided with training in entrepreneurial skills. In Kenya, the African Network for Prevention and Protection against Child Abuse and Neglect (ANPPCAN) has been involved, with IPEC support, in school-based income generation as a means of preventing children entering domestic work. The funds generated are used to help children in a variety of ways, determined by the communities concerned, with support from ANPP-CAN. IPEC has evaluated these experiences together with others in Kenya, Pakistan, the Philippines and the United Republic of Tanzania.

Experience shows that community-based strategies are cost-effective and sustainable in the long run, but require time-consuming facilitation, support and follow-up by the implementing agency. Other findings are that school-based income generation can be effective; and that attempts to reunite child domestic workers with their families are not always advisable. Overall, the evaluation emphasized the need for a strategic and integrated approach by IPEC. It encouraged IPEC to take up a networking role to strengthen links between organizations. This challenge is being taken up by IPEC through a global, multi-partner initiative to combat child domestic labour involving, in addition to ILO constituens, Anti-Slavery International. Save the Children Fund (UK) and UNICEF. The programme is active in selected countries in Africa, Central and South America and Asia, with financial support from several donors.

The problem of hazardous work has been a priority of IPEC since the programme began. In 1996-97, some two-thirds of IPEC's 700 action programmes in 20 participating countries in Africa, Asia and Latin America targeted children in hazardous work and hazardous working conditions. The challenges of tackling these forms of child labour were recognized early on: the difficulty in identifying and locating the children, the lack of precise and universal definitions of what constitutes hazardous work and the need to find appropriate partners to work with these children.

While knowledge in this area is far from complete, enough is known to act immediately to reduce hazards at work, particularly for children in the 15- 17-year age group, as well as for younger children who cannot be immediately removed from work. Such interventions include technological change to replace the hazardous substance or process, changes to isolate the children from the hazard, training children and adults in what constitutes an occupational hazard, and how to reduce exposure to it. Providing personal protective equipment, such as gloves and helmets, is not usually a viable option. Such equipment is rarely developed specifically for children; therefore it will not fit, it will be inefficient and uncomfortable and the children will probably not use it regularly, if at all. Medical checkups should accompany evaluation of workplace hazards, so that the links can be traced and appropriate interventions made. When the hazards cannot be reduced or removed or there cannot be adequate protection, children should be removed immediately from that hazardous environment. Labour inspection services can play a crucial role in monitoring for hazardous child labour, as well as in its prevention and in more proactive interventions for withdrawal and rehabilitation.

In the Dominican Republic, child labour has increased in the cultivation of flowers and vegetables, despite the hazards of pesticide use. Many children drop out of school, others never attend. Education, together with legal action, monitoring and social mobilization were the main components of a recent programme. Children were assessed, given health checks and their family situation was evaluated. They completed a threemonth educational bridging programme during which they received food supplements and medical care.

Grants were given to help with school clothes and other supplies, and families signed a written agreement to give priority to school attendance, while receiving loans to compensate for loss of income from child work. Selected finalyear school pupils provided individual help to each of the 374 children from 17 rural communities. The presence of these "promoters" aided active monitoring and demonstrated the value of capitalizing on the strengths and enthusiasm of young people at community level.

IPEC is establishing national, regional/subregional and global networks to address hazardous child labour. These include occupational safety and health specialists and other related groups. Those non-traditional IPEC partners that already have knowledge and skills on identifying and reducing hazards for adult workers are invited to broaden the scope of their action to children. The first preparatory Asian Network meeting took place in November 2001; a pilot project on agriculture, stone-crushing and footwear has started in Indonesia, the Philippines and Thailand. Research findings and practical solutions are shared between the different countries and institutions in the network. Similar network efforts are under way in anglophone and francophone Africa and in Latin America. The main collaborators include the ILO InFocus Programme on Safety and Health at Work and the Environment, the World Health Organization, the

International Commission on Occupational Health and the International Occupational Hygiene Association.

Almost all new projects on hazardous child labour and other worst forms are multidimensional, containing project elements that address family poverty, education of the child workers and, sometimes, the trauma that they have experienced.

For example, the South-East Asia fishing project is working with fishing communities and employers to stop children working on jermals (fishing platforms far out at sea) in Indonesia. Children removed from the jermals are placed in shelters where they receive counselling, food and nonformal education, until they can be placed in vocational training programmes.

The seven country study by IPEC describes a number of good practices in dealing with hazardous work, which do not necessarily involve total withdrawal from work for the older children, for example, offering children alternative, safer income-earning opportunities combined with schooling, removing the hazard from the production process, providing health checks and services through mobile clinics, setting up "dropin" centres to strengthen children's ability to protect themselves through knowledge of their rights, involving trade unions to bargain for better working conditions, encouraging community empowerment through organization of village committees and awareness raising, producing training manuals and curricula on hazardous occupations and workplaces for use with government officials, and creation of "rapid response centres", with government, trade union and NGO involvement, empowered to respond immediately to serious child labour violations.

IPEC works with the ILO Social Protection Sector in the field of occupational safety and health. A new edition of a manual on children and hazardous work has been published, joint advice on labour inspection is provided and a network of national institutions to undertake research, training and advisory services concerning children in hazardous work is being jointly developed.

The Report of the expert of the United Nations Secretary-General, Ms. Graça Machel, submitted to the General Assembly, recommended that ILO standards, in areas such as vocational rehabilitation, the employment of disabled persons, special youth employment and training schemes and human resource development, should form the basis of innovative rehabilitation and social integration programmes for adolescents in post-conflict situations, especially for former child soldiers, children with disabilities and children who have missed educational opportunities. Following the adoption of Convention No.182, the ILO InFocus Programme on Crisis Response and Reconstruction strengthened its work on child soldiers. For example, in the Democratic Republic of the Congo the ILO has been collaborating with UNICEF and the World Bank on the demobilization of child soldiers. The process starts with a rapid assessment and national workshops to develop a common policy framework.

Reintegration of child soldiers requires at least three to five years of committed resources for family reunification, psychological support, education and income-generating opportunities. The ILO is now collaborating with other partners to test a number of new approaches; the first phase of a regional project in the Great Lakes area of Africa is already under way.

Children in the 14-18 age group are provided with vocational training, on-the-job training and enterprise development assistance. Former child soldiers are typically semiliterate, lack skills for the labour market or even for agricultural work and have few material assets or kinship links to give them access to these. Nevertheless, they may also have built up social and financial capital during the war, including looted property and personal contacts, which might help them set up enterprises in the informal economy.

Improved socio-economic conditions encourage young soldiers to demobilize but they are likely to be more interested in work than in schooling. They need education opportunities with flexible hours and an emphasis on literacy, numeracy and life skills, such as nutrition, sexual health and managing finance. In post-conflict El Salvador, apprenticeships and micro-enterprise support "proved to be more effective than vocational training schemes in urban areas because they provided a more immediate way of acquiring skills and income. They also helped bring at least some economic activity to more rural and isolated locations".

For legislation on children's rights in general, and child labour in particular, to have an effect, people in all walks of life must know about it, including children and their families, government officials, parliamentarians, employers and employers' organizations, human rights institutions, community organizations, the media, and others. Legal literacy and education must be adapted to the needs of the particular audience.

The ILO has supported a range of interventions with respect to improving legal and policy frameworks, awareness and law enforcement. These include law reform, translation of domestic laws into local dialects and languages and para-legal education for community groups and provision of legal services to child labour victims. Some "good practices" identified in country programmes include the passing of local ordinances and by-laws that make it possible to monitor child labour directly in communities, capitalizing on external events (for example, adoption of international instruments) to bring about domestic policy change, NGOs or trade unions contributing to the law-drafting process and keeping the child labour issue on the public agenda so as to increase the commitment of political leaders.

Considerable effort has gone into capacity building of labour inspectors. Practical training materials, focusing on the particular inspection issues relating to child labour, have been developed by the ILO for adaptation and use in many countries, including for a subregional programme in Indonesia, the Philippines and Thailand.

The role of labour inspectors goes well beyond that of law enforcer. Labour inspectors can spread awareness about the consequences of child labour, work with employers to improve the situation and work with trade unions or NGOs to ensure that children withdrawn from work receive appropriate support and rehabilitation.

Other good practices include quality circles whereby labour ins pectors use non-confrontational methods to assist employers to carry out self-inspection, inspection groups affiliated with trade unions in workplaces with few employees, labour inspectors being involved in research to increase their understanding of child labour and labour inspectors being encouraged to use the information gained through their field studies to train their colleagues. Mobile inspection units can prove useful where child labour is found in remote and isolated regions of the country.

The effectiveness of government labour inspection in detecting and combating child labour is often constrained by the resources available, which are not equal to the task, by perceptions of their role and by the hidden nature of much child labour, especially its worst forms, in informal and illegal activities. New approaches and partnerships are clearly needed for an integrated solution to child labour monitoring. Different models have already been developed and tested.

8

Educational Strategies to Eliminate Child Labour

All children should—'but do not have'—the right to education. Problems in guaranteeing free and compulsory education to all children revolve around funding. The worlds of human rights and fiscal allocations are separated by an abyss at the global or domestic level. Funding for education tends to be treated as discretionary, contrary to what international human rights law demands.

Few countries in the world have effective constitutional guarantees which oblige the government to allocate to education a determined proportion of its budget. A rare example is the 1947 Constitution of Taiwan which has specified: Expenditures of educational programmes shall not be in respect of the central government, less than fifteen percent of the total national budget, in respect of each province no less than twenty-five percent of the total provincial budget, and in respect of each municipality, no less than thirty-five percent of the total municipal budget.

The purpose of human rights law is to transform allocations for education from discretionary into obligatory. This process entails acceptance of human rights correctives in decision-making, which is a political process at all levels, from local to global. Securing a match between governmental human rights obligation in education and fiscal allocations requires another step-according priority to primary education.

The objective of international human rights law is to alter political choices by bestowing legal rights upon those actors who have the least access to decision-making, such as children. Primary-school aged children who should be 'but are not' in school are easily marginalised hence their legal claim upon governments. This claim is detailed in a number of international and domestic legal instruments. These are, as the term 'instrument' indicates, tools whose value increases with their utilization. The inverse is also true, such tools have no value unless they are known and used.

The European Social Charter, whose revision in 1996 has included a far-reaching guarantee of the right to education, has added the previously missing economic and social dimensions, and the Council of Europe is no longer the single exception mentioned above. The 1962 UNESCO Convention against Discrimination in Education is the oldest global treaty guaranteeing free and compulsory education. It was followed by the International Covenant on Economic, Social and Cultural Rights, adopted in 1966 and abbreviated as ICESCR.

Within the Organization of American States (OAS), similarly to the Council of Europe, the American Convention on Human Rights had included only civil and political rights to be in 1988 supplemented by the

Protocol of San Salvador on economic, social and cultural rights. The Organization of African Unity created its own human rights treaties and organs, starting in 1981 with the African Charter on Human and Peoples, Rights, which merged collective and individual as well as civil/ political and economic/social/cultural rights. The Charter on the Rights and Welfare of the African Child was adopted in 1990 to come into force ten years later, with the committee that should be established on the basis of this Charter expected in the year 2001.

The Convention on the Rights of the Child (CRC) was ten years old in 1999 and has thus far been ratified by the largest number of states (191). These treaties map out the international legal framework of the fundamental requirement of right to education, to secure free and compulsory education for all children.

From the Universal Declaration of Human Rights in 1948 to the (Revised) European Social Charter of 1966, the requirement for education to be free and compulsory never wavered. However, changes have been in the specific designations of various stages of education. The Universal Declaration has used the term 'elementary' which later became 'primary' and in the African Charter 'basic.' Although the wording of international treaties demands only primary education to be free, compulsory education has been prolonged in practice, thus lengthening free-of-charge education.

Because law is symmetrical, the right to education entails corresponding obligations. Making education compulsory requires parents and governments to perform their obligations towards children. This logic was aptly summarized in 1956:

> Just as school legislation imposes upon the parent the duty of sending his children to school, States should accept the obligation of providing enough schools to educate all children.

Nobody can be required to do the impossible and thus parents cannot be obliged to ensure that their children attend school if they cannot afford the cost of schooling. Making education compulsory was thus contingent on making it free.

In the drafting of the foundation for all human rights treaties, the Universal Declaration of Human Rights, there was never a question about education being made compulsory without being free. Records of early discussions within the Commission on Human Rights or later in the Third Committee of the General Assembly testify to this linkage from the very beginning of the drafting process to its very end. Its rationale was followed in all subsequent human rights treaties. Thus far the (Revised) European Social Charter has provided the most generous definition of the right of children and young people to free and compulsory education, requiring that both primary and secondary education be free and compulsory. This has remedied the previous exceptionalism of the Council of Europe, whose Convention on Human Rights dealt only with selected civil and political rights, providing safeguards only against denied access to education.

The mosaic of diverse pre-state schools existing in Western Europe at the time when the provision on the right to education was drafted (1950-1952) influenced the approach to the role of the government under the European Convention on Human Rights. The Secretary-General of the Council of Europe at that time had this to say about the substitution of the originally proposed 'every person has the right to education' by a negative formulation in the final text of the Protocol to the European Convention on Human Rights:

> The right to education has been asserted in the negative formulation: 'No person shall be denied the right to education' because the positive formulation proposed by the [Consultative Assembly in August 1950] might be interpreted to impose on the State the positive duty to provide education. While education is provided by the State for children, as a matter of course, in all member States, it is not possible for them to give an unlimited guarantee to provide education, as that might be construed to apply to illiterate adults for whom no facilities exist, or to types or standards of education which the State cannot furnish for one reason or another.

This reasoning has influenced reservations to that negative formulation, which have affirmed the reluctance of governments to finance diverse schools which are due to emerge through the exercise of parental freedom of choice-he need to balance parental freedom of choice with governmental obligation to ensure that education is available and accessible to all children which includes interpretations of best ways to attain this balance by the European Court of Human Rights. The adoption of the (Revised) European Social Charter in 1996 and its entry into force in 1999 'almost four decades after the initial guarantee of the right to education' signified a changed attitude within the Council of Europe. With this change, the uniformity of requirements that primary education be free, compulsory and all-encompassing has been fully accomplished, underpinning the universality of the right to education. The process of concluding international treaties includes two stages. Treaties are first negotiated amongst governmental delegations and the text is formally adopted to be signed by representatives of those states who have decided to formally record their political commitment to the adopted treaties.

The second stage takes place within each state, whose parliament (the body empowered to create domestic law or accept international treaties) has to decide whether a treaty should become legally binding for that country and, if so decided, a formal ratification signifies the end of the second stage. With sufficient number of states ratifying a specific treaty, it enters into force for them. Lawmaking is based upon sovereign equality of states hence each one specifically and explicitly accepts to be bound by any international treaty. During the second stage, when international treaties are discussed within individual countries with a view to making them legally binding for the country concerned, some of their provisions may not be deemed acceptable because the government does not wish to or cannot comply with their requirements. Ratifications are then accompanied with reservations, and quite a few relate to the right to education. The reservations to those treaty provisions which require primary education to be free and compulsory indicate the general acceptance of this postulate by signalling, most often, that compliance cannot be assured immediately but gradually. The International Covenant on Economic, Social and Cultural Rights has prompted more than a dozen states parties to submit reservations to its provision on the right to education.

These range from acknowledgments that financial constraints to access to primary education were beyond the capacity of the state, to assertions that education should be treated as the monopoly of the state, or that parents should be allowed to educate their children themselves, in their own home. The Convention on the Rights of the Child lays down the full scope of the right to education. The principle of nondiscrimination is followed by general provisions on the access to education, its purposes and objectives, which is accompanied by specific requirements upon education to protect children from abuse and neglect or illicit use of narcotic drugs, and followed by safeguards against work that interferes with children's primary education. An illustration of the demanding nature and scope of states' obligations concerning education is the number and variety of reservations.

The consequence of the number and variety of reservations is that a mere ratification of a treaty does not mean that it is binding in its entirety for a particular country. Information on ratifications then has to be supplemented with indications of their limited scope through reservations. Moreover, some reservations, especially those relating to the human rights of children and women, are so wide-reaching that their compatibility with the spirit and wording of the treaties has frequently been challenged and their withdrawal urged. A brief explanation is then necessary to point out common gaps between appearance and reality.

A mere ratification of a human rights treaty may be of little value to the domestic population because the rights guaranteed therein cannot be accessed and enjoyed. The remark 'UN Special Rapporteur' in the right-hand column denotes countries for which the United Nations Commission on Human Rights has established a country-specific mechanism, which reflects the Commission's concern about the overall human rights situation in that country. Within the United Nations, there are two treaty-based procedures: the Human Rights Committee (HRC) deals with communications related to the International Covenant on Civil and Political Rights, while the Committee for the Elimination of Racial Discrimination examines communications alleging breach of the Convention on the Elimination of All Forms of Racial Discrimination (CERD). The third one is starting under the Convention on the Elimination of All Forms of Discrimination against Women (CEDAW), whose Protocol establishing such a procedure has recently come into force for the first dozen states parties. Within regional organizations, two distinct procedures exist within the Inter-American human rights system, one before the Commission and another before the Court. The Council of Europe has recently altered this pattern and there is only the European Court of Human Rights for violations of civil and political rights guaranteed by the European Convention.

The European Committee of Social Rights has recently started processing collective complaints of violations of social rights. For African countries (which include all the geographical region, thus also Africa north of Sahara), access to the African Commission on Human and Peoples' Rights follows from the ratification of the Charter, which also does not allow reservations; access to international remedies is thereby automatically broadened. The coming into force of the Charter on the Rights and Welfare of the African Child entails setting up a committee which will also receive complaints. Experiences at the regional level, in Europe and the Americas, and more recently in Africa, have undoubtedly contributed to the internationalization of human rights enforcement.

The interplay between international and domestic human rights guarantees represents a fascinating area for research because assumed correspondence between the two tends to be an exception rather than a rule. It would be easy to assume that human rights safeguards from ratified international treaties are reflected in domestic constitutions but this assumption is belied by facts.

Those states that have ratified all international treaties which guarantee free and compulsory primary education to all children, without any reservations, do not necessarily repeat this commitment in their constitutions. This inconsistence may exemplify two different situations:

- In countries where international human rights treaties are directly applicable, the absence of explicit domestic human rights guarantees is legally irrelevant. Quite a few countries have constitutions which are more than hundred years old, do not even mention the word 'human rights', and direct application of international human rights treaties supplements lacking constitutional guarantees. Making international human rights law directly applicable is the model best suited to ensuring the universality of human rights.
- Where international treaties are not directly applicable nor is there a provision whereby they override domestic law, there is incongruity between international and domestic human rights guarantees, with the latter often falling far behind the former.

The postulate of the Convention on the Rights of Child whereby all children should have guaranteed access to education regardless of their legal status, or that of their parents, is gradually being translated into the practice of states. In 37 countries, however, the right to education is formally restricted to citizens.

Access to education for those children who are likely to be facing legal obstacles, such as asylum-seekers and refugees, as well as children who are stateless and children of migrant workers, thus may not be assured as a matter of right. Putting into practice free and compulsory education for all children requires ensuring that primary schools are available for all children, which necessitates a considerable investment. While the state is not the only investor, international human rights law obliges it to be the investor of last resort.

In Africa, children of primary-school age may constitute close to half of the population and the majority is living in rural areas. Making primary schools available to dispersed rural communities, some of whom may be nomadic, illustrates the scope of the challenge. If the intake capacity of primary schools is below the number of primary-school aged children, legal provisions on compulsory education will not be translated into practice and access to education will remain a need or a wish rather than, being a right. Investment in educational infrastructure requires considerable initial capital but yields benefits after a long time. The recurrent costs and maintenance of schools as well as teachers' salaries add to the cost. The requirement that primary education be free of charge is thus costly.

Economists often apply the criterion of affordability to free-of-charge education, and questions have been raised in the past two decades about compatibility between fiscal and educational policy, that is, between fiscal targets defined in terms of reducing public expenditure and funding necessary to ensure universal primary education free of charge for all children. These have often been directed at the World Bank.

While international law requires primary education to be free of charge, education cannot be free-of-cost in theory or in practice. For governments, it is one of the major items in their budgets. Parents finance their children's education through general taxation, and routinely pay the cost of books, transportation and school meals, uniforms, pens and pencils, or sports equipment. The requirement upon governments to make primary education free implies that governments should eliminate financial obstacles in order to enable all children 'no matter how poor to complete primary schooling.

A great deal of controversy has been generated regarding the human rights obligation to finance primary education. The requirement that primary schooling be free of financial cost for the child has generated a great deal of consensus, but that it also be free of financial cost for parents triggers dissent. One reason is parental primary responsibility, financial as well as any other, for their children, affirmed in the Convention on the Rights of the Child. Another reason is parental freedom to choose non-state schools for their children, or establish their own or else educate their children at home, routinely at their own expense. Primary education should be free for children because they cannot possibly pay for themselves. This does not imply that education is free for parents, community, society or the state because schools and teachers' salaries have to be financed. Rather, this means that primary education should be prioritised in resource allocation.

Direct charges in primary education, under whatever name, impose upon parents the obligation to fully finance the education of their children. School fees are named differently, as user charges, registration fees, school maintenance or development levies, but whatever name they bear, their effect is to openly question the explicit requirement of international human rights law that at least primary education be free.

The duty to financially contribute to the cost of primary education is spread among the whole population where education is financed by the state out of general taxation, which is the model envisaged in international human rights law. Unless the state can generate revenue, it cannot comply with its obligation to secure that primary education is available for all children and free of charge.

International human rights law assumes that states are both willing and able to generate resources needed for education through general taxation. There are few which are unable to impose and enforce taxation upon their wealthy population, many more are unwilling to do so. This is precisely why human rights have been defined as governmental obligations. The assertion of the Universal Declaration of Human Rights that all individuals have duties towards their community has, regretfully, fallen into oblivion. And yet, states cannot finance education unless they generate resources, they cannot generate resources unless companies and individuals pay tax. Today's dominant ideology seeks the withdrawal of the state from generating and allocating resources, thus jeopardizing access to education, particularly in the poorest and youngest countries. The financing of education is in many countries within the remit of local or regional authorities, whose tax base and tax revenue may be profoundly different from those of the central government.

Nevertheless, no internationally comparable data have been generated in this area. From the human rights viewpoint, the state is responsible for human rights hence its obligations encompass the whole territory and all the people. Because local communities may not be able to raise revenue sufficient to guarantee to all children free and compulsory primary education, the state ought to redress their lack of capacity. The same rationale extends to the world at large because human rights are universal. International co-operation has been envisaged as the method for redressing inability of individual states to comply with their human rights obligations.

Distinguishing between inability and unwillingness thus obtains a great deal of importance. Those who do not earn enough to be liable to taxation are not taxed, thus taxation applies the logic of distributive justice. Where fees are charged in primary school, those who are too poor to afford the cost nevertheless have to pay the charges. If they cannot afford them, their children will be penalized by denied access to primary school. Where exemptions are nominally provided, they may be too cumbersome to comply with or too expensive to administer.

The Convention on the Rights of the Child has specified for health that children should not be denied access to health services because of the inability of their parents to pay its cost, and there is no indication that the Convention envisaged a lower standard for primary education, on the contrary.

The Committee on the Rights of the Child requires governments to report on 'the measures taken to ensure that children, particularly those belonging to the most disadvantaged groups, are protected against the adverse effects of economic policies, including the reduction of budgetary allocations in the social sector.' The cost of primary schooling is considerable. Mark Bray has estimated that at least 20% and often as much as 90% of the financial cost of primary education is borne by the parents and/or families.

Parental financial contributions towards primary education of their children depend on their ability to contribute, not only their willingness to do so. Their inability to afford sending their children to school deprives their children of access to primary education and highlights the essence of governmental human rights obligation to be the provider of last resort. Parental choice may be exercised to the detriment of girls and requires governments to act so as to alter parental choices. Efforts to increase primary school enrolment for girls have included subsidizing direct, indirect, and opportunity costs (namely, the loss of the value of the girls' work) for their parents and/or families. The distribution of the cost of primary education between the government and parents depends on budgetary allocations. The budget exemplified the translation of political choices into financial commitments.

Education is often the single largest item in governments budgets although in heavily indebted countries it tends to be dwarfed by debt repayments. A group of senators in the Philippines challenged in 1991 the constitutionality of the budgetary allocation of P86 billion for debt servicing, while P27 billion was allocated for education. The Constitution of the Philippines obligates the government to assign the highest budgetary priority to education.

The issue to be decided was whether debt servicing, exceeding three times the budgetary allocation for education, was unconstitutional. The Court found that education had been the highest budgetary priority, while debt servicing was necessary to safeguard the creditworthiness of the country and thus the survival of its economy. This rare case of attempted legal challenge of priorities in financial allocations has affirmed the need to design international solutions for international problems. The process of negotiating debt relief has hastened at the beginning of the new millennium, providing an opening for insertion of human rights.

The purpose is to illustrate convergence and divergence in the current pattern of expenditure worldwide. The figures are, of course, an indication of magnitude rather than precise measurements because of the immense complexity of compiling all necessary data and making such data comparable. Suggestions for an optimal level of public expenditure for education tend to converge at about 5—7% and reflect the practice of a large, but regretfully decreasing number of countries. There is, however, increasing agreement on three points:

- firstly, that public funding for primary education is necessary;
- secondly, that primary education should be prioritised within education, and,
- thirdly, that public funding is particularly important in those countries that have low net enrolments.

The correspondence between low enrolments in primary school level and low budgetary allocation is typical for the poorest and most indebted countries which also have large proportions of children in their population. The inevitable consequence of insufficient public funding for primary education is slanting financial obligation to bear the cost of schooling towards parents and families.

There are, of course, exceptions, such as United Arab Emirates with a low allocation out of a sizeable budget, while Lesotho has a proportionally large allocation and yet primary education is not free of charge. Piecing together the mosaic needed to portray the full panorama of free primary education in today's world demands a great deal of painstaking search for important questions and answers. Regretfully, this has not yet been done despite the crucial importance of securing free education for all primary-school children.

The documentation generated by the reporting procedures under human rights treaties or reports by ministries of education have been used so as to keep the sources authoritative. The documentation of the World Bank and other international agencies has been used where no governmental reports have been found. For countries, such as Angola, where no recent information is available, reports by journalists have been the only available source. Education should be compulsory until children reach the minimum age for employment Similarly to the requirement that primary education be free of charge, information about the requirement that education be compulsory is routinely confined to international treaties and domestic laws while there is no review of the gap between normative and empirical worlds.

Compulsory education has much longer tradition than the right to education. This was reflected in the 1959 Declaration of the Rights of the Child, which laid down the entitlement of the child to receive education, articulating the vision of the child of the time as a passive recipient of education. The changed vision of the child as a subject of rights, embodied in the Convention on the Rights of the Child, is slowly being translated into domestic laws and policies.

The requirement that primary education be compulsory forms part of international human rights treaties and this is reflected in domestic laws of a vast majority of countries in the world. The capacity of governments to implement their laws on compulsory education varies, as do enforcement measures. Many target parents by fines for their failure to secure enrolment or school attendance by their children. Some target children, however.

Enforcement of compulsory education thus raises important human rights issues. The Convention on the Rights of the Child goes no further than obligating States to encourage school attendance; enforcement is not mentioned. Older human rights treaties, such as the European Convention on Human Rights, provided for detention of a minor by lawful order for the purpose of educational supervision, which mandated compulsory schooling in the narrowest sense of this term. The specific offence of truancy was created to punish the child for breaching the duty to attend school. The explicit wording of international human rights treaties requires primary education to be compulsory and free of charge. Categorizations of education and the terms used to describe the first stage of formal schooling (elementary, primary, fundamental, or basic) have changed during the past decades.

A division of schooling into primary and secondary was challenged by UNESCO as early as 1961. It held that primary and secondary schooling should be deemed to constitute 'successive phases of a continuing process' rather than two different entities. With the lengthening of compulsory education, this division is no longer valid in many countries.

Countries are categorized in two groups: those in which compulsory education equals the length of primary schooling, and those that have prolonged compulsory education beyond primary schooling. In the majority of countries for which data is available, compulsory schooling has been lengthened beyond primary schooling.

Countries in which the two remain equal in length have become a minority; in more than 40 compulsory education is six years long or less, while just below forty countries have lengthened compulsory education to ten or more years. The only countries where primary schooling is reportedly longer than compulsory schooling are Jordan, Rwanda, and Tuvalu. This trend of lengthening compulsory schooling follows a twofold rationale:

- the raising of school-leaving age through prolonged compulsory education prevents children from venturing into adulthood too early, which is particularly important in combatting child labour or child marriage;
- prolonged compulsory education provides all children with the common core schooling which is becoming increasingly demanded by the shift towards knowledge-based societies and economies, reinforced by the interplay between globalisation and localization in education; in an ideally inclusive model of schooling, all children socialize in the same

school and classroom regardless of their sex, race, provenance, religion, wealth or poverty, or disability.

Countries in which compulsory schooling is the shortest (such as Bangladesh, Laos, Nepal or Viet Nam) share financial obstacles to lengthening education, while the tendency in Western Europe to extend compulsory education beyond ten years (in Belgium, Germany, and the Netherlands, for example) reflects the necessary merging of the willingness and the ability to do so. This issue has obtained increasing importance at the turn of the millennium with the switch towards knowledge-based economy, increasing inequalities in access to education, and equally increasing international trade in education services.

Integrating key human rights dimensions in education, especially the principle of nondiscrimination, remains an unmet challenge. Education strategies and statistics are not based on international human rights law and there is no internationally collected data on access to education by race, ethnicity or religion.

Consequently, it is impossible to monitor progress and retrogression in access to school using internationally prohibited grounds of discrimination as the yardstick. Moreover, education strategies tend to merge two different categories lacking access to school-the unreached and the excluded. Difficulties in providing schools for dispersed mountainous villages are easy to understand, as are those in providing schooling for nomadic children.

It is well known in primary education, much as in primary health care, that the cost of assuring full coverage of the entire population is not uniformly spread-the last 5% to be reached is usually the most costly. The rationale for denying access to school to some children is rarely, if ever, based on cost. Children may be excluded from schooling because they are female, indigenous, refugees, or because they do not have identity papers hence they legally do not exist. Asylum-seeing and refugee children may be difficult to reach, but some may be excluded because the right to education is confined to citizens. C

hildren with disabilities may be in practice excluded from school, whatever the law may say, because the buildings and classrooms make their access impossible. Children who are institutionalized may be excluded from schooling because the mandate and funding of the institution housing children excepts education. The existing figures reported by governments and international agencies are often estimates of the numbers of out-of-school children and create an illusion of precision.

The commonly used statistics on enrolments tell us the number of children who are in school (or at least who registered at the beginning of school year) but not how many should be in school. This is a consequence of large, but unknown, numbers of children who are precluded from schooling because they live in remote areas or are displaced, children of illegal aliens or migrants workers, street children, domestic servants, and many others. The largest category of children without access to school are those in countries where no registration has been carried out and nobody knows even an approximate number of these children.

Although the International Covenant on Civil and Political Rights as well as the Convention on the Rights of the Child demand that all children be registered when they are born, this has not yet been put into practice. Few cases of denied access to school have been addressed as human rights problems. The notorious recent example of denied access to education have been girls in Afghanistan.

The Commission on Human Rights has condemned this as a human rights violation, insisting on "the right of women and girls to education without discrimination, the reopening of schools and the admission of women and girls to all levels of education." Denial of access to school to poor children in poor countries is often deemed to be corollary of poverty and not treated as a human rights problem. Herd boys in Lesotho are a case in point:

The employment of herd boys, an inherited and enduring tradition, is widespread in Lesotho but no one knows their exact numbers. Spending weeks at a time alone with their herds, the boys travel long distances away from their villages. This time away from home results in missed opportunity for education, poor socialisation and inadequate nutrition.

In the past, there was no age limit for enrolment in primary school. Herd boys typically began work at a young age and continued into their early teens, at which point some would enrol in school. As a result, the herd boys were much older than their classmates, and these age differences in the classroom created social tensions.

In an attempt to address these tensions, the GOL [Government of Lesotho] implemented a policy of non-registration of overage children. As a result, when herd boys complete their duties in their early teens, the possibility of enrolling in school is closed off and they are excluded from formal education.

Internally displaced children are on the borderline between being unreached and excluded. Armed conflicts and man-made disasters make the provision of schooling difficult, often impossible. When the provision of schooling becomes possible and previously unreached children can be reached, some may prove to be excluded, as mentioned above with regard to girls and women in Afghanistan. The right to education of the internally displaced was reaffirmed in the Guiding Principles on Internal Displacement with the 'as soon as conditions permit' qualification, thus implicitly reaffirming the practice of suspending education in emergency and/or human-itarian programmes which encompass food, shelter, water and sanitation and basic medical services.

The preparatory work for these Guiding Principles included stocktaking of obstacles which often need to be overcome and four were singled out:

- the inability of parents to pay any fees or expenses which may be required due to the loss of property and livelihood,
- the absence of identity papers which are required for school enrolment;
- the lack of knowledge of the language in which schooling is provided;
- fear of the identification of children for what they are and repression or reprisals that may target the family if children are sent to school.

ILO's Educational Programmes

The International Labor Organisation (ILO) and its International Programme on the Elimination of Child

Labour (IPEC) has supported action research on many issues related to educational policies and programmes. It has also analysed the impact of action programmes with educational components on child labour, such as those providing non-formal education, (pre-) vocational training and other social support services for (former) working children and promoting their enrolment in formal schools. There are many examples of effective educational programmes that are successful in preventing and eliminating child labour. The challenge is to mainstream such innovative initiatives into larger formal and/or non-formal education systems.

Improvements in education systems are not enough, however. First, children who have been traumatised by work need rehabilitation. Secondly, the worst child labour abuses take place among the most vulnerable socio-economic groups in society. These groups can seldom afford education, even if it is available, relevant and less costly. Their children are sent to work, because the children's contribution and earnings are essential for family survival. Measures to improve education need to be part and parcel of integrated programmes for disadvantaged population groups, programmes which aim to empower the poor and abolish social discrimination by providing income-earning opportunities. These can be employment creation and poverty alleviation schemes, small enterprise development, minimum wage systems, credit systems and social safety nets for the most needy. The programmes should address both the need for income for adults and schooling for children at the design and implementation stages, so that they do not inadvertently encourage the employment of children along with or instead of the employment of adults. Finally, given that the supply of child labour is so large, actions to provide alternatives to children need to be combined with intensive awareness-raising in workplaces, among employers, managers and young and adult workers, and in communities. Workplace and community child-watch or monitoring systems need to be set up to ensure that new children do not enter the vacated jobs.

A whole range of interventions in education is necessary to attract children to school, and to keep them there and out of work. Investment in a country's human resources is crucial, not only for younger generations, but for socio-economic development as a whole. Therefore, renewed national commitment, policy reform and massive investment in basic education are vital to meet the challenge. A holistic approach to education is required. Children should be provided with access to quality education from early childhood onwards up to at least 15 years of age. In the long term, this will be the most durable solution. However, given that many countries are still far from providing quality education for all, immediate remedial measures are needed. ILO-IPEC experience shows that even in countries where substantial progress has been made and average school enrolment ratios are high, there are still children from poor population groups who do not benefit from this progress.

Transitional education has to be provided to prevent such children from taking up hazardous work or to wean them away from it. They need to be equipped with basic education, practical knowledge and skills. Such education should consist of an integrated package of basic education, life skills and practical skills training and should ideally aim at main-streaming the children into formal education and vocational training systems.

However, options also have to be provided to the children who are unable to continue formal education and training, so they do not re-enter the labour market as unskilled workers.

The younger children may require skills that are useful in improving their quality of fife and can be developed further, while the older children generally require vocational counselling and practical training that can lead to income generation either through wage labour or self-employment in a broad array of employable skills. A measure which can be undertaken relatively quickly and which does not require massive investment is the incorporation into children's and parents' education of explicit messages on the dangers of premature work and the rights of children to education, wherever there is a high risk of child labour.

Education on children's rights can and should be integrated into the curriculum through social studies, health education, literacy and language learning. In this way children are also in a better position to protect themselves, express themselves, negotiate and assert their rights. Education on rights teaches them about their responsibilities to themselves and to others; it helps them become productive citizens of their own communities while receiving adequate care and protection.

Integrated early childhood development programmes that address the physical, social, emotional and cognitive development of young children have in recent years received more attention and visibility because of their evident impact. Children who participate in various forms of these programmes are healthier, socially well adjusted and better prepared for learning experiences in later childhood. Thus, the programmes help prevent school failure, which contributes to children dropping out and being recruited for full-time hazardous work. The more successful children are at school, the more persistent parents tend to be about keeping them there. At the same time, most early childhood development programmes involve a parent education component and are good entry points for educating both parents and children about the detrimental effects of full-time and dangerous work of children.

More schools are needed in communities with high concentrations of child labour, especially in rural areas, and these schools need to provide the complete basic education course and the necessary ingredients to meet the basic learning needs. Both formal and non-formal education systems can be made more responsive to children who are at risk of premature work or who are already working.

The structure of educational programmes, the content of the curriculum and the teaching approaches applied in schools should include relevant, useful knowledge and skills, which meet the developmental needs of children and prepare them to earn income later in life and become responsible adults in their communities. Innovative education methods which have been tried out successfully on a small scale in experimental non-formal education programmes should be incorporated and expanded in the formal education system.

Many initiatives have been undertaken in recent years to adapt educational programmes and make them more suited to the needs of former child workers. It has been found that quality non-formal education can act as a bridge between work and school and facilitate the entry of children into formal schools. However, the initiatives have been small scale to date and are often isolated from the mainstream educational programmes within the country.

Serious efforts still have to be made to further streng-then flexible non-formal remedial education programmes which provide adequate entry points into a country's educational and vocational training system. Non-formal education programmes have been established alongside the formal education system and accreditation and equivalency programmes have been developed to allow for an easier transition between formal and non-formal education. In most countries, however, stronger linkages need to be created between the formal and non-formal education streams. For some older children, a few years of non-formal education will be the only option. These children need to be provided with an integrated package of general education, along with practical life and work skills so that they can re-enter the labour market at an appropriate age with more knowledge about their rights as workers and skills that will allow them access to better jobs.

Vocational training is often very popular among families which are prone to resort to child labour. Short-term vocational training is often combined with or delivered after functional literacy training and can provide immediate economic alternatives. However, there are issues to resolve in the definition and approaches to vocational education.

A distinction must be made between more formal vocational training, which is usually longer term and systematically linked to apprenticeship programmes, and less formal training. Most formal vocational programmes require close adult supervision and the available slots for students are limited. There are also non-formal vocational training programmes linked to both formal and non-formal education programmes which are often short term and deal with specific skills and topics that are not necessarily marketable or highly productive.

Non-formal education programmes can teach children skills that will provide immediate economic alternatives as well as psycho-social support. But these should not be viewed as a complete substitute for formal education, rather as transition programmes to facilitate the child's re-entry into the formal school system. In situations where there are no local institutions or schools offering such vocational education programmes, it may be necessary to provide scholarships.

Practical skills training in the form of "learning by doing", experiments and arts and crafts are an integral part of basic education. Vocational training should be geared to the provision of marketable skills that can be adapted to the changing needs in the job market. The gender bias in education is even more pronounced in the field of vocational training and specific attention needs to be given to facilitate girls' access. In most countries, better linkages need to be created between education and vocational training, and between non-formal and formal vocational training.

Many of the most abusive types of child labour are hidden and few organisations have the capacity to identify and handle them. Child victims may also have developed various coping mechanisms and often there will be differences in the needs of boys and girls. Thus, special efforts are required to first identify the groups for priority action and then develop a range of appropriate interventions. It is essential to prevent children from becoming engaged in extreme forms of child labour. This involves intensive awareness-raising, and the provision of viable alternatives.

In cases where organisations aim to withdraw children from the worst forms of child labour, the types of intervention need to include identification and rescue of children working under forced labour conditions, legal aid, intensive counselling and other rehabilitation measures for the children and their families.

Victims of human rights violations such as children in bondage and children forced into prostitution, domestic work or sweatshops in their own or other countries are often damaged and traumatised beyond recovery. It is therefore critical that these types of child labour abuse be prevented through effective law enforcement and large-scale awareness-raising in schools and communities where there is a high incidence or risk.

Local community monitoring mechanisms should be activated to identify those at high risk and to monitor the situation of those who have been rescued. Girls and women bear a major share of the burden of poverty. Giving girls access to quality education is a first essential step towards empowering them and enabling them to break through the vicious cycle of poverty.

Successful strategies include intensive awareness-raising in communities where there are social and cultural constraints, provision of schools and childcare facilities near the girls' homes, recruitment of female teachers, promotion of gender fairness and equality at schools and investment in the education and skill training of mothers. Prevention through family life education for boys and girls at school is still the most cost-effective measure. Special programmes to allow pregnant girls and young mothers to continue their education are also needed as these young women are otherwise forced to start working themselves and involve their children from an early age in meeting basic survival needs.

The lifestyle of street children has to be taken into account when designing education and rehabilitation programmes. In the first instance, peer or adult street workers reach out to street children to establish contact and gain their trust by involving them in street education activities, motivating them to participate in educational programmes and helping them acquire the basic skills that will enable them to learn in a structured environment. They need help to adjust to adult authority after being used to surviving on their own and developing a variety of defence mechanisms against adults who may have exploited them or who may have violated their rights. Street education programmes which provide an atmosphere of freedom and democratic consultation and which build up rapport gradually and develop trust, have been more effective than enrolment in formal schools, especially at the initial re-entry stages.

Non-formal education programmes are usually needed for a smoother transition between life and work on the streets and formal schooling. Special attention has to be paid to matching the learning methodology and process to the learning styles of street children. Hands-on-learning, experimentation and observation, and learning-by-doing are what they have been doing to survive. Many street children may not be "school smart" but they are certainly "street smart". They are adept at problem- solving and assessing situations from the perspective of survival. They have worked and will assess the relevance of schooling to their immediate future in the world of work. It must be worthwhile for them to decrease their time on the streets and spend it in the classroom learning skills that help them improve their life.

Many street children also need counselling services to cope with traumatic experiences of violence, sexual exploitation or other harassment at home or on the street. Rehabilitation for substance abuse may also be necessary. Children who belong to ethnic groups need to be educated both in their own and in the national language and they should be taught about their own culture from the point of view of their community and not from an outsider's point of view.

It is clear that children learn best in their mother tongue, in particular when they start school. At the same time, they should learn to express themselves in the dominant language of their country to be able to fully function in society. The need to learn the dominant language—written and oral—has to be balanced with respect for the child's own language and culture.

Adults in the community need to be actively involved as resources for the school in this respect. Several successful programmes have highlighted the importance of providing teachers who have the same socio- cultural and economic background as the children and of offering young people employment opportunities in their own communities.

Indigenous communities usually belong to the most disadvantaged groups and seldom have access to basic services such as education, health, housing and employment. Education Programmes

There are various forms of parent education programmes offered by governmental and non-governmental agencies as part of early childhood development, literacy or health programmes. The provision of information on child labour and on child rights and the organisation of workshops for extension workers from these programmes, can be ways of incorporating child labour concerns in these adult training programmes.

Other forms of adult education through workers' organisations or trade unions and cooperatives which provide educational programmes for their members, and through other community-based structures or committees, should also be further utilised. Women's literacy programmes that emphasise child development, family life and children's and women's rights offer great potential for preventing and eliminating child labour and improving school enrolment. There is a tendency to look at women's and children's programmes separately or, at best, an incidental connection is made.

However, women and children's rights are intimately linked. Thus, women's programmes should include components to promote children's rights and address child labour exploitation and—vice versa—programmes geared towards children should pay attention to the situation of mothers as women with their own needs and rights.

In addition, more and better jobs and social protection are needed for adults through the provision of income-earning opportunities for the poor, employment creation and poverty alleviation schemes, small enterprise development, minimum wage systems, credit systems and social safety nets for the most needy.

Women's economic empowerment is an especially effective measure to strengthen vulnerable families. Programmes that enable them to learn skills (such as improved agricultural practices, entrepreneurship, specific crafts or food production) that provide them with resources to earn a stable income for the family and manage households by using labour-saving devices, or increase their access to credit schemes.

Systematic efforts to ensure that workplaces and communities remain child labour free mean first of all that awareness raising activities should not be limited to the children and parents, but extended to all groups involved: employers, managers, and adult workers in workplaces, community leaders, service providers and enforcement agencies. In a second stage, monitoring mechanisms need to be set up to ensure that the children withdrawn from work remain and complete school and that new children do not enter work. This can be done in the schools or educational centres, in the workplaces and in the children's communities.

In any workplace monitoring programme, the active participation of the concerned employers, manu-facturers, contractors and subcontractors is critical, as the commitment to free all manufacturing and production processes from child labour may call for a change in established and traditional manufacturing and production practices. The involvement of the concerned workers' repre-sentatives and local community groups as well as the concerned governmental agencies, is also critical.

The involvement of children in the production and manufacture of goods for export has become a matter for international concern. Faced with outside pressure, some producers and manufacturers have turned to the ILO for advice on action to eliminate child labour from their particular industry. This has resulted in three instances in concrete prevention and monitoring programmes in the garment industry in Bangladesh, the football industry in Pakistan and its international counterparts and the carpet industry, also in Pakistan. The result has been partnerships that span geographical and cultural boundaries, as well as positive changes in the attitudes and practices of the communities, in that the families have been willing to withdraw their children from work and send them to school.

The basic elements of the ILO-IPEC prevention and monitoring programmes are:

— Ensuring cooperation and collaboration of employers/manufacturers, workers' organisations, district administration and other government departments;

— Assessing child labour involvement in the particular sector or industry;

— Assisting the participating employers/manufacturers in setting up their internal monitoring system;

— Operating an external monitoring team involving ILO project staff;

— Identifying and zoning monitoring area for visits;

— Establishing a monitoring database to collect, analyse and synthesise data, to indicate schedules, of surprise monitoring visits, and to prepare reports on progress; and

— Establishing linkages with the social protection component of the programme.

Social protection programmes provide viable and practical alternatives to the children and their families affected by the prevention and monitoring programme. These programmes support the withdrawal of the children from workplaces and prevent them from working by sensitising and mobilising the communities. They also provide services to rehabilitate the children withdrawn so that they can be integrated into mainstream educational systems and other developmental activities. The basic elements of a social protection programme are:

— Awareness-raising, mobilisation and counselling families through one-to-one contact and group meetings to prevent child labour and to encourage them so that their children participate in the activities of the village education and action clusters set up under the project; communicating with the families on an ongoing basis;

— Group training of adults to form the family clubs/ committees for mothers and fathers to encourage them to play an active role in the programme;

— Non-formal education to provide literacy, basic education and practical skills training to the children withdrawn and their younger siblings.

— Recreational activities to foster social and physical development;

— Health services through linkages with local health facilities;

— Mainstreaming of younger children into formal schools;

— Training in income-generation activities (adults): to follow up training in the credit/savings facility and training in various income-generation activities for the adults in the family;

— Provision of a credit/savings facility to the adults in the family; and

— Mainstreaming of children of employable age and adults into the labour market.

The establishment of local child welfare and vigilance committees is an effective tool which is increasingly being utilised in many countries. These committees can monitor, undertake action and even provide limited resources and services where necessary. Programmes which stress a participatory approach and actively involve the children, their, parents, community leaders and teachers are the most successful. Decentralisation of authority to local governments and community structures also has a positive impact and results in effective community participation.

Given the socio-economic situation of some countries and the lack of adequate resources and infrastructure, the complete elimination of child labour will be a lengthy process. But there can be no excuse for ignoring flagrant cases of child abuse that are an outright breach of human rights and an affront to the dignity of children. Clearly the children who fall into this category are those engaged in activities that pose a serious danger to their health, or physical or moral integrity; those who work in slave-like conditions or are subjected to forced tabour and those caught up in illicit networks such as prostitution, drug trafficking and pornography.Some children are particularly vulnerable to this type of exploitation because of their age and sex, because they live and work on their own, or because they belong to socially excluded groups. Appropriate measures need to be adopted urgently to rescue children from these worst forms of child tabour. Prevention is crucial; but children must also be withdrawn from such activities and both they and their families provided with alternatives. Sometimes, especially if a country is only starting to address child labour problems, there is resistance to begin to combat some of the worst forms, because of political and social sensitivity.

The existence of these types of child labour is even denied and very few partners come forward who can effectively address the problems. None the less, at a minimum, the worst forms of child tabour need to be tackled immediately. The most strategically positioned programme partners or initiators, governments have the main responsibility to make action a top priority. They need to take the lead in designing national policies and programmes and in allocating the necessary resources to enable implementation.

When the policy framework is in place, care should be taken to translate it into feasible programmes and implementation guidelines and to inform and enable all stakeholders to take the required action. Without such a commitment, countries will have great difficulties in overcoming the problem. However, the task is too enormous to be handled by governments alone. A participatory approach and concerted action by all stakeholders is needed to eliminate child tabour. Successful examples of effective cooperation between different sections of local government, NGOs, employers' and workers' organisations, and local communities are emerging. Effective programme delivery has taken place through proper coordination between government structures at the national and local levels.

However, the implementation of multi-sectoral programmes by a range of different service providers is sometimes difficult. It has become clear that institutional mechanisms need to be set up to encourage joint planning and implementation for an effective convergence of services in countries where a start has been made in developing and implementing specific measures to combat child labour through education. Participation should ideally begin at the planning stages.

Often, the lack of consultative mechanisms at the various stages of programme implementation or the exclusion of stakeholders from the processes of planning, problem solving and decision making engenders a sense of remoteness and powerlessness of the participating groups in relation to the programme managers and leaders. Active participation—not just token participation—is a critical element to developing a sense of ownership for programmes.

The main issues when starting a direct action programme is related to the partial or total withdrawal of children from work. But national goals must be defined in a clear, achievable and time-bound manner. If either the partial or the total withdrawal from work is defined as an objective and made a precondition for the children's participation, the programme design and content must reflect this. In other cases, stipends are provided for the children to participate and withdraw from work. For programmes which opt for partial withdrawal, the design either provides for a schedule which allows children to study and work part time or, alternatively, less hazardous income-generating, opportunities are made available. The ground rules are as follows:

— If children are involved in hazardous or exploitative forms of child labour, they need to be withdrawn completely. Child victims of human rights violations cannot be helped by the provision of support services while they continue to be in a slavery-like position. They must be rescued.

— If children are involved in work that harms them because of the working conditions or environment, a gradual phased approach may be used. The work hazards should be removed and children should gain access to education, but they can in a transitional phase continue to be involved in light work that is not dangerous.

Parents react positively to programmes where children work part time in light work and are involved in non-formal education. Even if this means a decrease in their income, it is more viable because of the continuing income. The parents also feel that the children are getting an education and learning practical skills which improve their employment opportunities for the future. Another approach that can be seen as a step towards the ultimate goal of children's withdrawal from hazardous working conditions involves campaigns for making the workplace safer. Adult workers as well as owners of workplaces can be recruited as volunteers to participate in training workshops so that they can monitor safety.

Improvements in education are not sufficient to attract and keep children from very poor families at school. Many families of child labourers live on the brink of survival and many millions of children in the world do not go to school because they are malnourished or frequently ill. Many more go to school hungry and are unable to pay attention, concentrate and learn.

Child Nutrition Programmes

A nutritious meal makes a tremendous difference to a child's health and ability to learn. The school is also an important entry point for providing essential health services such as immunisation, detection of disabilities and childhood illnesses. Many organisations provide nutrition and health care to children through the education system and these have proved to be powerful incentives for parents to send their children to school. Besides school-based food and health programmes, organisations have experimented with providing other economic incentives, such as school uniforms, books or transport.

Cash payments, such as regular stipends or scholarships, have also been provided. Schiefelbein has reviewed examples of such incentives in Latin American countries. These include cash payments for students, provision of school materials and allocating additional funds to schools or municipalities which provide services for child labourers or children considered at risk of child labour to enable them to provide more responsive and flexible programmes.

The various income-replacement strategies that have been tried in Latin America offer interesting examples of how effectively to provide for the needs of child labourers. Most require a combination of responsive local schools and the political will of national and/or local governments, which provide the necessary policy support and resources to implement income-replacement measures.

An ILO survey on economic incentives for children and families to eliminate or reduce child labour also aimed to identify whether income replacement and substitution activities offered viable options in the battle against child labour. Many of the incentives used by the NGOs which participated in the survey were directly related to schooling. Payments in kind were the most common form of benefits extended to children or their families. These included provisions for school uniforms or clothing, books, schoolbags and materials, school lunches or other food items, transport, or payment of school fees.

Evidently, organisations which provide income-replacement services for child labourers, or for children who are at high risk of child labour, do so because the cost of schooling or the forgone income deters children from entering education. Thus, they raise the question of whether replacing the lost income of children who attend school full time would in fact be adequate to keep them in school. Another important finding was that the provision of cash incentives could lead to abuse and therefore many NGOs preferred to provide in-kind incentives rather than cash payments. Support services are sometimes provided as incentives to attract parents and children to participate in action programmes. But it has been observed that some programmes offer too many incentives which make them more like welfare programmes. Among the disadvantages are:

(i) high programme costs;

(ii) the programme is not sustainable in the long term;

(iii) child workers are perceived as privileged, because non-working while equally poor and disadvantaged children do not receive such benefits elsewhere;

(iv) the practice may encourage more parents to remove children from school and send them to work in the hope of becoming eligible for similar benefits; and

(v) parents of children who may not be part of the target group will insist on their children's participation, thus creating confusion and divisiveness in the community if they react negatively when their children are not admitted.

The major disadvantage is the difficulty of sustaining and replicating the programme since the participation of parents and children will be heavily reliant on the availability of incentives; thus the motivation for participation is mainly external. A careful balance must therefore be struck.

One option is to encourage children's participation in running the programme. They can also work with younger children as peer teachers and participate in home visits, especially to other children who have been absent for a while. After they complete, their courses of study, they can also be asked to help with the programme activities and work as resource persons or volunteers with the other children. In this way they can serve as positive role models and share their own experiences. Parents can be asked to work as volunteers for the programme and the activities can depend upon their individual talents and skills. Whatever time and energy they can contribute should be discussed with them from the outset and also clarified so that they will not view incentives as a hand-out but feel that they have something meaningful to contribute.

Parents who actively participate in the action programmes are also more likely to better appreciate the impact or the benefits of these programmes for their children and ultimately their families. It is important to assess whether direct action programmes should focus only on the objective of generating income for the children and their families, or should also serve as income-saving or expense-reduction measures for the family. If the children can use what they make, or if the family, can eat what is produced through the programme, there may also be value added to encouraging such cost-saving measures towards self-reliance.

The approach of helping children and their families opt for participation in courses that also involve the production of goods that meet the basic day-to-day needs of the children and helping them to manage existing resources, may ultimately be more beneficial for the children. This approach will help them practice problem-solving and planning for very practical life needs and at the same time help them achieve a sense of fulfilment in being able to meet their immediate requirements.

One of the more frequent reasons children drop out of programmes for their, education and protection is the difficulty they have in delaying the gratification of their needs. Another important issue in setting expense-reduction measures alongside income-generation or replacement is the possibility that children and their parents can be helped to learn to be more realistic about earning possibilities and about basic needs versus additional or emerging needs.

It is necessary to work closely with them and their parents, and clarify objectives with them at every step of the way.It is important to determine whether the schools where the children are expected to enrol are actually receptive to the re-entry or the integration of working children. If they consider it as an imposition or a burden rather than as a responsibility, their attitude towards the children will be passive at best and negative at worst.

In relation to the mainstreaming of children into formal schools, some specific issues need to be considered:

— *The age of the children:* If children are older than the other children in the grade level for which they qualify, they usually feel uncomfortable, and often embarrassed, not only because they are older but because in most cases they also have difficulty in coping with the academic requirements. Former working children also find it difficult to adjust to the rigid structure and the regimen of formal schools.

— *Parents' expectations and attitudes.* Parents may react negatively or may be impatient with apparently slow progress through formal school, especially when they are used to their children being economically productive. With the loss of income, any activity that replaces their child's work will be viewed badly if they have not yet fully accepted the fact that it is a better situation for their children, a worthwhile investment even from their family's economic viewpoint, and a responsibility that they should fulfil. Another problem that affects the parents' attitude is the burden of school-related expenses.

— *Provision for follow-up and support programmes.* The need for follow-up support programmes, especially after the first year of re-entry into the formal schools is evident in the trends of programme experiences. Action programmes in different countries show that many children tend to drop out after the first year, especially when assistance for meeting expenses is discontinued.

There are some questions to consider in connection with the issue of mainstreaming working children into regular schools. In developing countries where job opportunities are still limited and where a large number of youths with college or university degrees are unemployed, it is not surprising that many disadvantaged parents doubt whether their children can compete in the job market with a primary or secondary education certificate. Few parents expect their children to be able to proceed to tertiary levels of education. That is why they may appreciate vocational training because they consider it more realistic for work opportunities. The experiences in education and child labour and the strategy for maximising education in the fight against child labour, clearly identify the expansion of early childhood development programmes as critical to meeting the needs of working children or those at high risk of recruitment in the near future.

Research and case studies also show that disadvantaged children, who did not receive adequate health, nutrition and psychosocial cognitive and language stimulation in the early years of childhood are highly likely to experience developmental and learning problems and will have difficulty catching up.

A number of mainstreamed children have to drop out because they cannot compete with other, often younger, peers and do not enjoy doing so. If there are younger siblings in the families of working children, they should be supported by facilitating their access to community-based early childhood development programmes and convincing parents that this is an important step to take for their children.Mainstreaming of former working children or children who continue to work part time is only viable if there are support services for them. Parents need support and information so that they will be able to support their children. Teachers need help to understand the perspective of former working children and the pressures of adjusting to formal schools. It is critical if a country programme chooses to adopt this as the primary approach to the education and social protection of working children.

Most action programmes include various forms of awareness-raising activities directed at parents, community members, local school authorities, the business sector, and policy makers. These have been included based on the realisation that the understanding by these groups of child labour issues will be their basis for supporting the programme's objectives and activities. Ultimately, the programmes will also be the basis of their continued participation in concerted actions to prevent child labour, protect working children through community action, engage in needed policy reform and support effective law enforcement.

When awareness-raising efforts are not considered investments of the programme, there can be problems. For example, teachers in formal schools may not develop a positive attitude towards non-formal education programmes provided by these action programmes if they are not informed in any way, especially in the planning processes. Two Articles in the Convention on the Rights of the Child address the issue of nutrition. Article 24 says that "States Parties recognise the right of the child to the enjoyment of the highest attainable standard of health" and shall take appropriate measures "to combat disease and malnutrition" through the provision of adequate nutritious foods, clean drinking water, and health care. Article 27 says that States Parties "shall in case of need provide material assistance and support programmes, particularly with regard to nutrition, clothing, and housing". India is making steady progress in limiting malnutrition, but the numbers are still too large and the rate of progress is too slow.

In 1948 the Universal Declaration of Human Rights said in Article 25(1) that "everyone has the right to a standard of living adequate for the health and well-being of himself and his family, including food...."The International Covenant on Economic, Social, and Cultural Rights, which came into force in 1976, says in Article 11: "The States Parties to the present Covenant recognise the right of everyone to an adequate standard of living for himself and his family, including adequate food, clothing, and housing..." and also recognise "the fundamental right of everyone to be free from hunger...." While the idea of the right to food appears in many different contexts in international law, most are not binding. In some cases, as in the International Covenant on economic, social, and cultural rights, the obligations are technically binding on the states parties. However, because the obligations lack specificity and because there are no effective mechanisms for implementation and accountability, they are not binding in practice.

On reviewing the hunger data, Philip Alston and Katarina Tomasevski observed that "these statistics make hunger by far the most flagrant and widespread of all serious human rights abuses". The idea that people should have a right to adequate nutrition is an old one, one whose vision has not been fulfilled. However, its articulation in the Convention on the rights of the child suggests a new approach: Implementation of the idea of the right of adequate nutrition may be more politically feasible if it focuses on children.Our principal obligation towards children is to promote their development, to be understood as empowerment or increasing self-reliance. The task is to increase children's capacity to define, analyse, and act on their own problems until they can become independent participants in society.

Who is responsible for children? The question is not whose fault is it that children suffer so much (who caused the problems?) but who should take action to remedy the problems? Many different social agencies may have some role in looking after children, but what should be the interrelationships among them? Most children have two vigorous advocates from the moment they are born and even before they are born. Their parents devote enormous resources to serving their interests. In many cases, however, that bond is broken or is never created. Fathers disappear, many mothers disappear as well. In some cities, hundreds of children are abandoned each month in the hospitals in which they are born. Bands of children live in the streets by their wits. Often children end up alone as a result of warfare or other political crises. Many children are abandoned because they are physically or mentally handicapped. Often parents become so disabled by drugs or alcohol that they cannot care for their children.

Children ought to get their nurturance from their parents. Failing that, they ought to get it from their local communities. Failing that, they ought to get it from the local governments. Failing that, it should come from their national governments. Failing that, they ought to get it from the international community.

Childhood malnutrition is one of those issues for which there should be a recognised obligation of government to provide some sort of services. As a matter of principle, there should be a recognised legal obligation of government to provide services to assure that every child is adequately nourished. The point is that there should be a clear duty of government, enshrined in law, to do what needs to be done if the family's and the community's response is inadequate. If the principle is accepted, there will still be a need for discussion of the exact nature of the services and the conditions under which they must be provided.

Community groups working on the local malnutrition problem should be able to rely on their local and state governments for help, whether for money, contacts, transportation, or moral support and encouragement. It is the responsibility of government to help such community groups. Moreover, the government should be grateful for the opportunity to help the community use its resources to deal with local malnutrition.

There have been efforts to gain recognition of a right to nutrition within individual countries and internationally. Unfortunately, this has often been equated with the general effort to alleviate malnutrition, and advocates of the right to nutrition have simply recommended ways of improving the production and distribution of food. Nutrition rights in international law are vague and soft. If the nutrition rights idea is to be implemented within nations, its meaning will need to be clarified in their national law. It is there, in national law making, that the specific, hard commitments can be made. It is important to distinguish between the achievement of adequate nutrition and achievement of a right to adequate nutrition. Nutrition rights are based on the quality of protection one has against the occurrence of malnutrition. To assess the quality of the protection one has to look into the institutional arrangements that are in place, ready to act if and when disaster threatens. Past efforts to ameliorate malnutrition have all been valuable, but they have been matters of charity.

The motivating idea underlying the nutrition rights vision is that extreme malnutrition can be reduced by establishing clear rights to adequate nutrition in the law, and assuring the implementation of that law. The nutrition rights approach does not replace existing programmes for alleviating malnutrition, but rather it builds on and uses them. It can make feeding, health and education-based nutrition programmes more efficient and effective by making them more decisively goal-directed to end malnutrition. According to UNICEF's 1993 report, *The Progress of Nations,* on average, developing countries have been devoting only about 10 per cent of their annual budgets to human priority issues: nutrition, water supply, primary health care, primary education, and family planning. Thus even poor countries could do more with their existing resources. The main argument of the rights approach, however, is not that nations should spend more but that they should spend better.A clear distinction should be drawn between the broad notion of children's interests involving many different things such as shelter and a nurturing environment, and the more limited subset of those things that are—or should be—formally recognised as rights in law. Soft rights are not spelt out in the law, or if they are there is no strong and effective mechanism to assure their implementation. The CRC and other international human rights instruments in themselves establish only soft rights. They can be transformed into hard rights which are clearly articulated in the law and are accompanied by effective implementation and accountability mechanisms. Hard rights have a history of case law through which the meaning of the right is tested and refined. There is clear recourse in law for individuals whose rights are not fulfilled and clear public accountability.

Rights are important because without clear rights, those who are more powerful, more highly educated, or better connected have an advantage in obtaining services. Clearly established rights empower the weak, levelling the playing field a bit so that the weak are not so disadvantaged. Rights can be truly hard only where there is a strong and effective legal system in place. In many countries there is no such system.

However, where it is absent it is nevertheless worth advocating the hardening of rights as part of the broader effort to pursue a civil society. Many nations are divided into smaller jurisdictions, perhaps provinces or states; these smaller units might be able to establish their own nutrition rights systems. Provinces could then be assessed in terms of their nutritional status and the most needy provinces entitled to specific services. In some cases provinces, in turn, might manage their nutrition rights system by focusing on still another administrative layer—districts within the province.

Laws, rules, guidelines and principles can be introduced or adapted to conform to a nutrition rights system at the global, regional, national, state or district levels. Even the rules of access to individual service programmes can be modified to assure that clients are treated as if they had rights to the service. Just as different levels have different responsibilities, they also can have different rights. For example, some services might be assured to individual children while others are assured for households, villages, or districts.

The nutrition rights idea, while based on the use of the law, is not based on punitive sanctions against wrongdoers. There may be some cases in which children go hungry because they have "bad" parents. In such cases, the law should be more concerned with ensuring that children do not have to pay for the sins of their parents than with ensuring that their parents do have to pay for them. In much the same way, it would be foolish for the international community to think about punishing bad governments. To the extent possible, government's approach to its citizenry should be in positive forms. Similarly, the citizenry's "holding the government to account" should be positive.

In a negative approach to accountability, a government agency assigned the duty of preventing abuse or ending malnutrition could be sued or fined in some way. In a more positive approach, designated non-governmental organisations could be given an award or "bounty" of a small sum of money for each needy child they find and present for services. It is important to distinguish between monitoring and reporting on nutrition status and monitoring and reporting on nutrition rights. In my view, reporting on the status of nutrition rights should cover five distinct but interrelated components:

(a) the nutrition problems;

(b) government's service programmes in response to the nutrition problems;

(c) the law relating to nutrition rights;

(d) implementation, the extent to which the law is effectively carried out; and

(e) the institutional arrangements for holding government to account in fulfilling nutrition rights.

It is important to know what categories of individuals suffer from what sorts of malnutrition problems. The most important form worldwide, protein-energy malnutrition, can be gauged by measuring the heights and weights of children and comparing them with the heights and weights of well-nourished children. If nutrition rights exist, there must be government-sponsored services to assure that people are adequately nourished. Services should be preventive, to keep malnutrition from occurring, and remedial, to undo malnu-trition after it occurs.

Preventive services may include such things as health, education, water supply, or immunisation programmes, or programmes to keep people from being displaced from their land. Remedial services for those who are malnourished or at risk of malnutrition may include feeding programmes, clinics or land reform programmes.There are several things one would want to know about government-supported service programmes related to nutrition.

It would be useful to have information about their targeting and selection of beneficiaries; staff selection, supervision and training; community participation; manage-ment information systems; sustainability and replicability; and their impact and cost. In systematic reporting, nutrition service programmes should be listed and then characterised, following a simple outline to specify their main features.

Given the magnitude of the malnutrition problem and the level of resources available, judgements should be made as to whether the eligibility criteria are too high (excluding many who should be served), too low (including many who should not be served), or about right. Many nutrition programmes concerned with protein- energy malnutrition as indicated by low weight or low height are misdirected in terms of their intended coverage. Growth failure is most active between six and 24 months of age, which is thus the main "window of opportunity" for prevention. Actions targeted to children beyond, say, three years of age are not likely to be very successful in reversing their growth retardation because their low weight or height is likely to have originated in their first two or three years of life. Nutrition rights must be enshrined in the law with as much clarity and detail as possible, specifying not only the rights of citizens but also the specific duties of government to fulfil those rights. Of course one must also look further to see if what is written in the law is effectively implemented.

CHILD LABOUR

CHILD LABOUR
(Volume—II)

GOPAL BHARGAVA

Publications

KALPAZ PUBLICATIONS

DELHI–110052

CHILD LABOUR

(Sociology)

Rs. 1800 (Set)
Rs. 900 (Each Volume)

© Gopal Bhargava

ISBN: 81-7835-200-1 (Set)
ISBN: 81-7835-242-7 (Vol. II)

All rights reserved. No part of this book may be reproduced in any manner without written permission.

Published in 2003 in India by
Kalpaz Publications
C–30, Satyawati Nagar
Delhi–110052
E-mail: kalpaz@hotmail.com

Laser Typesetting at: Varsha Graphics, Delhi
Printed at: Mehra Offset Press, Delhi

Contents

9

Child Labour in India

The complex issue of child labour is a developmental issue worth investigating. The notion that children are being exploited and forced into labour, while not receiving education crucial to development, concerns many people. India is the largest example of a nation plagued by the problem of child labour. Estimates cite figures of between 60 and 115 million working children in India—the highest number in the world.

What are the causes of child labour in India? How do governmental policies affect it? What role does education play in regard to child labour in India? A critical analysis of the answers to these questions may lead in the direction of a possible solution. These questions will be answered through an analysis of the problem of child labour as it is now, investigating how prevalent it is and what types of child labour exist. The necessity of child labour to poor families, and the role of poverty as a determinant will be examined. Governmental policies concerning child labour will be investigated. The current state of education in India will be examined and compared with other developing countries. Compulsory education policies and their relationship to child labour will be investigated using Sri Lanka and the Indian state of Kerala as examples of where these policies have worked. Finally, India's policies concerning compulsory education will be assessed.

The problem of child labour in India

It is difficult to cite a current figure for the number of children engaged in child labour. This difficulty is attributed to the fact that the Indian Government "has been negligent in its refusal to collect and analyze current and relevant data regarding the incidence of child labor. As of 1996, official figures continue to be based on 1981 census figures". The 1981 Indian census reports that there were 13.6 million child labourers in India.

Indian government extrapolations of this 1981 data place the current number of child labourers at between seventeen and twenty million. This extrapolation seems highly unlikely as "The Official National Sample Survey of 1983 [of India] reports 17.4 million child labourers, while a study . . . sponsored by the Labour Ministry, concluded that the child-labour force was 44 million". UNICEF "cites figures ranging from seventy-five to ninety million child laborers under the age of fourteen". A universal difficulty in obtaining accurate data may be that individuals fail to report child labour participation during surveys, for fear of persecution.

Although the figure for the number of child labourers varies, they are all significantly high when considering that the Child Economic Activity rate for

1980-1991 was 13.5% for males and 10.3% for females. In comparison, other developing countries such as Sri Lanka and Malaysia (where data is available), have lower activity rates: 5.3% for males and 4.6% for females in Sri Lanka, and 8.8% for males and 6.5% for females in Malaysia.

Historical census data shows an overall child work participation rate of 12.69% in 1961 and 7.13% in 1971. This data is misleading because the definitions of child labour are different in the two censuses (unpaid workers are not included in the 1971 census), thus a comparison cannot be completely valid. The data shows that in a span of twenty years, the proportion of children who are working has not changed significantly, but since comparisons with this data are not valid, this conclusion is questionable.

The 1981 Census of India divided child labour into nine industrial divisions:

I. Cultivation,

II. Agricultural Labour,

III. Livestock, Forestry, Fishing, Plantation,

IV. Mining and Quarrying,

V. Manufacturing, Processing, Servicing and Repairs,

VI. Construction,

VII. Trade and Commerce,

VIII. Transport, Storage and Communication, and

IX. Other Services

The percentage distribution of child workers by these industrial divisions in 1981. From this table it is observed that the majority of rural child workers (84.29%) are employed in cultivation and agricultural labour (divisions I and II). Urban child labourers are distributed differently. There are 39.16% of them are involved in manufacturing, processing, servicing and repairs.

Although more children are involved in agriculturally related jobs, human rights organizations tend to focus on the manufacturing types of child labour because most children in these situations are bonded labourers. Bonded labour refers to the phenomenon of children working in conditions of servitude in order to pay off a debt. Estimates place the number of bonded child labourers in India at close to one million.

Child labour is a source of income for poor families. A study conducted by the ILO Bureau of Statistics found that "Children's work was considered essential to maintaining the economic level of households, either in the form of work for wages, of help in household enterprises or of household chores in order to free adult household members for economic activity elsewhere".

In some cases, the study found that a child's income accounted for between 34 and 37 percent of the total household income. This study concludes that a child labourer's income is important to the livelihood of a poor family. There is a questionable aspect of this study. It was conducted in the form of a survey, and the responses were given by the parents of the child labourers. Parents would be biased into being compelled to support their decision to send their children to work, by saying that it is essential. They are probably right: for most poor families in India, alternative sources of income are close to non-existent. There are no social welfare systems such as those in the West, nor is there easy access to loans, which will be discussed. What is apparent is the fact that child labourers are being exploited, shown by the pay that they receive. For the same type of work, studies show that children are paid less than their adult counterparts. A comparison of child wages to adult wages obtained by a study of child workers in the Delhi region of India. Although 39.5% of employers said that child workers earn wages equal to adults, if the percentage of employers admitting that wages are lower for children are added up, a figure of 35.9% is found. This figure is significant when taking the bias of employers into account.

Employers would have been likely to defend their wages for child workers, by saying that children earn the same wages as adults. The fact that no employers stated children earned more than adults, should be also be noted. Other studies have also concluded that "children's earnings are consistently lower than those of adults, even where there two groups are engaged in the same tasks"

The percentage of the population of India living in poverty is high. In 1990, 37% of the urban population and 39% of the rural population was living in poverty Poverty has an obvious relationship with child labour, and studies have "revealed a positive correlation—in some instances a strong one - between child labour and such factors as poverty". Families need money to survive, and children are a source of additional income. Poverty itself has underlying determinants, one such determinant being caste. When analyzing the caste composition of child labourers Nangia observes that, "if these figures are compared with the caste structure of the country, it would be realised that a comparatively higher proportion of scheduled caste children work at a younger age for their own and their families' economic support. Scheduled caste (lower caste) children tend to be pushed into child labour because of their family's poverty. Nangia goes on to state that in his study 63.74% of child labourers said that poverty was the reason they worked.

The combination of poverty and the lack of a social security network form the basis of the even harsher type of child labour—bonded child labour. For the poor, there are few sources of bank loans, governmental loans or other credit sources, and even if there are sources available, few Indians living in poverty qualify. Here enters the local moneylender; for an average of two thousand rupees, parents exchange their child's labour to local moneylenders.

Since the earnings of bonded child labourers are less than the interest on the loans, these bonded children are forced to work, while interest on their loans accumulates. A bonded child can only be released after his/her parents makes a lump sum payment, which is extremely difficult for the poor. Even if bonded child labourers are released, "the same conditions of poverty that caused the initial debt can cause people to slip back into bondage".

Even though poverty is cited as the major cause of child labour, it is not the only determinant. Inadequate schools, a lack of schools, or even the expense of schooling leaves some children with little else to do but work. The attitudes of parents also contribute to child labour; some parents feel that children should work in order to develop skills useful in the job market, instead of taking advantage of a formal education.

Indian Government Policy on Child Labour

From the time of its independence, India has committed itself to be against child labour. Article 24 of the Indian constitution clearly states that "No child below the age of fourteen years shall be employed to work in any factory or mine or employed in any hazardous employment". Article 39 (e) directs State policy such "that the health and strength of workers . . . and the tender age of children are not abused and that citizens are not forced by economic necessity to enter avocations unsuited to their age or strength".

These two articles show that India has always had the goal of taking care of its children and ensuring the safety of workers. The Bonded Labour System Act of 1976 fulfills the Indian Constitution's directive of ending forced labour. The Act "frees all bonded laborers, cancels any outstanding debts against them, prohibits the creation of new bondage agreements, and orders the economic rehabilitation of freed bonded laborers by the state". In regard to child labour, the Indian government implemented the Child Labour Act in 1986. The purpose of this act is to "prohibit the employment of children who have not completed their 14th year in specified hazardous occupations and processes". ILO convention No. 138 suggests that the minimum age for employment should not be less than fifteen years, and thus the Child Labour Act of 1986 does not meet this target.

A recent advance in government policy occurred in August of 1994, when then- Prime Minister Narasimha Rao announced his proposal of an Elimination of Child Labour Programme. This program pledges to end child labour for two million children in hazardous industries as defined in the Child Labour Act of 1986, by the year

2000. The program revolves around an incentive for children to quit their work and enter non-formal schooling: a one hundred rupee payment as well as one meal a day for attending school. Where the funds for this program will come from is unknown. The government needs eight and a half billion dollars for the program over five years, and yet "about 4 percent of the five-year estimated cost was allocated for child labour elimination programs in 1995-1996".

All of the policies that the Indian government has in place are in accordance with the Constitution of India, and all support the eradication of Child Labour. The problem of child labour still remains even though all of these policies are existent. Enforcement is the key aspect that is lacking in the government's efforts. No enforcement data for child labour laws are available: "A glaring sign of neglect of their duties by officials charged with enforcing child labor laws is the failure to collect, maintain, and disseminate accurate statistics regarding enforcement efforts". Although the lack of data does not mean enforcement is nonexistent, the number of child labourers and their work participation rates show that enforcement, if existent, is ineffective.

Education and its effects on child labour

What is the current state of education in India in comparison to other developing countries? India's state of education lacks effectiveness in yielding basic literacy in the population. It has been observed that "the overall condition of the education system can be a powerful influence on the supply of child labour". The 1991 Census of India shows that 64% of males and 39% of females are literate—an increase of 17% and 14% respectively from the 1981 census. These increases seem significant, but

India's overall literacy rate of 40.8% lags behind other developing countries such as China (72.6%), Sri Lanka (86.1%), and Indonesia (74.1%), all of which have Per Capita Incomes comparable to India's.

India's primary-school survival rate of 38.0% is also lower than China's rate of 70.0% and Sri Lanka's rate of 90.8%. This indicates that few students are reaching fifth or sixth grade, and dropout rates support this conclusion. Dropout rates measured by the Department of Education show that 35% of males and 39% of females dropout. What is the reason for these high dropout rates and poor school survival rates? One possible argument given by Nangia is that "the pressing need for the child's earnings as well as low perceived advantages of school" cause parents to withdraw children from school and deposit them in the labour force.

In this case, poverty and the inadequacy of the school system play significant roles in causing child labour, but also affect each other. Poverty forces high dropout rates, and thus no matter how good schools are, school survival rates and literacy rates will still remain low.

Compulsory Education

The concept of compulsory education, where all school aged children are required to attend school, combats the force of poverty that pulls children out of school. Policies relating to compulsory education not only force children to attend school, but also contribute appropriate funds to the primary education system, instead of higher education.

An example of a country where compulsory education has worked to reduce child labour is Sri Lanka.

The Sri Lankan government decided to enforce compulsory education in the 1920's and 1930's. With this compulsory education policy, school participation rates rose from 58 percent in 1946 to 74 percent in 1963. The literacy rate also increased from 58 percent in 1946 to 86 percent in 1984. The corresponding result has been that the employment rate of children in the ten to fourteen age group has shown a substantial decline from 13 percent in 1946 to 6.2 percent in 1963, and currently stands at 5.3% for males and 4.6% for females. These trends lead Weiner to the conclusion that "Sri Lanka has achieved a remarkably high enrollment rate, high retention rate, and a corresponding decline in child labor"..

The Indian state of Kerala distinguishes itself from the rest of India with its educational system. The government of Kerala allocates more funds to education than any other state, with a per capita expenditure of 11.5 rupees compared to the Indian average of 7.8 rupees. It is not only the expenditure of more funds, but where the funds are used that make the difference. Kerala spends more money on "mass education than colleges and universities". No correlation exists between expenditure on education and literacy when comparing different countries because some countries, such as India, spend more funds on higher education than primary education.

Kerala's emphasis on primary education has lead to a dropout rate of close to 0%, a literacy rate of 94% for males and 86% for females, and a low child work participation rate of 1.9% compared to the Indian average of 7.1% in 1971. Weiner points out that "The Kerala government has made no special effort to end child labor. It is the expansion of the school system rather than the enforcement of labor legislation that has reduced the amount of child labor".

Article 45 of the Constitution of India states that "The State shall endeavour to provide within a period of ten years from the commencement of this Constitution for free and compulsory education for all children until they complete the age of fourteen years". It is obvious that "the State" has not achieved this goal, shown by the literacy, dropout, and child work participation rates discussed previously. A National Policy on Education was adopted in 1986, and it addresses the need to "expand and improve basic education".

Recently, the central government implemented The District Primary Education Program (DPEP), in an attempt to act on the recommendations of the National Policy on Education. The program involves the subsidizing of approved investments, by the Government of India. The central government will provide a grant of 85% on expenditures by the states. Since these measures have been implemented very recently, results cannot be obtained and the effectiveness of the DPEP cannot be commented on at this time.

Child labour is a significant problem in India. The prevalence of it is shown by the child work participation rates which are higher in Indian than in other developing countries. The major determinant of child labour is poverty. Even though children are paid less than adults, whatever income they earn is of benefit to poor families. In addition to poverty, the lack of adequate and accessible souces of credit forces poor parents to engage their children in the harsher form of child labour—bonded child labour. Some parents also feel that a formal education is not beneficial, and that children learn work skills through labour at a young age. These views are narrow and do not take the long term developmental benefits of education into account. Another determinant is access to education. In some areas, education is not affordable, or is found to be inadequate. With no other alternatives, children spend their time working.

The Constitution of India clearly states that child labour is wrong and that measures should be taken to end it. The government of India has implemented the Child Labour Act in 1986 that outlaws child labour in certain areas and sets the minimum age of employment at fourteen. This Act falls short of making all child labour illegal, and fails to meet the ILO guideline concerning the minimum age of employment set at fifteen years of age. Though policies are in place that could potentially reduce the incidence of child labour, enforcement is a problem. If child labour is to be eradicated in India, the government and those responsible for enforcement need to start doing their jobs. Policies can and will be developed concerning child labour, but without enforcement they are all useless.

The state of education in India also needs to be improved. High illiteracy and dropout rates are reflective of the inadequacy of the educational system. Poverty plays a role in the ineffectiveness of the educational system. Dropout rates are high because children are forced to work in order to support their families.

The attitudes of the people also contribute to the lack of enrollment—parents feel that work develops skills that can be used to earn an income, while education does not help in this matter. Compulsory education may help in regard to these attitudes. The examples of Sri Lanka and Kerala show that compulsory education has worked in those areas. There are differences between Sri Lanka, Kerala and the rest of India. What types of social welfare structures do these places have? What are the attitudes of the people? Is there some other reason why the labour market for child labourers is poor in these areas? These are some questions that need to be answered before applying the concept of compulsory education to India?

India is making progress in terms of educational policy. The DPEP has been implemented only four years ago, and so results are not apparent at this time. Hopefully the future will show that this program has made progress towards universal education, and eradicating child labour.

Table 1
Percentage distribution of child workers (in India) by industrial divisions in 1981.

Type of Worker Industrial Divisions	*Urban*	*Rural*	*Total*
I	5.32	38.87	35.93
II	14.73	45.42	42.74
III	3.07	6.61	6.30
IV	0.20	0.25	0.24
V	39.16	5.72	8.65
VI	3.27	0.47	0.72
VII	15.03	0.96	2.19
VIII	2.45	0.10	0.30
IX	16.77	1.60	2.93

Child labour cannot be eliminated by focusing on one determinant, for example education, or by brute enforcement of child labour laws. The government of India must ensure that the needs of the poor are filled before attacking child labour. If poverty is addressed, the need for child labour will automatically diminish. No matter how hard India tries, child labour always will exist until the need for it is removed. The development of India as a nation is being hampered by child labour. Children are growing up illiterate because they have been working and not attending school.

A cycle of poverty is formed and the need for child labour is reborn after every generation. India needs to address the situation by tackling the underlying causes of child labour through governmental policies and the enforcement of these policies. Only then will India succeed in the fight against child labour.

India has the largest number of urban and rural child workers in the world. The Government of India acknowledges at least 17.5 million working children. Estimates by various organizations range from 44 million 2 to over 100 million child workers. The exact number of child workers in India's export industry is not known. Major export industries which utilize child labor include hand-knotted carpets, gemstone polishing, brass and base metal articles, glass and glassware, footwear, textiles and silk, and fireworks. Children are also exploited as bonded laborers, particularly in the carpet industry.

Other industries in India alleged to use child labour are: locks; leather; pottery; granite, mica, slate mining and quarrying; auto parts and accessories; cashew processing; coir (coconut fiber) products; iron and steel products; wood, rattan, and walnut furniture; suitcases and trunks; sports goods; garments; tile; and shrimp and seafood processing. Further research is required to determine the nature and extent of child labor in these industries, as well as their link to export markets. Some of these industries, such as pottery and locks, probably produce solely for the domestic market.

Child Labour in Export Industries

Hand-knotted carpets are exported in large quantity from India to the United States and Germany. In 1993, India exported more than $170 million worth of carpets to the United States. Although there are weaving 5 centers scattered throughout India, the largest centers are located in the 'carpet belt' of Uttar Pradesh. Carpets are also produced in the Jammu-Kashmir region, as well as outside Jaipur in Rajasthan. The South Asian Coalition on Child Servitude (SACCS) estimates that there are approximately 300,000 children working in the industry. In 1992, the American Embassy in New Delhi noted that estimates of children in the carpet industry range from 300,000 to 400,000.

Children work in almost every stage of carpet-making. In a comprehensive May 1994 report on child labor in India, the International Labor Rights Education and Research Fund (ILRERF) asserts that children's tasks include sorting, knotting, cutting, washing, and dyeing. They also rear sheep, roll yarn into balls, string the looms, and weave and bind carpets. Often children begin work at six or eight years old as unpaid 'apprentices.'

Child carpet weavers typically fall into four categories: unpaid children working on family looms, unpaid children working with adult family wage earners, unpaid apprentices (for approximately one year), and wage earners. A 1992 survey conducted for the Government of India by the National Council for Applied Economic Research (NCAER) estimated that 8 percent of the total work force in the hand-knotted carpet industry is child labor.

A 1993, the International Labor Organization estimates that the ration of adult to child workers in the carpet industry of Mirzapur-Bhadohi is 1:2.254. Of the 500 carpet children surveyed by the NCAER, the average daily wage was 12.20 rupees (approximately 42 cents); the survey found that wages were not promptly disbursed. Often both adults and children are paid per square yard, which makes the weavers work very long hours.

A review of current literature indicates that children work an average of six to twelve hours a day. Most looms are located in earthen shacks or sheds scattered throughout villages. These sheds are similar to a typical lodging for a family in a rural village. Only a small percentage of carpet production actually occurs in factories (housing multiple looms). The NCAER study found that 91 percent of the children sampled lived and slept in weaving sheds, and basic amenities, such as light, ventilation, and toilets were deficient or unavailable.

Anti-Slavery International described loom sheds as small, seldom more than twelve feet by nine feet, with very little light. Trenches about 3 feet deep and 21 feet wide are dug into the floor to accommodate the looms which are too high for the sheds. During the weaving process, three to six children and/or adults sit shoulder to shoulder. Usually there are one adult and two boys per loom, sitting in damp pits, which fill up with water during the monsoon season. Children are charged for meals, which include a few chapatis (bread), onions, and salt. They also suffer health- related problems.

The NCAER 1993 study found that cuts and injuries were common. Over 90 percent of the children complained of swelling of lower limbs and severe pain in the joints. Children also came into constant contact with woolen fluff causing skin troubles including scabies and respiratory ailments. Work in ill-lit sheds impacted the eyesight of 40 percent of the children. Similarly, SACCS reveals that bonded children rescued from the carpet looms say they were overworked and beaten.

When children suffered cuts to the fingers during weaving, the loom owners scrape sulphur from matches heads into the wound and then set the wound on fire to stop the bleeding. In addition, children have also been known to suffer loss of eyesight due to poor lighting and deformed backs due to long hours of sitting in cramped conditions. Children suffer from psychological distress, and are beaten and even tortured if they attempt to escape from the looms. Some reports describe children beaten to death by loom owners for making mistakes. Numerous stories about children published in newspaper reports and non-governmental periodicals describe bonded child labor in the carpet industry.

Many children who work in the carpet belt are sold into debt bondage by their parents, or merely taken with promises of future payments. A Fact Finding Committee commissioned by the Order of the Supreme Court of India confirmed that a large number of children work as bonded laborers in the carpet industry. The vast majority come from the poorest part of Bihar, the most impoverished state in India. In the bonded labor system, recruiters give parents a cash advance or 'loan.'

The child is often taken far away to weave carpets in order to work off the family debt. The debt is rarely paid off and indebtedness may carry on for generations. The child is, in effect, an indentured servant with virtually no rights and no protections. In cases where a bonded child is sent to work with a family, his treatment is significantly worse than the other non-bonded children.

When parents are in fact paid, the going rate for an eight year old boy is 1,500-2,000 rupees ($50-$60), a substantial sum for many families. Once the deal is struck, the recruiter will take a group of children at a time by bus and train to the 'carpet belt', usually to the town of Bhadohi, where loom owners come to pick up their new workers. Reports have surfaced alleging that Nepali women and children are now also working in the Indian carpet industry.

The Bonded Labor Liberation Front, together with local authorities, raided a small carpet factory in Mirzapur earlier this year, finding 86 Nepalis locked into a tin shed. Eyewitness reports confirm that children from Nepal are working in India's carpet industry. It is unclear, however, whether they arrive in India with their families voluntarily or whether they are forcibly brought into the carpet centers of India. News reports abound of similar carpet 'factories' in Mirzapur and Bhadohi housing large numbers of migrant laborers locked into their place of work.

Gemstone Polishing

In 1993, India exported more than $1 billion worth of gems, which is the largest export by value from India to the United States. The majority of these exports are diamonds, which are processed and polished in Surat, Gujarat, and emeralds which are polished in Jaipur, Rajasthan. Some sources allege that anywhere between 6,000 and 100,000 children are working in the diamond industry, cutting and polishing diamond chips. These 34 figures are uncorroborated. The Operations Research Group in its 1993 report singled out the diamond-cutting industry in Surat, Gujarat, of special concern for child labor. It found children, mostly boys between 12 and 13 years old, polishing diamonds for an average of seven to nine hours a day in unhygienic conditions.

This study also found major health and safety problems, including eye strain, headaches, leg and shoulder pain, malaria, discoloration of hair, rotten teeth, and dysentery. Wage rates were similar to adults; children, who received wages based on the number of diamonds they polished, reported a monthly income of 930 rupees (approximately $30). The Indian government, under its National Plan of Action, has targeted, on a priority basis, the diamond polishing industry in Surat as one of nine industries in which it will develop a Child Labor project.

In addition to diamonds, children also polish emeralds, sapphires, rubies, lapis lazuli, turquoise, corals, garnets, amethysts, and topaz. Estimates of child workers in the gem industry in Jaipur range from 7,000 to 13,000. A 1991 study by the Institute of Development Studies in Jaipur provides extensive documentation of child labor in the gem industry of Jaipur. For example, the study cites a 12 year old girl using a drilling machine, children stringing gems, a 14 year-old girl cutting tiger stone, turquoise, amethysts and garnet, and a 9 year-old boy polishing stones.

According to noted academic Neera Burra there are two categories of children working in the gem industry in Jaipur: 1) Children from 6 to 10 years old belonging to families of manual laborers and poorly paid people. These children work from 8 a.m. to 6 p.m. and are completely illiterate; and 2) Children from 10 to 14 years old belonging to families with a fairly steady income. These children go to government schools and work about four hours a day after school.

According to Burra's 1991 study, children are involved in large numbers in the making of the 'ghats'(rough cut stones), faceting and polishing of semi-precious stones. In the precious stone industries, children use oxides in the final stages of gem-polishing. In fact, in the final polishing with oxides, the entire labor force consists of children below fourteen. Burra found that although children in the gem polishing industry are engaged as 'apprentices,' they are in fact a source of cheap labor.

The learning process takes five to seven years-during the first two years children receive little or no remuneration. Children work for 10 hours a day. After the two years, a child worker is paid 50 rupees per month. According to the Burra, local doctors revealed that more than 30 percent of the children get tuberculosis, presumably due to unhygienic conditions, overcrowding, and malnutrition. Children complain of body ache and finger tips grazed by the polishing disc.

The most common complaint was eye strain and allergic dermatitis due to constant use of dirty water. Brass products, such as vases, figurines, planters, plates, dinner services, and tea sets are made in Moradabad in Uttar Pradesh, and exported all over the world, including to the United States. It is reported that more than 90 percent of the goods produced in Moradabad are intended for export. The brass industry is made up of numerous unregistered shops in the guise of household units, thereby skirting child labor regulations. The

Operations Research Group documented occupational hazards of children working in the brass industry in 1993 and found that the average income of a child was 174 rupees per month (approximately $6) for eight to 10 hours of work six days per week. A dated, but detailed, study by Neera Burra in 1989 estimated that 40,000 to 45,000 children work in the brass industry in Moradabad. Children were recruited by middlemen called 'dalals,' who receive a commission from the employers for finding child workers. Contractors, or 'thekedars,' and workshop owners prefer children because they are easy to control. Burra notes that, except for the process of engraving and coloring, child workers in the brass industry do not work with their families.

Almost all the children in Moradabad work as wage laborers and are unrelated to workshop owners. Children work in almost all aspects of brassware production for long hours and low wages, and are exposed to health hazards. Children remove molten metal from molds near furnaces. Burra observed these children standing, without protective gear, on top of furnaces with a temperature of 1,100 degrees celsius (approximately 2,000 degrees fahrenheit). Burns were a constant danger. Children were also observed working in electroplating, polishing, and applying chemicals to the wares. The constant inhalation of fumes from the furnaces and metal dust leads to tuberculosis and respiratory problems. During acid washing of the brassware, Burra noted that green and blue vapors rising into the air cause irritation to the eyes.

In 1992, India exported more than $2 million worth of glass and glassware to the United States. Estimates of the number of children working in the glass industry range from 8,000 to 50,000. The glass and glassware industry in India is concentrated in Ferozabad. The glass factories of Ferozabad produce a number of glass items, such as bangles, chandeliers, wine glasses, beads, crockery, bulbs, and cut glass items. The factories also produce test tubes, beakers, and laboratory glass products. The ILRERF Report referred to a glass-factory floor as Dante's 'Inferno' due to the intense heat of the furnace (between 1,400-1,600 celsius), lack of ventilation, broken glass everywhere, dangling electric wires, and workers with no protective equipment (no shoes, gloves or goggles).

Both adult and child workers stand outside furnaces dipping iron rods into molten glass, bringing it out, and throwing it to glass molders or blowers. Boys as young as 11 or 12 sit on the floor for long hours in front of the pot furnaces, melting and fastening glass bangles and beads. Often glass splinters injure the workers, and pieces of glass cut into the bare feet of the children. The children bump into each other as they have to run very fast before the molten glass can cool, and may scorch each other's bodies. An earlier study in 1987 by Cox newspaper reporters found boys under 14 running from the furnaces to the glass blower carrying molten glass.

The glass blower would then throw the hot iron pole, javelin style, to a child several feet below him, who would put water on it. The reporters observed children walking barefoot over glass littered floors, some with scarred eyes and burnt scalps. In addition, children of the glass factories in Ferozabad suffer mental retardation, asthma, bronchitis, eye problems, liver ailments, skin burns, chronic anemia, and tuberculosis. A recent study by Dr. Asha Singh of the Maulana Azad Medical College in New Delhi revealed genetic damage in the body cells of the laborers working close to furnace heat for three years or more.

In 1993, India exported more than $107 million worth of footwear to the United States. The American Embassy-New Delhi advises that "child labor is known or widely believed to be used in the shoe export industry. The American embassy further states that children are employed in the manufacture of shoes in the Agra area and that Agra shoe manufacturers are beginning to find markets in the West, possibly including the United States. Some sources estimate that as many as 25,000 children may be involved in shoe making, both for the domestic and international markets.

Children between 10 and 15 years old are assembling shoes. Some 80 percent of the children work for contractors at home. Children work on soling (fixing upper portions of shoes to leather or rubber soles) with glue. Children in cramped poorly lit rooms suffer from continuous skin contact with industrial adhesives and breathing vapors from glues. The ILRERF report found children working in shoe factories throughout Agra, including road stalls, and in small factories. It is reported that children also work in larger factories.

Silk

Children are allegedly found in sericulture, silk weaving, and in the silk handloom industry. The May 1994 ILRERF report states that children, mostly girls, work in the silk industries. Children work in sericulture and silk thread spinning in the villages of southern Karnataka, as well as in silk handlooms in Varanasi and Kanchipuram. There are approximately 5,000 children employed in the silk thread industry in southern Karnataka. ILRERF observed factories with children ranging in age from 5 to 16 who work from 7 a.m. to 9 p.m. spinning silk. Another factory was found to employ young bonded workers, mostly girls. In contrast to the sericulture and silk thread weaving industry, it is difficult to witness child labor in the silk handloom industry, as it is a household industry.

A 1994 study mentions that because of scant governmental attention paid to child labor in the silk industry, a growing number of children are working in the industry in Bhagalpur. The study was drawn from a sample of 250 child workers under 14 years of age in the silk industry in Bhagalpur. Most child workers were between 11 and 13 years old, the smallest children being 5 years old. The majority of the child workers received 5,000 to 10,000 rupees per year ($170-$340). The largest number of children belonged to a disadvantaged class or are Muslims.

Moreover, data revealed that there were more boys than girls in this industry, and girls were generally below the age of 10. Some of the health hazards include poor work conditions (lack of sanitation, water, and fresh air), diseases of the lungs and sight problems. The Central Tessar Research Training Institute in Ranchi stated that silk weavers suffer from heart and skin diseases, and various other lung diseases.

Children are involved in virtually the entire process (about 14 phases) of silk manufacturing. Specifically, children dye the silk. This process involves boiling the skeins in water to remove the gum. The children then place the yarn on bamboo hangers for drying, after which, it is starched. Children about 14 years old commonly put prepared yarns on beams, weave the silk and then take it to the market. 81 The Times of India in Patna on March 27, 1988 reported that silk made in Bhagalpur Tassar is exported to the United States, as well as to some European countries.

The fireworks and match industries of Sivakasi exist side by side, and therefore, reports study the industries together. The United States' importation of matches and fireworks/pyrotechnics from India is minimal. According to the available literature, it is estimated that there are 50,000 to 100,000 child workers in the Sivakasi area working in the match and fireworks industries. Overall, there are approximately 2,700 to 3,000 match units in Sivakasi and the Sivakasi-Sattur belt which produce 55 percent of the matches in India.

An ICFTU/APRO study in 1992 estimated that 55 percent of the workers are below 14 years. Many begin working at age five to seven. According to findings by the ICFTU-APRO study in 1992, there are approximately 300 licensed fireworks factories and several hundred unlicensed units. These units account for 90 percent of India's fireworks production. Most of the items are used for Diwali (Festival of Lights). Estimates of the number of children working in Sivakasi's fireworks industry range from over 30,000 to 70,000, according to SACCS.

Working in the fireworks industry at the age of 10 or 12. According to Manjari Dingwaney of the Rural Labor Cell (India), children are carried in buses from their villages to the work sites between 3 a.m. and 5 a.m. in the morning and return home between 6 p.m. and 9 p.m. Children dye outer paper, roll gun powder, make firecrackers, dip material into chemicals, and pack the final products for seven to twelve hours a day every day.

According to the ICFTU, children in semi-mechanized industries earn 15 to 18 rupees a day to 62 cents), but those who work in tiny sector match units or unlicensed fireworks units only receive 8 to 15 rupees (approximately 28 to 51 cents). The ILRERF found that children were paid on a piece rate basis which varied between boys and girls. Hazardous work environments in match and firework factories, including highly inflammable chemicals spread on the unprotected floor have resulted in fatal accidents.

Laws of India

Article 24 of the Constitution of India prohibits employment of children under 14 years in factories, mines, or other hazardous employment. India has numerous laws pertaining to child labor which span over 100 years. The Children (Pledging of Labor) Act, 1933 prohibits any agreement to pledge the labor of a child. Pledging means the taking of advances by parents and guardians in return for bonds. In 1986, the Child Labor (Prohibition & Regulation) Act, was promulgated to consolidate the various other child labor laws. It provides penalties for employing child labor; a uniform definition of 'child' (14 years or under); machinery for proclaiming a list of prohibited occupations for children; and permission for any person to file a complaint against anyone employing children. Proscribed occupations include: carpet weaving, cloth printing, dyeing, weaving, manufacture of matches, fireworks, and explosives.

The 1986 Act also limits child work for six hours between 8 a.m. and 7 p.m. with one day of rest per week, and provides penalties of imprisonment and fine up to

10,000 rupees for violations. For repeated offenses, imprisonment can be up to three years.

Critics of the Child Labor Act of 1986 note that the determination of age is left to the Inspector, and that the Act lowers some higher standards established by earlier acts. More specifically, the 1986 Act: lowers the age of entry for employment in motor transport, merchant shipping, and factories; puts child workers in agriculture or the unorganized sector outside the reach of the Act, and provides exemptions for family-based work.

According to the Advocate Supreme Court of India, labour statistics for 1992-1993 show that there were 349 prosecutions and 162 convictions under the Child Labor (Prohibition and Regulation) Act of 1986. The record shows that Uttar Pradesh was the only state with convictions under the Child Labor Act of 1986.

The Government of India has reportedly approved draft legislation to tighten provisions of the Child Labor (Prohibition and Regulation) Act of 1986 and improve enforcement. The amendments would make violations of the law subject to the provisions of India's 'Code of Criminal Procedure 1973,' increase penalties, and empower Magistrates to dispose of cases speedily.

The enforcement of child labor laws, however, is weak in India. The Standing Committee on Labor and Welfare and the Ministry of Labor found inadequate enforcement of the Child Labor Act of 1986 by the States. This Committee questioned the commitment of the Central Government to eliminating child labor. The 1993 Operations Research Group study was even more critical; it concluded, "[S]heer callousness, almost bordering on sadism, on the part of government officials is the main reason for the exacerbation of the sufferings of the child labor. The implementation of child labor legislation in India is entrusted to labor inspectors, representatives of the Ministry of Labor at the district level. Labor inspectors are responsible for ensuring that no child below the stipulated age is employed.

The judicial department inquires into complaints. Enforcement is divided; some labor inspectors enforce the Factories Act; others enforce the Child Labor Act of 1986. While conducting seminars for enforcement officials, the National Labor Institute's Child Labor Cell instructors found that many inspectors were uninformed about the laws.

Moreover, credible sources maintain that rampant corruption further compromised enforcement of child labor laws. Finally, there is a lack of labor inspectors. For example, in the carpet industry, Varanasi Deputy Labor Commissioner, D.P. Singh said his office had only six inspectors (two of them for Bhadohi). Inspectors were generally not welcome in the loom sheds and found that children were shifted out of sight when they arrived.

Education Laws

Although the Constitution of India directs the States to provide free and compulsory education to all children up to 14 years of age, it is not implemented. India has one of the highest illiteracy rates in the world, in addition to a very high drop out rate from school. Myron Weiner, professor at Massachusetts Institute of Technology who has written extensively on education in India, attributes the prevalence of child labor in India largely to the failure of the educational system.

Professor Weiner notes that, due to a lack of compulsory education, half the population of school age children between 6 and 14 years old is at home or in the labor force. Weiner argues that it is not poverty which prevents India from investing more in its children, but rather the caste prejudices and value systems of those who create and implement policy in India. Professor Weiner notes, however, that the central government is calling for a substantial increase in expenditures for elementary education, though responsibility for funding remains primarily in the hands of state governments. Alec Fyfe of the International Labor Organization also emphasizes the importance of viewing child labor and educational policies as reciprocal within the context of India.

International Conventions

India is a party to ILO No. Convention 5 Concerning Minimum Age for Admission to Employment in Industry and the U.N. Convention on the Rights of the Child. India is not a party to ILO Conventions No. 59 Concerning Minimum Age for Industry [revised]) or No. ILO Convention 138 Concerning Minimum Age for Admission to Employment. Programmes and fforts to Address Child Labour

According to the written testimony submitted by the Embassy of India to the Department of Labor, the Indian government has followed a 3-pronged strategy for child labor eradication under the National Policy of Child Labor in 1987:

The Legislative Action Plan to tighten and improve enforcement of the law. A Child Labor Advisory

Committee was set up to advise the Central Government on the addition of occupations and processes to the schedule contained in Child Labor (Prohibition & Regulation) Act of 1986.

General development programs benefitting child labor are being undertaken by State Governments. The National Policy on Education (1986) set the target of providing five years of schooling or its equivalent, through a 'Non-Formal System of Education' (NFE), to all children who attained the age of 11 by 1990. Approximately 490,000 NFE centers were to be set up offering part-time and vocational courses. Voluntary agencies and local institutions were to be involved as well.

Project-based Plan of Action in areas of high concentration of child labor engaged in wage and quasi-wage employment. This plan includes the adoption of specific projects/programs in areas where child labor is endemic. Nine National Child Labor projects are being implemented in five states and special schools have been set up which provide non-formal education. Child workers in the many sectors were to receive priority attention because either the employment processes in which they work were prohibited under the Factories Act, or the Child Labor Act of 1986, or the work was such as it was likely to affect the child's well-being.

The International Labor Organization and the Government of India are working in cooperation under the International Programme on the Elimination of Child Labor (IPEC). The priorities for India in 1994-1995 will continue to be in the areas of bonded child labor and hazardous work, including the carpet industry, and the match and fireworks industries. The ILO, through its

Child Labor Action and Support Program (CLASP), is concentrating on target groups which mirror the Indian Government's child labor policy. The ILO's programmes covered approximately 33,000 children between 1992 and 1993. The total funds committed by the IPEC for 59 action programs in India, up to March 1994, is $1,532,857. Many of these programs are run by community-based non-governmental organizations which establish special schools for working children.

No information on the curriculum, attendance rate, or effectiveness of these schools is available. Many of the schools are open only for a few hours per day so that the children are able to work and attend school. The Carpet Export Promotion Council (CEPC) has adopted a code of conduct to eradicate the use of child labor in the carpet industry. To enforce this code, the CEPC has begun to register its looms. The registration certificate is to be compulsory for membership in the organization which oversees the majority of exports of carpets and floor coverings.

The CEPC and the All-India Carpet Manufacturers Association (AICMA) have agreed to send all children employed in the carpet industry to their homes and stop fresh recruitment of workers below 14 years of age. Only carpets made by complying factories will be sold overseas. The CEPC claims to have registered at least 50,000 looms where no children are employed. It warned that it would inspect factories to make sure that the labor code is not violated. At the moment this industry initiative lacks an independent oversight mechanism to insure its accuracy and effectiveness.

The Indian National Trade Union Congress (INTUC) adopted a resolution in May 1993 voicing concern over the increasing employment of child labor. The Conference called upon all INTUC branches to identify child labor in their own regions/branches and explore ways to evolve strategies and an effective Action Plan to mitigate child labor. Other plans for action are unknown.

Out of the countries studied for this report, India has perhaps the largest number of non-governmental organizations concerned with child labor. The South Asian Coalition Against Child Servitude, by far the most well-known, initiated a 'Not Made by Children' campaign to effect India's carpet export earnings since carpets are frequently made by children. SACCS also has a program to release, and sometimes rehabilitate, bonded children. There have been several well-publicized raids conducted by SACCS targeting carpet factories. After the children are liberated, Satyarthi and SACCS attempt to provide them with social support, return them to their families, and pressure the local government to respect India's constitutional commitment to free and compulsory education. Throughout the years, SACCS has also organized several marches across India against child servitude. SACCS focuses on all industries which it believes utilize child labor, particularly bonded child labour.

The Indo-German Export Promotion Programme (IGEP), in cooperation with the Indian government, NGOs, international organizations such as UNICEF and the ILO, and leading carpet exporters was developing a system called 'rugmark' to certify and label carpets made without child labor. The negotiations for this project recently faltered, but the 'rugmark' project has reportedly moved forward, on a reduced scale, in cooperation with a number of smaller carpet exporters who belong to an association called the Carpet Manufacturers' Association Without Child Labor.

Some other non-governmental organizations include: The Children's Emancipation Society, which has set up schools near the looms so that children can study in the morning and weave in the afternoons; The Campaign Against Child Labor, Youth for Voluntary Action (YUVA) in Bombay; Action for the Rights of the Child (ARC) in Pune; and Terre des Hommes (Germany) India Programme, and a public awareness campaign with the support of approximately 300 non-governmental organizations, the ILO, and UNICEF.

Concerned for Working Children (CWC)

The Concerned for Working Children (CWC) has been working in the field of child labour since 1980. In its early years, CWC was involved in the unionisation of the informal sector where children below the age of 14 years comprised nearly 40 percent of the total work force. These children, who in many ways were more militant than the adult members were deeply disappointed when they found that the agreements as a result of collective bargaining had not given them any benefits as laws did not recognise them. They wanted to change the law to one that recognised them as workers and protected them as children at the same time. The children and the members of the union embarked on an exercise to draft an alternative legislation for working children in 1985.

The children approached the question from the premise that the reasons why they worked could not be changed and proceeded to address the work situation. The adult office bearers of the union approached the problem from a different angle, as they were not willing to accept the causes of children's work as given. They wanted to find ways to tackle these by inducing structural changes. These two visions were integrated and a Draft Bill was developed. In 1985, the Central Labour Ministry agreed to convert the draft into an official Bill of the Ministry. In 1986 the official Bill was presented to the Central Cabinet for approval.

A watered down version of this draft was presented to parliament and passed in October 1986. Though the Legislation was fraught with loopholes and definitional difficulties, it did generate a major debate on child work in independent India for the first time. The children also proved that they could engage in policy debates and make major contributions in this area.

Strategic objectives

— Solve the child labour problem and be able to declare areas 'child labour free'

— Facilitate protagonism of working children so that they may enrich their lives and contribute towards building a more just and equitable society

— Create the 'time and space' for children to be empowered by making an impact on National and State policy, legislation and programmes.

— Develop theoretical and practical models that effectively and efficiently deal with the problem and can be replicated both by the state and by NGOs.

— Influence state and National Governments and International agencies and organisations to focus on child labour as a major part of their political agenda.

— Influence state and National Governments and International agencies and organisations to focus on child labour as a major part of their political agenda.

— Participate and influence in National, Regional and International forums in order to bring the issue of child labour into the political spotlight.

— Use all forms of media, including main stream, to sensitise the public to the issue and change perceptions in order to create a climate where child labour is not acceptable.

— Build relations with NGOs, institutions, trade unions, social and political movements and individuals in order to build a strong lobby in support of the rights of children.

— Develop with others, an alternate agenda for India where there will be no exploitation of children.

South Asian Coalition on Child Servitude (SACCS) India

A total number of 39,240 bonded/child labourers have been identified

4,155 child/bonded labourers have been released

Documentation of liberation Processes.

To strengthen Bachpan Bachao Andolan (BBA) as a movement

— Setting up of a central Secretariat

— Setting up of BBA offices at States/ District levels

— Training and upgrade of skills

— Generating adequate resources and skilled manpower

— New offices have been set up and Elections have taken place to elect the regional leaders for State co-ordinators

Various training and meetings

Evaluation of the work done by the organisation through external evaluators

— To provide transitory rehabilitation to the freed bonded children

— To carry forward the initiatives of transit rehabilitation at Mukti Ashram

— Opening of Bal Ashram for rescued bonded labourers and a Girls' collective for working girl children

Bal Ashram, which became operational in April 1998, has so far trained 104 former bonded child labourers and at present 73-rescued child labourers are undergoing the training.

— At the Girls' Collective, 30 working girls have undergone training

— To lobby, advocate and campaign for the rights of child labourers

— To carry forward campaigns

— Organise various protest marches

— To take this issue to higher forums of Legal interventions

— School campaigns

— Fire Cracker boycott campaigns

— Campaign during Elections

— Various press conferences

— Organisational representation in various forums

— Legal interventions through NHRC and other legal bodies

— To broad base the movement by increasing the membership and networking with other NGOs

— Identification of organisation totally committed to child's rights.

— Support to improve the organisational skills of SACCS partners.

— Increasing the visibility of the organisation.

— Coming in broader alliances with other movements.

— Incorporating SACCS objectives into other networks and movements.

— The number of SACCS associates has increased from 300 in 1996 to 480 in April 1999.

— The individual membership of BBA has increased from 5000 in 1996 to 80,000 in 1998.

— Broader alliance and incorporation of issues into networks and associates.

— Research and documentation of all activities of SACCS and BBA.

— Research into newer industries

— Research into ongoing activities

— Documentation of all the initiatives of SACCS

— Research has been conducted in the areas of sarees, glass industry, bidi, domestic child labour, brass, hosiery and sports goods.

— Separate unit for documentation has been set-up in the central secretariat

Groups/individuals

1. Bonded Child Labour, Child Labour, their parents and family members.
2. Associate partners NGOs working in this field.
3. Trade Union leaders, parliamentarians, religious leaders, students, teachers, policy makers, and government officials. 4. Consumers association, employers association.
5. National & international organisation, state & central governments.
6. Electronic/print media, street theatre groups,
7. Cultural association doctors and members of Panchyat Raj institutions.
8. Judiciary police and law enforcement agencies.
9. 100,000 individuals to be involved through membership drive.

States

Bihar, Uttar Pradesh, Madhya Pradesh, Rajasthan, Maharashtra, Tamilnadu, Punjab, Haryana and Delhi.

Industries

Carpet, Brick kiln, Glass Industry, Sports, Saree, Bidi, Stone Quarries, Domestic Child Labour and Firecrackers.

Peace Trust India

Peace Trust started its work during 1986 in the slum of Saveriarpalayam adjoining Dindiguaal Town, in a modest way among the Tannery working children. It highlighted the hazardous nature of their occupation and provided them with education. Slowly, it spread out to other slums and suburbs such as Peiryar Nagar and MGR Nagar during 1987 and subsequently to semi urban areas and villages located in the hinterlands of Dindigul town in the year 1988 and 1989.

These centers gathered working children and provided them opportunities for literacy, social awareness, health care, nutrition, entertainment and creativity. They came together every day in the evening after their work and shared their experience at work places and learnt from others; tried to find a solution to their day-to-day problems and there by slowly gained awareness on their rights and tried to improve their working conditions.

The centers also provided newspapers, children's literatures, radio, sometimes television, video and thus access to information. Many programmes were organised to enable the children to demonstrate their talents and skills. These children were guided by trained animators and health workers who were in charge of the centers. The programmes and activities of Peace Trust thus grew more day by day.

Activities

The following is a random list of basic activities undertaken by Peace Trust.

- Non-formal education for working children.
- Supplementary education for school-going children
- Skill training for adolescent boys and girls
- Camps and campaigns for child labour elimination
- Medical camp, Health care services
- Women Sangam-Saml savings and credit management
- Campaigns for Environmental protection
- Nursery raising and reforestation
- Environmental awareness to school students and general public
- Awareness raising on Neww Panchayat Raj
- Campaign against Tanery Pollution
- Efforts for obtaining drinking water facilities to tannery affected villages
- School health programmes
- Kitchen gardening by school-going children
- Ante-natal and post-natal care
- Referral Services
- Smokeless chulah
- Soak-pit construction
- Sharamdhan by School Children

— Cultural programmes-Street play, songs, dances

— Healthy Baby show

— Small credits for women (through DWCRA)

— Free notebook, school fees and uniform for children

— Participatory Rural Appraisal workshops in Villages for planning purposes

— Legal Aid Camps

Mahita is a Sanskrit term meaning rejuvenation or regeneration. Mahita is a commitment of group of individuals for development through education, empowerment and environment awareness. Our focus is on the deprived areas of urban slums and rural villages with emphasis on women and girl children.

Mahita was registered in 1994 as a non-profit society with secular and non-political outlook. Over the years we have been working in the urban slums of Hyderabad and interior villages of Ranga Reddy District of Andhra Pradesh, India.

Our interventions are aimed at poverty alleviation amongst the urban and rural poor through self-help concepts and by collective action. Our interventions include:

— Education through empowerment programmes for working girl children and women groups

— Skill development training programmes for adolescent girls

— Micro entrepreneur development of marginalised women through thrift & credit management

— Reproductive health awareness

— Health and sanitation for the deprived communities

— Natural resource development programmes through women groups

— Information and dissemination for community awareness and development

— Networking with like minded NGOs

Community linkages to government programmes

— Every child, especially girls, must have the opportunity to go to school rather than to work.

— Create community-acceptable ways to provide formal and non-formal education intervention.

— To involve people, especially women from planning to implementation

— To undertake dissemination of information, develop opportunities, conduct workshops for community awareness.

— To empower women and adolescent girls through micro entrepreneurhsip and vocational training

— Strengthening the efficiency of delivery of civic services i.e. health, education, and legal rights through women participation.

— To prevent child labour through education.

Main activities

— Educational Centers for Working girl children

— Vocational centers for Adolescent girls

— Self help groups for women economic development

— Mainstreaming children in to formal schools

— Training in self-help management groups, reproductive health, Sanitation and other environmental issues

— Linkages to government welfare schemes for community members

— CRC Camps and workshops at community level

— Networking with other NGOs on child issues.

10

Child Workers in Pakistan

Although most Pakistani children work in the agricultural sector, a large number of children work in urban centers weaving carpets, manufacturing surgical instruments, and producing sporting goods for export. There are allegations of children working in other industries including leather, footwear, and mining. Further research is required as the connection between child labour in these industries and the importation of such items to the United States is not clear. Data on the Pakistan labour force and child labour is unreliable. Nevertheless, there is little doubt that child labour has assumed massive proportions in Pakistan. The actual total number of working children in Pakistan is probably somewhere between 2 and 19 million.

Millions of children in Pakistan suffer under a system of bonded labour. The bonded labour system consists of giving advances of "peshgi" (bonded money) to a person. As long as all or part of the peshgi debt remains outstanding, the debtor/worker is bound to the creditor/employer. In case of sickness or death, the family of the individual is responsible for the debt, which often passes down from generation to generation. In the case of children, the peshgi is paid to a parent or guardian, who then provides the child to work off the debt.

Bonded labour has long been a feature in brick kilns, carpet industries, agriculture, fisheries, stone/brick crushing, shoe-making, power looms, and refuse sorting.

Some of these children reportedly come from Afghanistan, Bangladesh and Burma. In September 1988, the Pakistan Supreme Court, in a well-publicized case against brick kiln owners, legally abolished the "peshgi" (bonded) system. This Supreme Court decision, however, stopped short of forgiving past debts. The Bonded Labour (Abolition) Act of 1992 abolished and made illegal bonded labour in Pakistan, and cancelled all obligations of bonded labourers to their employers.

The most widely recognized export product from Pakistan using child labour is carpets. In a meeting with an official of the U.S. Department of Labour, the Pakistan Secretary of Labour maintained that carpet weaving is the only major export industry employing children. The U.S. State Department Country Reports on Human Rights Practices for 1993 concurs. In 1993, the Provincial Labour Departments compiled statistics on child labour in nine industries. The study found that in carpet industries, 2,463 children under 14 years of age were found, and another 4,246 were between 14 and 17 years old.

A 1992 UNICEF-Punjab report asserted that according to conservative estimates, one million out of 1.5 million workers in the carpet industry in Pakistan were children. A separate 1992 UNICEF/Government of Pakistan study reported that 90 percent of the one million workers in the carpet industry are children, many of whom began working in the industry before 10 years of age.

The Human Rights Commission of Pakistan found that weaving thrives in self-contained homesteads, where labour is cheap and readily available. The Pakistan Carpet Manufacturers and Exporters Association (PCMEA) describes the Pakistani carpet industry as follows: "A Study on Child Labourers in Pakistan Hand-Knotted Carpet Industry" Pakistan Carpet Manufacturers and Exporters Association (PCMEA), included as attachment in "Replies to the Questions-Points Raised in the Non-Paper on GSP Worker Rights.

The Pakistan carpet industry is primarily a cottage-based industry employing around 1.5 million people, with heavy concentration in Punjab and Sind provinces. Of this an estimated 8 percent are children of which the major portion is comprised of family unit labour. Only 10 percent of the looms are in factories of 10-30 looms each, while 90% of the weaving is based in village homes where the amount of work done is by choice of the family unit and beyond the manufacturers and contractors control.

Despite legal limitations, child labour is widespread in the carpet industry, where much production comes from the family-run cottage industry. The Government of Pakistan is fully aware of the existence of child labour in the carpet industry. In March 1992, the Centre for the Improvement of Working Conditions and Environment, within the Labour Department of the Government of Punjab, in conjunction with UNICEF, reported that over 80 percent of the carpet weavers in Punjab are children under 15, including 30% under 10.

Child weavers suffer work-related injuries and illnesses, such as injuries due to sharp instruments, respiratory tract infections, and body aches. They also remain uneducated, 42 percent never having attended school and 58 percent having dropped out.

In May 1994, the Asian-American Free Labour Institute (AAFLI) investigated five carpet factories in the Lahore area and found child labour in four of them. None of these factories was a "parent-child" operation. The AAFLI report found that carpet exporters did not deny the existence of child labour in the carpet industry and acknowledged that the bonded labour system or "peshgi" is regularly practiced, even though it violates the 1992 Bonded Labour Abolition Act.

The 1992 UNICEF-Punjab report details the conditions of child labour in the carpet weaving industry in Punjab. The study surveyed 10 villages and interviewed 175 children in carpet weaving centers in Punjab. It concluded that carpet weaving is done mostly by children. Eighty-three percent of the survey were male children, but access to predominantly female carpet weaving centers was restricted. The study found the earnings depended on the number of knots per square foot.

The maximum wage was 40 rupees (approximately $1.50) per day. The majority of the children 19 worked between 9 and 10 hours per day with a one hour break. They ate three meals a day, consisting of bread/rice, dal (lentils) or vegetables. Fifty-one percent of the children expressed dissatisfaction with their jobs.

Ninety-four percent of the children suffered one or more work-related illness or injuries, which included fingertip and hand injuries due to handling sharp knives, as well as physical abuse. Finally, the report states that contrary to expectation, conditions of work for children weaving at homes were found to be no better and often even more detrimental to the child's welfare than for those working in private workshops. Parents tended to keep their children at the loom for longer hours and the working environment at home was on the whole not as well ventilated nor adequately lit.

Carpet manufacturers often avoid labour regulations by subcontracting to "thekedars," or middlemen, who control several looms set up in the weavers homes scattered throughout the countryside. Since factories employing less than 10 workers are not covered by most labour laws, large carpet enterprises have divided up into smaller units.

The Human Rights Commission of Pakistan states that work units in rural areas have more child labour than urban areas. In these village units, the children are mostly girls, some only six or seven years old; boys are barely eight. Working conditions are poor, lighting and ventilation inadequate, hygienic conditions substandard, and the work area hot and humid. Workers complain of coughs and sickness. The workers usually work 10-hour days, with no holidays and are paid on a piece-rate basis. Child workers pay is as low as 10 rupees (approximately 37 cents) per day; teenagers, however, earned 20-30 rupees (74 cents to $1.13) per day, and can even get 50 to 75 rupees ($1.87 to $2.81) per day for superior quality carpets.

UNICEF describes the work as painful and unhealthy; children sit in cramped positions for long periods of time, breathing wool dust, working under poor lighting conditions, straining their eyes and working with chemical dyes. The children also develop spinal deformities.

Human Rights Watch/Asia notes many of the children in the carpet industry are bonded. In some situations, parents force the children to work. In other situations, children are separated from their families and kept in small buildings which house several carpet looms. Human Rights Watch/Asia interviewed several children in such factories who were beaten frequently and rarely allowed to return home. It was noted that if the children attempted to escape they were forcibly returned to the looms with the help of the local police.

The United States imports surgical instruments from Pakistan, especially from the Sialkot area. Although there 28 are no comprehensive studies on child labour in the production of surgical instruments for export, the International Textile, Garment and Leather Workers Federation claims that children between the ages of 10 and 15 years spend eight hours a day grinding and sanding surgical instruments. The Government of Pakistan's chart on child labour compiled by the provincial governments in 1993 shows 3,670 children under 17 working in this industry. The South Asian Coalition Against Child Servitude also maintains that there are thousands of children working in this industry.

According to the South Asian Coalition on Child Servitude, children are working in the sporting goods industry in Sialkot and adjoining towns and villages. The Pakistan Human Rights Commission found no child labour in factories that supply international sporting goods firms, but children have been found stitching soccer balls for export in cottage-level family units. Children constitute approximately 20 percent to 25 percent of the work force in this sector, and range in age from 12 to 15 years. They work five to six hours per day. The wages are either fixed at 800-900 rupees per month (approximately $30-33) or on a piecework basis at 20 rupees (approximately 75 cents) per football). A child can usually stitch three footballs (soccer balls) a day.

National Child Labour Laws of Pakistan

In Pakistan, a "child" is defined as a person younger than fifteen. The legal minimum age for employment is 14 for shops and commerce, industry, and work at sea, and 15 for mines and on railways. The Constitution. The Government of Pakistan twice agreed to provide information to the Child Labour Study 39 on the number of prosecutions and convictions carried out under the Bonded Labour Act and the Employment of Children Act. To date, no information has been received.

The Bonded Labour (Abolition) Act declares all customs, traditions, practices, contracts or agreements concerning bonded labour, whether entered into or in operation before or after the effective date of the legislation, void and inoperative. Any obligations on the part of the bonded labourer to repay any bonded debt were cancelled and no suit could be brought for the recovery of such a debt. Special provisions in this Act provide for setting up of Vigilance Committees to advise the district administration on matters relating to the effective implementation of freed bonded labourers, application of the law, and providing the bonded labourers with necessary assistance. The penalties for violating this law are imprisonment from two to five years and/or a fine of 50,000 rupees. According to the

U.S. Department of State, little progress was made in 1993 in the industries employing bonded labourers.

The Employment of Children Act 1991 prohibits the employment of children in certain occupations and regulates their conditions of work. No child is allowed to work over-time or during the night.

An earlier law prohibited the employment of children in the following industries: bidi (cigarette) making; carpet making; cement manufacturing (including bagging of cement); cloth dyeing, printing, and weaving; manufacturing of matches, explosives, and fireworks; mica cutting and splitting; shellac manufacture; soap manufacture; tanning; and wood cleaning. The 1991 law added the following industries: shoe-making, leather, power looms, fishing, glass, garments, precious stones, metal and wood handicrafts, furniture, and paper.

Enforcement of child labour laws in Pakistan is hampered by the lack of manpower and expertise in the Department of Labour and a general acceptance of child labour, according to Professor Omar Noman. Pakistan has appointed a Task Force for Labour to consider improving enforcement mechanisms and increasing penalties. It also directed provincial governments to provide data on the number of cases prosecuted and fines imposed under existing child labour and bonded labour laws.

However, according to the Government of Pakistan, only one case of bonded labour was found in the Punjab province. A National Committee on the Rights of the Child has been established within the federal government specifically to monitor enforcement and protection issues related to child workers.

The Constitution of Pakistan, in Articles 37 (b) & (c), declares public policy to: remove illiteracy and provide free and compulsory secondary education within the minimum possible period [and to] make technical and professional education generally available and higher education equally accessible to all on the basis of merit. Among Asian countries, Pakistan ranks 27 out of 28 countries in its literacy rate of 26.2 percent. Despite a 1962 law requiring each province to designate areas where primary education is compulsory, none of the provinces have complied. The Government of Pakistan recently noted, however, that the Punjab government has decided to provide compulsory primary education free of cost to every child.

According to the U.S. State Department Country Reports on Human Rights Practices for 1993, schools are available in most localities, but they have very limited staff, space, and resources. Government figures show that less than 65 percent of children between five and nine attend primary school, and more than 50 percent of those drop out before finishing their primary education. Many observers believe that even these figures are optimistic.

In its 1993 Manifesto, the Pakistan People's Party stated that contract labour, bonded labour, and child labour will be abolished. Pakistan claims to have taken concrete steps to protect the rights of the child and to eliminate child labour in all sectors of the economy, including the carpet industry. Secretary of Labour, Sultan Hameed, maintains that the present government has demonstrated the "political will at the highest level" to address the issue. He also stated that the federal government held a meeting with the provincial governments and has asked for periodic progress reports from the provinces on prosecutions and convictions of child labour violations.

According to the Labour Secretary, the Labour and Commerce ministries are considering setting up an agency to certify that products manufactured for export are not made by child labour. The government would like to identify a foreign non-governmental organization to act as the certifying authority to lend more credibility to the process. Recently, the Government signed a Memorandum of Understanding with the International Labour Organization to cooperate in establishing a national program on child labour. It has also worked with UNICEF in preparing studies and hosting a conference on child labour.

In other efforts to address the problem of child labour, the Pakistan Carpet Manufacturers & Exporters Association (PCMEA) has suggested the formation of a Committee for the Eradication of Child Labour (FECL), comprised of members from the PCMEA, government agencies, non-governmental organizations, and human rights organizations. The objective would be to coordinate efforts to erase all illegal and exploitative forms of child labour by setting up individual welfare projects which would provide primary education, basic medical facilities, conduct surveys, and issue labels certifying that a carpet was free of illegal child labour.

UNICEF has conducted several studies in Pakistan on child labour and publicizes the hazards of child labour in many public settings. The Bonded Labour Liberation Front promotes education for child workers through their program, "Struggle Against Slavery Through Education." It has set up 122 small schools with

5000 freed bonded children between 6 and 12 years. The BLLF plans to have 200 schools by the end of 1994.

In July 1993, the Kamalayan Development Centre (KDC) and the National Bureau of 5 Investigation (NBI) raided a sardine factory in Navotas, and found seven children under 17 years of age working in sweatshop conditions. Children in the sardine factories filled cans with sliced fish parts.

In May 1994, the Philippine Department of Labour and Employment (DOLE) and the NBI raided this sardine factory again, as it continued to operate despite an order to shut down. Labour officials and NBI agents reportedly found about a hundred 'exploited' children working in the Sardine factory during the second raid. The child workers, whose ages range from 10 to 17 years, have not been paid regularly or sufficiently. According to Labour Secretary Nieves Confessor, the company, which was ordered to close down by the NBI, has continued to operate because its owner is being protected by a local official of the Philippine National Police.

According to the ILO, fishing corporations employ children between 12 and 14 years of age, who spend 10 months a year out at sea, swimming and diving to a depth of 100 feet to attach nets to coral reefs. These children have no protective swimwear and are subjected to needlefish and shark attacks, and diseases like typhoid.

The Working Women Association came into existence as a response to meet the housing and other needs of young professional women of federal capital. The Association established its first working women hostel in 1975 on self help basis and organised first ever women mountaineering expedition in 1978 with the help of Alpine club of Pakistan.

The Association got itself registered with Federal government of Pakistan in 1987 as a non-profit social welfare organisation in order to do contract researches for funds generation.

Association has come long way in its networking and other development activities for girls and women. Currently it has its membership spread in all the four provinces and enjoys the observer status with UN Economics and Social Development division New Your. Its main functions consist of networking, holding of workshops and conferences and doing research on critical issues facing working women. It also runs some projects of working girls Education and Skill Enhancement besides working women hostels.

Aims and objectives

— To enhance the status of working women in the urban as well as rural areas through recognition of their economic role.

— To enhance the consciousness level and self-awareness amongst Pakistani women in general and working women in particular.

— To encourage women to take up job to raise the socioeconomic standard of self, family and nation.

— To undertake socio-cultural studies which determine and define the role of women in national development.

— To highlight the economic role of women relating to their participation in household work, farm activities. Wages and employment in the country.

Services

In order to meet these objectives, the following services are provided by the association.

— To provide hostel and other support facilities to working women to facilitate them in their job.

— To hole seminars, lectures and workshops to raise the consciousness level of women.

— To carry out researches and exploratory studies on the needs of special categories of women e.g. professional women, white collar.

— Workers in public and private sectors and women with special needs.

— To establish education and skill enhancement Center for girls and women at grass roots.

— To organise healthy recreational activities like mountaineering, tracking, participation in national and international conferences. A contingent of 25 women members of TWWA participated in Beijing NGO Conference. Two members of TWWA participated in World Conference as observers.

Research

The Association has been undertaking research in following areas:

— The data collection surveys and policy studies on development of women and girls in urban and rural areas.

— The attitude and impact surveys of special

populations.

— Joint Ventures with other consulting agencies in multinational projects for social impact human resource development and environment.

— The monitoring and evaluation studies of development projects

— The studies to quantify the economic contribution of women relating to their participation on household, farm activities, handicraft and employment sector studies are carried out.

— Action research to sensitise the society regarding the plight of rural girls and women in domestic services.

Training

The Association promotes and carries out training programs, which prepare women for non-traditional occupations and there by expand their job opportunities. Human resource development, environment, income generation skills and teachers training programs are carried out regularly.

SPARC's Mission

"SPARC's mission is to speak...and ... act for the youngest, the weakest, the least empowered members of our society, our Children"

SPARC seeks to:

Protect every child from work that threatens his or her

health, education or development.

— Encourage the government to set minimum ages for employment and regulate working conditions.

— Safeguard every child from all forms of exploitation.

— Oppose sexual exploitation and abuse of children, including prostitution and involvement in pornography.

— Oppose children's use of narcotic and psychotropic drugs, and oppose the involvement of children in their production or distribution.

— Advance every child's right to education.

— Lobby the governments to primary education is tree and compulsory

— Endeavour that different forms of secondary education and accessible to every child.

— Safeguard that higher education must be made available to all on the basis of capacity.

— Establish and help develop education institutions.

SPARC's Aspirations

SPARC strives to function as a catalyst for change by introducing new ideas and new ways of doing things in the society.

SPARC aspires to

— Protect the right of every child to express his or her opinion freely and to have that opinion taken into account in any mater affecting the child.

— Protect the child's right to freedom of thought, conscience and religion, subject to appropriated parental guidance.

— Protect the right of every child to join or form associations.

— Oppose child abuse, and stand for establishment and promotion of appropriate social programs for the prevention of abuse and the treatment of victims.

— Promote every child's right to protection from interference with privacy, family, home and correspondence.

— Prevent the sale, trafficking and abduction of children.

— Provide appropriate assistance to parents in child raising.

— Champion every child's right to leisure, play and participation in cultural and artistic activities; and to help develop recreational activities for children.

— Defend children against all forms of discrimination and to take positive actions to promote their rights.

— Promote every child's right to a standard of living adequate for his or her physical, mental, spiritual, moral and social development.

— Influence the mass media to disseminate information beneficial to the child, and to protect the child from harmful materials.

— Defend the right of every child to express his or her views, obtain information, make ideas or information known, regardless of frontiers.

SPARC's Plan

— Advocate the rights of the child.

— Keep public effectively informed of issues relating to children through mass media.

— Lobby for legislation.

— Monitor arrangements to ensure that policies and programs for children are successfully carried out.

— Mobilise public opinion for the rights of the child.

— Undertake research, analysis and investigation into issues relating to children and disseminate widely the findings of such research.

Formulate specific legal provisions to solve child-related issues.

Take-up children's issues with the concerned authorities, and urge them to take appropriate timely actions.

SPARC, as a member of IBFAN (International Baby Food Action Network), subscribes to its Manila Declaration (1989) which Called for Action all concerned people to join efforts to:

Ensure full Implementation of the International Code of Marketing of Breastmilk Substitutes, related resolutions and strong national codes.

Pressure corporations to abide by the International Code and national legislation and to stop immediately the practice of giving free or low-cost supplies to hospitals. The boycott of corporations and products is the most powerful weapon people have.

Support health professionals to eliminate industry pressures that interfere with their decisions and actions.

Improve maternity leave, social support for mothers and facilities for working mothers.

Promote breast feeding as the safest and best means of infant feeding, even in situations of disaster, through community actions, education and training.

11

Child Workers in Nepal

There are an estimated three million working children in Nepal. Most working children in Nepal are in the agricultural sector and in the export-oriented carpet industry. The percentage of child workers in the carpet industry varies from an official estimate of 0.76 percent to a non-governmental organization estimate of 50 percent. There are also reports of children working in the garment industry, "thanka" painting, and in handicrafts, but the extent of child labour in these industries and their direct link to exports is not documented.

In 1992, Nepal exported approximately $17 million worth of carpets to the United States. In Nepal, the carpet business is classified as a tax-exempt cottage industry. A substantial number of children under the age of 14 work in Nepal's carpet industry.

In the beginning of 1993, the Government of Nepal inspected 23 carpet factories, estimating that nine percent of the industry's work force were children. Another government survey, carried out in July 1993 on 419 registered and unregistered industries in the Kathmandu Valley, found that of the 23, 418 workers, 178 were children below the age of 14. The American Embassy in Kathmandu reported that the July 1993 survey lacked credibility as many factories refused entry to labour inspectors, while others did not fill out the forms, and still others lied about the ages of child workers.

The Embassy also noted that the 1992 Child Workers in Nepal Concerned Centre (CWIN) study reported a figure of 50 percent child labour based on a relatively large 1992 study, as compared to the nine percent figure mentioned by the government in its first survey based on smaller sample. Furthermore, a report by the Asian-American Free Labour Institute (AAFLI) contends that the government finding of only 178 child workers was uniformly greeted with skepticism.

According to the 1992 CWIN study, major districts for carpet factories are Kathmandu, Lalitpur, Rasuwa, Dhading, Nuwakot, Kavrepalanchowk, Sindhupalchowk, Dolka, Ramechhap, Kavrepalanchowk, Illiam, Jhapa, Sankhuwasabha, Terhathum, Panchthar, Dhankutta, Bhojpur, Morang, Solukhumbu, Okhaldunga, Khotang, Sindhuli, and Chitwan.

During visits to carpet factories, Marcia Lieberman found children sleeping in crowded rooms with 12 a water tap and latrine outside. International Child Labour Hearing, U.S. Department of Labour (Statement of Marcia Lieberman) [hereinafter Testimony of Lieberman]. Lieberman found that children pay 200 rupees per month (approximately $4.54) for rent 13 which is paid to the factory owner. Testimony of Lieberman. CWIN's study found more than 95 percent of the children sleep on factory premises while the rest rent rooms outside the premises. About 28 percent of the children sleep on the floor, without mattresses.

AAFLI researched 17 carpet factories in Nepal, interviewed over 400 children, and found at least 30 percent of the workers to be under 14 years of age. In 1992, CWIN conducted a survey of carpet factories, finding 3,322 children below the age of sixteen. Based on its study, CWIN estimated that 150,000 children work in some 2,000 factories in Nepal. CWIN found that most child workers are between 11 and 14 years old with about 7.8 percent below 10 years of age. Most children in the carpet industry are wool spinners and weavers, some also dye and wash carpets.

In 1992, CWIN found that over 47 percent of the children come to the factories alone or in groups with a "naike" or labour recruiter. These children, sometimes as
young as five years old, work long hours in cramped 11
and stuffy rooms or sheds which lack air and light. Some
child workers sleep in another shack or a "garage- 12
like" room with no windows for which they have to pay rent. Children also pay for their food.

Child workers in the carpet industry indicate that they work very long hours. Marcia Lieberman, a freelance journalist, interviewed a girl in Kathmandu, who looked to be 12 years old, knotting carpets from 7 a.m. to 10 p.m. The foreman said he too worked those same hours. In a visit to another factory, Lieberman interviewed a 10-year old girl who worked from 7 a.m. to 11 p.m. or midnight. CWIN's 1992 study also found children working an average of 15 hours a day.

In a visit to centers for street children in June 1994, Lieberman interviewed a 17 year old boy who worked for nine months in a carpet factory without pay, even though he was promised 600 rupees per month. Another 15-year old boy stated that he worked for three years in a carpet factory without pay. Many of the children (approximately 48 percent) had no idea how much they earned. Telephone Interview with Marcia Lieberman by Department of Labour official.

More than 15 percent of the rape incidents registered in the police department are reported to involve carpet workers. Recently carpet factories have attracted the attention of the media with the disclosure that many of them run a side business of trafficking young girls across the border to India, where they are sold to brothels.

According to CWIN's 1992 study, after the training period the naike may or may not pay the child workers. Child weavers generally work in unhealthy conditions. According to CWIN's 1992 report which extensively documents children's health in the carpet industry, health hazards include swollen knuckles, arthritis, eye strain, and lung diseases. Moreover, 32 percent of those interviewed were frequently sexually abused by male co-workers, naikes, and factory managers. CWIN maintains that among the 5,000 to 7,000 Nepali girls between 10 and 20 years old who are sold to brothels in India ever year, many are trafficked via carpet factories. Many young carpet girls in Kathmandu are also forced into prostitution.

A 1993 study by the International Centre for Integrated Mountain Development in Kathmandu reported cases of young girls and boys that have no choice but to render services to a factory under the constant threat of breach of contract and harassment. CWIN estimates that seven to eight percent of the carpet children surveyed are working to pay debts incurred by their parents, which ranges from 100 to 15,000 rupees.

According to the 1994 AAFLI report, none of the children surveyed were "bonded," meaning that they were being held against their will to pay off a family debt. Of the children interviewed, 100 percent were from rural villages outside Kathmandu, brought either by a naike or some relative.

The children were not aware of the amount of payment made by the naikes to their parents, but this is widely understood to be the situation. The naikes pay some amount in the range of $40-$100 to the families to take the children to Kathmandu to work in the carpet factories. The primary benefit to the parents or family is the initial payment from the naike, as few of the children reported sending money to their families.

According to the State Department Country Reports, this Act calls for the establishment of Child Welfare Committees and orphanages. Many of these facilities are not yet in place.

National Child Labour Laws of Nepal

According to the ILO, Nepal's law establishes a minimum age for employment of children at 14 years. The Constitution of Nepal stipulates that children shall not be employed in factories, mines, or similar hazardous work. The Constitution also forbids slavery, bonded labour, and the trafficking of individuals. Other important child labour laws include the Children's Rights and Welfare Act 1992. This Act defines child as a person who has not reached the age of 16. Article 17 prohibits the employment of children who have not attained the age of 14 years. This legislation prohibits forced labour, requires equal remuneration for equal work, and prohibits employment of children in hazardous work.

Child labourers are entitled to leisure for a half-hour for every three hours of work, and one day off every week. The Labour Act 27 of 1992 prohibits employment of minors under 14 years of age and regulates the work hours of 'minors' between the ages of 14 to 18. This Act applies to children working in urban industries and provides for labour inspectors in each district.

The Nepal Department of Labour has a 'spotty' enforcement record. In 1993, the Labour Ministry fined 23 factories for employing children. Overall, however, the government's action has been inadequate to reduce the incidence of child labour. The Labour Secretary of Nepal states that there are 11 regional labour offices throughout Nepal and approximately 22 officers with responsibilities encompassing occupational safety and health, industrial relations, negotiations, training, and education, as well as the enforcement of the child labour law. The Secretary stated that in reality, inspectors do not look for child labour. And although factories were 'penalized'

In late April 1994, a German television show on child labour in the 35 carpet industry allegedly caused a cancellation of carpet orders, leading to a flurry of industry debate and dissension. As a result, AAFLI reports that in one town, Phaperbari (Makawanpur District), 50 percent of children previously working in carpet factories have been fired from their jobs and have returned home. AAFLI further alleges that previous interest by factory owners to set up model schools for child workers has dissipated.

In the meantime, a small group of carpet factory owners plan to establish a certification system for child-free carpets sooner and separate from the NASPEC program. Letter from Asian-American Free Labour Institute-Nepal to International Child Labour Study.

Education is not compulsory in Nepal. The government has a stated policy of providing free education through the 6th grade, but this policy reportedly is not implemented. Anti-Slavery International and Child Workers in Nepal (CWIN) states that the government offers free tuition and textbooks and tuition for children in grades one to three, and grades four and five for children in rural areas. Parents, however, still have to provide stationary, which can amount to rupees 200 (approximately $4.54) per child per year. This is a substantial financial burden, especially on poor families. Moreover, access to schools is limited, especially in rural areas, and most schools have no latrines or drinking water.

Responding to the threat of an international ban on carpets made by child labour, the government, on-governmental organizations, and the private sector have expressed interest in creating a "child labour free" certification to be used in the carpet industry. According to the Minister of Commerce, the Rugmark certification will be implemented by the end of 1994. Carpet manufacturers, non-governmental organizations, and the Nepal-German Chamber of Commerce and Industry have formed the National Society for Protection of the Environment and Children (NASPEC) to eliminate child labour in Nepal and rehabilitate child workers.

NASPEC will work to eliminate child labour in all sectors, but initially will focus on the carpet industry. It plans to establish a "Producers Group" to implement a program to certify that carpets are produced without child labour. The group's first stated task is to establish an independent agency to inspect carpet factories. Carpet manufacturers who do not employ children or receive any materials produced by children under 14, and who pay at least the minimum wage, will be eligible to receive an internationally recognized "rugmark" certification to affix to their carpets. NASPEC also pledges to establish a non-governmental organization to support the health, education, and welfare of child workers who will lose their jobs.

The non-governmental organization, Child Workers in Nepal (CWIN), has been conducting a series of studies on children working in Nepal and is active on child rights. The International Textile, Garment, and Leather Workers Federation alleges that children 10 and 11 years old are sick and deformed from years of sniffing glue in a shoe factory.

The Pakistan Labour Force Survey put the number of child workers in the age group 10 to 14 at two million. The Pakistan Institute of Development Economics maintains that two million is a gross underestimate because a) of serious under-reporting due to the fact that child labour is illegal, and b) working children below 10 years are not included.

UNICEF study estimated the total number of children at not less than 8 million. Pakistan's Secretary of Labour, Mr. Sultan Hameed, stated that the UNICEF figure was "on the high side," but appeared to accept the figure as being in the general range. Interview with Sultan Hameed, Pakistan Secretary of Labour, by Department of Labour official. Economists at the Pakistan Institute of Development Economics estimate there are 19 million working children, 7 million below the age of ten, and 12 million between 10 and 14 years old.

The American Embassy-Islamabad, questioned the 19 million figure given the fact that the total labor force in Pakistan is 33 million (or 29.8 million according to the World Factbook). The Embassy observed that the 19 million figure "seems high unless the number of workers in the labor force is widely underestimated." Unclassified memorandum from American Embassy-Islamabad to International Child Labor Study. Child Workers in Nepal (CWIN) is an activist non-governmental social organisation for the child. Concerned with the rights, dignity and development of children working and living in the most difficult circumstances, CWIN works for the social emancipation of children from servitude. In brief, CWIN is:

— The first child's rights organisation in Nepal
— Initiator of alliance building work for the Rights of the Child
— Is a non-profit making initiative to strengthen and empower the rights of the child movement with a mission of "action through advocacy"
— Is an independent and non-partisan social movement against child labour exploitation and child servitude
— Is a solidarity in action rather than a charity institution for the welfare, development and dignity of children, especially those at risk
— Is a community conscientisation and empowerment process in order to make children a reliable source of hope for future prosperity
— Is a research/information dissemination, training/education/advocacy and development programme for child rights and child development
— Is an action for children with children.

Establishment of CWIN

CWIN was formed by a group of university-student activists. They aspired to raise the issue of child labour and child rights for the social emancipation of children from all forms of exploitation, and for the integration of child's rights into the broader social movement for freedom, peace and equality. They decided to start a concern group to help protect children living and working in the most difficult circumstances.

To hold the torch to forward the child's rights movement, however, there was a complete dearth of appropriate philosophy and vision. Children, the neglected majority, did not have much standing on the adult dominated society. Welfare and service for the children were merely viewed as charity and had conservative approaches. The initiators of the CWIN wanted to change that perception owing to their knowledge of the international declarations and convention on the rights of the child, which recognised the child as an integral component of the society with their inherent rights to survival, well being, protection and freedom. Children are to be nurtured with the best the mankind has to offer and need special treatment because of their vulnerable disposition.

Objectives of CWIN

Strongly believing in and supporting the UN declaration on the Rights of the Child and UN Convention on the Rights of the Child, CWIN aims to build up and empower a nation wide social conscientisation movement, so that children of Nepal and elsewhere my be able to enjoy a dignified childhood.

Specific Objectives

Work for the immediate abolition of child bonded labour/children in servitude and for the progressive elimination of child labour in general. Promote and protect the rights of the child with a mission of "action through advocacy. Keep abreast of the realities of working children and children living at risk through regular action research, lobbying, empowerment activities and solidarity in action. Organise both local and international concerned groups and campaign against all forms of child servitude, including child labour, trafficking and sale of children, child marriage, child-bonded labour and all forms of crime against children. Formulate and conduct basic child development and support activities for underprivileged children at both local and national levels.

Vision

CWIN recognises the Child as an inherent component of society deserving the best that it has to offer. CWIN believes that every child has an inherent right to justice, peace and freedom, and deserves access to all fundamental human rights including education, health care, love respect, security and protection. CWIN recognises child labour as a form of socio-economic exploitation of children covering the denial of basic education, long working hours, under or no payment, forced labour, and health hazardous working conditions.

Mission

Develop and establish a model of "Action Through Advocacy" for the social conscientisation movement on the rights of the child based in the Nepali context. Develop and establish a model of socialisation center for children working and living in the most difficult circumstances. Develop and establish a model for the rehabilitation of the children at risk through community conscientisation and Family Reunion Process

Initiate Alliance for the rights of the child

Thereby develop an alternative movement for the rights of the child through a sustainable, self-reliant and participatory way.

Lobbying, campaigning & social conscientisation on rights of the child, social mobilisation, child's rights forums, publication and media sensitisation, and production of campaign materials.

Child Rights Forum

The child rights forum is the forum of children for children to contribute in the broader movement of the rights of the child.

Action Research & Training

About 30-action research, studies and survey studies undertaken, published and disseminated publicly.

Information maintained on 150 child-related titles. Collection of about 2000 books and reports, 205 different periodicals, 40 different newspapers, 200 videos, about 5000 articles, photographs on 40 different titles, slides on 25 titles and 150 different posters on children and related issues.

Concern for Children and Environment

After the restoration of the Multi–Party "Democracy" system in Nepal in 1990, Nepal's government ratified the UN Convention on the Rights of the Child. The new constitution of Nepal, in conjunction with the UN Convention, banned any form of child slavery in Nepal. We now, have the Children's Rights Act 1992 and the newly amended Labour Act of 1991 in addition. Both Acts strongly prohibit any form of child labour and/or child exploitation. However, despite the existence of these child rights protection acts, millions of children are still forced to work under slave-like conditions for their day to day survival.

Concern for Children and Environment, Nepal (CONCERN-Nepal) is a non-profit and non-political organisation whose principal purpose is to advocate the general situation of children and cause of child labour in Nepal. It also aims to highlight the cause and effect of the environmental impact on children's over-all physical and mental development and well being.

The concept of CONCERN was conceived and developed by a group of child rights activists and renowned environmentalists fully dedicated to the alleviation of the present harsh situation of children living under difficult circumstances. CONCERN'S emphasis lies in action-oriented programmes and is fully determined to work for the physical, mental, social and overall development of deprived and destitute children.

CONCERN is undertaking this process as part of a social movement for the sake of liberating children from all forms of exploitation, discrimination and oppression. CONCERN also recognises that this is not an easy task and will face several obstacles throughout the movement.

Objectives

CONCERN is concerned with both children and the environment, and as such it aims to:

— raise awareness among people of all ages regarding the situation of Nepalese children through different mediums;

— abolish all forms of child exploitation and protect their rights, welfare and dignity;

— encourage policy makers to develop long term and short term plans for the welfare of children living under difficult circumstances;

— educate people through in-depth observation and research studies;

— emphasise local people's empowerment and sustainability for independence and self-reliance;

— study the magnitude of the problems generated from the degraded environmental impact on children's health;

— launch action-oriented programmes for the alleviation and improvement of the child carpet workers living in the highest risk situations;

— conduct a variety of activities for the protection of children's health caused by the degradation and destruction of the environment, polluted water and polluted habitation;

— Emphasise the preservation of nature and necessity of pure drinking water.

Action Programmes

Nation-wide advocation of the rights of the child; highlighting the plights of children' developing action strategies for practical application. Monitoring and organising national and international pressure groups; formulating bilateral, collateral and multilateral campaign programmes against all forms of child oppression. Conducting rescue and rehabilitation programmes for the children living under the most difficult circumstances, such as street children, squatter children and girl children at risk. Opening a resource library center, which would benefit students, teachers and researchers. Conducting community awareness and development activities regarding environmental conservation and children related issues in urban and rural areas of the country. Conducting environmental education programmes for both campus and school level students.

Informal Sector Service Center (INSEC) was founded in 1988 in order to cater human right services to the grass-roots people and general public. INSEC is an independent, non-profit-making and non-partisan human rights organisation. It is based in Kathmandu and has branches in all regional centers of Nepal.

Protection and promotion of human rights through advocacy, lobby, training, education, information, campaigns and projects and national, regional and grass-roots levels.

Specific Objectives and Regular Activities

Monitoring human rights through INSEC District representatives and Fact Finding Missions.

Catering 'information for awareness' through Human Rights Year Book, Situation Report and publications.

Catering 'human rights education' through programs conducted by 40 district networks within Nepal, bi-monthly human rights campaigns and radio programmes.

Intervention in human rights law-making and human rights mechanisms through seminars, workshops and mass meetings.

Realisation of women's rights implementing the decisions of "women's forums", specifically implementing the Pasand Lhamu Pledge of the first Women's National Assembly through "gender justice programmes" based on the Pledge

Combating against all forms of slavery with a special focus on Damaiyas (Bonded labourers in Agriculture) implementing the decision of the first National conference of Kamaiyas, facilitating the activities of Kamaiya Liberation Forum formed by the Conference.

Catering formal and non-formal education for out-of-school children of Kamaiyas.

Conducting action researches on various social topics.

Maintaining documentation of human rights violations and human rights bibliography to facilitate researchers and students.

Standing for solidarity actions for democracy, national liberation and human rights around the globe.

General protection of human rights education programs targeted at the 'untouchable' community in 15 districts.

Underprivileged Children's Educational Program (UCEP)

Underprivileged Children's Educational Program (UCEP) was incepted in 1978 as a national Non-governmental Organisation. UCEP-Nepal was subsequently established after the successful program of UCEP Bangladesh, one with an international image. The objective of UCEP is to provide primary education to underprivileged children and then further to job oriented vocational skills training at its complex in Sano Thimi Technical School. The main target group is the working and street children.

UCEP was established in Dhaka Bangladesh in 1972 by the late Allan Cheyne, a New Zealander with the objective of providing opportunities for street and working children to attend school, learn technical skills and enhance their income generating capability. UCEP extended its program to Nepal in 1978. After conducting a case study of working children in the Kathmandu Valley, five schools were started in 1980 followed by Sanothimi Technical School in 1983 with financial aid and technical assistance from the Danish International Development Agency – DANIDA. The program, which saw over 1500 skilled technicians in the technical sector and over 5000 student in non-formal education sector being produced, was for various reasons terminated in June 1993.

Objectives

— To provide special school facilities to the working and street children.

— To impart vocational and technical training in different trades to the underprivileged Nepal children to make them self-reliant, and enable them to live a respectable and dignified life.

— To raise their awareness about family well-being democratic values and norms.

— To assist those who have completed education and skills training at UCEP to find suitable employment or help establish links with potential employers.

— To disseminate the problems of Underprivileged children of Nepal and to conduct/implement appropriate programs.

Target group

UCEP-Nepal works for underprivileged street and working children up to 14 years of age who have previously not received any education or are school dropouts in the stage of their primary education. The major categories of such underprivileged children are :

— Direct worker: those who are directly involved in some kind of manual job such as waiters, day labours, house servants, garment worker and carpet weavers.

— Non-working street children including beggars.

— Indirect workers: children who help parents in household works, traditional handicraft/farming etc.

Jagaran group is a team of former street children working for street children. Jagaran group was formed as a result of a group of street children who worked together on and off on street drama with support from Arohan drama group (a professional actors' group) in the early 1990s. As the founding members of Jagaran Group expressed interest in forming an independent children's street acting group, Ajuni (Development Communications) Constancy supported them with the necessary training on development work and basic organisation development.

In early 1997 Jagaran was formed with a loose structure, getting together and performing street drama in schools and at the offices of development organisations. The Group then decided to seriously start gathering support for starting a full time project for helping street children and preventing new children from joining the streets. The group decided on starting a scrap collection center in order to be a contact point for street children – majority of who scavenge the garbage sites and sell recyclable items at scrap collection centers. The Group felt convinced that this would be a good way to keep in touch with the "target group" and also to slowly become self-dependent.

Objective

— To prevent new children from becoming street

children.

- To help build self-respect among street children through constructive activities.
- To guide street children towards a positive attitude towards life so that they can adjust in their home and society.
- To perform the 'pity life of the street children' to the school children so that they can understand the real life of street children.
- To rehabilitate those who are in interested to returning home.
- To inform the INGOs/NGOs about the real situation of the street children.

Activities

Establish a scrap collection center for sustainable income and also an easy access to reach street children.

- Provide welfare including medical facilities.
- Healthy food canteen for street children
- Shelter for street children.
- Street drama.

Group for International Solidarity

Founded in 1990, Group International Solidarity (GRINSO-Nepal) is committed towards peaceful neighbourhood, equitable social system and respectful life all over the globe. GRINSO-Nepal understands that

Human Rights is indivisible, inter-dependent and universal, and is indifferent from democracy and people's development. GRINSO-Nepal in inspired by the strength of group actions, and therefore aims to work with other organisations at national, regional and global level dedicated for the cause of peace, equity, human rights and development. It is committed to be an active partner in the above process in a formal/informal global network environment.

In the context of changed political environment and based on its experience as a Human Rights activist, since 1994, GRINSO-Nepal is also supporting grassroots, development action and community initiatives in Nepal. Organised communities have become imperatives for the consolidation of democracy, people's development and promotion of Human Rights. Therefore, GRINSO-Nepal works very closely with sustained group action and empowerment of marginalised and deprived people. It also works as a support institution to community based activists, group and local organisations and helps them in capacity building, training and service delivery.

Programme Areas

— Global support for Human Rights and Democracy

— Joining hands in arranging all kind of support to initiatives and movements for democracy and Human Rights in any part of the globe,

— Advocating and mobilising people and people based organisations for the promotion and protection of Human Rights.

— Working as a vigilant organisation for the detection of Human Rights violations in Nepal and mobilising international support against such violations

- Empowerment women through social awareness, economic independence and local women group,
- Safeguarding and supporting the interest of the marginalised and indigenous people,
- Supporting people's access and control over opportunities and natural resources.

Capacity Building

Strengthening formal/informal networks and forums working for the people,

Providing information and training support to activists, groups, communities and organisations working for the protection and promotion of Human Rights in Nepal.

- Preparing and inspiring activists groups, communities and organisations for social development and change,
- Institutional support for community action and service delivery.

Elements of Strategy

Programme implementation strategies of GRINSO-Nepal are founded on the following elements:

- Using Human Rights/Women's Rights and Child Rights as a tool and norms in the pursuit of people's development.
- Assisting communities/women to organise and

inform themselves and to work as a group for common future

— Strengthening partner organisations/formations/actions and individuals dedicated for the people.

Action in Progress/proposed

Integrated Programme for the Liberation of Bonded Labour in Nepal

— Tharu Women's Project.

— Research on Human Rights Violation in Tharu community (indigenous population of Nepal)

— Monitoring of Economic, Social and Cultural Rights.

— Development Works on Untouchable Community

— Human Rights Net (on e-mail) in South Asia

— Seminars/Workshops/Training of trainers

— Solidarity Campaign

Rural Reconstruction Nepal (RRN)

RRN envisions a world where all human beings enjoy opportunities for their progress with justice, equality, peace and prosperity for all citizens.

RRN has a mission to improve the lives of the poorest rural people, particularly rural women, small farmers and the most disadvantaged and socially oppressed strata of Nepalese society through providing them opportunities for their own socio-economic empowerment. RRN aims to empower the people so that they can attain self-reliance and confidence for long-term sustainable development. It believes that not temporary relief from poverty but the permanent release through releasing the people's boundless potentials which enhance people's productive and organising abilities for their own development. Empowering People's Organizations as the core implementation instrument, the development activities RRN initiates are very much integrated and community based.

The Objectives of RRN are to:

— conceptualize, develop and execute income generating livelihood programmes,

— create awareness in diverse sectors such as health, education, environment, human dignity (rights), self-governement, resources mobilisation, etc.,

— advocate, lobby and form national and international networks for the great cause of the people,

— implement development projects on sustainable agriculture, community based social and agro-forestry, livestock husbandary and production, safe drinking water, irrigation, institutional development, etc.,

— carry out action oriented and people's participatory research on issues related to social and economic situation of the communities,

— assist local people to evolve new organisations and strengthen the existing ones so that the self-organisation, self-government and self-reliance are promoted and sustainable rural development is assured in the long-run.

— disseminate issue-based information pertaining to contemporary national concerns, sustainable development, democracy, human rights, gender, bonded labourers, health effects and impacts of agricultural chemicals, etc.,

— promote indigenous knowledge, traditional skills and resources of the deprived local people to speed up the process of self-development, considering learning as a continuous process.

— publish people-oriented IEC materials that are relevant to people's development and can be used by the majority of rural people.

Development Projects and Project Areas

RRN implements integrated rural development projects on livelihood, sustainable agriculture, kitchen gardening, social forestry, irrigation, drinking water, community health, savings and micro-credit, child and adult education, community mobilisation, people's institutional development, resources development and management, etc.

The RRN activities

Training and education

RRN has a three tier strategy of training and education. First its project activities are supported with intensive training and educational packages for the project beneficiaries. Second, with a view to deliver quality services, both at field and management level, staff are given opportunity to participate in various relevant training courses within or outside the organisation. Third, RRN also shares the learnings of development organisations by organising training programmes at national and regional level.

Advocacy, lobbying, and networking

RRN is actively involved, on behalf of the rural poor, on the issues of national concerns, hence participates in different networks and campaigns. Some of these undertaken in the past include a campaign against the proposed hydroelectric megha dam as well as those advocating for land reforms, environmental conversation, women's and human rights.

RRN has also organized and hosted some national and regional seminars and conferences which include The Role of Nepalese Women Peasants, Global Economy and Sustainable Agriculture, South Asian Forum Against Destructive International Aid and PP21, Asian Women Conferences etc. RRN has also worked as the Secretariat for Nepal NGO Initiatives for World Summit on Social Development 1995 (NIWOSD), and the Secretariat of NGO Action Committee for World Food Sumit 1996 (ACTCOM)

RRN's Publication and Documentation Unit contains a variety of publications produced by itself and other organizations. RRN publishes a regular newsletter, the Punarnirman in English and Nepali; periodicals and technical books synthesized from field experience on sustainable agriculture and kitchen gardening, community health and sanitation, human rights, saving and credit, etc, and books and primers of national concern such as Peasant Women in Nepal, Structural Adjustment Policy in nepal and Arun III Hydroelectricity Dam, Cartoon Book on The never-ending Third World Debt, etc. The unit also produces posters and video films based on rural reconstruction issues. It has books, journals and documents on a variety of areas ranging from gender studies, environment and development, agriculture, to political economy and current affairs.

12

Child Labour in Bangladesh

According to the Bangladesh Bureau of Statistics Labour Force Survey, there are 5.7 million 10 to 14 year old children working in Bangladesh. Another estimate puts the number at 15 million. Nearly all the child labour in export industries is found in the garment industry. According to the Bangladesh Ministry of Labour, "children are found working in garments, bakeries and confectioneries, hotels and restaurants, transport, bidi (cigarette) factories, small engineering workshops, fish-processing, and other informal and unregulated sectors." There are also allegations of children catching and processing shrimp in Chittagong for export.

The garment industry, including those enterprises producing accessories for finished garments, is without doubt the most significant industry in Bangladesh which utilizes child labour and exports to the United States. It is also a relatively young industry, established in 1977 and developed rapidly after 1983. In 1993, Bangladesh exported nearly $750 million in apparel to the United

States. The garment industry's main products include shirts, trousers, jackets, T-shirts, shorts, and briefs. Garment workers make sports caps and sweat suits for export to the United States.

The BGMEA estimates the work force at approximately 800,000 persons. Interview with Mr. Redwan Ahmed, President, Bangladesh Garment Manufacturers and Exporters Association, by Department of Labour official. Based upon surveys of the garment industry, the Asian-American Free Labour Institute (AAFLI) reports that females constitute about 90 percent of all adult workers, and roughly 60 percent of all child workers.

Determining precise ages of child workers in Bangladesh, as in many developing countries, is sometimes difficult. Children rarely if ever have a birth certificate, and many will lie about their age for fear of being dismissed.

Interview with Redwan Ahmed, President, Bangladesh Garment Manufacturers and 12 Exporters Association and Member of Parliament, by Department of Labour official . Interview with Humayan Shamsul Kabir, Joint Secretary, Bangladesh Ministry of Labour, by Department of Labour official. At the same time, the Joint Secretary for Export, Mr. Shoaib Ahmad, estimated the percentage of children in the garment industry at two to three percent.

Estimates vary on the total number of factories and workers in the garment industry. One estimate puts the figures at 1,500 factories and over 700,000 workers, of whom 75 to 90 percent are women. Representatives of the garment factories located in and around Dhaka frequently cite the figure of 1,800 factories registered with the BGMEA, with 1,000 actively producing garments, of which approximately 300 lead in production. However, these figures do not include a growing subcontracting sector, which frequently goes unnoticed and unregulated.

Children ranging in ages from eight to fourteen work in the garment industry. It is reported that most of the children are girls with an average age of just over 13 years — 10 percent of whom are already married. Reported figures on the incidence of child labour in the garment industry vary from source to source. On the one hand, Dr. Farida Akhtar, Executive Director of the Srama Bikesh Kendra, claims that one-fourth of the workers in the garment industry are children.

On the other hand, in May 1994 the President of the Bangladesh Garment Manufacturers and Exporters Association (BGMEA) stated that one percent of the total work force are children, numbering an estimated 8,000 - 10,000. A recent study by the Asian-American Free Labour Institute (AAFLI) estimates that 25-30,000 children work in the industry, mostly in subcontracting industries.

Still others maintain that child labour does not exist in the garment industry. Some estimates suggest that the number of child garment workers may be near 55,000. A June 1994 report of the International Confederation of Free Trade Unions lists the percentage as ranging from 20 to 40 percent. Recent observations made during site visits by U.S. Departments of Labour and State officials suggests that anywhere from 5 to 20 percent of the work force are under age. In short, children are working in the garment industry, even though various observers differ as to the precise numbers.

As a result of international attention paid to child labour in the garment industry in the recent past, both the Government and the BGMEA have made efforts to encourage manufacturers to abide by the law which prohibits the employment of children under the age of 14.

Fearing the imminent passage of the Child Labour Deterrence Act (otherwise known as the Harkin Bill), garment employers dismissed an estimated 50,000 children from the factories in the fall of 1993, approximately 75 percent of all children in the industry. No follow-up study has been undertaken to determine where the children went, but it is widely thought that most of them have found employment in other garment factories, in smaller, unregistered subcontracting garment workshops, or in other sectors.

Observers estimate that approximately 75 percent of all child workers in the garment industry were dismissed following governmental and industry warnings. International organizations and NGOs pressured the industry to retain the remaining children in order to have an opportunity to establish "safety nets" for them.

In its written testimony to the U.S. Department of Labour's International Child Labour Hearing, the Embassy of Bangladesh noted operations are simple and technology is uncomplicated in the garment industry. Most of the work is performed by women. These women, in the absence of any guardian at home, bring along their children, particularly female ones, for security and day-care, to their places of work. U.S. Departments of Labour and State officials, AAFLI representatives, and other non-governmental organizations, however, have witnessed children on their way to work in the morning, without parents, carrying their tiffins (tin lunch boxes) and holding their timecards. AAFLI's study found that very few children interviewed had an immediate family member (father, mother, brother, or sister) working in the same factory, but most had a friend or some distant relative who arranged for them to get the job.

Garment factories are located in multi-storied buildings throughout Dhaka including Mirpur, Malibagh and Rampura districts (allegedly one of the worst areas), and the Free School District area. Working conditions in general in Bangladesh are far below western standards. On a par with other factory settings, garment factories are often dimly lit, with poor ventilation, and open for very long hours.

However, some factories operate with good lighting and are not overly hot or crowded. The workers, mostly female, work without a break during their shift. Too often the factory doors are locked. Sometimes guards with keys stand by the locked gate; other times no one able to unlock the iron grating is near. Many times the locked gate is the only entrance or exit to a factory.

A *Toronto Star* article described children working in oppressively hot conditions, where the air was thick with cotton dust, there was constant clatter of machinery, and children were allowed only three-minute bathroom breaks.

Overtime hours occur during peak periods in the production cycle when manufacturers are rushing to fulfill their export quotas. AAFLI's 1994 survey of garment factories found that, like adult workers, children typically work 10 to 14 hours a day, with a half-day off on Friday. Children generally are given the less skilled tasks; adults are normally found operating the sewing machines and cutting fabric. Children are confined to cutting and trimming loose threads from completed garments, serving as "helpers" to the sewing machine operators and ironers, as stockers, transporters of garments from one station to another, and finishers who pack the products.

In contrast to some other industries in the Indian subcontinent, children in the garment industry are indeed paid, albeit very little and many times late. Each factory worker must carry an employment identification card which gives the person's name, hours worked per day, and the daily signature of a supervisor. It is only by presenting this card that an employee can receive his or her monthly wage.

In some cases, the employer withholds issuance of the card for the first month or two of employment, and the child is not paid during this period. Interviews with child workers found that supervisors regularly punish misbehaviour such as talking while working by docking a day's pay. Eventually the child will earn a wage. Children in some factories do not receive time cards, and often are unaware of their compulsory working hours, monthly salary, or hours of overtime work. Since there are no trade unions for the child workers, they have no bargaining power or recourse to a grievance system.

The study of 143 garment factories in Bangladesh, the Asian-American Free Labour Institute (AAFLI) reported the salary range is 300 to 500 taka per month (about \$7.69-\$12.82), except for the case of sewing machine operators or ironers who were reportedly paid 750-1,800 taka per month (\$19.23-\$46.15), and that the children are generally paid less than adults. In a recent visit to Bangladesh, a Department of Labour official spoke with children who reported receiving anywhere from 250 to 700 taka per month. Children also reported that, like adult workers, they are often paid two to four weeks late, and rarely paid extra for overtime. In some factories, the child workers are appointed as "apprentices" or "helpers" for months and are not issued identification/time cards even after completing their apprenticeship period. In some factories, the child workers are appointed as "apprentices" or "helpers" for months and are not issued identification/time cards even after completing their apprenticeship period. There is no paid leave for holidays, and salary is deducted if the child is absent, or for unproductive periods when the electricity in the factory temporarily goes out.

National Child Labour Laws

Bangladesh has some 25 special laws and ordinances to protect and improve the status of children. The current laws, however, present a confusing maze of conflicting provisions regulating child labour. Under existing law, the minimum age for employment may be variously interpreted as anywhere between 12 and 16. In 1993, the Government of Bangladesh created a National Labour Law Commission to revise and harmonize labour laws.

The first draft of the recommendations, completed on March 31, 1994, proposes to eliminate the inconsistencies regarding the minimum age for employment by defining a child as "a person who has not completed his fourteenth year of age." The draft further provides that "no child shall be employed or permitted to work in any occupation or establishment."

According to the Joint Secretary for Labour, these provisions, if enacted, would supersede and control all other labour laws related to children.

Current laws include The Factories Act of 1965, which prohibits the employment of children below the age of 14 in any factory. This law also stipulates that young workers (i.e. children and adolescents) are only allowed to work a maximum 5-hour day and only between the hours of 7 a.m. and 7 p.m. The penalty for violation of this Act (Article 44(1)) is a fine up to 1,000 taka. The Employment of Children Act, 1938 (as amended in 1974) prohibits employment of children under 14 years in a factory. Other laws include the Shops and Establishments Act 1965 and the Children's Act 1974 and Children's Rules, 1976.

The government agency responsible for enforcing child labour laws, the Bangladesh Department of Labour and Inspectorate of Factories, lacks sufficient resources, staff and logistical support to adequately perform the task of monitoring child labour laws. The Government of Bangladesh also maintains that employers and factory owners/managers evade labour laws. It should be noted, however, that the government has instructed the garment industry not to use child labour. The Labour Ministry was unable to provide information to the Department of Labour official regarding inspections of garment factories or prosecutions or convictions of factory owners for violating the Factories Act or the Employment of Children Act.

Under Bangladesh law, children must attend school through the fifth grade. Primary education is free and compulsory, although not compulsory for girls in the rural areas. The implementation of compulsory education has fallen short in part because parents keep their children out of school, finding school accessories too expensive or preferring their children to be working for money or helping with household chores. The current government policy is to implement compulsory education in 50 percent of the country by 1995 and 100 percent by the year 2000.

The 1994 report by the Asian-American Free Labour Institute, however, maintains that, despite this policy on compulsory education, there has not been much progress. The Government of Bangladesh contends that it does not have the resources. A UNICEF sponsored study on non-formal education and child labour in Bangladesh noted that parents find purchasing uniforms, books, and other supplies a significant burden, especially for poor families, and presumably a major disincentive for sending their children to school rather than to work.

Bangladesh is a party to ILO Convention No. 59 Concerning Minimum Age for Admission to Employment in Industry and the U.N. Convention on the Rights of the Child. Bangladesh has not ratified ILO Convention No. 138 Concerning Minimum Age for Admission to Employment.

In the past year or two, there has been significant action taken by the Government of Bangladesh, the BGMEA, international organizations, and NGOs to create solutions and alternatives for child workers. In its written testimony to the U.S. Department of Labour, the Government of Bangladesh listed official efforts either taken or planned for the future. Some of the efforts include a realization of the objectives of the Rights of the Child Convention (a National Program of Action for Children was launched on June 2, 1992); examination by the National Labour Law Commission on existing labour laws with the goal of updating and consolidating them into a "Labour Code,"; strictly enforcing child labour laws; continuing to publish notices containing the provisions of laws relating to child employment in daily newspapers and broadcasting prohibitory messages over TV and radio; and distributing posters prohibiting child labour.

The government is cooperating with international organizations such as UNICEF to develop non-formal educational and other support programs for working children. The government has reportedly also agreed to allow the ILO to conduct a national survey of child workers. On July 4, 1994, the Bangladesh Garment Manufacturers and Exporters Association (BGMEA) announced that it would eliminate child labour from all garment factories by October 31, 1994.

On May 5, 1994, Mr. Redwan Ahmed, president of the BGMEA, announced that in addition to setting up a hospital for garment workers, the BGMEA also planned to give informal education, professional training, and to provide health care facilities to the employees of the apparel sector by setting up seven clinic/hospitals and seven training centre/schools in Dhaka and Chittagong. On many occasions both publicly and privately, the BGMEA has expressed its willingness to work with NGOs, international organizations and the government to establish programs for children.

Although the BGMEA presumably has a vital interest in ensuring that the garment industry is free of child labour, as of this writing, only one of the above-mentioned programs or cooperative efforts proposed by the BGMEA recently have been implemented. At its July

4, 1994 news conference, the BGMEA inaugurated one small school/clinic for children in Dhaka. Other programs or cooperative efforts recently proposed by the BGMEA have not yet been implemented.

George Brown, would ban the importation to the United States of products which are manufactured or mined in whole or in part by children. Since the Bangladesh garment industry is wholly export-oriented, the threat of a U.S. import ban had a significant impact in the country.

There has been tremendous public reaction in Bangladesh to the proposed Child Labour Deterrence Act, which, combined with serious concern for the welfare of the children, has resulted in the formation of a child labour coalition, consisting of representatives from international organizations, NGOs, labour unions, various government ministries, and representatives of the garment industry. The work is being spearheaded by UNICEF, which has researched and reviewed a number of private non-formal education programs for possible use in setting up schools for working children. In addition, numerous child welfare and education NGOs are active in the effort to provide assistance to working children.

Underprivileged Children's Educational Programs (UCEP)—Bangladesh is traced back to a study on child labour in Dhaka city conducted in 1970 and published in 1972 under the title 'Our Unfortunate Children as Labourers'. The study described and analysed the life situation of urban poor children who did not have any schooling and instead were engaged in selling physical labour in order to earn a subsistence. The same study provided guidelines for a program aimed at alleviating the deprivations of working children.

The problem was magnified in the post-liberation war situation of 1972 with an enormous increase in the number of destitute children. It was in this context that UCEP came into being to provide opportunities for schooling of the poor working children in urban location and thereby increasing their access to better socio-economic opportunities. With a rapid rise in the number of urban poor families in the recent years the number of illiterate poor children has increased at an alarming rate. But for the opportunities that UCEP seeks to provide the poor working and illiterate children would have grown as poor illiterate adults and would have no chance for changing their poverty situation. Consequently poverty would perpetuate over successive generations.

Thus UCEP is an effort to break the vicious circle of poverty. The project addresses itself, on the one hand, to the educational need of the urban poor children which is their basic right and on the other, to the improvement of the overall living conditions of themselves and their families.

Goals

In keeping with the national priorities to remove illiteracy and to alleviate poverty, UCEP seeks to establish opportunities for the poorest children and adolescents, so that they can enhance their chances for having a better socio-economic status.

The Strategy

The operational strategy of the project consists of measures for encouraging school enrollment and retention of the working children and attaining such social and vocational skills, which enable them to be useful/productive citizens. Thus UCEP strategy has the following arrangements:

The children continue to work and earn, while they attend UCEP school. UCEP admits working/street children of 10+ years-minimum 10 years in case of female and 11 years in case of male-to UCEP general schools for basic education. After four years of basic education the students are admitted to technical schools for employable skill learning in various trades.

UCEP general school basically follows the curriculum and textbooks as prescribed by the National Curriculum and Textbook Board. UCEP runs two academic sessions in one calendar year, each session having 135 school days. Thus UCEP shortens the duration of schooling period which increases the motivation of the students and their families for education. UCEP school seeks to function as a social service unit, and as such social work is undertaken to:

— Keeps the attendance rate high

— Revent student's tendency to drop-out

— Provide special assistance to slow learners or those who have behaviour problems

— Improve the general teaching—learning environment

— Provide special assistance to bright students encouraging them to further academic training and

— Establish a cooperative relationship between school, family, community/neighbourhood and employers of the children.

— CEP schools are located where there are large concentrations of the target group.

UCEP established links with other agencies and groups of people including industrial and business communities to promote education/training facilities and employment of the UCEP's target group.

Provide special schooling facilities for the urban working and street children (boys and girls) who have had no opportunity to attend public school or dropped out in the very early stage of primary education.

Provide such children and adolescents with training opportunities to acquire employable technical skills after they have had their basic education in UCEP general schools. Assist those who have completed education and skills training at UCEP to find suitable employment and, find that purpose, establish links with potential employers. Undertake social work services to ensure cooperation of families and other concerned in promoting education and social rehabilitation of the working and street children.

Programmes and Services

The following activities are implemented in order to achieve the objectives of UCEP:

- General School Programme to impart basic education and to provide skills training.
- Technical Education Program
- Employment Promotion or Job Placement Services
- Social work as a supportive service to education, training and job placement

— Human Resource Development to ensure effective implementation of the above activities.

Ain O Salish Kendra (ASK), formed in 1986, is a legal aid and human rights centre dedicated to creating a critical awareness of civic and human rights to build a democratic society. It provides legal aid to the powerless, especially the poor, women and working children, and supports legal action through advocacy and public campaigns. ASK registered under the Societies Act in 1986 and with the NGO Bureau in 1993.

ASK seeks to reach the powerless—primarily women, working children and workers—through its legal aid programs to enable them to access justice and to negotiate for their rights in a holistic manner.

Objectives

The objectives of this cell are twofold:

— To investigate, monitor and document violations of law and human rights; and

— To disseminate this information through the media, public campaigns and publications.

— Training, Education and Publication (TEP)

— To provide legal literacy and human rights education in order to:

—empower the disenfranchised; and

—create a public awareness of human rights and knowledge about national laws.

Law and Policy Reform forum (LPRF)

The Law and Policy Reform Forum seeks to:

— examine the impact of the state (law and policies) and the market on people's livelihoods at the micro-level;

— engage in consultations and dialogues with grassroots activists, researchers, academics, policy makers, and public representatives to analyse the consequences of the application or neglect of specific laws, policies and programs;

— broaden consensus among concerned groups and individuals (linking local level dialogues with national and international debates) around the need for alternative perspectives and ethics for law and policy formulation, based on the criteria of gender equality and justice, protection of human rights and provisioning of basic needs;

— prepare reports or position papers to reflect such a consensus; and

— support advocacy with public representatives and policy planners as well as mobilise public opinion around critical issues for law and policy reform.

Child Rights Cell (CRC)

To increase the basic education level of working children, assist in their social and emotional well-being, and develop awareness of their rights amongst children themselves by providing access to health, education and legal protection in cooperation with the community of employers and guardians.

To develop the socio-economic conditions of disadvantaged children, women and poor of the rural and urban areas, by applying their decisions for their own development.

Strategy

The strategy of Bikash Bangladeh is integral, community development particularly empowering the disadvantaged i.e.:

— Promoting the UN convention on the right of the child (CRC).

— Organising the people as a community through association and credit support.

— Increasing awareness, knowledge and skills through appropriate education and training.

— Improving socio-economic condition on the disadvantaged in the community.

Main (Current) Activities

Pre-primary school for children's from the poor families.

— Non-formal Education for young adults
— Cultural activities for school children
— Group formation and institutional building
— Savings scheme
— Health Education
— Education on Safe drinking water & Sanitation
— Kitchen Gardening
— Disaster Management program (the Warm clothes distribution for children and women).

13

Globalisation and Child Labour

There is no empirical evidence that globalisation increases child labour. If anything, globalisation reduces child labour. In a country that starts out with a largely uneducated workforce, globalisation raises the wage rate of uneducated, relative to educated workers. Unless the government takes steps to counter the reduction in the incentive to educate children, the net effect of globalisation is likely to be an increase in child labour. By contrast, in developing countries that have spent sufficiently for education to have a relative large number of workers with at least a basic education, globalisation raises the wage rate of educated, relative to uneducated workers.

In these countries, public intervention is needed not to raise the incentive for parents to educate their children, but to loosen liquidity constraints. Developing countries can turn globalisation into an opportunity to reduce child labour by spending more on education and public health. Developed countries can help them by financing these policies, compensating them for short-term adverse effects, and stopping agricultural protectionism.

Globalisation is the process by which an increasing share of world production is traded internationally, and the productive systems of different countries become increasingly interdependent. It started soon after the end of the second world conflict, but gathered momentum in the 1980s, as rapid progress in information technology compounded the effects of falling transport costs and trade liberalisation. It thus seems reasonable, in trying to understand the consequences of globalisation, to look at what has happened over the last couple of decades. Most of the existing analyses are concerned with the effects of globalisation on wages and employment in the developed world. Child labour is concentrated mainly in the developing world.

The measure of child labour that figures in the Development Indicators is the participation rate of individuals aged 10 to 14. The limitation of this measure is that it does not count children working at younger ages (the participation rate for the age group 6-10 is far from negligible), and children engaged in unofficial, especially if illegal, work activities. It thus leaves out what are probably the most undesirable forms of child work. In addition to this measure of child labour, we thus consider the primary school non-attendance rate (the complement to unity of the primary net enrolment rate reported in the Development Indicators).

The problem with using the latter as an indicator of child labour is that children not attending school are not necessarily working (in the home or elsewhere). However, since children not attending school are more difficult to monitor by the authorities than children who do, and thus more exposed to the worst forms of abuse (from hazardous or very hard work, to soldiering and prostitution), the non-attendance rate is at least a danger signal.

Poverty is generally assumed to be the main cause of child labour. There is a negative association between income and child labour. For similar levels of per-capita income, however, both indicators of child labour show very large variations. That may be partly due to the fact that countries with similar levels of per-capita income can have very different income distributions, but partly also to the effects of different policies.

To measure a country's relative position in the globalisation process, we use the standard measure of trade openness: the sum of imports and exports, expressed as a percentage of GDP. Later, we shall also use the classification of trade openness in Sachs and Warner. According to this very stringent criterion, a country may be called open if it has none of the following characteristics:

1. Non-tariff trade barrier covering 40 per cent or more of trade
2. Average tariff rates of 40 per cent or more
3. A black market exchange rate that is depreciated by 20 per cent or more relative to the official exchange rate, on average, during the 1970's or the 1980's.
4. A socialist economic system
5. A state monopoly on major exports.

On the contrary, higher foreign trade appears to be associated with a lower incidence of child labour. Here again, however, we find considerable national differences. At low levels of trade, countries similar in terms of exposure to trade can be very different in terms of child labour incidence. A clearly negative association between trade openness and child labour is evident only for Africa and Latin America. In Asia, the relationship between trade and child labour is much weaker (especially if the latter is measured as a complement to the school enrolment rate). This seems to indicate that the type of activity in which a country specialises, and the policies it pursues, shift the relationship between child labour and globalisation.

There is, therefore, no prima facie evidence that globalisation will necessarily result in more child labour. Indeed, there are signs that international trade and economic integration offer governments the opportunity to reduce child labour. Since trade promotes economic growth, the opportunity could come in the form of higher income. Or it could be that the relative wage changes brought about by international trade are conducive to less child labour.

The children do not normally choose to work. Most have that decision taken for them by their parents. Even in the case of the child who was expelled or run away from home, the reasons for his or her present working can be traced back to parental actions that made it impossible for the child to remain in the home. The only real exception are children who were abducted, and children who lost, or were separated from, their family of origin because of war, or of some natural disaster.

Parental actions affect the number of working children under their control in three ways. By conditioning the probability that a child is born. By conditioning the probability that the child will survive to an age, as early as 6, when he or she can be made to work. By actually making the child work. On all three accounts, household economics is the appropriate conceptual framework within which to examine the emergence of child labour.

Parents care about their own, as well as their children's consumption, the decision whether to send a child to work or to school does in fact depend on essentially three things: the cost (including the opportunity-cost) of education, the expected return to education, and the extent to which parents are able to finance educational investments. Conceptually, parental decisions may be described as a two-stage process. Parents decide whether to procure the birth of a child, and how much to spend for the child's health and nutrition, under conditions of uncertainty about whether the child will survive to school age. The probability that the child will survive is conditioned not only by external causes, but also by how much the parents spend for the child. If the child survives, parents decide how the child's time should be allocated between work and study. They also decide how much of the family budget (augmented, if the child is sent to work, by his or her earnings) is spent on the child. If the child is sent to school, parents also decide how that sum is to be divided between consumption and educational expenditures.

The decision process can have one of three possible types of outcome. One occurs if the marginal cost of human capital (say, the cost of increasing the child's future earning capacity by one dollar) is higher than the maximum that parents are willing to pay. If that is the case, the child is made to work full time. Another arises if the marginal cost of human capital is lower than the minimum, at or below which parents are willing to buy as much education as possible. If that is the case, the child does not work at all. Between these two extremes, there is a third possible type of solution, where the child works and attends school at the same time. Parents, in that case, allocate family income, and the child's own time, to the child's education up to the point where the marginal cost of human capital just equals the price that parents are subjectively willing to pay for it.

An important role is played by the capital market and educational policy. Suppose that, by acquiring education, a child could substantially enhance his or her future earnings. If they could borrow against those future earnings, parents could finance the child's education and current consumption, and leave also something for everyone else. If that is not possible, however, the child's education and current consumption would have to be financed out of the parents (and other members of the family's) current income. This liquidity constraint establishes a direct link between current income and child labour participation: only families with above subsistence income can contemplate investing in a child's education.

Educational policies such as free schooling or subsidised educational material can help relax the constraint, but not eliminate it. To eliminate it altogether, there would have to be scholarships generous enough to cover the child's current consumption, and on a large enough scale to reach all liquidity-constrained families. Capital market imperfections thus help explain the finding of a negative effect of income on child labour at the aggregate level: as GDP rises, the proportion of liquidity-constrained families falls, and the extent to which a government is able to finance educational policies (if it so wishes) rises. Now take a step back, to the first decision stage.

Since the child's survival probability is conditioned not only by external causes, but also by the actions (parental expenditure for the child's nutrition and health) taken by the parents themselves, the latter face a trade-off between procuring an extra birth, and improving the survival chances of the children that they already have. In taking their first-stage decisions, parents take into account not only this, but also the other trade-off, between work and education, that they will face at the next decision stage (if the child lives that long).

The external causes that condition the probability of a child's survival include not only climate and genetic factors, but also government expenditure on sanitation, and public health. The higher this expenditure, the higher, other things being equal, the probability that a child will survive to school age, an later to adulthood; the higher, consequently, the return to investing in that child's education. If public health expenditure is a complement for private expenditure on the child's health and nutrition, an increase in the former will induce parents to raise the latter; if it is a substitute, the effect may be the opposite. An increase in public health expenditure could thus induce parents to have fewer children, and spend more for each of them, first on health and nutrition, then on health, nutrition and education.

A lump-sum increase in household income (e.g., a government subsidy) tends to reduce the proportion of school-age children that works. It also tends to raise the amount spent by parents for the health and nutrition of each child, and for the education of each child that attends school. These effect are stronger if parents have difficulty in borrowing, because the increase in current income relaxes the liquidity constraint. The effect of income on fertility is ambiguous, because it raises the expected marginal utility, but also the expected marginal cost of children. The effect on the absolute number of children who work is also ambiguous, because the proportion of school-age children that works falls, but the number of school-age children may increase (either through an increase in fertility, or through a reduction in infant mortality large enough to more than compensate for the fall in fertility). If the income change is the product of an increase in someone's wage rate, and of a change in someone's labour supply in response to the wage rate increase, there will be substitution as well as income effects, and the signs and sizes of both will be different depending on whose wage rate has increased.

Suppose that the wage rate for unskilled labour rises. This means that not only unskilled adult workers, but also child workers, are paid more per unit of time. As the opportunity-cost of time spent in education will consequently go up, the marginal cost of education will rise. At the same time, as the remuneration gap between educated and uneducated labour will become smaller, the return to education will fall. Both these changes will reduce the incentive for parents to invest in their children's education. If the income-effect is not large enough to compensate for the substitution-effect, an increase in the unskilled wage rate will then raise child labour. Evidence related to the farm productivity child labour in India suggests that this may indeed be the case.

By contrast, an increase in the remuneration of skilled, or just literate, adult workers would raise the return to education, and thus the incentive for parents to produce fewer, better educated children. In households where the parents themselves are skilled workers, or if parents are able to borrow against their children's expected future earnings, the substitution-effect will be reinforced by the income-effect. That makes it likely that a skilled wage rate increase would reduce not only the number of children, but also the labour force participation of each school-age child. Wage rate increases encourage also the labour participation of women with children. This introduces yet another effect on child labour.

In the short run, a wage increase will tend to raise the number of working children, as young girls will be called upon to substitute for their mothers in the performance of domestic chores; in particular, looking after younger siblings. As the opportunity-cost of their time increases, however, women will be less willing to give birth to more children. In the long run, the supply of potential child workers could thus fall. Public expenditure on health, sanitation, etc., induces parents to have fewer children, and to spend more for each child, if private and public expenditure are complements; the other way round if they are substitutes.

A country can increase its welfare if, instead of directly producing all the goods its members wish to consume, it specializes in the production of those goods that it can produce at relatively lower cost than other countries, and exchanges the surplus for the goods it does not produce. Since the cost of a good depends on the prices of the factors used for its production, and the prices of traded inputs are the same everywhere, differences in the relative costs of traded goods reflect differences in the relative prices of non-traded goods used as factors of production. In turn, the relative prices of these immobile factors reflect differences in factor endowments.

Standard trade theory predicts that countries specialize in the production of traded goods that make more intensive use of the non-traded factors of which they have relatively greater abundance. In traditional classroom accounts of this theory, the non-traded factors are labour and capital. Countries with a relative abundance of labour (developing countries, the so-called South) will thus export labour-intensive products, countries with a relative abundance of capital (developed countries, the so-called North) will export capital-intensive products.

Since, within each country, an increase in trade raises the price of the abundant factor relative to that of the scarce one, an implication of this vision of the world is that "globalisation" will make workers worse-off relative to capitalists in the North (hence the alarm of trade unions), better-off in the South. This vision of the world has somewhat changed over the last couple of decades. Partly, this reflects a general rethinking of the development process. While early growth theory equated economic growth with the accumulation of physical capital (buildings and machinery) per head of population, modern theory does in fact attach much greater importance to the accumulation of human capital (knowledge and personal skills). Partly, however, the change of emphasis comes also from a recognition that physical capital is not immobile.

Machinery can be moved around, and buildings can be taken down and rebuilt anywhere. All that is needed is the financial capital (equity or debt instruments) to pay for plants and machinery. Since financial capital is highly mobile, physical capital is then mobile too. Human capital is embodied in skilled workers. These are more mobile than unskilled workers, but they, too, have their international mobility restricted by immigration rules and sentimental ties. As a broad generalization, one might then say that the fixed factors determining the comparative advantages of different a countries are their different endowments of labour skills.

Of course, in the same way as capital endowments can be modified by investment, so skill endowments can be modified by education. But education takes much longer than the purchase of a new machine, or the construction of a plant, and workers are by and large more durable than physical capital. Starting from this premise, Adrian Wood has reformulated the theory of comparative advantage in terms of relative skill scarcities: countries export the products which make greater use of the relatively more abundant type of labour. Within each trading country, the benefit of increased world trade will then accrue to members of the relatively larger skill group.

In developed countries, where there are comparatively more skilled than literate workers, and the number of illiterates is insignificant, globalization widens the gap between skilled and unskilled wage rates. By contrast, in developing countries with a relative abundance of literate workers, what widens is the wage gap between literate and illiterate workers; the wage gap between skilled and just literate workers becomes narrower. In developing countries with relatively more illiterates, the wage gap between this and other categories of workers will narrow. There is ample evidence of increasing wage dispersion, and of a consequent increase in income inequality in developed countries.

Evidence on developing countries is sparser, but it, too, appears to support the predictions of reconstructed trade theory. There is a negative correlation between changes in income inequality, as measured by the Gini coefficient, and changes in the income share of manufactured exports to developed countries. Since the exporting countries have all got relatively more unskilled (literate or illiterate) workers than the countries to which the exports go, evidence that inequality and exports tend to move in opposite directions is consistent with the hypothesis that comparative advantages reflect relative skill endowments. This has important implications for child labour. Their parents are more likely to be illiterate than literate, and very unlikely to be skilled.

In developing countries with comparatively more literate than illiterate workers, trade then leads to an increase in the gap between literate and illiterate wage rates. If parents cannot borrow against their children's future earnings, however, educational investments are subject to liquidity constraints, and these constraints are all the more stringent in families where the parents are illiterate.

In developing countries with comparatively more illiterate than literate workers, trade reduces the ratio of literate to illiterate wage rates. Here, the argument is the exact opposite of the one used for countries with a relatively large literate population. On the one hand, the incentive for parents to have fewer, better educated children is reduced. On the other, poorer families become less poor, and this may tend to reduce the number of working children, though not by much. The net result is likely to be a rise in the number of working children. In a developing country, trade expansion could thus help reduce child labour. Whether it actually does depends to a large extent on education.

In countries that start out with too few educated people, parents will see their incentive to produce more educated people reduced, rather than increased. The opposite is true of countries that start out with enough educated people to give them a comparative advantage in exporting goods with a high content of this type of labour, but the greater incentive to produce better educated children will translate into actual school enrolments only to the extent that poorer families, where child labour is mainly concentrated, can afford the investment.

Income redistribution would thus help reduce child labour, but simulation experiments suggest that it would have to be carried out on an unrealistically large scale to have any noticeable effect. Public school provision, educational subsidies, and generous maintenance scholarships are more effective.

As adult female labour participation increases in response to rising female wage rates, gender-specific educational policies may be required to counter a possible short-run tendency by female children to substitute for their mothers in the performance of domestic work. As explained in the last section, public health expenditure, which directly and possibly indirectly reduces mortality, and thus increases the incentive to make human capital investments, also would help.

Globalisation does not simply mean more international trade for final goods. It also means more trade in intermediate goods. Falling transport costs and advances in information technology facilitating the coordination of dispersed production activities, are in fact favouring the segmentation of production processes, and the location of different segments of the same process in different countries. Although much of the resulting intra-industry trade is among developed industrial countries, the potential implications for developing countries, and thus for child labour, cannot be lightly dismissed.

The growing literature on this new aspect of international trade emphasizes the effects of market size on the international division of labour. The emergence of clubs of developed countries who speak only to one another is associated with the availability of educated workers in sufficient numbers to make it possible to create integrated productive systems spanning more than one country. Developing countries with a largely uneducated workforce thus face a double risk: that exposure to international trade may reduce the incentive for their inhabitants to educate their children, but also that they may be excluded from trade and economic integration with the richer countries. Clearly, for all these countries, globalisation presents great risks. That reinforces the conclusion reached in the last section about the importance of accompanying exposure to international trade with vigorous educational and health policies, capable of rapidly increasing the proportion of educated workers in the country's total labour force.

We have seen that exposure to international competition may result in more children going to school, rather than to work. We have also seen that a necessary condition for this to happen is that a country opening itself to international competition should have a sufficiently large share of educated workers. We have seen, finally, that policies aimed at lowering mortality are likely to also reduce child labour.

To test these propositions, we must measure the effect of trade on child labour while holding all the other variables (income, health expenditure, skill composition of the labour force) constant. Using the data in our Global Panel, we regressed child labour on trade openness, real per-capita income, health policy, and skill composition. It would have been desirable to control also for differences in income distribution. Child labour is alternatively measured by the 10-14 labour participation rate, or by the primary school non-attendance rate.

Trade openness is alternatively represented by the trade ratio (exports plus imports, divided by GDP) or by a dummy taking value one if the country is open according to the Sachs-Warner definition, zero otherwise. Real per-capita income is measured as GDP (in constant PPP terms) per head of total population. Health policy is represented by the share of public health expenditure in GDP. Skill composition is represented by the share of the 15-65 workforce which completed primary education only, and by that which attained secondary or higher education (the share of those who did not even complete primary education is used as the reference group). Skill composition captures essentially the cumulated effects of past educational policies. In view of the fact that current educational policies may affect the incentive to send children to school, it would have been desirable to measure the effects of these policies on child labour.

Since child labour is a close correlate of school attendance. If skill composition is not controlled for, trade raises the 10-14 labour participation rate, but has no significant effect on the primary school non-attendance rate. Income and public health expenditure reduce both measures of child labour. If skill composition is controlled for, trade has no significant effect on either measure of child labour. The effects of the skill composition have the expected signs.

The proportion of workers with completed primary education has a negative effect on child labour, and so does that of workers with secondary or higher education. If the dependent variable is the 10-14 labour participation rate, however, the share of workers with secondary or higher education reduces the significance of the workers with completed primary education. Conversely, if the dependent variable is the primary school non-attendance rate, what is nonsignificant is the share of workers with secondary or higher education.

Openness reduces child labour, however measured, even if we do not control for skill composition. The share of workers with primary education is nonsignificant if the dependent variable is the 10-14 labour participation rate, while that of workers with secondary or higher education is nonsignificant if the dependent variable is the primary school non-attendance rate.

Interestingly, the more optimistic scenario is associated with the more stringent definition of trade openness, the one that takes into account the conditions under which trade takes place, rather than the actual volume of trade. Since the beneficial effects of international exposure come through relative price changes, it is in fact not irrelevant whether internal prices are subject to government control, or free to adjust to international prices, and whether foreign trade is distorted by quotas and state monopoly or not. The estimated coefficients of the skill composition variables measure the effects of increasing the proportion of educated (or of more highly educated) workers, holding all the other variables, openness included, constant at their mean values.

A notable feature of the growth of international trade since World War II is that the share of agricultural goods in the total exports of developing to developed countries has fallen from nearly a quarter in 1955, to barely a fifth in 1989.

Over the same period, agricultural exports from developed to developing countries have staid roughly constant at just under a fifth of the total. That may be judged positively, from the viewpoint of developing countries, if one believes that industry is where technical progress occurs, and that industrialization at any cost is thus the only key to development.

A closer look at what many developing countries export, however, reveals that much of the growth in manufactured exports consists of low-tech goods, made internationally competitive by the low wage rates prevailing in the exporting countries.

By contrast, the Green Revolution experience, and agricultural productivity growth in developed countries, suggest that developing countries with a high ratio of cultivable land to population may have forgone the opportunity of exploiting their comparative advantages, for no great benefit in terms of productivity growth.

The resulting agricultural surpluses have been sold below cost, or donated in times of food crises, to developing countries. This policy has discouraged agricultural production in developing countries. By holding food prices, and thus wages, low in developing countries, it has also made it easier for these countries to produce and export manufactures with a high content of unskilled labour. Ending agricultural protectionism would bring efficiency gains. It would also cause a redistribution from European and North American farmers, to European and North American consumers, and to Third World farmers.

Since child labour is predominantly supplied by farming families, or by former farming families who have emigrated to the cities, in the developing world, the welfare of working children would undoubtedly rise. Under certain conditions, child labour would fall. We have seen that simply making parents richer has ambiguous effects on child labour. To be sure that child labour will fall, the return to education has to rise. That would happen spontaneously in the longer term, as increased international demand for agricultural imports, and the higher quality standards required by first world markets, induce farmers in developing countries to adopt modern production methods. That can in fact be expected to put a premium on skilled, or at least literate, labour. The process could be accelerated by deliberate policy, by spending on education and health on the one hand, and encouraging technical development in agriculture on the other. There is empirical evidence of an enhanced effect of educational policies on school enrolment in parts of India that had been touched by the Green Revolution.

In short, there is no empirical evidence that globalisation increases the incidence of child labour. If anything, the available cross-country evidence shows that globalisation can reduce child labour. There is evidence also that educational and health policies affect child labour. The theoretical explanation may be summarised as follows. The parental decision to make a school-age child work depends on the costs and benefits of education. Due to capital market imperfections, parental investments in their children's education are limited by liquidity constraints. Wage rate changes affect both the costs and the benefits of education, and the liquidity constraint. Exposure to trade raises the wage rate of the comparatively larger skill group, relative to that of the others.

In a country that starts out with a largely uneducated workforce, globalisation raises the wage rate of uneducated, relative to educated workers. The cost of education, that includes the opportunity-cost of time spent in education, will then rise relative to the benefit, that reflects the wage differential between educated and uneducated workers.

This will reduce the incentive to educate a child, and raise the incentive to have more children. On the other hand, the wage change may relax the liquidity constraint on the poorest families (if the wage rate of uneducated workers, children included, increases in absolute terms). Unless the government takes steps to counter the reduction in the incentive to educate children, the net effect of globalisation is likely to be an increase in child labour. Indeed, according to some variants of new trade theory, these countries are at risk of uncoupling from the more developed countries, as the latter form exclusive clubs that trade only with one another. In a country that starts out with a relatively large educated workforce, globalisation raises the wage rate of educated, relative to that of uneducated workers. If we distinguish between basic education, and higher (or basic plus technical) education, we can then expect the wage rate of the higher educational category to rise relative to that of the lower category in developed countries

By contrast, the wage rate of the lower educational category can be expected to rise relative to that of uneducated workers in developing countries that spent sufficiently for education in the past, to have a relative large number of workers with a basic education. In this elite of developing countries, the benefit of education will rise relative to the cost, thereby making it more advantageous to have fewer, better educated children. On the other hand, the wage change may tighten the liquidity constraint on the poorest families (those with uneducated parents, if the uneducated wage rate falls in absolute as well as relative terms), where most child workers originate.

14

Role of Governments in Child Labour Abolition

National political commitment is the key to the effective abolition of child labour. In the absence of firm policy commitment by the government, backed up by resources and translated into effective action, the best efforts of other partners in the fight against child labour are likely to result in making little more than a small dent in the problem.

The obligation to establish, implement and monitor policies and legislation, and to translate international commitments into domestic action, rests firmly with governments. Inclusive, accountable systems of governance and sound macroeconomic management provide the foundations on which effective, well-resourced policies and programmes to combat child labour can be built and sustained.

Many countries have established distinct child labour policies, programmes or plans of action. For example, of the 36 governments addressing this issue under the 2002 follow-up to the Declaration, 75 per cent (27 countries) indicated that a national policy or plan aimed at ensuring the effective abolition of child labour was in place. The focus of these policies differs from country to country.

Commercial sexual exploitation of children has moved developing, transition and developed countries alike to take action. In its annual report under the follow-up to the Declaration, the Czech Republic notes that a national plan includes a set of long-term measures aimed at eliminating child trafficking, prostitution, abuse and pornography.

The Government of Ghana's national programme focuses on children in prostitution, street children, domestic workers, porters and children working in small-scale mines, with priority given to girls, children working in very hazardous conditions and children under 12 years old. The youth programme adopted by the Government of Kazakhstan aims to create legal, economic and organizational machinery for the implementation of a policy to safeguard the rights of youth in work, education and health. The Government of Mexico established a special council to promote the development of children and adolescents through implementing an agenda which guides action by government and society in favour of children.

Of the 38 countries under the 2002 review of annual reports that mentioned specific measures or programmes of action to combat child labour, 20 countries gave special attention to the needs of particular groups of children: disabled children (e.g. Australia, Canada, Cuba, Kazakhstan, Syrian Arab Republic); street children (e.g. Ethiopia, Mexico); children performing hazardous work (e.g. Lebanon, Pakistan); girl children (e.g. India); children with disadvantaged backgrounds (e.g. Belgium, Russian Federation); orphaned/abandoned children (e.g. Kazakhstan, Russian Federation, Syrian Arab Republic); children in rural areas (e.g. Canada, Mali, Thailand); and children working in the informal sector (e.g. Mali, Mexico).

At the same time as maintaining a specific policy on child labour, each government must mainstream the issue within overall policy frameworks in, for example, employment, poverty reduction, education and vocational training, labour and social protection. Such mainstreaming has been a feature in, for instance, Colombia, Kenya, Mexico, the United Republic of Tanzania and Thailand.

For its part, the Government of Jamaica acknowledges that strategies for poverty eradication must address the problem of child labour within a child-focused framework. These strategies must:

— be a part of public policies for children, developed jointly by government and civil society;

— see the child in his/her social context, including the family;

— promote gender awareness;

— improve the income levels of poor families through targeted policies to ensure children's access to and completion of primary school.

The need for an integrated approach to children's issues, involving the many different parts of government that have a role to play, is frequently acknowledged but less frequently found in the structures of governance. A child-focused approach helps to bring about an integrated framework for action, as reflected in "children's policies" that create an improved basis for different ministries to focus together on meeting the various development needs and rights of children. This approach has been successfully adopted in Colombia, Kenya, Mexico and the Philippines.

Child labour policy often directs that a formal structure be created with a mandate to oversee the work on this issue. The combination of IPEC action and the provisions of the CRC have resulted, in many countries, in the establishment of national steering committees, national commissions for child labour or child labour units to coordinate action, instigate consultations and create a critical mass of knowledge and expertise at the national level. Child labour units have been set up, with IPEC support, in Egypt, Turkey, Kenya and the United Republic of Tanzania.

Other than the Ministry of Labour, ministries with a stake in fighting child labour may include those responsible for national development, economic policy, finance, rural and industrial development, public health, social welfare and protection, women's issues, education and law enforcement.

The child labour unit may act as the secretariat to a high-level institution that brings together this wider group of actors, sometimes charged with articulating and monitoring child labour policy. High-level committees consisting of representatives of government, employers' and workers' organizations, NGOs and academics have been set up in Argentina, Colombia, Kenya, Nicaragua, Portugal and Thailand, among other countries.

In Colombia, for example, the National Commission for the Elimination of Child Labour, active since 1995, monitors the country's national policy across a wide range of economic sectors and government institutions. It extends to the work of the Colombian Institute of Family Welfare, and NGOs working with it, to provide psychological counselling, training and income-earning opportunities. Action by trade unions complements the national plan by urging employers not to take on anyone under the age of 15. As a result of this work, Colombia has seen a reduction in child labour in several sectors.

Establishment of a legal framework for the abolition of child labour, along with mechanisms for its enforcement, is a responsibility that many governments have taken up. The vast majority of ILO member States have enacted legislation to set a basic minimum age for admission to employment, and to address other aspects of the employment of under 18-year-olds. Even in the absence of ratification, ILO Conventions still have an influence on national legislation. A coherent, national normative framework provides a stable point of reference for the various policy actors responsible for different aspects of children's rights. It also provides the basis on which violators of these rights can be held accountable.

While considerable progress has been made in establishing coherent national legal frameworks, inadequacies remain in many countries. The ILO provides advice on how legislation can be improved, for example, by harmonizing the provisions of the laws relating to education and child labour, by increasing the scope of legislation to cover sectors such as agriculture and work in the informal economy and by defining how to determine the types of hazardous work to be covered by legislation. For example, the ILO Multidisciplinary

Advisory Team for Andean, in Lima, commissioned studies in the Andean subregion to help governments identify the gaps and inconsistencies in their legislation as a basis for law reform. It is equally important that legal processes are reformed, for example, to introduce "child-friendly" court processes and treatment of child witnesses in ways that respect the dignity of the children involved.

Legal instruments in a wide range of areas have a bearing on child labour, its causes and its consequences, including those relating to discrimination and equal opportunities at work, freedom of association and collective bargaining, forced labour and trafficking, minimum wages, labour inspection, social security, health and safety, small enterprises, education, family law, criminal law and child protection. The framework should be reviewed in its entirety for its coherence, balance and coverage with respect to child labour. Countries can draw on the experience of others. Useful sources are the ILO's Labour Legislation Guidelines and the NATLEX database on national labour and social security law, both of which have recently added more examples of national approaches and full-text legislation.

Putting the legal framework in place, however, is clearly only a first step, albeit a very important one. The more challenging aspect is how such legislation can be effectively put into practice, particularly as child labour is so often hidden in the informal economy and government labour inspectorates in developing countries may be severely under-resourced in terms of staff numbers, capacity and equipment to carry out their work effectively. Practical, effective mechanisms for enforcement are needed to define the responsibilities of each party involved, to allow information to circulate freely among them and to create innovative mechanisms to generate critical information, particularly for the more hidden forms of child labour. People must also know about the law to be able to use it; raising awareness and legal literacy among children, families and communities about their rights and how to pursue them is an indispensable complement to legal reform.

Governments need to provide for universal birth registration for children. Without this, children cannot access social services or schools, and minimum ages for employment can be neither monitored nor enforced. Yet many nations lack effective systems for recording births. Every year, about 40 million children or one-third of all births, go unregistered around the world. Migrant children are particularly vulnerable to all forms of exclusion, which is compounded by their lack of official existence, increasing the likelihood that they will end up in child labour and often in its worst forms. Awareness-raising campaigns are essential to ensure that parents are aware of the importance of registration and know how to go about it.

One of a government's prime responsibilities is to provide for essential services to children and their families. Such investment is needed to fulfil children's rights to survival and development, and it is a crucial factor in long-term poverty reduction and the elimination of child labour. Yet, investment in children through health, education and social assistance usually represents only a small proportion of national budgets. Health care for mother and child, maternity protection schemes and immunization programmes, as well as social assistance and childcare for working mothers all have a role to play in combating poverty and child labour.

A "child budget" seeks to establish what proportion of social services expenditure actually reaches the children who need it. For example, the Hunger Eradication and Poverty Reduction Programme in Viet Nam is reported not to reach the most needy groups, so that children may perceive no option but to work.

Systematic tracing of funds invested in child-related programmes, from national level to point of delivery, can reveal how much reaches the targeted children and how much is lost along the way. The fact that several ministries often share responsibility for children and the existence of substantial official and unofficial development assistance and domestic programmes outside the regular budget make such analysis difficult. But such a process can help improve the planning and delivery of public expenditure in the future.

The provision of quality education for all children, as we have seen, is of crucial importance for the abolition of child labour. This means that:

— Primary education must be accessible to all children: available where children live, adequately equipped, for example, with heating, light and sanitation, at very low or no cost to the family, with quality curricula and teaching materials.

— Campaigning is needed to change prevailing negative attitudes to schools, alongside an improvement in their quality and relevance.

— Special efforts are needed to counter the factors that keep girls and disadvantaged and socially excluded groups, such as disabled children, migrants and the very poor, away from school.

— Teachers must be supported to do their job better, through good training and improvements in their status, pay and working conditions; respect for their rights to freedom of association and collective bargaining is critical in this respect.

— Primary education and secondary education up to the minimum age for employment should be made compulsory, and students' attendance monitored and supported where necessary.

Education must not stop at primary level if young people are to be adequately prepared for the labour market and for decent work within it, rather than being confined to low-skilled, unprotected jobs in the informal economy. Yet in the least developed countries as a whole, secondary educational enrolment is only 19 per cent. For Africa, secondary enrolment is 34 per cent and for developing countries overall the rate is barely over 50 per cent.

Vocational training also needs to be better resourced, of higher quality and better integrated into the education system. Governments thus need to look carefully at the education system in its entirety, including both its quantity and its quality, if it is to meet the needs of children and society as a whole and contribute its proper part to the abolition of child labour.

Under the 2002 annual review under the follow-up to the Declaration, free compulsory education was cited as a measure being implemented to bring about the abolition of child labour by 33 per cent of governments replying (for enforcement of the minimum age for employment) and by 25 per cent (for elimination of the worst forms of child labour).

The Government of India plans to introduce free compulsory education; a Bill providing for education as a fundamental right for children aged 6-14 years is pending approval by Parliament. The Government of Lesotho introduced free primary education in January 2000 as part of its efforts to eliminate child labour.

Countries that have yet to ratify the international covenants which are part of the international bill of rights, have ratified the Convention on the Rights of the Child (CRC). In a world full of conflict and violent confrontation, we have found a single issue that can evoke a positive sense of agreement. If we widen this small window of reconciliation and realise even a few of the core values of humanism that the CRC articulates, we may well succeed in having an impact on the quality of life of all people.

Most international instruments refer to "the people" on whose behalf these instruments have been ratified. Yet it is only recently that the people are becoming aware that international law has been transformed. It is no longer exclusively a matter for diplomatic relations between States but rather a set of norms that can be used to promote accountability in government within the state and at the national level.

The European Convention of Human Rights has adopted a radical procedure in this regard and even gives individuals right of relief and redress for any infringement of the standards of the convention by their governments.There are those who will argue that a rights strategy and realizing justice through the use of law are superfluous or irrelevant concepts, particularly in developing countries which suffer problems of poverty, social divisiveness and economic limitations. Yet the history of the past and the realities of today must surely convince us that the State has to be a presence in governance. It cannot "wither away" if we are to prevent anarchy. It is therefore vital to recognize that reality and develop structures and institutions that will humanise the interaction between the State and the people. Laws and a legal system fashioned according to norms of justice and international human rights standards which reflect the anguish and inspiration of human experience in struggling with authoritarianism are important for all peoples and their governments. They represent a universal and common heritage for ensuring that State power does not emerge as authoritarianism, but is exercised in a democratic environment.The CRC envisages an important role for the legal system in realizing those rights. International agencies such as UNICEF, which are committed to the interests of children, have a critical role in helping to interpret those rights and in refining them within the context of international human rights law standards. It is the responsibility of both the State and the people to ensure that these rights will not remain aspirations or concepts of international law that we have no hope or expectation of realizing.

We cannot afford to create an impression of international consensus, a common vision and a value system, where there is no real commitment to move our societies towards fulfilling their promises to children. Accepting treaty commitments under international law often becomes only a gesture, because most of our countries do not recognize that international law and domestic law are one system. According to this dualist approach, international law can be enforced domestically, only if treaty standards are incorporated into the national legal system. National courts therefore perceive treaty standards as having moral rather than legal authority.. This is why it becomes vital to ensure that the standards set by the CRC are incorporated into the national legal systems. The CRC, like certain other human rights treaties, recognizes the concept of cultural pluralism and diversity. Nevertheless, Articles 2 and 3 of the CRC, which can be described as the "non-discrimination" and "best interests of the child" clauses, require that States Parties commit them selves to realizing the same framework of core rights for all children. Article 2 in particular clarifies that a child's right of survival and development, protection from exploitation and aggression, and the right to participate in matters that concern the child, consistent with evolving maturity , must be realized for all children within ratifying countries. Factors such as the child's or the parent's or guardian's birth, economic class, disability, ethnicity, religion or gender, cannot be a justification for denying these rights or diluting them. The commonality of the core standards set by the CRC in Articles 24, 26, 27 and 28 must stimulate uniformly applicable policies on education, health and a safe environment.

We can no longer justify different standards in the treatment of children on the basis of a different vision of the nutrition, health, safe environment or education needs of "our children" and " others' children." It is difficult if not impossible to adopt a culturally relativistic approach which would argue that the State had no right to intervene or impose common standards. The articles in the CRC on compulsory education and attaining the highest standards of health, mandate policy intervention by the State to prevent or undermine social practice that would be an obstacle to the realisation of those standards for all children. We must also remind oursel not priorities one set of rights but treats them all as indivisible and interdependent.

It is not possible to realise the child's right to survival without projecting towards and committing efforts to realise the rights of development, protection from exploitation and participation. This inevitably means that law making becomes not merely a task for the legislator and the law reformer. Laws have to be put in place with a holistic perception of their linkages, and a commitment of the resources necessary for implementation. It is not therefore possible to prohibit child marriage or child labour by setting minimum ages by law, without legislative and administrative decisions that provide for compulsory education, facilities for registration of marriage, and the general implementation of relevant socio-economic policies.

Resource allocation for education, immunization, nutrition and sanitation, and legislative and regulatory mechanisms to ensure the proper delivery of these services becomes as much a part of law reform as legislating on minimum age for marriage, employment, and juvenile justice. These social and economic policies can no longer be considered issues of political choice outside the realm of law and enforceable rights. Many developing countries in Asia and Africa face problems of infant mortality, child marriage, maternal mortality, and the phenomena of child widows, child trafficking even across national borders for prostitution, and child labour. We are used to consider these children as high risk, exceptional categories who as children placed in difficult social and economic circumstances need protection by law. Yet the reality is that these children are a product of our countries' inability to realise their rights and the right of their families to national resources. When families are given minimal allowances to care for children, when maternity leave is grudgingly granted or perceived as a "benefit" to the working mother, we are perpetuating the myth of alleviating poverty and destitution while supporting a welfare payments and benefits ideology. Many of our countries have vagrancy laws that perceive poverty as a fault. Juvenile justice laws which deal with neglected street children speak of the need to rehabilitate them, and impose sanctions on parents for their poverty and neglect. Because we do not provide adequate resources for education or registration of marriage, we are reactant to impose sanctions on parents and the family for infringement of laws on child marriage and child labour. We recognize the validity of child marriage even as we set a standard of a minimum age of marriage by law. In a vicious cycle the inadequacy of the facilities is used as a justification for not imposing sanctions for violations.

In the process we do not begin to touch the fringes of the problem of gender discrimination and denial of children's access, girls in particular, to minimum standards of health and education. We cannot ameliorate adult female illiteracy or the health of the working mother. Maternity leave laws make it more difficult for a woman to compete with men for employment. Law making is perceived as ambivalent, and fails to have an impact on these problems. The CRC focuses on our past failures in recognizing that we should shift from the "poor law" and "welfare benefits" approach that has fertilised the jurisprudence of our countries for many centuries. Access to basic education, health care and a safe environment become the socio-economic rights of all children and their families who are entitled to resources allocation for these purposes. State parties are required to "take measures" to diminish infant and child mortality, combat malnutrition, ensure pre-and post-natal care for mothers as a social responsibility, and make at least primary education composure. It is only if these policies can be put in place, that it will be possible to realise the protection and participation rights of children. A reduction of the level of gender-based and other types of violence in our societies against children cannot be expected unless prohibitive sensations are combined with socio-economic policies that encourage responsible parenting and life chances for all children.

The concept of people's and children's core right to basic services in the area of health, education and environment is not as radical for national legal systems as it seems. Indigenous norms and even laws often recognised the concept of "community rights" in land. Even the legal systems derived from Roman law accepted that "the people" had certain rights in public rivers ad the sea shore. We already have on the statute books of countries, composure education laws, or laws on immunization, sanitation, community health and maternity leave that are often not monitored or enforced. Countries with written constitutions also have powerful mechanisms for using their chapters on fundamental rights to promote social action in areas such as health and education. Many of these constitutions adopt the typical standpoint in the traditional human rights discourse and treat civil and political rights as enforceable rights and social and economic interventions as uneforceable guidelines to state policy. However, the Indian Supreme court with its extensive power of judicial review has developed the concept of using rights litigation to link the directive principles to justifiable fundamental rights. Social sanction litigation has expanded the scope of Constitutional redress for violation of child rights in areas such as child labour, adoption, children in prison, prostitution and trafficking. The right to life has been recently interpreted as broader than a negative duty of the State to refrain from infringement of personal liberty. It has been interpreted as a positive duty to provide the basic conditions for survival. These initiatives reflect the same perspective, that core needs in the area of health, education and the environment are part of the basic justiciable fundamental rights that accompany citizenship. Citizenship laws which discriminate on the basis of gender have been challenged in the courts of Pakistan and Bangladesh.

The new Constitutional Bill proposed for the Republic of South Africa is unique in the area of constitution making for its integration of international law standards on children's rights and for recognising socio-economic needs as justiciable rights. Children's rights to nurturing, basic nutrition and health, are recognised as their particular fundamental rights to basic education and a safe environment. This constitution is also unique in making the link between child labour and education, following International Labour Organization standards and the standards of the CRC. Unlike many other constitutions, the South Africa Constitution defines the right to protection from hazardous labour as a right to be protected from labour that is prejudicial to health and education. The CRC therefore provides an incentive to the people, legislators, courts and lawyers to expand the scope of fundamental rights by constitutional amendments and/or interpretations of the law that link national constitutional standards to obligations of their states under international law. If an ethos is created in which there is widespread awareness of the CRC, courts and lawyers can be motivated to interpret constitutional and legal standards so as to incorporate the concept of child rights into dispute settlement. In countries that face problems of divisiveness it is important to remember that common legal values have already been forged by certain processes. Many countries continue to recognize the "choice concept" which permits persons to be governed by State law instead of personal laws based on ethnicity or religion. Certain laws and policies apply to all citizens, irrespective of choice.

The cords in most countries have used the concept of the "child" best interests" in guardianship litigation to forge uniform standards that undermine gender discrimination, discrimination against nonmarital children and the separateness of personal law that can have a negative impact on children. Constitutional standards already recognize equality before the law and even provide for affirmative state action on behalf of women and children so as to achieve substantive rather than formal equality.

Gender discrimination and discrimination against non-marital children is a remarkable feature of the jurisprudence of many countries. With constitutional closes on equality and non-discrimination, the standards of the CRC can be used to bobby for those areas that have been ignored in law reforms, since they strengthen and relate to the constitutional standards of domestic legal systems. Where Judicial discretion is exercised, an understanding of the framework of rights can stimulate dynamic interpretations of law that will give the child access to justice through the court system, and influence other methods of dispute settlement.

The absence of a childcentred focus in legal proceedings in largely due to the tendency to treat the child as a miniature adult before the courts of law. A child-centred approach stimulated by the standards of the CRC can help to create spaces for providing the child access to justice even within the constraints of existing laws. It may be argued that this kind of judicial activism is in consistent with the traditional role of the judiciary as an agency concerned with interpreting rather than making law. Yet the judiciary has expanded and expounded the content of major areas of law precisely because the arrival at a decision in legal proceedings involves policy choices. To day, written constitutions are the basic law of the land, and courts must interpret them to realise fundamental right's. It is hardly possible to argue that they can not interpret the constitution to promote the realisation of rights.

The obligation of State to publicise the CRC and the regular country report, as well as the concept of national and international cooperation in realising child rights prevents arguments of State sovereignty being used to restrict the monitoring of state performance. Nationally and internationally, the CRC envisages a partnership between many actors and encourages dialogue and cooperation. Just as it requires and assumes a joint parental and family responsibility, it assumes a shared state and family responsibility for realising the rights of children. This concept of a shared commitment makes law making and law enforcement something more than the exclusive preserve of lawyers, judges and law enforcement agencies or their critics. There is indeed no places for professional exclusiveness in formulating strategies to realise these rights.

As we see the massive violations of rights in many of our countries it is easy to lose faith in a strategy of rights and their advancement through legal processes. Yet a rights strategy has been usually forged through the experience of human anguish in containing the abuse of power. Rather than allow social and economic injustice to continue and spawn the terror of violence and disillusionment which impacts all our lives, civil society and governments can work together to promote State, community and family accountability in the use of power and authority.

If we can ensure accountability and humanism in the process of governance on an agenda of child rights based on the value system of this new and important human rights convention, we will have found a path to improving our past record on rights and move from rhetoric to action. We can then truly say to children, "you are indeed the wonder tree plant, grown of ruins."Ours is a deeply perplexing age in relation to rights. On the one hand there is a virtual explosion of human rights annotations; on the other hand, there is growing disregard of rights and cynicism about their future.

The proliferation of human rights instruments seems to have caused critics of human rights to form a rights-weariness and a rights-wariness. They insist that only a lean and sparse articulation of rights provides hope for their enforcement. Thus we are in a situation where there is a notable increase in affirmation as well as violations of human rights, where all struggles articulate themselves in the language of human rights and invoke the "politics" of rights; making human rights into bargaining points for the enhancement of power. Even so, the convention on the Rights of the Child, the World Summit Plan of Action, as well as the Jomtien World conference on Education for All, mark triumphant inaugural articulations of human rights. "Human rights," of course, in some way or other, have tacity included children's rights. But the range of inclusion was never so comprehensive and caring as is the case now.

The Vienna Declaration on Human Rights accelerates, in so many ways, the dynamics of the international movement for the promotion of "respect for the rights of the child to the CRC by 1995 and urges State to withdraw "reservations to the Convention" which are "contrary to the objects and purpose of the Convention or otherwise contrary to international treaty law." In particular the Declaration insists that all States, with international cooperation, should:

— combat "exploitation and abuse of children by addressing their root causes:,

— devise "effective measures against female infanticide, harmful child labour, sale of children, child prostitution, child pornography, as well as other forms of sexual abuse",

— organise "means of improving the protection of children armed conflicts" and programmes of "aftercare and rehabilitation of children in war zones" as well as those in "especially difficult circumstances." The minimum age of recruitment to armed forces is also addressed.

It is difficult to imagine even the most conscientious critics of human rights enuncitations as having any cogent critique of the expansion of child rights. Critics of human rights enunciations must surely respect the achievements of these measures and realise that inaction would be costly. The neglect of the rights of children would mean the confiscation of our common future: the world's children. Human rights articulations represent human hope in a brutal and brutalizing world. They provide arenas for he struggle for a just national and international legal order in relation to the child; hey mark an insurrectionary protest against the savage uses of power in the state and society. Even if we fail to achieve our collectively formulated human aspirations, not to try to achieve them is, starkly put, to belie our claim to be and to remain, human. For as state and society which is callous to the right of the child can never aspire to be a just society.

Adult illiteracy about children's rights is widespread among policy makers, intellectuals, ideogogues, opinion makers (e.g. the media), and even among human rights communities. This illiteracy also makes possible the comprehensive and continual ignorance about linkages between the rights of the child and human rights enunciations which are not child-centred and yet affect heir and our common future. Promotion of adult literacy about children's rights is a sine quo non for their realisation. It must be realized at the outset that the problem of adult illiteracy with respect to children's rights is as massive, complex and in need of urgent resolution as the problem of general illiteracy addressed at the Jomtien World Conference on *Education for All.* Second, we must acknowledge and develop linkages between the rights of the child and other instruments of human rights. There is no danger in such an endeavor of losing the focus on children's rights. Rather; awareness and advocacy of such linkages will enable us to advance the plan of action on children's rights. The World Health Organization had in 1993 activated the advisory jurisdiction of the International

Court of Justice on the use of nuclear weapons by a state in war or other armed conflict as constituting a breach of international law. The World Court accepted the reference and asked all states to make submissions by June 10, 1994. Whether or not explicit so far, the right of all persons, especially children, to immunity from a world with nuclear arms, as a part of the right to peace, is the matrix of all other rights. But there is little awareness of enthusiasm in children's rights communities (indeed, human rights communities in South Asia) on this laudable intuitive. Similarly, we have little appreciation of the implications of the Dunkelt text on the life and world of children. It should not require any apologies to seek to review world economic development from the standpoint of children's rights.

At the same time, we can not defer action on children's rights until the outcomes of scholarly and scientific engagement emerge. It may even be said that the lack of such involvement is among the "root causes" of the plight of the world's children! At any rate, reorientation of education and research traditions in "children's rights-friendly" directions is a task which ought to be high on our educational policy agenda.

In India, legislative initiatives for the promotion and protection of children's rights are sparse and their enforcement impoverished; some recent movement does, however, point to an emergence of a more active involvement. But insofar as rights are to be enforced by courts, the whole nature of the adjudicatory system and lowering manifests itself as among the prime "root causes." For India at least, the need to rethink its adjudicatory system, to retool it, to recreate it, is a need which emerges most sharply in the context of child rights. If the rule of law is to have any meaning for tens of thousands of India's children as they grow into "adulthood," then legal education and research, the transaction of the legal profession and court-craft, and the reogranisation of the court system should engage the attention of children's right advocacy in India. In a profound sense, the career and future of a rule-of-law society and state in India remains closely linked to children's formative perceptions about "rights," law" and "democracy". This remains unexamined but even so it may be said that a nation determines the reproduction or repudiation of legality by the formative experiences of justice and injustice that it imposes on its children.

Fourth, human rights instruments on children's rights stress "participation" as a core value, along with "survival," "protection" and "development." What strategies should be devised to encourage "participation" by children in designing policies for "survival", "protection" and 'development" is, indeed, a most critical question. Policy and legal paternalism is the very basis of the movement towards the enunciations of children's rights. The ideology of "participation, "however, interrogates the institutionalized paternalism of policy, law, administration. Even to raise this kind of question may seem to be a kind of luxury given the misery and powerlessness of masses of children, especially in many parts of the Third World. But it seems tome that giving children a voice, a forum, empowering their opinion, may accelerate the adult world's pace of progress towards realising their rights. To delink though and action on "participation" in my opinion, is to contribute, knowingly or otherwise, to a strategy or to a deferment of policies regarding the rights of "survival," "protection" and development."

It seems imperative to me that India should develop resources - intellectual, ideological, institutional and praxeological - for sustained children's rights advocacy. But given the nascency of the movement for children's rights, the persistence of historic formations that suppress and exploit children, and the need to accelerate history, some sort of institutional arraignment might enhance the capabilities of concerned citizens in their struggle to redeem our common future.

Protein-Energy Malnutrition (PEM), Iodine Deficiency Disorders (IDD), Vitamin A Deficiency (VAD) and Iron Deficiency Anemia (IDA) are the major problems of malnutrition in less developed countries, attacking more than half of the young child population. In society, malnutrition in any form is a problem with medical manifestations. The biochemical and medical complexities of malnutrition are dealt with by the science of human nutrition, while the problem of malnutrition in society calls for a much broader approach, requiring sciences, and others.

Like all other societal problems, malnutrition has a scientific and ethical aspect. Science deals with what "can" be done, while ethics deals with what "should" or ought to" be done. It is a scientific fact that iodisation of salt increases the intake of iodine and reduces the risk of IDD. It is, however, an ethical question whether or not salt should be iodised. It is a scientific fact that early initiation of exclusive breastfeeding reduces morbidity and mortality among very young children. The extent to which manufacturers should be allowed to distribute free breast milk substitutes in hospitals is an ethical question.

Science and ethics are dialectically related. Scientific discoveries influence ethics. For example the new discoveries in nuclear science pose some very difficult ethical challenges. Ethics, on the other hand, may influence science, such as the way in which human beings may be used for medical experimentation. Both science and ethics progress through the constant interaction between theory and practice. Theory has no meaning without practice, and practice is "blind" without a theory.

The nutritional needs of young children have been known for a long, time, even if details continue to be debated. These needs are expressed in quantified daily requirements of energy, protein and micro-nutrients. The definition of these requirements is a scientific task. Unfulfilled needs pose an ethical challenges, depending on how serious the deficiency is judged. When a need is recognised as being worthy of sympathy and serious consideration, this need becomes a claim. A need becomes a claim when people find it unethical not to do something about it. Claims, however, are of different strengths. Some people may claim that young children should have their requirements of minimum intake of iodine fulfilled. This is no more than a descriptive statement. Nobody is identified as having the duty to fulfill this claim. Stating that children have a claim to adequate iodine intake is stronger, but still no duties are defined. Stating, however, that children have a claim against their parents, the community, or the government are expected to do something. Such claims are called justified claims, valid claims or duty-claims.

The World Summit for Children (WSC) and the International Conference on Nutrition (ICN) specified and agreed on a set of nutritional goals. These goals transformed well-known nutritional needs into recognised claims. Heads of Governments/States in the WSC and Governments in the ICN promised to achieve these quantified goals (objectives) before the year 2000. Rights are more than claims. Rights are entitlements to something, even if they do not constitute valid claims against a particular individual or entity of society. Most often, however, rights imply obligation with the respondent clearly identified. Human rights have been defined as rights which all persons equally have simply insofar as they are human. Gewirth defines human rights as "personally oriented, normatively necessary moral requirements." "Personally oriented," because they are morally mandatory and not a result of charity. "Moral requirements" refer to (a) necessary needs, (b) justified entitlements and (c) claims on others.

An example from nutrition may help clarify these distinctions. Every child needs a minimum intake of iodine ("personally oriented"). Every child should get an adequate intake of iodine, or his/her mental development will be negatively affected ("normatively necessary"). This moral requirement constitutes (a) the fact that iodine is necessary ("necessary needs"), (b) that children have a right to optimal mental development ("justified entitlement") and (c) that the governments have an obligation to ensure the availability of iodised salt ("claim on others"). Human rights are primarily claim-rights, because they imply correlative obligation to other persons or groups. Eide et al. define these different aspects in the implementation of human rights: (1) to respect, (2) to protect and (3) to fulfill. They also suggest that human rights need to be implemented at different levels of society, from individual/household to international levels. This approach is used by Jonsson (1993) to operationalise the implementation of nutrition as a human right. Rights imply duties or obligations. Rights also imply goals. Goals, however, do not imply rights. A goal is a necessary, but not a sufficient condition for a right. This means that human development goals, including nutritional goals, can be achieved without any rights. Feinberg describes this in a thought-experiment "Nowheresville," where most of the human goals were achieved but where there was no self-respect, no dignity, no rights. The full implementation of the CRC requires or implies the achievement of all WSC goals. On the other hand, the achievement of the goals does not necessarily mean the full realisation of the CRC.

The challenge, therefore, is not only to achieve the WSC goals but to achieve them in such a way that the processes required for the realisation of the CRC are strengthened and accelerated. Such a rights-based approach combines elements from a goal-based strategy and a duty-based strategy. It constitutes a goal-driven, process-conditioning strategy. Kant stated that "ought' implies 'can' - or it is otherwise Utopia." Rescher questions this statement and suggests a new interpretation of Kant. He argues that if "ought implies can" this logically means that "obligation implies capacity", which in turn is equivalent to "incapacity removes obligation." This, however seems unacceptable. He qualifies this problem by two arguments.

a) "To all appearances, an obligation can persist despite an incapacity. We have to be prepared for the prospect of undischargeable duties and unmeetable obligations."

b) "...incapacity does not actually defeat an obligation, it can, however, negate all blame for a failure to carry it out."

He suggests a distinction between the weaker mode of "should" and the stronger mode of "must." Based on Rescher's analysis, a choice needs to be made between:

a) "Absolutistic" rules with "realistic" expectations, and

b) "realistic" rules with "absolutistic" expectations.

In this sense "ought" does not imply "can", while "must" does. In the ideal world, "ought" implies "can," while in the real world only "must" implies "can." Seen in this perspective the WSC goals represent "realistic" goals with absolute expectations, i.e. the goals must be achieved, and they can be achieved. The full implementation of the CRC, on the other hand, should be interpreted as "absolutistic" with "realistic" expectations. Rights are not divisible and cannot be graded; they are absolute. Many goals are "absolutistic" and not attainable. Rescher argues that it is completely rational to pursue unattainable goals. "Truth" has been the goal for scientific progress. As both Popper and Kuhn argued (and agreed for once!), this goal is not attainable.

Science, however, can come closer and closer to the "truth" (of. Popper's definition of "verisimilitude"). The same is true for democracy in political development. The CRC as a whole represents an unattainable goal, although many parts of the CRC can be defined is "absolutistic" goals, e.g. the WSC goals. It is very important to pursue morally important goals even if they are unattainable. By doing so, other attainable goals will be achieved faster. The promotion of the CRC contributes to the achievement of the WSC goals. Further, aiming "too high" often gives a better end result than aiming lower. Finally, pursuing unattainable goals gives a clear direction and can often mobiles and create new resources.

Rights implies duties and obligations, but most often nobody can be punished if the obligation is not met. When a right becomes a law, the respondent is identified and if the law is violated the respondent can be punished through the judiciary system. Practice, however, does not necessarily follow from law. There is therefore a need to enforce a law. Several countries have laws against distribution of non-iodised salt or against aggressive marketing of breast milk substitutes but their practices have not changed, because the laws have never been enforced. The World Summit for Children Declaration and the Convention on the Rights of the Child can be seen as "social contracts" between the Heads of States and governments and the states themselves and the world's children. More than 300 years ago, Thomas Hobbes (1651) defined in his Leviathan the concept of a "contract" as, "the mutual transferring of rights" and that "...he that is trusted to perform in time to come, being trusted, his performance is called keeping the promise." The challenge is now for leaders of governments to keep the promise they gave at the WSC and for states to keep the promise they made when they ratified the CRC.

Countries are used to being compared on their economic development. Now the time has come when countries should be compared for the way they take care of their children. Signing the WSC Declaration or the ICN Declaration or ratifying the CRC means an obligation to give "a first call on resources for children." Only the future will tell who will keep the promise. Hobbes, however, also stated "...covenants without the sword, are but words, and of no strength to secure a man at all." What "sword" do we have? An immediate action that can be taken is to establish national monitoring systems for the gradual achievement of the WSC goals, which are necessary for the implementation of the CRC.The WSC goals represent moral minima, supported by all major religions and political ideologies. A rights-based strategy aims at achieving such fundamental goals, but in such a way that their achievement becomes a right. This implies, for example, sustainability. Such a strategy will contribute to the development of a non-ethnocentric global development ethic. Gradually the information from monitoring systems will contribute to an increasing "global embarrassment" for those countries that have the resources but avoid the necessary political choices to achieve the goals. This will contribute to an environment where it becomes "good politics" to ensure the rights of children and "bad politics" to deny children their rights. In an increasingly democratic world more people will both know that the WSC goals can be achieved and think that the should be achieved. Ultimately this will not only influence what political leaders choose to do, but also why political leaders are chosen. As a Lawyer who has Discharged duties in the executive as well as in the legislative organs of the state, the Turkish legal system and existing practices in terms of the rights envisaged in the Convention on the Rights of the Child. The duties imposed upon the State by the Convention and some principles cited in the same document. The Convention obliges States Parties:

a. to make the principles and provisions of the Convention widely known to adults and children (Article 42);

b. to submit to the Committee on the Rights of the Child, through the Secretary General of the United Nations, reports on the measures they have adopted which give effect to the rights recognised and on the progress made on the enjoyment of these rights within two years of the entry into force of the convention for the state party concerned and every five years thereafter (Article 44/1);

c. to make their reports widely available to the public in their own countries (Article 44/6);

d. to take all legislative, administrative, economic and social measures for the implementation of the rights recognised in the Convention (Article 4);

e. to ensure that the institutions, services and facilities responsible for the protection of children shall conform, in terms of safety, health, the number and suitability of staff, with the standards established by competent authorities (Article 3/3); and,

f. to ensure that the best interests of the child shall be a primary consideration in all actions concerning children (Article 3/1).

Of course, this is not an exhaustive list of the obligations that States Parties have undertaken with respect to the Convention. Some duties that States Parties have to fulfill, particularly those which relate to the duty of making booth the Conventional and the reports widely known by the public, have the potential of mobilising the public. This mobilization can make a significant contribution to the material realisation of the rights included in the Convention. Besides emphasising the economic and social rights of children, the CRC lays down many principles relating to the rights of the child. The legislative, executive and judicial organs of States Parties have to take these principles into account in all activities relating to children. Among these principles are:

a. regarding the best interests of the child as a primary consideration in all actions concerning children (Article 3/1);

b. assuring the child who is capable of forming his or her own views the right to express these views freely in all matters affecting the child and giving due weight to these views in accordance with the age and maturity of the child;

c. showing respect to his or her basic rights while taking decisions concerning the child;

d. recognising the principle that parents have the primary responsibility for the upbringing and development of the child, and that appropriate assistance will be rendered to parents by the State in the performance of this responsibility (Article 18);

e. ensuring that a child shall not be separated from his or her parents unless such a separation is necessary for the best interests of the child (Article 9);

f. respecting the rights of parents or those who are responsible for the child (Article 3/2 and Article 5);

g. ensuring review of any penal decision concerning the child by an independent and impartial authority or judicial body (Article 40).

All these principles and provisions clearly show that there has been a change in the overall approach to the child. At the beginning of the present century, the relationship between the State, the child and parents was dominated and governed by quite different principles. Within the frame of these principles, the child was regarded as an "object" rather than a "subject." Throughout the first half of this century and even in the most advanced countries, the dominant view was that in all actions relating to the child, his or her needs could be best considered and met by "adults". If parents did not or could not fulfill their duties in relation to children, the State undertook to place the child in an institution under State surveillance or in another family. The child's view was not considered at all and there was little regard for the rights of parents.

Today there is a very different approach to the child, and due concern is also paid to the rights and duties of parents. It is accepted in principle that the child has the right to state his or her opinion freely and that this opinion should be properly considered in decisions concerning the child. The CRC is one of the documents which fully reflects this overall change in approach relating to the child. States Parties have the obligation to respect the rights and personality of the child and to ask for his or her opinion while they are engaged in legislative arrangements relating to the child and preparing the environment in which the child will be able to grow to his or her full potential.

The CRC was signed by the former Turkish Government on September 14, 1990. In order to ratify the Convention, the former Government immediately prepared a bill and presented it to the Parliament. However, in November 1991 the country had a general election and the composition of the Parliament, as well as the government changed. As a result, he provisions of the Turkish Parliament Proceedings Regulation, the bill that would provide for the ratification of the Convention, became void. Therefore, the new Government had to draft and present another bill to the Parliament. This New Bill is Currently on the agenda of the Turkish Grand National Assembly for ratification. Efforts are being made by a group of parliamentarians to ensure the speedy ratification of the Convention. When the Turkish legal system and related practices are analysed in terms of the provisions of the Convention, we can reach the following broad conclusions:

a. As far as some provisions of the Convention are concerned, there is no contradiction at all with respect to legislative arrangements or to legal practices. For instance, the child's right to a name and citizenship are guaranteed under the Turkish Civil Code, the Surname Act and the Act on Citizenship, which are all in effect currently. With these acts, it is impossible for a child in Turkey to be deprived of his or her right to a name or citizenship.

b. For some rights stipulated by the Convention, there are problems relating to practical aspects though no problem exists as far as the legislative frame is concerned. The child's right to education can be cited as an example. In Turkey, the child's right to education can be cited as an example. In Turkey, the child's right to education is recognised firstly by the Constitution (Article 42) and further elaborated by the Basic Law on National education and the Code on Primary Education in a manner fully conforming to Article 28 of the Convention. Under these acts, primary education is compulsory and free for all children irrespective of their gender. Furthermore, the State has the obligation to provide appropriate support to children who are talented but lack the material means to reach the highest stages of education in line with their specific interests and capacities. While these provisions are clearly stated in laws, there are some difficulties in actual implementation. For example, despite the face that primary education is compulsory and free for both boys and girls according to our Constitution, many families, especially in he region of southeastern Anatolia are reluctant to send their girls to school because of traditional beliefs.

c. In order to enable our children to benefit from some of the other rights stated in the Convention it is necessary to introduce new legislative arrangements, as well as certain administrative, economic and social measures. Some efforts in this direction have been made.

Article 32 of the Convention recognises the right of the child to be protected from economic exploitation. According to this article, States parties shall effect all legislative measures in conformity with the relevant provisions of other international instruments to provide the following: minimum ages for admission to employment; appropriate regulation of the hours and conditions of employment; and prevention of the performance of any work that is likely to be hazardous or to interfere with the child's education, or to be harmful to the child's health or physical, mental, spiritual, oral or social development. The same article obliges States Parties to take all relevant administrative, economic and social measures to protect children from economic exploitation. When the Turkish legal system is analysed in terms of the right to be protected from economic exploitation, it is seen that the relevant provisions are scattered among the various acts. In some cases provisions actually contradict each other.

The Labour Act stipulates the minimum age for employment as 15 (Article 67) According to the standards of the International Labour Organization (ILO) agreements. Nonetheless there are some exceptions to this rule. The very same Act states that children above 13 years can be admitted to employment if the nature of the work is such that it does not impair their health, development and school attendance. On the other hand, according to the Apprenticeship and Vocational Training Act, elementary school graduates may be given training at enterprises for the purpose of preparation for an occupation before the minimum age limit. This means that children around 11 or 12 years may be legally employed in light work.The working conditions of children are also taken into consideration by the Turkish legal system. According to the Labour Act, working hours of children must not exceed 7.5 hours and must not interfere with their school hours (Labour act, Article 67). Before employing children, employers must ensure, through a health check-up, that the child's health is appropriate for the job. The health examination has to be repeated every six months (Labour Act, Article 30). Employers who do not fulfill these obligations are liable to be fined (Labour Act, Article 104).

These legal provisions, which are designed to protect children from economic exploitation, cannot be enforced in most cases since relevant administrative, economic and social measures have not been taken. Moreover, since the Acts mentioned above do not cover children who work in the agricultural sector or in the streets, such children are vulnerable to conditions that are potentially harmful for their mental and physical health, education and development. Street children particularly are frequently subjected to physical, emotional and sexual abuse. As examples of the Provisions of the Convention which require new legislative arrangements and some economic, social and administrative measures, we can cite those which are related to delinquent children and others who are abused and neglected. The programme of the previous Coalition Government, in which, gave priority to human rights as well as children's and women's issues. Hence, that Government had, in addition to presenting the bill which provided the ratification of the Convention, prepared another bill which revised the current Juvenile Court Act. In preparing for the Juvenile Court Bill, the Ministry of Justice considered both the Convention on the Rights of the Child and the UNs Standard Minimum Rules for the Administration of Juvenile Justice.

The Cooperation Programme largely includes backward provinces, those which have been prioritised for development and big urban centres. The rationale behind this is the fact that these provinces are the ones in which children are affected much more adversely by such phenomena as poverty, unhealthy urbanization, intensive migration and distorted patterns of income distribution. In addition to those which are valid for all children, the CRC includes special provisions, which cover children in especially difficult circumstances. This category includes children who are:

— in need of protection or special education;

— subjected to abuse and neglect;

— used in crime, drug trafficking, prostitution and pornography; and

– working.

A point which we would like to raise here in relation to children in need of protection is the change taking place in the overall policies of the Social Services and Child Protection Institution in conformity with the provisions of the CRC. This agency no considers keeping children with their own families as the priority solution and strives to create supportive institutions for the family and to extend assistance to needy families. Alternative care such as placing children with relatives, protective family, adoption, etc. is resorted to only in the most pressing cases. It is now accepted also by the Ministry in charge that institutional care should be the last resort. In spite of this, more than 90 per cent of children who have been taken under protection by the State are placed in protective institutions. We hope that this situation will change soon with the introduction of new policies.

The Convention on the rights of the Child, represents an instrument of infinite significance which binds peoples everywhere to cooperate "for improving the living conditions of children in every country, in particular, the developing countries and to evolve a viable jurisprudence of juvenile justice." The Universal Declaration of Human Rights and the International Covenants on Human Rights, which together make the magna carta of making, confer rights without discriminating as to age, race, sex, religion, birth or other factors. The Universal Declaration of Human Rights rightly stresses that childhood is entitled to special care and assistance. It further maintains that the family, as a fundamental unit of society, should focus on children as the new hope of tomorrow and provide all the necessary conditions for their growth, the lack of which would result in the stunting of the community. So it is that the Universal Declaration specifies in Article 24 that:

1. Every child shall have, without any discrimination as to race, colour, sex, language, religion, national or social origin, property or birth the right to such measures of protection as are required by his status

as a minor, on the part of his family, society and the State.

2. Every child shall be registered immediately after birth and shall have a name.

3. Every child has the right to acquire a nationality.

The voiceless child has title to legal protection before or after birth, according to the canons of international justice. But the harsh truth is that the welfare of the child ranks tragically low in the agenda of State action. In our present day world, the trauma and torture, the illiteracy and deprivation, the hard labour and gross neglect which are the lot of the Third World's juvenile generation call for sensitive social action, united mass mobilisation and affirmative justice processes. Every child everywhere belongs to one global family and is entitled to a universal minimum of rights, fullness of expression and development of faculties.

One hundred and thirteen nations, by consensus, promulgated the Vienna Declaration and Programme of Action where the rights of the child and of the girl child in particular, have justly received humane emphasis worldwide. The Vienna Declaration and Programme of Action makes a humanitarian summons on nations in the articles relating to the rights of the child. Part D of the Vienna Declaration dealing with the rights of the child must become the locomotive of juvenile jurisprudence. The World Conference at Vienna emphasized the principle of "first call for children," and underlined "the importance of major national and international efforts especially those of the United Nations Children's Fund (UNICEF), for promoting respect for the rights of the child to survival, protection, development and participation."

The Vienna Conference Specifically refers to female infanticide, child prostitution, child pornography as well as other forms of sexual abuse and enjoins that measures be taken by specialized agencies "to ensure the effective protection and promotion of human rights of the girl-child" and "urges States to repeal existing laws and regulations and to remove customs and practices which disriminate against and cause harm to the girl child."

Childhood and youth are subject to many visible and invisible suffering and disabilities. Thus, several conventions and other instruments have included juveniles as part of International Jurisprudence by the United Nations. Each nation must have a special ombudsman for juvenile justice, with power, suo motu, to investigate, here cases, render verdicts and take action, including punishment. Cultural cooperation among nation, acceptance of common values and the introduction of a world watchdog, which will not become an instrument of imperialism, but will operate in the juvenile field as a functional and effective Human Rights Commission is an urgent desideratum.

If the Charter of the United Nations and the International Bill of Human Rights are to be taken seriously humanity worldwide, there is a need to transform the Declarations, Covenants, Conventions, Resolutions and Programmes of Action from pious wishes and paper projects into stern commands and operational obligations. The ideals and goals projected in the UN instruments are a global gain. But shaping children's future by law, and harmonising their lives with the right to health and a happy environment has a long way to go. Laws on the books and law in action often occupy different streets. If environmental degradation and betrayal of human health are not corrected by law and affirmative action by the executive, legislative and judicial wings of the State, tomorrow may castigate today as treacherous. So what we need is the development of a community conscience in the field of child justice, without which social justice and sustainable development will be a mockery of democracy.

The Constitution of India states specifically that affirmative discrimination in the form of special provisions for women and children is permissible. Article 39(e) of the India Constitution shows special concern for children and directs the State to secure conditions in favour of children so that in their tender age, they are not abused nor coerced by economic necessity to enter avocations unsuited to their age or strength. Article 45 directs the State to provide free and compulsory education for all children until they complete the age of 14 years. There is no doubt whatever that these obligations have been violated. There has been a chronic dereliction of duty on the part of the State. Vast numbers of children have been kept illiterate, uneducated and without protection against exploitations of childhood such as forced labour and unwholesome activities, which condemn them to moral and material abandonment. If the State betrays its obligation, the Court and the people must rise to monitor and correct this delinquency.

The needs of children and our duties towards them have been expressed in the Constitution. The Resolution on a National Policy on Education has been adopted by Parliament. It gives direction to State policy on the Educational needs of children. India is also party to the UN Convention of the Rights of the Child. Goals set out in this document can reasonably be achieved by judicious and efficient use of the available national resources.

The vision projected covers a comprehensive health programme, nutrition service of a formal or informal nature, free and compulsory education, special attention to the children of weaker sections and those who are socially handicapped, delinquet or otherwise in need of rehabilitation. Even in litigation involving them, children's interests are to be given paramount consideration.

Although nominally a National Children's Board was constituted in 1974 and reconstituted in 1981, the majority of Indian children in India belong to the via lnerable sections and poverty' stricken families. The International Year of the Child (1979) was followed by a whole decade dedicated to the redemption of children from neglect, destitution and deprivation. The International Year and the decade have come and gone, statistics have escalated and the dimension of the problem remains frighteningly colossal. The Constitutional obligation has not been implemented and although the international instruments, such as the Universal Declaration and the two Covenants and the Convention and Declaration regarding the rights of the child, have persuasive power over the State, their fulfillment continues to be a low priority. Nevertheless there has been at least one step forward, the Government is committed to the National Policy for Children which emphasises the importance of education in Human Resource Development The vicious circle of child illiteracy, cheap child labour, and poverty cannot be used to deny the child his/her basic right to develop as a full human being. In fact, other countries with repent poverty have fared better. China is far ahead of us.

African countries have advanced beyond us. Among the 21 largest developing countries, India ranks 15th in overall literacy and 12th in the percentage attending primary schools. The denial of education is the denial of the creative potential of the child and a culpable deprivation by the State since education of the young is a categorical imperative. India's future, bearing mind that there are over 20 million children below 14 years of age, depends a great deal on juvenile justice in its development dimensions. The National Policy is a printed tribute; but if, alongside it, ill-health and illiteracy, child labour, squalor, shanties and infant mortality flourish, the future remains bleak and the country's failure to provide juvenile justice, an ominous shock. The challenge of the child continues.

In 1979, the International Year of the Child, the Government set up the Gurupadswami Committee to submit a report on child labour. That Committee notwithstanding, the Ministry of Labour accepted child labour as a "harsh reality," taking the view that abolition of child labour is not an economic feasibility.

The culpability of the establishment is aggravated by the fact that, far from withdrawing children from labour, provision for training of children to labour better, is being organized. For example, in 1978, the Handloom and Handicrafts Exports Corporation (HHEC), a Delhi-based Government body, had set up a training centre to train children between ages seven and 14 to weave carpets. This job has been declared hazardous and forbidden by law since the woolen fibers are dangerous for the child's lungs, eyes and skin. These children, after undergoing training eight hours a day for one year, enter into the carpet industry for employment.

During February and May 1983 a series of reports appeared in the newspaper regarding rampant child labour in the fireworks and match factories of Sivakasi, a town in the Ramanathapuram district in the state of Tamil Nadu. The children in these factories are made to work nearly 15 hours a day, in spite of the fact that the occupation has been scheduled as hazardous for children. This issue of child labour is Sivakasi has ignited a national debate on the question of the legitimisation of child labour. Social paediatrics, in the sense of eliminating the infrimities - social, economic and other - of children, has received statutory consideration at the hands of our legislatures.

Public interest litigation in the area of bonded labour of children has made some change or at least awakened the people to their crime against the younger population. It is an equally well known fact that trafficking in children is becoming resistant to the law. Cheap labour through dalals is something blinked at by officials. girl children often end up in the flech trade. Indeed, the worst atrocities relate to the girl child. Middlemen buy and sell children while the law offers little resistance.

The legislature may reasonably claim that laws against employment of children have been made as partial implementation of the promise of justice to children. The minimum age of employment has been fixed by law and hazardous employment prohibited. The period beginning with 1950 has witnessed a spate of legislation based on the Labour Investigation Committee Report. Today it can be claimed that in the eye of the law the right to life, which includes the right to education and development, interdicts child labour. this labour not only risks life and opportunity for growth but also denies those freedoms and facilities without which a child is condemned to dwarfism, moronism and penury of creativity. The ILO Convention has gone a long way in the amelioration of children's status. The Plantation Labour Act, the Mines Act, the Factories Act, the Motor Transport Workers' Act, the Beedi and Cigar Workers (Condition of employment) Act, the Employment of Children Act (as amended in 1978) have provisions which are benignly disposed towards children. The present priorities of the government ignore the child. The minimum one expected was the implementation of the National Labour Commission recommendations of 1969. Scattered pieces of legislation are not equal to a uniform code which liberates the child and gives him his entitlement for development. A similar situation holds true regarding child labour, child education, child nutrition, and child development. A child's welfare cannot be compromised; a holistic approach to Project Juvenile Justice must deal with the negative and positive aspects, as in the English Children Act.

We cannot claim that the Children Act of 1960 and the Juvenile Justice Act of 1986 passed in India are as effective as the English counterpart although the inspiration for both came from the English statues. When we deal with the child we have to deal with parents too, especially in societies where divorce is frequent and poverty is omnipresent. The guardianship of the child must depend upon the interests and well-being of the child, not only on the personal law. Likewise, the question of criminal responsibility of a child when an offense is committed needs special attention. The question of neglect and delinquency vis-a-vis children is a delicate and sensitive branch of law, and depends very much on concern and commitment for the tender age of the juvenile. In India, more and more crimes are committed by adults using children as tools. Here we come upon the need for a Penal Code dealing with young persons which meets the manifold difficulties of the problems of juvenile culpability and curative methodology. Psychiatric inputs may be necessary to help the Court pass appropriate sentences, custodial or non-custodial. After care organizations also call for careful design, depending on the country and culture and social milieu. Certified schools, industrial schools, children's' homes and the like, along with foster care, adoption, sponsorship and other human techniques have to be compassionately created. In India there is not even an adoption law because religious differences have made it difficult for a facultative national legislation on adoption. Intercountry adoption has its own dangers although the India Court, at the highest level, has laid down guidelines. Even so, the fact remains that intercountry adoption deprives the child of its title to native culture and citizenship and promotes the likelihood of being a second-class citizen in later years in the foreign country. Cacism, cultural discrimination and the helplessness of the child in a foreign jurisdiction cannot be overcome by all that the Supreme Court has laid down.

The finest hour of Juvenile Justice Jurisprudence arrived in India when the Juvenile Justice Act, 1986 was passed. Prior to that, there were many imitative Children's Acts which when put into operation produced chaos. The Children Act of 1960 was preceded by the United Nations Declaration of the Rights of the Child in 1959. Concepts became more refined and juvenile justice was adopted by the UN General Assembly in 1985 followed in India by the Juvenile Justice Act of 1986. These is more scientific and comprehensive treatment of the subject in the 1986 law which deals with neglected juveniles as well as delinquent juveniles. Prostitution, narcotic drugs and psychotropic substances, observation homes and places of safety are relevant topics in the juvenile context and are receiving legislative attention now. The Indian Jurisprudence of Juvenile Justice is the wayward victim of legislative chaos and statutory slumber. And even when a fine piece has been put on the statute book, meaningful execution is distances away. If inaction is a form of action, the executive is culpable of non-enforcement of the law as any serious student of the subject will agree. The tragic irony is that the State Children's Acts continue de facto in many parts of the country, because the Juvenile Justice Act visualises various structures, functionaries and expenditures for which the States may not be ready. Neglected juveniles and delinquent juveniles fall under different categories and punitive provisions regarding each must therefore be different.

Many of miscellaneous matters regarding duties of parents, appointment of officers, people's participation through Advisory Boards, health care for juveniles and the like, find specific statutory expression in the Juvenile Justice Act. Had this justice legislation been brought into force throughout the country, the protection, development, correction and rehabilitation of younger delinquents would have received therapeutic jurisprudential attention sufficient to meet Constitution obligations. There are many sins committed by the State which cannot be forgiven but those which relate to the welfare of children deserve condign public censure because the child has the first call on the State's resources. Because children are voiceless and voteless they are neglected with impunity by those in power who will be held guilty by the future.

15

Child Labour and Human Rights

In the context of child labour, a working definition of 'child' may be a person below the internationally agreed age limit of 15 years. However, different countries have different basic minimum age of employment.The economic exploitation of children in India has always been an area of concern. In rural areas it is the fact that the child who does not attend a formal school is a working child. Collection of water, fuel, household chores and taking care of younger siblings all constitute important elements of a child's life. While many of these activities cannot be defined as hazardous work, inasmuch as they interfere with the normal development of the child and in the child's ability to reach his/her true potential they violate the Convention on the Rights of the Child. In the typical environment in which Indian children grow up the concept of a non-working, non-social going child simply does not exist. The issue of compulsory education has always been something of anenigma. At the theoretical level very few disagree that all children should receive education, at least upto the primary stage, or with the fact that children should not work. In fact, the state has committed itself not only to the universalisation of primary education but also to the abolition of child labour through various pronouncements, not the least of which are the Directive Principles of State Policy enshrined in the Constitution of India. Democracy and its three pillars—liberty, equality and fraternity—enshrined in the Constitution of India are relatively meaningless in view of the fact that 120 to 140 million children are working in this country. Of these, 55 million children between the ages of six and 14 are languishing in servitude. They are employed mostly in agriculture and industries such as carpet weaving, brassware manufacture, glass and banglemaking, leather, gem cutting and polishing, matches and fireworks, stone quarries, brick kilns and handloom.

Socio-cultural factors, including the abominable caste system and ethnic and gender discrimination, are responsible for the perpetuation of the scourge of child labour. These factors exercise a significant negative influence, worse even than socio-economic factors such as grinding poverty, unemployment and illiteracy. Little wonder that 90 per cent of bonded child labourers belong to untouchable castes and tribes. No government can scale down adult unemployment without curbing child labour. This is so because the maximum job opportunities created every year are preferentially given to children as their physical and mental vulnerability makes them easy to exploit. In addition, children represent the cheapest source of human labour. Our logical apprehension is that if we do not eradicate child servitude today, we will be responsible for perpetuating the poverty, abject misery and ill-health of 55 million adults in the country. It should be noted that the growth rate of the population is much higher among those communities in which unemployment is rampant. Obviously, if child labour is not controlled, impoverished parents will continue to succumb to the 'necessity' of enlarging the number of earning members in the family. In India, an aggressive anti-carpet campaign was launched; the premises of manufactures were raided, children were liberated and their rehabilitation started. In addition, the issue has been publicised widely and political will has been generated for the total eradication of this menace. The phenomenon of the sale of children is universal. The tragic circumstances leading to the abuse and exploitation of children cuts across the barriers between the developing and developed world. As child labour entails the sale of a child, the following concepts of sale could also be considered:

i) armed conflict;

ii) adult criminal activities: forced labour or abducted children;

iii) debt bondage;

iv) labour in the unorganised sector;

v) labour in the organised sector;

vi) child prostitution;

vii) pornography and sexual exploitation;

viii) forced marriage;

ix) disabled children in the labour force;

x) domestic labour;

xi) apprenticeship and family-supervised labour.

It is recognised that the exploitation of child labour is a form of sale of children. Generally speaking when one considers the notion "child labour" *per se*, it is not necessarily detrimental to children. However, when it gives rise to exploitation, usually be another party who has power over the child, it may result in negative consequences for children, both with regard to their rights and their development. It also constitutes sale because the child becomes the object of a transaction in cash or in kind. It appears that in many parts of the world, children are sold into several types of employment, either by their parents, guardians or other intermediaries. Recently, the International Labour Organisation (ILO) estimated that there were some 88 million working children between 10 and 14 years of age. Instances of exploitation are to be found in all regions of the world but Asia and South America figure high in the number of children in difficult circumstances. It is noted that the worst forms of child labour exploitation often take place in the informal sector and small-scale industries.

At the international level, various instruments provide an umbrella of protection for child labourers. Under the auspices of the ILO, a series of conventions and recommendations on the exploitation of child labour has been developed. One key convention is Convention Number 138 which establishes 15 as the basic minimum age of employment, although reduction to 14 may be possible in developing countries.

The ILO conventions and recommendations have been strengthened by the advent of the convention on the rights of the child. The CRC emphasises anew the issue of sale linked with child labour. Article 32 states that "children should be protected from economic exploitation and from performing any work that is likely to be hazardous or to interfere with the child's education, or to be harmful to the child's health or physical, mental, spiritual, moral or social development". In East Asia, the sale and trafficking of children for labour exploitation is still rampant both locally and across borders. The issue is closely linked with the sex market. In Africa, the exploitation of child labour in the informal sector was reported in various countries in 1993. In particular, the girl-child is a victim of exploitative domestic service. At times, there is a link with the remnants of slavery, such as the sale of children for forced labour, particularly from certain ethnic groups. In Central and South America, the number of children at work is large, especially as there is a vast population of street children. There were disturbing incidents of killings of street children during the past year. In this region, too, the problems of child domestic workers and the use of children in the informal sector are rampant. At the other extreme, children are at times employed to sell drugs. In Europe, the problem of child labour exploitation poses a challenge to many countries. This includes a specific linkage with children used as instruments of crime and as domestic workers.

In relation to child labour, the whole range of measures advocated by the UN Commission on Human Rights' Programme of Action for the Elimination of the Exploitation of Child Labour, 1993 should be implemented. There should be stricter law enforcement in the case of child labour, with more incentives for exemplary law enforcement personnel. All vestiges of bondage should be eradicated, and attention should be paid to the plight of the girl-child. The Programme of Action against Child Bondage, 1992, should also be placed as a priority for all parties concerned. Child labour only happens in the poor world—while the vast majority of working children are found in developing countries, children routinely work in all countries. In every country, rich and poor, it is the nature of the work children do that determines whether or not they are harmed by it—not the plain fact of their working. Few people in the industrialised world, for example, would look upon the employment of a child to deliver newspapers for an hour or two before school as an exploitative form of child labour, despite the fact that the child will certainly be paid less than normal adult rates for the job. Often such a job will be encouraged in the interest of the child's gaining experience of the 'real world' of work and commerce.

Child labour will never be eliminated until poverty disappears—it is true that the poorest, most disadvantaged sectors of society supply the vast majority of child labourers. The conclusion often drawn from this is that child labour and poverty are inseparable and that calls for an immediate end to hazardous child labour are unrealistic. The phrase 'child labour' conjures up a particular image: we see children chained to looms in dark mills and sweatshops, as if in a long and nightmarish line running from Lancashire in the 1830s right through to the South Asia of the 1990s.

Child labour has increased substantially in Central and Eastern European countries as a result of the abrupt switch from centrally planned to market economies. In industrialised countries, such as the UK and the US, meanwhile, the growth of the service sector and the quest for a more flexible workforce have contributed to an expansion of child labour. Understanding all the various cultural factors that lead children into work is essential. But deference to tradition is often cited as a reason for not acting against intolerable forms of child labour.

Children have an absolute, unnegotiable right to freedom from hazardous child labour—a right now established in international law and accepted by every country that has ratified the convention on the rights of the child.

Respect for diverse cultures should not deflect us from using all the means at our disposal to make every society, every economy, every corporation, regard the exploitation of children as unthinkable. Street child labour, virtually unheard of prior to the transition to a market economy, is now a growing problem in the Russian Federation. In Kyrgyzstan, in Central Asia, the numbers of children working on the streets, selling food and other products, have increased dramatically over the last three years. Many have dropped out of school or never attended classes. On the streets, they shine shoes, wash and guard cars, carry luggage, hawk flowers and trinkets, collect recyclables and find a myriad other ingenious ways to make money.

The amount they earn may be small but is sometimes more than they would receive from formal-sector work. In virtually every area of life and in every country as these annual state of the world's children reports have long noted, girls and women routinely bear burdens and endure treatment that reflect their unequal status. So it is with child labour. Working girls are often invisible, treated as if they did not exist.

All over the world, more girls than boys are denied their fundamental right to primary schooling. In some regions, including the Middle East and North Africa, sub-Saharan Africa and especially South Asia, the gender gap is still enormous. Educational equality between the sexes is being approached in East Asia and Latin America and the Caribbean, but elsewhere little progress has been recorded. The exploitation of children is one of the consequences of complex situations of insufficient progress. ILO observed that 98 per cent of the economically active children are found in developing countries. The Special Rapporteur of the United Nations Sub-Commission on prevention of discrimination and protection of minorities also observed that poverty and exploitation of child labour go hand-in-hand. It is the poorest populations, at the lowest levels of human existence, who are forced to work the most prematurely. Children may be forced to work due to poverty but child labour in turn accentuates poverty.

Children are engaged in jobs that can be done by adults too, thus depriving adults of jobs. Employers prefer to hire children because they can extract the same work from children at lower wages, in the process bringing down the overall wages for such jobs. Thus child labour increases adult unemployment and reduces their income and thus forces adults to send their children to work to supplement the family income. The poor are thus caught in a vicious circle. Rather than improving the household income, child labour helps to reduce it.

In a large number of developing countries, migration from rural areas has also intensified the problem of child labour. In most developing countries, developmental efforts have neglected the agrarian sectors, resulting in growing pauperisation of small farmers, increasing landlessness and rural differentiation. This has led to search for wage employment in commercial farms, as well as to rapid migration away from rural areas. Children from poor families are forced into the labour market to work either individually or as part of contracted family labour. When a rural family migrates to the town, the adults are straightaway faced with a new and unknown environmental and labour situation. As a result of the instability and insecurity that this causes, the children are often sent to work so that the family may survive.

Countries having low literacy and school attendance rates generally have the most acute child labour problems. It has been often stated that education can bring the dramatic exploitation of child labour to an end. The example of the developed countries confirms this conclusively. The historical record reveals an astonishing correlation between the progress of education in Europe and decrease in the volume of child labour and the transformation of its very nature. A glance at the educational statistics shows that it is almost always the same countries that admit to being the most behind in school enrolment and teacher-student ratio, that have the greatest problems as regards the exploitation of child labour.

Governments in developing countries lack financial resources for universal compulsory primary education and parents often find schools irrelevant to meet their needs. Many countries successfully made primary school education compulsory and universal when per capita incomes were low, poverty was widespread and parents would have employed their children had they been permitted to do so. The relationship between child labour and illiteracy may not be one of cause and effect. Some countries have largely succeeded in eradicating illiteracy but remain confronted by the child labour problem, which is sometimes very acute. Sri Lanka is an example of a country that massively expanded its primary school enrolments in the 1950s.

By 1981, 90 per cent of the primary school-age children were in school and 70 per cent of all children completed five years of schooling. Labour force statistics indicated a sharp decrease in the number of children in the age group of 10-14 in the labour force from 1946-63 as a result of school enrolment. Thus the importance of compulsory schooling in the struggle against child labour cannot be undermined. However, the educational system adopted by countries concerned must be meaningful and realistic and must adapt itself to the real needs of society.

The role of vested interests in perpetuating child labour also need to be highlighted. Employers often claim that there are types of work for which children are particularly suited. However, most work done by children can also be done by adults. The real reason behind employers preference in hiring children is the desire to maximise profits. Children can be made to work for long hours for low wages. Employers find it easier to deal with children because they do not organise themselves in trade unions, can be easily intimidated and are not capable of defending themselves and insisting on their rightful due.

The notion of child labour is also rooted in the traditions and attitudes of the regions where it is practised, as a remnant of the past, a form of resistance to change. In many societies, child labour is not considered a problem and is regarded as part of a child's normal socialisation even if exploitative work conditions are present. On the other hand, the attitudes and beliefs of policy makers in several developing countries regarding the respective roles of upper and lower classes have perpetuated the problem. It is often argued that the children of the poor should be prepared for their future roles from an early age.

Child labour persists in some countries because of lack of political will to deal with the problem and because child labour laws cannot be adequately enforced because of shortage of qualified labour inspectors. Thus children work because of poverty, lack of compulsory education, rapid rural-urban migration and because of prevailing social, cultural and political attitudes.

Family farming makes the greatest use of child labour in the context of unpaid family assistants. In this type of labour it is not so much the child who is exploited by the general social system as the whole family. The economic, social and cultural situation of the family obviously has repercussions on the child but he at least remains integrated in a social context that is in principle protective. Children are also engaged in family craftwork. The intricate rules governing the market for the crafts produced also makes possible exploitation and abuses. As in the case of family farming, there is no question of wage and the situation remains one of joint production at the group level. This type of activity, in which the exploitation of child labour is no less real because it is indirect, to be found in most parts of the world. Craft piecework is a more highly evolved form than the previous type. It meets the same needs, is carried out in the some places, and employs the same manufacturing techniques. However, a middleman or a capitalist is involved who picks up the products from the families to market them, having first secured a more or less extensive and more or less excessive sales monopoly. The family no longer has direct access to the market. To be in a better position to exert pressure he gives a small advance on the wage.

The threat of exploitation is clearly greater and affects the child along with the family. Since payment is made on the basis of amount and quality of work, to earn more money the family calls upon its children and becomes the more or less willing and conscious accomplice of the middleman. Children also carry out small tasks on their own account. However, two subtypes, differing radically, according to the level of development of the country, must be distinguished in this type of work.

In developing countries, the child usually works in order to live and in order to survive. In developed countries children usually work in order to satisfy secondary or even superfluous needs. Small tasks called out by the child for third parties are different in that they produce a relationship of dependence which can very easily become one of exploitation. The seasonal labour of children in agriculture is more organised and also more prevalent. Seasonal labour is in general remunerative and is carried out under widely varying conditions. However, to the extent that it is work that is very difficult to control and in which middlemen are fairly numerous, the loopholes for abuse are quite large. Learning how to work is a part of any sound and balanced education. Apprenticeship enables the child to try his hand at a task at a fairly early age and then to improve in skill until all operations have been mastered. But very frequently apprenticeship is simply subterfuge for evading legislation on minimum age.

The exploitation of child labour is perpetuated through apprenticeship. More often than not, supposed apprentices are in fact working rather than learning and not being paid for it. Such a state of affairs may sometimes last for years. There is too much fake apprenticeship, which is merely a facade behind which there is nothing at all, since the activities performed require no qualification, provide no training and at best are carried out for paltry sums. Maids-of-all-work in situation of virtual bondage are to be found everywhere. This type of child labour is very widespread. Bonded labour is the ultimate stage of exploitation of child labour. Debt bondage can arise in a number of ways. In agrarian societies land tenure patterns impose on tenants, sharecroppers and similar categories of workers obligations over and above household consumption requirements. In some cases, these obligations, may take the form of providing the landlord a share of the produce. But in others they may involve the provision of labour services, including those of children. The prevalence of such relations is known to lead to a severe and high incidence of debt bondage. Debt bondage is often also the result of the parents being given a loan to meet some urgent need. The debtor then has to repay by working. Parents may send children to work in the house of the moneylender.

In practice the debt does not decrease; it climbs ever upwards—a combination of usurious interest rates and outright fraud. These children may stay for many years, not knowing how long they must work or even the size of the debt they are paying off. While bonded labour is prohibited by law, it is still found for example, in parts of South and South-east Asia. Children in most countries have always been used as prostitutes but the situation in some Asian countries, like Thailand, has been aggravated by the expansion of mass tourism. Both boys and girls are used in the flesh trade. In Sri Lanka, for example, the majority of child prostitutes are boys. The problem can also be analysed by examining the sectors in which children are employed. Sectors employing child labour vary from one country to another but child labour is most common in agriculture followed by service sector, largely in street trades and in third place industry. Most child work is agricultural. Starting with light tasks, such as looking after animals, collecting firewood and fodder and drawing water, they later learn to sow and to reap. In commercial agriculture, on plantations for example, they often work as part of the family team: weeding, spreading fertilizer, tending plants, though they often share in the heavier tasks. The rapid urbanisation process of recent decades has led to a marked increase in child labour in the cities.

Children work in a wide variety of street trades: as shoeshine boys, messengers, sellers of magazines, food, flowers, lottery tickets, etc. These children are often termed as street children because they may be literally living on the streets or at the place of their work. The boys very often work as waiters in roadside cafes and restaurants and as pageboys and the girls as hotel maids or domestic servants. Children who work in industries are generally employed in the informal sector. While in some industries children perform secondary tasks, they may also directly participate in the main tasks of production. Where children work in a family undertaking, generally working conditions may not be too arbitrary. However, these traditional situations are declining in many areas, especially where plantation agriculture is becoming established or where there is massive out-migration.

When children are employed outside the family, the way they are treated, as well as their conditions of work, are usually determined by the employer. The possibilities of ill-treatment are unlimited. Ill-treatment may include corporal punishment, abuses of all kinds, humiliation and frustration. Children are usually employed in the informal sector, where conditions of work are appalling and welfare facilities are conspicuous by their absence. The tasks in which they are employed are generally monotonous and repetitive in nature and often they are ill- suited to the child's physical and mental capacities. The working conditions severely tax the child's physical and mental resistance as a result, for example, of suffocating heat in enclosed premises or exposure to rain or sun in open-air work. They may be forced to work in an awkward position in badly lit, badly ventilated, noisy or unhealthy premises, in damp and unhygienic surrounding, in an atmosphere contaminated with dust or gases, crammed together with other workers, in workshops without adequate safety devices, rest areas, medical and toilet facilities, having to carry excessively heavy loads, etc., all in violation of the principles set forth in international instruments to protect their rights. Children who are more or less self-employed and child street traders generally feel they are freer than other working children. Despite their relative freedom, they too are an exploited lot because they too have to bear the demands of the market.

Although many self-employed workers work in their own home, others have to travel varying distances to reach their workplace as many wage-earners do. When carrying out their activities they are hardly ever protected from the vagaries of the weather. They may be harassed by the police or by groups of youths or adults. The length of time that children work each day and over the year varies considerably according to their schooling status, their parent's wish to keep them at work more or less continuously, how long the employer needs them and so on. Some children work only during the school holidays, at weekends, early in the morning or late at night. Seasonal work is also often undertaken by children, in agricultural work for tasks such as sowing and harvesting.

In some countries, girls work longer hours than boys because boys spend more time at school. It is common knowledge that children in domestic service work long hours since they must be available at virtually any time to carry out their employer's bidding. Some wage earning, children are permitted to take work breaks at fixed intervals during the working day. Others are not allowed to do so despite the fact that a child needs a break more often than an adult if he is to recharge his physical and mental batteries. The period of daily rest is often not sufficient, especially in agricultural work, industry, some service industries and domestic service. The weekly rest is sometimes granted and paid, sometimes granted but not paid and sometimes not allowed at all, i.e., the working week is a seven-day week. When the child is a wage earner, he may be paid a salary, a daily wage or piece-rate wage. The wage that a child earns is much lower than those received by an adult for doing the same work. A still more flagrant example of exploitation of child workers is that of supposed apprentices who are in fact working than learning and are not being paid for it. Finally, in another types of exploitative relationship, payment is symbolic or non-existent or supplied in kind: food, lodging or 'presents' to the child or to the family.

Sending children to work may seem a rational approach to poverty but employment of children has profound repercussions. ILO research shows that child labour is almost universally recognised as being undesirable, harmful for the children themselves and harmful for the future of their nations. When a child joins the workforce at a young age, he is deprived of the opportunity to educate himself and acquiring qualifications which will help him in getting a better job in future. It is, therefore, very likely that a child who has been at work from an early age will spend his whole life at the bottom of the social ladder. Thus child labour has become a mode of perpetuating an unjust social system and of ensuring the continued availability of subservient, unskilled, illiterate labourers who do not have the bargaining power to question the system that marginalises them and deprives them of their right to lead a decent life. Many of the jobs that children do are harmful for their physical development. The physical susceptibility of working children also has a lot to do with the fact that they have very different capacities and needs from adults, and this fact is very rarely taken into account by employers. The manner of their employment, the nature of their work and the conditions under which they are often employed subject them to severe health and safety hazards. Work in agriculture is also characterised by certain hazards, particularly with the introduction of advanced farming practices, new techniques and chemicals. There is also prolonged exposure to heat, sunlight, dust, wind and insects and the high costs in terms of safety and health associated with work in commercial and plantation agriculture.

Children are particularly at risk from endemic and parasitic diseases, diseases of the respiratory tract, dermatosis and fatal accidents. However, these problems are multiplied several fold in industries. Work may be heavy and intense; it may be highly mechanised and extremely monotonous; it may involve the use of sharp and dangerous objects and toxic substances; it may be carried out in conditions of extreme heat, dust and noise. Child workers in industries are faced with serious risks to their health and physical development. They may be required to undertake tasks for which they are entirely unprepared physically. In a number of industries children are exposed to lead poisoning which may have no noticeable effect on adults. There are claims that children's brains are detrimentally affected due to exposure to lead poisoning. There are documented cases of paralysis caused by the use of toxic glues. There is documentation on the paralytic effects of a number of chemicals on children in Moroccan workshops where children were gluing suitcases and shoes. In these cases the toxic effects were accentuated by poor sanitation and ventilation and the younger the child, the more serious the paralysis. The risk of occupational diseases or accidents are higher among child workers because their growing bodies are not as strong as adult workers. Several studies show that child workers have greater health problems than adults even if both are placed in the same working environment.

There can be special risks associated with the working environment. Heavy loads and awkward body positions in particular can affect physical growth, especially the growth of bones, which are still soft in children. When a child is regularly bent under a heavy burden or is forced to stay in an unnatural position for long periods, deformation of the spinal column, pelvis or thorax may be the result. A World Health Organisation report on child workers cites health hazards such as bony lesions and postural deformity attributable to such work as carpet weaving, embroidery and lifting heavyweights. Children generally work for long hours, which results in excessive fatigue and stunted growth. Poor children are generally malnourished but their work increases their energy requirement and calorie deficit. Moreover, if they suffer from anaemia, fatigue and inadequate sleep, they become more susceptible to accidents and infectious diseases. Excessively hot, damp or dusty conditions also create a milieu which favours the transmission of communicable diseases. Many of these diseases, for example, tuberculosis, may be very difficult to cure and involve lifelong illnesses. Once again, malnutrition, anaemia, inadequate sleep, etc., lower resistance. Once infected at an early age, and through constant reinfection, it becomes difficult to break the vicious cycle of contact. In many cases workplaces do not meet hygienic standards. There is often no running water or toilet facilities. In these situations gastro-intestinal diseases nourish and it is difficult to break the oral-faecal cycle.

The self-employed child who has an accident or contracts a disease of occupational origin obviously benefits from no form of social protection. If the child is a wage-earner he is not usually protected either since in the vast majority of cases he is working illegally. If he is the victim of an occupational accident or disease he and his parents must be prepared for fearful and irreversible consequences. The official statistics reveal a very small proportion of the occupational accidents or diseases that affect children. Thus many jobs done by children are the cause of physical deformities and illnesses such as deformities of the spine, stunted growth, infections, burns, sores, etc., or else they may aggravate defects or maladies. Child labour involves both short-term and long-term health risks. Child labour has mental repercussions also since the age at which he usually starts to work coincides more or less with a period of profound mental change in the child. The mental consequences of child labour are not just the result of the work situation but the violent change to which the child is exposed. In many cases children are separated from their families when they migrate to cities and other places in search of employment.

An unfamiliar, often oppressive work situation, exacerbates the stresses and leads to socio-cultural disorganisation. There is a breakdown of effective communication, impaired human relations, insecurity problems of identification, a high prevalence of psycho-neurotic reactions and psychosomatic disorders. With the spread of compulsory schooling in developed countries, the rapid and considerable improvement in levels of living and the enforcement of anti-child labour laws there was a significant decline in child labour. However, child labour is still prevalent in the developed nations, according to an ILO report. In the poverty pockets of the industrialised countries there may be as many as another 10 million or more working children, many of whom are not in school full-time and many may not be reached by health services. These children are found particularly amongst illegal migrant families; but also in certain occupations in the entertainment or publicity industries.

The growing magnitude of the child labour has made it a cause for international concern. Efforts have been made at the global and national level by various international organisations along with their member nations to expose the problem and to cope with it. The beginning of the industrial revolution brought about the enactment of child labour laws.

In the international arena, the first conventions indirectly protecting children began in the late 19th and early 20th century. Children's right emerged as a sub-category in the development of the rules of war and of the international labour conventions. The idea of grouping children into a distinct category was gradually promoted. Children have been a silent and unrepresented minority, they used to belong to one of those groups in history which Martin Luther King Jr described as "nobodies". Non-governmental organisations played a very important role in giving shape to the rights of the child. The whole process started at the outset of 20th century, when some British women in Cambridge made a survey of the charitable societies at that time to determine what protection was provided to children. These pacifist women worked throughout the First World War to alert the general public to the plight of children in war-affected areas.

After the war, they founded the "Save the Children" movement, whose lobbying led to the recognition of the rights of the child in the League of Nations. In January 1924, a committee was set up in the league whose scope included the protection of children in general. This was later divided into two sections, one of which was specifically devoted to child welfare.

The Geneva Declaration of the Rights of the Child was adopted in 1924. The Geneva Declaration recognises the principle that childhood is entitled to special care, assistance and safeguards. The Geneva Declaration contains a sentence that has become the motto of all supporters of the children's cause: "mankind owes to the child the best it has to give." The General Assembly of the UN adopted on 10 December, 1948, a Universal Declaration of Human Rights. Portions of the Universal Declaration of Human Rights apply specifically to minors. It contains 30 articles, 21 of which spell out civil and political rights, and six articles deal with economic and cultural rights. The UN adopted a Convention on the Abolition of Slavery, the Slave Trade and Institutions and Practices similar to Slavery in 1956. This convention prohibits the exploitation of child labour in cases where children are delivered to another person for that purpose.

The International Covenant on Economic, Social and Cultural Rights imposes a general prohibition on the employment of children under a certain age and the employment of children in work constituting a threat to their health or morals. Though the Universal Declaration of Human Rights, 1948, implicitly included the freedom and rights of children, it was believed that this was not enough. It was felt that the special needs of children justified a separate document because children are particularly vulnerable to arbitrary deprivation of their human rights. This led to the adoption of the Declaration of the Rights of the Child in 1959.

The 1959 declaration enunciates general principles for the care and protection of children. It is mainly concerned with economic, social and cultural rights. It must be noted that it was in the preamble of 1959 declaration that the problem of implementation of children's rights was first mentioned. The preamble to the declaration states that the child because of his physical and mental immaturity needs special safeguards and care.

The Declaration of the Rights of the Child also prohibits the employment of children under a certain age and the employment of children in work which endanger their development. Principle 9 states: "The child shall be protected against all forms of neglect, cruelty, and exploitation. He shall not be the subject of traffic in any form. The child shall not be admitted to employment before an appropriate minimum age; he shall in no case be caused or permitted to engage in any occupation or employment which would prejudice his health or education or interfere with his physical, mental or moral development".

The Government of Poland submitted a draft Convention on the Rights of the Child to the General Assembly in 1978. In 1979, it submitted an amended version of the draft to the Commission on Human Rights. The General Assembly requested the Commission to give the highest priority to the question of completing the draft convention, "bearing in mind the children's rights are basic human rights and call for continuous improvement of the situation of children all over the world as well as their development and education in conditions of peace".

As a result, the General Assembly decided to set up a working group within the Human Rights Commission, which from 1979, the International Year of the Child, met regularly to complete the Convention. On November 20, 1989, the General Assembly at its 44th session adopted the Convention. It came into force on September 2, 1990, following ratification by the stipulated minimum of 20 member states.

The Convention recognises the exceptional vulnerability of children and proclaims that childhood is entitled to special care and assistance. It is guided by the principle of "first call for children"—a principle that the essential needs of children should be given highest priority in the allocation of resources at all times. It obligates the state to respect and ensure that children get a fair and equitable deal in society. The Convention's provisions can be categorised under the headings of civil and political rights, social rights and cultural rights. Article 3 states that "in all actions concerning children... the best interests of the child shall be a primary consideration". It implies that whenever a child's right is in the process of being affected, the focus must be on the child's welfare and not on the parents' or guardians' will. The extraordinary importance of Article 3 lies in the fact that for the first time it grants children the right to their best interests. Article 27 makes it obligatory for the state to recognise the right of every child to have a standard or living which may ensure requisite physical, mental, spiritual, moral and social development of each child. Article 28 of the convention imposes a liability on the state to recognise the right of the child to education and for that purpose it is expected on the part of each state to make primary education compulsory and it should be available to all children free of cost. The state is also expected to take measures to encourage regular attendance at school and the reduction of dropout rates.

Under Article 32 obligation has been imposed on each member state to recognise the right of each child for being protected from economic exploitation and from doing work of hazardous nature which may prove to be harmful to the health of the child or retard the physical, mental, spiritual, moral or social development of the child. Article 35 requires state parties to take all appropriate measures to prevent the abduction, the sale of or traffic in children for any purpose or in any form. As of 1995, 181 countries had ratified the convention. The ILO has concerned itself with the question of child labour since its foundation in 1919. The abolition of child labour has been one of its basic aims since its establishment. At the same time, it has pursued a systematic policy of protection of working children from undesirable conditions of work.

The ILO's traditional approach to child labour has been to lay down international labour standards through ILO conventions and recommendations. There are thus two main categories of ILO instruments concerning child labour: instruments prohibiting child labour, and protection of child labour The first instrument which set a minimum age for admission to employment was the Minimum Age (Industry) Convention (No. 5), adopted by the ILO General Conference at its first session in 1919. This convention fixed the minimum age for admission of children to industrial employment at 14 years. At subsequent sessions the ILO adopted various other conventions and recommendations fixing minimum age standards for admission to employment in different sectors of economic activity. In 1973, the ILO decided that the time had come, as stated in the preamble to the convention, to establish a general institution on the subject, which would gradually replace the existing ones applicable to limited economic sectors, with a view to achieving the total abolition of child labour.

Convention No. 138 provides that "each member should pursue a national policy to ensure the effective abolition of child labour and to raise progressively the minimum age for admission to employment or work to a level consistent with fullest physical and mental development of young persons". This age should not be less than 15 years. However, the above Convention provides the possibility of lowering these age limits in certain circumstances. Article 2 lays down that a country "whose economy and educational facilities are insufficiently developed may, after consultation with either the organisation of employers and workers concerned, where such exist, initially specify a minimum age of 14 years". Moreover, a member state whose economy and administrative facilities are insufficiently developed may initially limit the scope of application of the Convention and may extend the scope at a later date. However, the provisions the Convention must be applicable as a minimum to the following: mining and quarrying; manufacturing; construction; electricity; gas and water; sanitary services; transport, storage and communications, and plantations and other agricultural undertakings mainly producing for commercial purposes, but excluding family and small-scale holdings producing for local consumption and not regularly employing hired workers.

Article 7 lays down that "states which have ratified the convention may permit the employment of children 13 to 15 years of age (12 to 14 for states which have adopted 14 years as a general minimum age) and of older children who have not completed their compulsory schooling, in 'light work' which is not likely to be harmful to their health or development" and not such as to prejudice their attendance at school or their participation in vocational orientation or training programmes".

As regards work which is likely to jeopardise the health, safety or morals of young persons, the convention lays down that the minimum age for admission to any type of employment or work of this kind shall not be less than 18 years. Article 3 provides that a country may authorise employment in dangerous work as from the age of 16 years on the condition that health, safety and morals of the young persons concerned are fully protected and that the young persons have received adequate instruction or vocational training in the relevant branch of activity. In addition, the International Labour Conference adopted the Minimum Age Recommendation, 1973 (No. 146) to supplement the Minimum Age Convention, 1973. This recommendation invites states to give high priority to planning for and meeting the needs of children and youth in national development policies and programmes and to extend interrelated measures necessary to provide the best possible conditions of physical and mental growth for children and young persons. It recommends that members take as their objective the progressive raising to 16 years of the minimum age for employment or work specified in pursuance of the Minimum Age Convention. In countries where the minimum age for employment is still below 15 years, urgent steps should be taken to raise that level. In countries where the minimum age for admission to types of employment or work which are likely to jeopardise the health, safety or morals of young persons is still below 18 years, steps should be taken to raise it to that level. With a view to facilitating the goals set forth in the convention, the recommendation advocates the adoption of measures designed to achieve full employment of adults; the progressive extension of other economic and social measures to alleviate poverty so as to make recourse to child labour unnecessary; the adoption and extension of adequate facilities for educational and vocational guidance and training; the adoption of special measures for children who do not have families or do not live with them, as well as for migrant children; and the introduction of compulsory full-time attendance at school or participation in vocational training courses at least up to the age specified for employment in Convention No. 138.

While maintaining the long-term aim of achieving the prohibition of child labour, the ILO has also pursued a policy of fixing standards with the objective of protecting child labour against exploitation. This had led, since 1919, to the adoption of a number of conventions and recommendations prohibiting the employment of children and/or young persons in certain types of work and regulating their working conditions. Legislation alone is not enough to deal with the problem of child labour. There is a wide gap between the legal instruments and the actual state of affairs as is borne out by ILO case studies. Child labour seems to be effectively abolished in the formal sector characterised by large enterprises using highly mechanised or capital-intensive techniques. Even here, it is not clear whether this is due to a strict enforcement of child labour legislation or to the fact that child workers are of little use and uneconomical in a production system which uses advanced technology and less labour input. In any case, child labour continues to be widespread in the unorganised sector of industry, agriculture and services in much of the developing world, despite national legislation prohibiting it.

There are many factors, responsible for the poor enforcement of existing legislation. The availability and quality of education along with the poverty of the families of school age children act as a brake on the effectiveness of legislation. The inadequacy and low standards of education results in a very high school dropout rate and undermines the parents expectations concerning the benefits of schooling. Moreover, governments lack effective enforcement machinery to monitor regulations and standards governing child labour. Such machinery is seriously deficient in most developing countries. The inspectorate system is generally understaffed and thus unable to cope with child labour. The introduction of social security contributions in respect of young workers has reduced employers' reliance on child labour.

Since child labour is closely linked with poverty, lack of development and inadequate schooling in the countries in which it is prevalent, child labour legislation must be accompanied by a wide range of measures concerning employment and income generation programmes, and by a reform and expansion of education facilities. Keeping these realities in mind, the ILO has not confined its activity to the establishment of standards and monitoring of the application of conventions.

In recent years, the ILO has supplemented its standard-setting work with research, information dissemination and technical assistance. ILO extends technical cooperation to member states to enable them to bring national laws and practice closer to the model set out in international labour standards.

The ILO technical cooperation activities focuses attention on eliminating forced labour or bonded labour and child labour in industries and occupations which are detrimental to the safety, health or morals of children. It recognised that employment of children in certain dangerous types of occupations, such as work which involves exposure to toxic substances, use of pesticides or insecticides in agriculture and recycling of household waste in dumping sites, may not be prohibited by national legislation, but should be eliminated.

The ILO recognises the fact that though it has been playing a leading role in the struggle against child labour, some of the action required to attack the underlying causes of child labour-poverty, insufficient economic growth and deficiencies in the education system—is within the competence of other international organisations like the International Monetary Fund (IMF), the World Bank, the General Agreement on Tariff and Trade (GATT) and the United Nations International Children Emergency Fund (UNICEF).

The ILO proclaims that diversity of mandates for action in the struggle against child labour should therefore be reflected in strengthened cooperation between the ILO and these other organisations and most importantly, by close collaboration with the UNICEF. Another way the ILO addresses the problem of child labour is through programmes and projects at the national and local community level. The ILO has committed itself to a major effort to halt child labour. The International Programme on the Elimination of Child Labour (IPEC) came into being with a view to giving a new impetus to the ILO's operational activities in this field.

The operational structure of IPEC is based on ILO rules and procedures and on Memoranda of Understanding between the ILO and participating countries. The MoU finalises the agreement on the development and execution of national IPEC activities. It establishes the areas, principles and modalities of cooperation between the ILO and the government. IPEC seeks collaboration with other UN agencies, particularly the UNICEF, the United Nations Educational, Scientific and Cultural Organisation (UNESCO), and the World Health Organisation and also with international NGOs to avoid duplication of effort and to maximise the impact of all available resources against the problem. IPEC focuses on the worst abuses of child labour: hazardous work, forced labour, the employment of working children who are less than 12 or 13 years old girls and street children.

Organisations directly involved in initiating and implementing the action programmes include governmental institutions, policy makers and political leaders, in particular the ministries of labour, education, health and welfare and information and statistics. Partner organisations include NGOs, including voluntary agencies, workers and employers' groups, religious organisations and the media. The immediate objectives of the programme are: (i) to have enhanced the capability of ILO constituents and NGOs to design, implement and evaluate policies and programmes aimed at the elimination of child labour and the protection of working children; (ii) to have determined the comparative strengths and weaknesses of various types of intervention at the local and national levels for replication and adoption; and (iii) to have established mechanisms at both the national and international level capable of generating and supporting public awareness and social mobilisation campaigns to combat child labour.

In order to promote action against bonded child labour, the ILO, within the ambit of IPEC, organised the Asian Regional Seminar on Children in Bondage in Islamabad in November 1992. It was held in collaboration with the United Nations Centre for Human Rights and the government of Pakistan.

Elimination of child labour is also a key component of UNICEF's policy. UNICEF is the only UN agency devoted exclusively to the needs of children. Founded in 1946, initially to care for the children of war-torn Europe, its mandate was gradually expanded. UNICEF supports government efforts in providing services essential to the survival and development of children such as clean water, safe sanitation, immunisation and other health measures. It also seeks to provide to children skills essential for leading a healthy and productive life and thus education is a major priority of the UNICEF. UNICEF collaborates with governments, international agencies, NGOs, trade unions and legal experts to promote the elimination of child labour and integration of children released from labour into the educational system. It has been a major funding agency for improving the lot of children in general and child labour in particular. UNICEF has sanctioned $0.5 million for child labour programmes for the five-year period commencing from 1991.

The United Nations Educational, Scientific and Cultural Organisation (UNESCO) is another of the UN's specialised agencies. UNESCO has special responsibility for everything involving prevention of the various forms of discrimination and promotion of the educational and cultural rights. UNESCO has also been making efforts to combat with the problem of child labour.

Set up in 1946, UNESCO aims at promoting cooperation among nations through education, science and culture and thereby contribute to peace and security and enhance universal respect for justice, fundamental freedoms and human rights, including rights of the child. It has tried to attack the problem of child labour through the spread of education. Thus the efforts of these international organisa-tions are in the right direction and indeed commendable.

The goal of complete abolition of child labour is still a distant one. In order to be effective, it is essential that international organisations arrive at programmes and campaigns suited to national conditions. Moreover, there is a need for greater coordination of efforts of international organisations in the struggle against child labour. International organisations also need to develop their campaigns within the framework of a partnership with concerned governments and NGOs if their efforts are to have a lasting impact on the status of the working children of the world.

The problem of child labour has assumed serious proportions. Their continued and widespread employment in the workforce is a denial of their basic rights. The repercussions of child labour are confined not only on the children individually but on the society as a whole because the contribution of these children to society in future will suffer on account of the sacrifices made in terms of their health and education.

Child Labour Legislation

The International Labour Organisation (ILO) has, since its foundation in 1919, devoted an important part of its standard setting activity to the abolition of child labour. Unfortunately, national governments have only taken a few measures in the application of these laws. Today, child labour problem is getting the attention of all. This is because of a large number of children employed in hazardous industries and, secondly, because of lot of awareness among grassroots organisations, social movements in favour of abolition of child labour and so on.No doubt, the opening up of the international market and the orientation towards a liberal market economy in developing countries has contributed to *defacto* changes in the hiring of labour, resulting in high demands for vulnerable workers such as women and children. There is an upward trend in the number of children employed in hazardous occupations, more inhumanly in child prostitution, forced labour, and debt bondage.

Developing countries are no doubt working towards eradication of this evil from their societies, yet, there seems to be some problems like lack of resources on their way. They argue that legislative measures are difficult to impose and cheap labour is needed for growth. The link between growth of informal sector, poverty and the emergence or persistence of child labour is very well known. It is also the same in this region. Yet to remain content with these explanations is to ignore the nature of exploitation and the vested interests that create and perpetuate informalisation and poverty itself. It has been seen in some Western countries that increasing the minimum age of children for recruitment for jobs and abolition of employing children in hazardous occupations coupled with political will, reinforcement of family values, and active role by social organisations can contribute in eliminating child labour. The Christian Workers Movement (CWM) has decided to undertake a campaign on 'Child workers' to raise public awareness regarding the issues of child labour and child rights. This voluntary organisation has drawn up a common programme for South Asian countries with the purpose of sharing experiences and formulating strategies for abolition of child labour at regional level.

In doing so, the CWM has mobilised hundreds of voluntary workers in different countries to build up personal relationships with child workers to give them hope for a better world. Careful analysis, case studies and recommendations for action against child labour have been presented as far as the seven nations are concerned. This has turned out to be a movement engaged in supporting action programmes, based on substantial issues affecting the life of child workers. Through systematic reflection in small groups, CWM discovers its role and find inspiration to activities along with their partners to establish a new view of society based on justice, fraternity and peace. CWM concerns itself with the marginalised or informal worker, to end their isolation and total helplessness and to integrate them into society with dignity.

Sri Lanka's major industrial and agricultural enterprises do not employ children. Sri Lanka's achievements in the provision of education and welfare service are among the most impressive in the developing world. However, child labour continues to present a challenge in the country. Most children work in very informal sectors, in small unregistered concerns, in private homes or sometimes even in illegal enterprises. Children are concentrated in occupations in which wages are low, working conditions are dangerous, workers rights are not recognised and labour organisation is absent. Also, the civil strike in Sri Lanka as exposes children to new dangers and more exploitative forms of labour. Child prostitution and the traffic in children for use as camel riders in the Middle East are among most recent forms of child labour. The main thrust of public policy in Sri Lanka has been to allow a low (12 years) age threshold for admission to employment, while protecting older children by excluding them from certain specified occupations and regulating conditions of work. A distinction is made between prohibited, hazardous employment and permissible, non- hazardous labour which is controlled. In Sri Lanka, there is a need to complement the establishment of universal free education and the enforcement of labour legislation with a coherent welfare programmes. The Sri Lankan population of 15.3 million as recorded in the census of 1981, belong to three major communities: the Sinhala, Tamil and Muslim. In all the three communities, poor children are viewed by their parents and other as crucial members of the household workforce. Changes in Sri Lankan economy and society in recent decades have also resulted in the growth of child labour in a range of new activities, both exploitative and dangerous. A large number of children in Sri Lanka live and work in small unlicensed or unregistered concerns as hotels, tea kiosks, food and grocery shops, etc. However, legal prohibitions on employment of children under the age of 14 years in hazardous activities or in those which prejudice their education have effectively excluded them from formal employment in public sector. In an effort to combine education and employment, children are required to work extremely long hours outside school hours, often at night.

In manufacturing industry, plantation, agriculture, production targets are stringent and these places put severe strains on the workforce. The informally employed child labourers inhale pollutants such as tea, dust and industrial wastes, pesticides and other toxic substances. Children were also employed in large numbers in fishing industry until recently. They were recruited by job placement agents to clean, salt and dry fish in fishing camps. They were kept in virtual slavery conditions, ill nourished, harassed, physically abused. However, an official raid in the fishing camp at Trincomalee led to the release of a group of boys. Recent evidence indicates that children are perhaps no longer employed in the fishing camps. Children are also involved in a number of illegal occupation as prostitution. The use of children in armed combat by military groups occurs as a result of the abduction and forced conscription of the young boys. There is evidence that some children have fled to the south or even to Europe to avoid conscription.The interest of child welfare can be traced in part to the cultural ethos which holds that children are a source of adult fulfilment, to be loved and indulged. State policies on education, health and child care have helped to reduce child employment and counteract traditional perceptions of the child as an economic asset belonging to the family.

The fist welfare policy in Sri Lanka to affect child labour was the system of vernacular state education developed at the beginning of the 20th Century by the British for children from rural communities and the plantation sector. Pressure from some parents in rural communities to provide better equality education in English, which leads to securing an upward social and economic mobility, soon led to the creation of semi-vernacular schooling. The children and young persons ordinance of 1939 was the first intervention focusing specifically on children and stated that no child under the age of 14 years could be employed in such a way as to prejudice schooling. The concept of universal free-education from primary to tertiary level was introduced in 1945.

In the 1950's, the national languages became a medium of instruction in the secondary schools and universities. This along with the free education brought education to a wider population.Provisions under the constitution facilitate the introduction of measures to prevent the exploitation of child labour. Thus, it can be used to implement radical reform in law and policy on child labour and remove certain existing anomalies in labour legislation. The first legislation of child labour was passed in Sri Lanka in 1923 in line with the minimum age (Industry) convention, 1919, restricting child employment in industry. This existing legislation on child labour was revised in 1956 and included in the Employment of Women, Young Persons and Children Act. More recently, Sri Lanka has ratified the United Nations Convention on the Rights of the Child (1989).

A minimum age for employment 10 years was first introduced in 1927 in respect of plantation workers, which was later raised to 12 rather than 14 years. The government opposed a total ban on child labour under 14 years of age in the Employment of Women, Young Persons and Children Act, (1956), in the belief that a flexible policy was needed to accommodate the necessity of child labour among the poor. The present situation is that a minimum age for employment has been re-enacted. In the legal context, all work involving children under 12 years in considered hazardous. The employment Act specifies that no child aged between 12 and 14 years can be employed to lift carry or move anything so heavy as to be likely to cause injury. The Shop and Office Employees Act (1954) states the child labour in shops, offices and hotels is for bidden, even during the day. Despite all this, there are obvious gaps in legislation. Employment of boys in mines is only indirectly prohibited, while employment of children between 12 and 14 years in quarries and transport does not appear to be covered at all. Girls above 14 years are prohibited from underground work in mines. Boys under 16 are also prohibited from this type of work. Young people above 16 years can work 10 hours a day or an additional five and half hours a week. According to a special provision children between 14 and 15 years of age may not be employed in work at sea except with the written permission of the Commissioner of Labour. Young people between the ages of 14 and 18 years are allowed to work during the day in industry. Considerable importance is attached to the regulations and their absence provides a rationale for failure to implement statutory provisions. The importance given to the promulgation of regulations can also result in mis-understandings of the content of the law. The prohibition on the employment of children under 12 years has been removed from the statute and enacted in the form of a regulation. While this regulation is known and applied to the formal sector, the informal sector employees and public are largely unaware of it. The government has created several agencies to deal with children's problems in general.

But there remain several serious obstacles to the implementation of a consistent policy in child labour. The failure of any single body to assume direct control in cases concerning child labour has been the major factor behind the inability to obtain any action in respect of child labour, child prostitution, child camel riding and child labour in fishing camps. Child labour is one of the major human right violations in South Asia. As a part of UNICEF's mandate and duty to protect, promote and ensure the rights of children, the purpose of this study is to gain a better understanding of the laws which can potentially protect the rights of children from exploitation, specifically child labour laws. The study was conducted in two phases with the first phase being a documentation of Labour legislation from 1881 to 1995 in Bangladesh, India, Nepal, Pakistan and Sri Lanka. Legislation is limited for Bhutan and the Maldives. The second phase of the study set out to analyse regional patterns in terms of patriarchy, religion and the type of laws.

South Asia has a dual legal tradition: national Laws and customary laws. The first phase which examined the national labour laws, reveals a region which has a strong history of child labour legislations. Analysis was conducted by the development of a taxonomy which was used to trace the progression of the legislation. From 1881, there has been basic coverage for employment of children. Over the years, the legislation has progressed such that there has been an increase in the role and responsibility of the state; increase in the minimum age; increase in the coverage of sectors; specificity of processes and occupations; decrease in the total work hours and size of unit; prohibition of night work; and increase in the number of exceptions, specifically dealing with family businesses. Regional differences and unique features in the laws were also noted.

Initially, the intent of the second phase was to analyse the differences in the legislation in the region by three explanatory variables: patriarchy, religion, and the type of the law. These variables were identified by Therborn in his study on the development of children's rights in western nations. Since the results of phase-I of the study revealed very little regional differences, the explanatory variables were merged with UNICEF's child survival, development and protection framework to form a framework for understanding child labour.

This proved to be useful, not only in demonstrating the universality of Therborn's explanatory variables but also raising awareness of the ideology that is at the root of child labour. The solutions are not only a matter of providing educational opportunities or improving the socio-economic structure—these must also involve changing certain patriarchal and religious attitudes and values. These attitudes and values support equitable control of resources resulting in misinterpretation of customary laws and providing very little incentives for the enforcement of national labour laws, which in turn give rise to care practices that destroy childhood for a large number of children.

With respect to laws, the analysis revealed that patriarchy and religion work strongly through the customary laws (that deal with family matters), which through the suppression of women perpetuate child labour. The major problem of the national labour laws is their lack of enforcement. This is in part because they do not hold any legitimacy for a practice that is reinforced by cultural traditions of patriarchy and religion. Customary laws take precedence and their legitimacy is permanently through nationalisation and fundamentalism rather than human rights.

Human rights in South Asia have achieved legitimacy in conducting political life, however, they do not hold the same legitimacy when it comes to community and family. This is in effect analogous to the split in the civil and political rights and the economic, social and cultural rights.The foundation has now been set in order to take the next step of translating law into practice.

Child Labour Surveys and Public Awareness

Child labour surveys have been carried out nationally or in selected areas of 19 countries or territories. These include Bangladesh, Cambodia, Costa Rica, Georgia, Ghana, Indonesia, India, Kenya, Namibia, Nepal, Pakistan, the Philippines, Senegal, South Africa, Sri

Lanka, Thailand, Turkey, Ukraine and the West Bank and Gaza. New child labour surveys are either under way or in the process of starting or are being planned in the following countries: Angola, Belize, Benin, Brazil, Burkina Faso, Cambodia, Colombia, Costa Rica, Mali, Mongolia, Peru, Uganda, Vietnam and Zimbabwe. Child labour surveys will be carried out as far as possible in all IPEC participating countries to optimise the complementary effects of IPEC and the Statistical Information and Monitoring Programme on Child Labour (SIMPOC).

Given the effectiveness and popularity of the newly developed survey methodologies for quantifying child labour in all its different facets, an externally funded programme (SIMPOC) was formulated and launched at the beginning of 1998.

SIMPOC, an interdepartmental programme between the ILO's International Programme on the Elimination of Child Labour (IPEC) and the ILO's Bureau of Statistics, is designed for a five-year period with the major aim of assisting individual countries in generating comprehensive quantitative and qualitative statistical data on child labour at the national level that is comparable among countries, sub-regions or regions. SIMPOC is also aimed at capacity building of national statistical offices and ministries of labour for the production and use of such data on a regular basis in the future.

For this purpose, under the SIMPOC programme, the staff of IPEC and SIMPOC are to be trained to design and carry out child labour surveys and analyse the data collected. The surveys are expected to become an integral part of the regular national statistical programmes; so that statistical information on child labour can be produced and disseminated at regular intervals. A large majority of the countries listed above have undertaken the surveys under the auspices of SIMPOC.

Through SIMPOC, comprehensive child labour information systems consisting of both quantitative and qualitative data will also be developed at national, international and regional levels with a computer programme that facilitates updating the database as new information becomes available. Such a database provide policy and decision makers with more detailed and better-quality information for the design, implementation, monitoring and evaluation of policies and programmes. The dissemination of this data, through the publication of a regular trend report, is planned under SIMPOC—which will contribute considerably to raising public awareness and enhancing the understanding of the problem of child labour. Since 1992, the ILO has taken the lead in developing methodological child labour sample surveys at national levels.

The survey methodologies were developed to enable countries to obtain benchmark statistics on children's work in general or to produce statistics on specific core variables. These methods were first tested in four countries (Ghana, India, Indonesia and Senegal). Following their refinement and recommendations for quantifying child labour, several countries collaborated with the Bureau of Statistics in adopting the methodologies and conducting national surveys for collecting comprehensive data. Based on detailed results of the experiments and national child labour surveys conducted in several countries using the newly developed methodologies, the ILO was able to:

— Produce regional and global estimates;

— Identify and quantify not only the different forms of hazard and risk working children face, but also the extent and nature of the injuries and diseases suffered while working; and

— Acquire much knowledge and experience, thereby enhancing considerably its competence for providing technical assistance to individual countries in designing and undertaking comprehensive child labour surveys and processing, analysing and using the statistical data obtained for formulating and implementing appropriate action programmes to combat the worst forms of child labour at the national and global levels.

To obtain a complete picture of the child labour situation, the information sought through surveys at the national level involved answers to the following questions, among others:

— Who are the working children and how many are there in the various countries?

— How old are the children when they start to work for the first time and how do they live?

— Why do they work and in which sectors are they engaged?

— What types of exploitation and abuse do they face at work?

— How safe are they physically and mentally at their workplace or in their occupations?

— Do they also go to school? If so, what are the consequences of their work on their schooling? And if they do not go to school, why not?

— Who are their employers? Why do they employ them? And how do they treat them in comparison with their adult workers?

— How many children are engaged on a full-time basis in housekeeping activities of a domestic nature in their own parents' or guardians' households, thereby sacrificing their education?

— Do any children live away from their parents' or guardians' home, and if so, where do they live and what do they do?

— What are the perceptions of parents about their working children? What are the perceptions of the children themselves and their employers?

The ILO Bureau of Statistics designed four survey approaches and tested them in a number of countries together with a supplementary inquiry. Three of the survey approaches were implemented, respectively, at the level of households, employers/establishments/enterprises, and street children. The fourth method tested was a "time use" approach. The supplementary inquiry was applied at the community level (cities, towns, villages). The main purpose was to determine which survey methodology would yield the best results. The surveys measured as many variables as possible, particularly in relation to the various non-schooling activities of children in the 5-14 age group, their characteristics and those of their parents or guardians, and so on.

The principal variables considered for the investigation related to the following subjects as expressed in broad terms:

- The demographic and socio-economic characteristics of the children, including their schooling and training status, occupations, skill levels, hours of work, earnings and other working and living conditions and the reasons for working, as well as the hardships and risks, especially work-related or environmental injuries and diseases they face at their workplace which are detrimental to their health, education, and physical and mental development;
- The socio-economic situation of their parents or guardians, or other relatives with whom the children live, as well as the particulars of their employers;
- The migration status of the children and how they live (in particular those on the streets); where the children have been working, for how long and why they are working, their own immediate and future plans and those of employers using child workers; and
- The perceptions of the parents or guardians about their working youngsters and those of the children themselves and their employers.

The concepts, definitions, classifications and the like, used for the purposes of the experimental surveys in all the countries, were generally in line with internationally recommended standards concerning such elements as the economically active population, the labour force, classifications of industry, occupation, status in employment, age grouping, households, enterprises and establishments and so on, with some variations to reflect the unique circumstance of child work and the peculiarities of the individual countries. Depending on the availability of basic information or demarcations regarding the general characteristics of the areas covered and the availability of appropriate sampling frames, the different elements considered for the stratifications included development levels of the selected, rural and urban areas—for example, poorly developed/well developed, slum/non-slum blocks, income classes (low, middle, high), overall rates of literacy/illiteracy of the general population, school attendance levels and so on. For the purposes of the experiments, a "child" was defined as a person between five and 14 years of age. In the absence of a universally endorsed definition of "child labour", all activities of children were enumerated and quantified so that the data could be tabulated according to the different characteristics or categories of the variables included in the questionnaires.

Depending on the level and nature of the quantified activities or variables, those which were judged or expected to have negative effects or consequences on the health, education and normal development of the working child were considered as falling within the boundaries of "child labour". The main focus of the surveys in all four countries was on the economic activity of the children, whether paid in cash or in kind, or in unpaid family work, thus respecting the international definition of "economic activity". Some types of work or production for own household consumption, such as carrying water, fetching firewood, pounding and husking food products, were also considered as failing within the boundaries of economic activity. While the dividing line between economic and non-economic activities for cases such as the above is rather thin and not always obvious, these and many others, were considered to fall within the margin of economic activity or the "production boundary" as defined by the System of National Accounts.

While schooling activities were measured in the majority of cases, in some instances non-schooling activities of a non-economic nature (especially household chores or housekeeping services provided in the child's own parents' or guardians' homes) were also estimated separately. Both the "current" and the "usual" economic activity approaches were applied, the first in reference to activities during a short period such as the week (or seven days) prior to the date of the interview, and the second in reference to a long period such as the 12 months (or 365 days) preceding the inquiry date. The latter reference period takes seasonality into account, which is an important factor since a considerable proportion of children's activities is seasonal, including activities undertaken when schools are closed. In all the selected areas the household-based surveys were carried out strictly on a relatively rigorous sample basis using a multi-stage (two-or three-stage) stratified sampling design.

Using the household listing as a sampling frame as well as the basic information that was collected during the listing, all the listed households in each unit of the segment were then grouped into three strata as follows:

— Households with at least one paid child worker (in the specific age group);

— Households without a paid child worker but with at least one child working as an unpaid family worker (in the same specific age group); and

— Other households (in the same age group).

A specified number of households in each of the above three strata were selected by means of systematic sampling which formed the final stage sampling units.

Through these sampling procedures or slight variations, between 4,000 and 5,000 households were selected to represent the sample size for the surveys in each of the four countries.

Where suitable statistical software packages were not available in the statistical offices of the countries concerned, a self-weighing systematic sampling design with probability proportional to size (PPS) was adopted. This approach helped by providing a uniform weight for estimating totals. It also facilitated the computation of percentages, means and ratios of the population parameters directly from the sample data. The questionnaire that was applied at the household level consisted of two parts. The first part was addressed to the head of the household to obtain information on the demographic and socio-economic composition of the household, including such aspects as housing facilities, household migration status and living standards and the education level and economic activity status of the household members. The second part was used to collect the required information from the individual children themselves. As a supplement, a simple questionnaire was used to interview elected and appointed leaders, administrators and the like, in the communities or towns and villages of the selected areas so as to identify the major local socio-economic characteristics, assess development levels and determine the differential in the incidence of child labour.

During the household listing stage, basic information on a limited number of variables relating to each household and its members was also obtained to facilitate the stratification of the households in each segment and the sample selection of households. The employer's questionnaire was addressed to the owner of the business or a designated respondent, seeking information on the particulars of the ownership, the goods produced and services rendered, the number of children and adults engaged, their working conditions, the reasons for using child workers, facilities and health care at the workplace and so on. Probability sampling became prohibitive due to the absence of basic information which could serve as a master frame, such as an exhaustive list or directory of employers in respect of the areas selected for the surveys. In view of this problem, only those employers identified by the children themselves or their parents during the interview at the household level, or those enterprises known or suspected to be using child workers, were located and interviewed on a random basis. In this way, up to a total of 200 entities were identified and enumerated in urban and rural area selected in each country. Special problems of collecting data on children working and living on the streets, an individual questionnaire was formulated and used to assemble information on variables relating to the schooling and non-schooling activities of such children, their living and working conditions, parents, migration status and so on. Therefore, for the children on the streets, a "purposive" or "convenience" approach was applied and as far as possible, enumerators who were selected and trained for the interviews were those who knew the core areas where such children were found. The children were visited in their localities in the evenings and in some cases at night if that proved to be more convenient.

Variations exist in the results of the surveys conducted in the four countries owing to their differences in terms of social, cultural, political and economic development levels, average family size, household income and expenditure, literacy or illiteracy levels of the adult population and especially the school enrolment and attendance ratios of young children. The findings are also influenced by the differences in the reference period of the surveys, for example, whether it covers a schooling period, agricultural season and so on. For the same reasons, the findings also vary between any two areas covered by the survey within each country. The statistical results from the surveys have proved the existence of a positive correlation—in some instances a strong one—between child labour and such factors as poverty, illiteracy, the level of rural community under-development, urban slum conditions, school truancy or dropouts, abandoned or runaway children, large family size, female-headed households, the parents'—especially the father's—occupations, and permanent absence or death of the father, among others. The household-based survey has been found to be the most effective means of investigating the child labour phenomenon in all its facets. As a result the data obtained through household surveys did not include information on such children who might have been working on the streets, although the number of such youngsters would be relatively very small in most countries. The best time to visit the sample households was found to be late afternoons or early evenings. While finding an adult respondent was relatively easy in the daytime, there was difficulty contacting the children themselves in the households during the daytime and proxy informants tended to be unreliable, especially concerning certain questions or variables.

In many cases the establishment-based investigation was not particularly successful, notably where it was difficult to identify employers and managers of workplaces. While it was hoped that the information obtained from the household heads and the children themselves would allow a list to be compiled of establishments where the children work, this proved difficult, mainly because many children were not available during the household inquiry and many adults were unable to provide the precise address of the children's place of work. Where a list or directory of establishments does not exist or cannot be compiled on the basis of the information obtained from the household-level survey, a micro-level approach can be taken in which the type of formal sector activities (industries, services) where children may be working are identified and the enterprises engaged in these activities are investigated. In view of the fact that a large majority (90 per cent) of economically active children are unpaid family workers and some others are self-employed or casual labourers, this approach may often suffice. In a few of the countries where a proper sample survey of establishments proved difficult, small purposive or convenience inquiries were carried out which produced some interesting statistical results, though for the most part these were qualitative and not representative of enterprises as a whole. Another problem regarding the establishment-based inquiry was the lack of full, or even any, cooperation on the part of the employers, especially where the employment of youngsters under a specified age is illegal. For this reason, the use of the term "child activity" or "child work" instead of "child labour" in the survey instruments and by field personnel during interviews, may lead to a better response rate at all levels.

Conducting a well-formulated campaign, prior to the launching of the survey, in the various localities and at the national level to publicise the importance of the data to be collected for improving children's welfare could make respondents much more cooperative. Homeless children are not represented in household samples since they have no usual place of residence or home. These children, however, face daily risks, hazards and exploitation that are detrimental to their mental and physical development.

A purposive approach was applied using well-trained interviewers who were well acquainted with the inner city where such children usually work or congregate. In one country in particular, a micro-level inquiry was conducted successfully taking as a starting point the fact that most homeless children are usually found in large urban centres. The interviewers were sent out in the early evening and often at night with a detailed questionnaire to interviewers at random the children they found. In many cases, the informal sector operators for whom the children work were also interviewed. The exercise resulted in useful statistical data, enabling the survey team to analyse the various characteristics of street children: age; sex; educational background; migration status and reasons for being on the streets; types of economic activity and occupation; earnings; living conditions (food, sleeping place, etc.); difficulties encountered; skills; future plans; activity patterns and background information of their parents; and so on.

The survey experiment based on a "time use" module was not successful for the purposes of investigating children's activities and the intensity of their work. Even when presented with a long list of economic and non-economic activities, many children could not recall the activities in which they had been engaged during the 24 hours preceding the date of the survey. Most children seem to remember only those activities which they most like, especially those in which they made "good" earnings.

In many instances, it was difficult to consult the children themselves, and approaching proxies for this purpose was found to be futile since they could not account for the children's daily activities or their time allocation on each. Consequently, the results obtained from the "time use" exercise were found to be unsatisfactory. However, better-quality data may be obtained if the investigators or interviewers spend time in the area where the children can be found and interact with them and/or observe them throughout the day. Unfortunately, this approach is neither practical nor feasible where the geographical coverage is wide and the sample size is large in order to make estimates at the national level. It is therefore recommended that, with the exception of a micro-level time allocation exercise, the application of a "time-use" approach to individual children to identify all their activities over a specific period of time (such as 24 hours) and to quantify the time devoted to each should be discouraged.

The overall recommendation is to conduct a household-based sample survey which should be supplemented by surveys of employers (establishments and enterprises) and street children.

Household based surveys: The justification for these surveys and their suitability lies in the fact that by definition a household is a unit consisting of either an individual living alone or a group of two or more persons living together with a common provision for food and other essentials necessary for living. The only persons who are not represented through household-based sample inquiries are the homeless, nomads, and household members who are absent from the household permanently or for a long period at the time of enumeration. If such persons do not live in another household within the country, they will not be represented in a household-based national sample survey. However, such groups normally only constitute a very small proportion of the total population within any specific age cohort. Even then, much in formation could be collected on those who are away from the households by addressing various relevant questions to the household head or a proxy. This information could, in turn, be used to design a more appropriate investigation of such persons to find out more details on all aspects of their activities, occupations, living conditions and so on. The use of households as units of enumeration could permit the gathering of a wealth of statistical information on all or any segment of a country's population, subject to the availability of resources. The ILO methodological experiments carried out in 1992-93 and national surveys undertaken since then concerning child labour in several countries have proved the household approach to be the most effective means for it profound assessment of the level, nature and determinants of the practice at the national level.

During such surveys, information could also be collected on the activity patterns of adults not only because the additional cost involved would be marginal, but because such data are important for studying the interrelation ship between the activities of children and the activities of other members of the same household and in particular, those of their parents or guardians. Besides providing a national picture, another advantage of a comprehensive household-based survey is that, if implemented through well-designed sampling and stratification procedures, it would permit segregation of the statistical information not only into rural/urban areas and informal/formal sectors, but also, and more importantly, into small geographical areas within any large geographical region or province. The information on small localities would be crucial for formulating and implementing policies and action programmes appropriate for combating child labour in specific geographical areas or communities where the problem may be quite serious.

The latter approach is much more efficient in many ways, particularly if the module is implemented as a supplement to an established programme of a labour force survey (LFS) conducted on a sample basis at the national level. This undertaking will not only result in substantial cost savings, but the operation could be achieved in less time. Operationally, it means that the module would be piggybacked into one of the rounds of the US and that the interviews for both the LFS and the module would be carried out at the same time. Since the LFS questionnaire always seeks to enumerate the demographic and socio-economic composition of household members, there would be no need to repeat this part in the module for children. Through empirical studies it has been demonstrated that the incidence of child labour and the demographic and socio-economic characteristics of the "adult" household members are correlated positively or negatively depending on the different variables considered. Therefore, information on other household members has to be collected as well.

The attractiveness of the modular option stems from the fact that there would be no need to list all the households selected in the initial stage of sampling, representing the primary-stage sampling units (PSUs), or to collect the basic information required for the stratification and selections of the second stage sampling units (SSUs). Since there would be no repeat questions on the demographic and socio-economic characteristics of the children, the entire module would be considerably shorter. In addition, where the ILO and national statistics offices have collaborated closely in attaching a comprehensive child labour module to ongoing household-based surveys, significant savings have been realised. For example, in Turkey, where the module was attached to one of the two rounds of the national LFS, the cost of the operation amounted to only one-fifth (20 per cent) of the total resources that would have been needed if a stand-alone child labour survey had been conducted. A similar approach was carried out in Cambodia where the cost of the child labour survey component was about one-tenth (10 per cent) of the estimated total resources. To avoid limiting the coverage of the incidence of various forms of child work, all types of activities (schooling and non-schooling, economic and non-economic activities) of children within a specified age group would be represented through sampling and enumerated and the volume or workload of their activities quantified, so that the assembled statistical information could be cross-tabulated by the different characteristics of the variables included in the questionnaire.

Depending on the level and nature of the quantified activities or variables, those which are judged or expected to have negative effects or consequences on the health, education and normal development of the working children could be considered as falling within the boundary of "child labour". The data should then be further dissected into various categories of affected children based on the degree of harm caused by the quantified activities.

Since the comprehensive household survey would investigate all the activities of children in the particular age cohort, the data collected would make it possible to identify the specific occupations of the working children, their working conditions, accidents/injuries/illnesses suffered—including their frequency and gravity—problems related to the workplace environment, particulars of employers using children, the specific industries in which children work, the effect of their work on their normal life (including their schooling) and other related matters which would assist in assessing more fully the extent, nature and causes of child labour.

Declarations and resolutions seek to protect all children under 18 years of age from different types of harmful activities, it is strongly recommended that the survey of child labour should cover children from 5 to 17 years of age. One advantage of using this broad age cohort is that it would allow breakdown of the data obtained by different age groups, thereby satisfying the requirements of the various instruments, as well as national needs for respecting compulsory schooling regulations, labour codes and other legal requirements of individual countries. Examples of groupings are: 5-14, 15-17 and 5-17 years, the 5-14 age group broken down further by 5-9 and 10-14 years, all commonly used by most countries. It may be useful to have the results also separately classified for children under 11, 12-13 and 14 years, in view of ILO Convention No. 138 and Recommendation No. 146 concerning Minimum Age for Admission to Employment (both adopted in 1973).

Convention No. 138 generally prohibits economic activity of children under the age of 15, while making exceptions for those aged 14 years and for those between 12 and 13 years, depending on different circumstances in individual countries.

It is also recommended that work of a domestic nature (household chores) performed by children in their own parents' or other relatives' homes where they actually reside should be included in the investigation of children's schooling and non-schooling activities. The final data compiled on these children should then be tabulated separately from those relating to children who are economically active. Non-economic work of a domestic nature in the parents' or guardians' household would then be classified and tabulated into various ranges according to the number of hours during which such work was performed. A threshold could then be established beyond which the activity could be deemed as constituting child labour. The above is based on the argument that many non-school-going children perform housekeeping activities in their parents' or guardians' households for various reasons, one being to make adult household members available for economic activity elsewhere. For many of these children this is a full- time occupation involving preparing and serving meals, washing clothes, cleaning floors, taking care of younger siblings, serving as messengers in and around the household and so on, all this at the sacrifice of the education and playtime to which each child is entitled under the United Nations Convention on the Rights of the Child. Even those who attend school are found to be spending several hours a day performing such activities which are detrimental to their schooling, health and normal development to adulthood. Such children suffer fatigue which affects their school performance and many are exposed to hazardous situations, for example, cooking food over an open fire.

Children who are put under the guardianship of relatives or other persons are especially susceptible to much abuse in these areas of work. The sampling approach to be adopted for surveys on children's activities should in principle be a multi-stage stratified sampling design to capture a good number of working children. Conversely, where there is a homogeneity of activities (in rural areas, for example), under-sampling (a smaller sample) could be considered. Where statistical software packages are not readily available, a self-weighting systematic sampling design with probability proportional to size (PPS) of the population being considered should be adopted, since this will have a uniform weight for estimating totals and will also facilitate the computation of percentages, means and ratios of the population parameters directly from the sample data.

The sampling and stratification procedures to be adopted depend on the availability of basic information on various factors and at different levels. Uptodate information or demarcations regarding the general characteristics of the areas to be covered, the composition of the population and/or the households within each area, and so on, would be required to serve as a master frame in designing several phases of sampling and stratification. In the experimental surveys, the various elements or classifications considered for the stratification included: development levels of the selected rural and urban areas (e.g. poorly developed/well developed, slum/non-slum blocks); income classes (low, middle, high); overall rates of literacy/illiteracy of the population; school attendance levels; family size, and so on. Again, depending on the sample size and the other factors, an over-sampling may be needed to capture adequately the incidence of child labour, which is more rare than finding an adult in the labour force.

According to ILO-IPEC experimental surveys carried out in Ghana, India, Indonesia and Senegal, the proportion of employed children among total child workers was found to be around 10 per cent. Thus, a survey of employers or establishments can give statistical information about only a small segment of child workers to supplement the results obtained through the household approach. However, these child workers might form the most vulnerable section of all working children; some of them may be exposed to danger, maltreatment by employers, underpayment and environmentally bad working conditions. Such facts may not, however, be revealed through the survey of establishments as most employers will not divulge such information.

Nevertheless, a survey of establishments employing child labour may be undertaken as a supplementary effort to find out more about the employers who have recourse to it. The most important was the difficulty in identifying the establishments that employ child labour. Most developing countries do not have an updated or exhaustive national list or directory of employers. The task of preparing such a list and identifying those employing children in the ultimate areal unit is time consuming and requires considerable resources, both human and financial. Also, many establishment owners try to hide the fact that they actually engage children, and even if they admit to it, they may provide only partial information. The alternative is to survey the establishments which employ the children belonging to the sample households. In spite of the problems that may arise, a survey of employers should be attempted. The following alternative operational procedures, which can be modified according to national requirements and circumstances, may be considered:

— Constructing a list/directory of employers using a child workforce based on the responses provided by the children and their parents during a household-based child labour survey;

— Preparing, through local inquiries, a frame of enterprises employing child labour in the areas known to have a concentration of such units. For each unit, some broad information relating to the type of productive activity and the scale of operation may be ascertained;

— Selecting a sample of enterprises engaged in different activities in which children are known or suspected to be working; and

— Collecting the required information by interviewing all owners or operators of enterprises.

The main difficulty in applying the above operational procedures is the preparation of a proper framework. An alternative could be to list all the enterprises along with the listing of households in the selected areal units and elicit information as to whether or not they employ child labour. All the enterprises/establishments in each geographical unit in the sample for the household survey can be taken up. Such a scheme might also permit estimates of total child workers employed in enterprises.

But it may call for a large number of ultimate areal units in the sample to obtain an adequate number of sample enterprises for the survey. Therefore, the strategy may be formulated according to the national circumstances of a country. The three possible strategies are:

1) As undertaken in the experimental surveys, a verification of the establishments in which the child workers identified during the household survey are reported to be employed;

2) A survey of all the establishments (employing child labour) located in the ultimate areal units in the sample for the household survey; and

3) A survey of establishments selected purposely from a list (prepared through local inquiries) of enterprises employing child workers.

Surveys of street children : Certain activities of children can prove difficult to quantify through sample surveys; for example, prostitution, trafficking and other illegal activities are not easy to investigate given that, for the most part, such activities are hidden. A purposive or convenience survey approach may have to be used to collect qualitative information. It may be possible to contact a few of the children involved in these activities who are willing to be interviewed. However, much information can be gathered through the "key informants" system—contacting and interviewing knowledgeable persons in the community where the activities are known to exist.

The investigators would have to be sociologists, psychologists, and social workers. Questions addressed to youths in the streets should relate to most of the variables directed at the children aged 15 years mentioned under the household-based survey. Additionally, street children should be asked to provide information on their migration status and reasons for being homeless or for coming to the present place, on living conditions (food, sleeping places and facilities, health and safety), on the background characteristics of their parents/guardians and siblings, on whether or not they are in regular contact with their parents/guardians and/or siblings, on their present difficulties or problems, and on their prospects or plans for the future.

The actual fieldwork for collecting data from street children may be operationally difficult within the general framework of a survey. There may even be some resistance from the group and in some cases it may even be dangerous to visit such spots for survey purposes. If so, help should be sought from local influential persons, social workers and the like and sometimes even from police personnel. The first operational step in the survey of street children is to identify the different places in the city where groups of street children usually gather to sleep.

After identifying these spots, a sampling of them can be undertaken if they are numerous, but otherwise they should all be surveyed. If a city has a large number of such places where street children gather, an alternative procedure could be to survey those which fall in the areal units selected for the household survey in the city.But since such places are not generally uniformly spread throughout the city, this scheme may not cover enough sample spots for the survey unless a special stratification is adopted. Therefore, an initial identification of such spots and a sampling of them may be more fruitful, particularly when such a survey cannot aim at statistical estimates for a larger geographical area. In the selected spots, a complete enumeration of all the children can be attempted if their number is small.

The children congregating at a particular place may often be homogeneous with respect to their activities and, therefore, if there is a large number of children in a given spot, a sample can be selected. To draw the sample, a list of all the children has first to be drawn up. Each child in the sample can then be interviewed to fill out the questionnaire. However, a survey of street children would have a number of limitations:

— The survey may not provide a reliable estimate of total street children by various categories, as the sample selected may not be representative;

— Children living individually on the streets may not be covered since many of them move from place to place continuously;

— It may not be possible to get reliable information on some of the activities (illegal or disreputable) pursued by street children, which they may not want to report to the investigators; and

— If there is resistance in some places (or even threats of violence), the investigators may try to avoid collecting data in such places unless security is provided.

Interviewers of street children should be those who are reasonably acquainted with the areas and streets where the children are usually found, who may even know some of the children themselves and who are well trained in putting the children at ease, for example, by providing them with soft drinks.

The obvious way of collecting the information is by interview. A standard context for research interviews is the household-based surveys. But for reasons already explained, it is impossible to conduct indepth interviews with child workers inside an employer's workplace (or premises). The atmosphere is wrong, the timeframe is wrong, the employer may be obstructive; the child is most unlikely to be forthcoming and—fearing repercussions from the employer—may even give answers which please the employer, especially if the employer is present at the interview. This may also be true even at the household level, which makes it important to interview the child alone, particularly away from his/her parents or so-called "guardians".

Indepth interviews with children should therefore be conducted in a setting outside the place of work, preferably a place where the child feels safe and comfortable. Unless the interviewer has a great deal of experience in interviewing children, it will also be necessary to build up the child's confidence in the person concerned. Training in working with children will also be needed because creativity is needed to elicit correct information. Thus, interviewing children in depth, as opposed to asking broad questions, is best done over a period of time in a relatively unstructured and informal way.

The ideal setting is an existing project in which (ex)-working children are participating, for example, a drop-in centre or an education programme. If no such project currently exists, it is suggested that any attempt to collect in-depth information from the child workers at the employer's workplace or premises is postponed until it does. Here is a case where "action" should precede "research". However, there is no need to feel that the task is impossible.

Some NGOs have set up projects with the twin purposes of action and research in mind and have trained those who work with the children to collect information from them as part of their job. Alternatively, researchers might identify—with help from social welfare departments and others—an existing institution such as a children's home where some children are to be found, and conduct research among them.

In interviewing children about the effects of terms and conditions of work on their physical and mental well-being, it would be a good idea to seek advice from professional child care workers, as well as follow the suggestions below.

First, if you ask a child questions in a way which leads to a "yes" or "no", the child will probably answer accordingly. If you say: "Please tell me about . . . ." or "Please describe to me. . ." you are likely to get more information. Similarly, sometimes a "leading" question such as "What do you think of ... ?" or "What do you know (or "Do you know") about the difficulties (or other situation) at your school, or where you work, or with your employer, or at your home ...?" will result in more information.

Second, much information can only be gained indirectly. A child will not understand these words very well. So ask him or her to describe the whole day's activities, from the moment he/she gets up in the morning, right through until bedtime. Questions can be included about what the employer says and does; and about meals, sleeping space, rest breaks and so on. From the very specific, the child could then be asked more general questions about visits from family members, holidays, outings, pay, and the like.

Effects on well-being is more difficult. As far as health is concerned, you could include "before" and "after" questions such as: "How does ... compare to ... at home?" (food, bedtime, getting-up time, aches and pains). For psychological impact, you could ask about "my happiest times", and "my saddest times" and about contact with friends and relations. The most important thing is to create an atmosphere in which the child feels sufficiently comfortable to tell stories about his or her intimate experiences and reveal his or her feelings. This is why time, trust and the advice of child specialists are needed. Bearing in mind the delicacy with which interviewing should proceed, work out ahead of time what kind of subjects are relatively easy to open up and what kind should not be opened without caution. For example, you can start with questions about tasks, pay, and "gifts" such as shelter, clothing, home, and medical expenses.

Then proceed to working hours, where the child sleeps, food and care, how often he/she has a day off. From these responses you may spot natural openings to questions about the treatment the child receives and how he or she feels about it. If at any time the child becomes distressed, you can stop. In addition to noting the child's responses to specific questions, you may also want to write down some of your observations: "observation" is a useful research technique. Immediately after the interview is over, write a few paragraphs about the child. But in this case the colleague should be very unobtrusive and sit somewhere off to the side. If the interview is conducted in a separate room with just the child present, there should only be one adult interviewer or the child is bound to feel overwhelmed. Have your observation headings ready ahead of time. For example: dress, cleanliness, facial expression, willingness to speak up, body language, signs of emotion, personality, ability to express him/herself. You may think you will remember all these things later when you read your interview notes, but very quickly one interviewee blurs into another. Drawing, painting, acting out and storytelling are revealing methods of eliciting information. They are especially useful in cultural settings where people are not used to being bombarded with questions. Many NGOs use these kinds of techniques within non-formal education programmes.

Convention on the Rights of the Child

Adopted by the General Assembly of the United Nations on 20 November 1989

Preamble

The States Parties to the present Convention,

Considering that, in accordance with the principles proclaimed in the Charter of the United Nations, recognition of the inherent dignity and of the equal and inalienable rights of all members of the human family is the foundation of freedom, justice and peace in the world,

Bearing in mind that the peoples of the United Nations, have, in the Charter, reaffirmed their faith in fundamental human rights and in the dignity and worth of the human person, and have determined to promote social progress and better standards of life in larger freedom,

Recognising that the United Nations has, in the Universal Declaration of Human Rights and in the International Covenants on Human Rights, proclaimed and agreed that everyone is entitled to all the rights and freedoms set forth therein, without distinction of any kind, such as race, colour, sex, language religion, political or other opinion, national or social origin, property, birth or other status,

Recalling that, in the Universal Declaration of Human Rights, the United Nations has proclaimed that childhood is entitled to special care and assistance,

Convinced that the family, as the fundamental group of society and the natural environment for the growth and well-being of all its members and particularly children, should be afforded the necessary protection and assistance so that it can fully assume its responsibilities within the community,

Recognising that the child, for the full and harmonious development of his or her personality, should grow up in a family environment, in an atmosphere of happiness, love and understanding,

Considering that the child should be fully prepared to live an individual life in society, and brought up in the spirit of the ideals proclaimed in the Charter of the United Nations, and in particular in the spirit of peace, dignity, tolerance, freedom, equality and solidarity,

Bearing in mind the need to extend particular care to the child has been stated in the Geneva Declaration of the Rights of the Child of 1924 and in the Declaration of the Rights of the Child adopted by the General Assembly on 20 November 1959 and recognised in the Universal Declaration of Human Rights, in the International Covenant on Civil and Political Rights (in particular in articles 23 and 24), in the International Covenant on Economic, Social and Cultural Rights (in particular in Article 10) and in the statutes and relevant instruments of specialised agencies and international organisations concerned with the welfare of children,

Bearing in mind as indicated in the Declaration of the Rights of the Child, "the child, by reason of his physical and mental immaturity, needs special safeguards and care, including appropriate legal protection, before as well as after birth",

Recalling the provisions of the Declaration on Social and Legal Principles relating to Protection and Welfare of Children, with Special Reference to Foster Placement and Adoption Nationally and Internationally; the United Nations Standard Minimum Rules for the Administration of Juvenile Justice (The Beijing Rules); and the Declaration on the Protection of Women and Children in Emergency and Armed Conflict,

Recognising that, in all countries in the world, there are children living in exceptionally difficult conditions, and the such children need special consideration,

Taking due account of the importance of the traditions and cultural values of each people for the protection and harmonious development of the child,

Recognising the importance of international cooperation for improving the living conditions of children in every country, in particular in the developing countries,

Have agreed as follows:

Part I

Article 1

For the purposes of the present Convention, a child

means every human being below the age of eighteen years unless under the law applicable to the child, majority is attained earlier.

Article 2

1. States Parties shall respect and ensure the rights set forth in the present Convention to each child within their jurisdiction without discrimination of any kind, irrespective of the child's or his or her parent's or legal guardian's race, colour, sex, language, religion, political or other opinion, national ethnic or social origin, property, disability, birth or other status.
2. States Parties shall take all appropriate measures to ensure that the child is protected against all forms of discrimination or punishment on the basis of the status, activities, expressed opinions, or beliefs of the child's parents, legal guardians, or family members.

Article 3

1. In all actions concerning children, whether undertaken by public or private social welfare institutions, courts of law, administrative authorities or legislative bodies, the best interests of the child shall be a primary consideration.
2. States Parties undertake to ensure the child such protection and care as is necessary for his or her well-being, taking into account the rights and duties of his or her parents, legal guardians, or other individuals legally responsible for him or her, and to this end, shall take all appropriate legislative and administrative measures.

3. States Parties shall ensure that the institutions, services and facilities responsible for the care or protection of children shall conform with the standards established by competent authorities, particularly in the areas of safety, health, in the number and suitability of their staff, as well as competent supervision.

Article 4

States Parties shall undertake all appropriate legislative, administrative, and other measures for the implementation of the rights recognised in the present Convention. With regard to economic, social and cultural rights, States Parties shall undertake such measures to the maximum extent of their available resources and, where needed, within the framework of international cooperation.

Article 5

States Parties shall respect the responsibilities, rights and duties of parents or, where applicable, the members of the extended family or community as provided for by local custom, legal guardians or other persons legally responsible for the child, to provide, in a manner consistent with the evolving capacities of the child, appropriate direction and guidance in the exercise by the child, appropriate direction and guidance in the exercise by the child of the rights recognised in the present Convention.

Article 6

1. States Parties recognise that every child has the inherent right to life.

2. States Parties shall ensure to the maximum extent possible the survival and development of the child.

Article 7

1. The child shall be registered immediately after birth and shall have the right from birth to a name, the right to acquire a nationality and, as far as possible, the right to know and be cared for by his or her parents.

2. States Parties shall ensure the implementation of these rights in accordance with their national law and their obligations under the relevant international instruments in this field, in particular where the child would otherwise be stateless.

Article 8

1. States Parties undertake to respect the right of the child to preserve his or her identity, including nationality, name and family relations as recognised by law without unlawful interference.

2. Where a child is illegally deprived of some or all of the elements of his or her identity, States Parties shall provide appropriate assistance and protection, with a view to re-establishing speedily his or her identity.

Article 9

1. States Parties shall ensure that a child shall not be separated from his or her parents against their will, except when competent authorities subject to judicial review determine, in accordance with applicable law and procedures, that such separation is necessary for the best interests of the child. Such determination may be necessary in a particular case such as one involving abuse or neglect of the child by the parents, or one where the parents are living separately and a decision must be made as to the child's place of residence.

2. In any proceedings pursuant to paragraph 1 of the present Article, all interested parties shall be given an opportunity to participate in the proceeding and make their views known.

3. States Parties shall respect the right of the child who is separated from one or both parents to maintain personal relations and direct contact with both parents on a regular basis, except if it is contrary to the child's best interests.

4. Where such separation results from any action initiated by a States Party, such as the detention, imprisonment, exile, deportation or death (including death arising from any cause while the person is in the custody of the State) of one or both parents or of the child, that State Party shall, upon request, provide the parents, the child or, if appropriate, another member of the family with the essential information concerning the whereabouts of the

absent member(s) of the family unless the provision of the information would be detrimental to the well-being of the child. States Parties shall further ensure that the submission of such a request shall of itself entail no adverse consequences for the person(s) concerned.

Article 10

1. In accordance with the obligation of States Parties under article 9, paragraph 1, applications by a child or his or her parents to enter or leave a State party for the purpose of family reunification shall be dealt with by States Parties in a positive, humane and expeditious manner. States Parties shall further ensure that the submission of such a request shall entail no adverse consequences for the applicants and for the members of their family.

2. A child whose parents reside in different States shall have the right to maintain on a regular basis, save in exceptional circumstances personal relations and direct contacts with both parents. Towards that end and in accordance with the obligation of States Parties under article 9, paragraph 1, States Parties shall respect the right of the child and his or her parents to leave any country, including their own, and to enter their own country. The right to leave any country shall be subject only to such restrictions as are prescribed by law and which are necessary to protect the national security, public order (order public), public health or morals or the rights and freedoms of others and are consistent with the other rights recognised in the present Convention.

Article 11

1. States Parties shall take measures to combat the illicit transfer and non-return of children abroad.
2. To this end, States Parties shall promote the conclusion of bilateral or multilateral agreements or accession to existing agreements.

Article 12

1. States Parties shall assure to the child who is capable of forming his or her own views the right to express those views freely in all matters affecting the child, the views of the child being given due weight in accordance with the age and maturity of the child.
2. For this purpose, the child shall in particular be provided the opportunity to be heard in any judicial and administrative proceedings affecting the child, either directly, or through a representative or an appropriate body, in a manner consistent with the procedural rules of national law.

Article 13

1. The child shall have the right to freedom of expression; this right shall include freedom to seek, receive and impart information and ideas of all kinds, regardless of frontiers, either orally, in writing or in print, in the form of art, or through any other media of the child's choice.
2. The exercise of this right may be subject to certain restrictions, but these shall only be such as are provided by law and are necessary:

a) For respect of the rights or reputations of others, or
b) For the protection of national security or of public order (order public), or of public health or morals.

Article 14

1. States Parties shall respect the right of the child to freedom of thought, conscience and religion.
2. States Parties shall respect the rights and duties of the parents and when applicable, legal guardians, to provide direction to the child in the exercise of his or her right in a manner consistent with the evolving capacities of the child.
3. Freedom to manifest one's religion or beliefs may be subject only to such limitations as are prescribed by law and are necessary to protect public safety, order, health or morals, or the fundamental rights and freedoms of others.

Article 15

1. States Parties recognise the rights of the child to freedom of association and to freedom of peaceful assembly.
2. No restrictions may be placed on the exercise of these rights other than those imposed in conformity with the law and which are necessary in a democratic society in the interests of national security or public safety, public order (order public), the protection of public health or morals or the protection of the rights and freedoms of others.

Article 16

1. No child shall be subjected to arbitrary or unlawful interference with his or her privacy, family, home or correspondence, nor to unlawful attacks on his or her honour and reputation;
2. The child has the right to the protection of the law against such interference or attacks.

Article 17

States Parties recognise the important function performed by the mass media and shall ensure that the child has access to information and material from a diversity of national and international sources, especially those aimed at the promotion of his or her social, spiritual and moral well-being and physical and mental health. To this end, States Parties shall:

a) Encourage the mass media to disseminate information and material of social and cultural benefit to the child and in accordance with the spirit of Article 29;

b) Encourage international co-operation in the production, exchange and dissemination of such information and material from a diversity of cultural, national and international sources;

c) Encourage the production and dissemination of children's books;

d) Encourage the mass media to have particular regard to the linguistic needs of the child who belongs to a minority group or who is indigenous.

e) Encourage the development of appropriate guidelines for the protection of the child from information and material injurious to his or her well-being, bearing in mind the provisions of Articles 13 and 18.

Article 18

1. States Parties shall use their best efforts to ensure recognition of the principles that both parents have common responsibilities for the upbringing and development of the child. Parents or, as the case may be, legal guardians, have the primary responsibility for the upbringing and development of the child. The best interests of the child will be their basic concern.

2. For the purpose of guaranteeing and promoting the rights set forth in the present Convention, States Parties shall render appropriate assistance to parents and legal guardians in the performance of their child-rearing responsibilities and shall ensure the development of institutions, facilities and services of the care of children.

3. States Parties shall take all appropriate measures to ensure that children of working parents have the right to benefit from child-care services and facilities for which they are eligible.

Article 19

1. States Parties shall take all appropriate legislative, administrative social and educational measures to protect the child from all forms of physical or mental violence, injury or abuse, neglect or negligent treatment, maltreatment or exploitation, including

sexual abuse, while in the care of parent(s), legal guardian(s) or any other person who has the care of the child.

2. Such protective measures should, as appropriate, include effective procedures for the establishment of social programmes to provide necessary support for the child and for those who have the care of the child, as well as for other forms of prevention and for identification, reporting, referral, investigation, treatment and follow-up of instances of child maltreatment described heretofore, and, as appropriate, for judicial involvement.

Article 20

1. A child temporarily or permanently deprived of his or her family environment, or in whose own best interests cannot be allowed to remain in that environment shall be entitled to special protection and assistance provided by the State.
2. States Parties shall in accordance with their national laws ensure alternative care for such a child.
3. Such care could include, *inter alia*, foster placement *kafalah of Islamic law*, adoption or if necessary placement in suitable institutions for the care of children. When considering solutions, due regard shall be paid to the desirability of continuity in a child's upbringing and to the child's ethnic, religious, cultural and linguistic background.

Article 21

States Parties that recognise and/or permit the system of adoption shall ensure that the best interests of the child shall be the paramount consideration and they shall:

a) Ensure that the adoption of a child is authorised only by competent authorities who determine, in accordance with applicable law and procedures and on the basis of all pertinent and reliable information, that the adoption is permissible in view of the child's status concerning parents, relatives and legal guardians and that, if required, the persons concerned have given their informed consent to the adoption on the basis of such counselling as may be necessary;

b) Recognised that inter-country adoption may be considered as an alternative means of child's care, if the child cannot be placed in a foster or an adoptive family or cannot in any suitable manner be cared for in the child's country of origin;

c) Ensure that the child concerned by inter-country adoption enjoys safeguards and standards equivalent to those existing in the case of national adoption;

d) Take all appropriate measures to ensure that, in inter-country adoption, the placement does not result in improper financial gain for those involved in it;

e) Promote, where appropriate, the objectives of the present article by concluding bilateral or multilateral arrangements or agreements, and endeavour, within this framework, to ensure that the placement of the child in another country is carried out by competent authorities or organs.

Article 22

1. States Parties shall take appropriate measures to ensure that a child who is seeking refugee status or who is considered a refugee in accordance with

applicable international or domestic law and procedures shall, whether unaccompanied or accompanied by his or her parents or by any other person, receive appropriate protection and humanitarian assistance in the enjoyment of applicable rights set forth in the present Convention and in other international human rights or humanitarian instruments to which the said States are Parties.

2. For this purpose, States Parties shall provide, as they consider appropriate, co-operation in any efforts by the United Nations and other competent inter-governmental organisations or non-governmental organisations co-operating with the United Nations to protect and assist such a child and to trace the parents or other members of the family of any refugee child in order to obtain information necessary for reunification with his or her family. In cases where no parents or other members of the family can be found, the child shall be accorded the same protection as any other child permanently or temporarily deprived of his or her family environment for any reason, as set forth in the present Convention.

Article 23

1. States Parties recognise that a mentally or physically disabled child should enjoy a full and decent life, in conditions which ensure dignity, promote self-reliance and facilitate the child's active participation in the community.

2. States Parties recognise the right of the disabled child to special care and shall encourage and ensure the

extension, subject to available resources, to the eligible child and those responsible for his or her care, of assistance for which application is made and which is appropriate to the child's condition and to the circumstances of the parents or others caring for the child.

3. Recognising the special needs of a disabled child, assistances extended in accordance with paragraph 2 of the present article shall be provided free of charge, whenever possible, taking into account the financial resources of the parents or others caring for the child, and shall be designed to ensure that the disabled child has effective access to and receives education, training, health care services, rehabilitation services, preparation for employment and recreation opportunities in a manner conducive to the child's achieving the fullest possible social integration and individual development, including his or her cultural and spiritual development.

4. States Parties shall promote, in the spirit of international cooperation, the exchange of appropriate information in the field of preventive health care and of medical psychological and functional treatment of disabled children, including dissemination of and access to information concerning methods of rehabilitation, education and vocational services, with the aim of enabling States Parties to improve their capabilities and skills and to widen their experience in these areas. In this regard, particular account shall be taken of the needs of developing countries.

Article 24

1. States Parties recognise the right of the child to the enjoyment of the highest attainable standard of health and to facilities for the treatment of illness and rehabilitation of health. States Parties shall strive to ensure that no child is deprived of his or her right of access to such health care services.

2. States Parties shall pursue full implementation of this right and, in particular, shall take appropriate measures:

    a) To diminish infant and child mortality;

    b) To ensure the provision of necessary medical assistance and health care to all children with emphasis on the development of primary health care;

    c) To combat disease and malnutrition, including within the framework of primary health care, through, *inter alia*, the application of readily available technology and through the provision of adequate nutritious foods and clean drinking water, taking into consideration the dangers and risks of environmental pollution;

    d) To ensure appropriate pre-natal and post-natal health care for mothers;

    e) To ensure that all segments of society, in particular parents and children, are informed, have access to education and are supported in the use of basic knowledge of child health and nutrition, the advantages of breastfeeding, hygiene and environmental sanitation and the prevention of accidents;

f) To develop preventive health care, guidance for parents and family planning education and services.

3. States Parties shall take all effective and appropriate measures with a view to abolishing traditional practices prejudicial to the health of children.

4. States Parties undertake to promote and encourage international cooperation with a view to achieving progressively the full realisation of the right recognised in the present article. In this regard, particular account shall be taken of the needs of developing countries.

Article 25

States Parties recognise the right of a child who has been placed by the competent authorities for the purposes of care, protection or treatment of his or her physical or mental health, to a periodic review of the treatment provided to the child and all other circumstances relevant to his or her placement.

Article 26

1. States Parties shall recognise for every child the right to benefit from social security, including social insurance, and shall take the necessary measures to achieve the full realisation of this right in accordance with their national law.

2. The benefits should, where appropriate, be granted, taking into account the resources and the circumstances of the child and persons having

responsibility for the maintenance of the child, as well as any other consideration relevant to an application for benefits made by or on behalf of the child.

Article 27

1. States Parties recognise the right of every child to a standard of living adequate for the child's physical, mental, spiritual, moral and social development.
2. The parent(s) or others responsible for the child have the primary responsibility to secure, within their abilities and financial capacities, the conditions of living necessary for the child's development;
3. States Parties, in accordance with national conditions and within their means, shall take appropriate measures to assist parents and others responsible for the child to implement this right and shall in case of need provide material assistance and support programmes, particularly with regard to nutrition, clothing and housing.
4. States Parties shall take all appropriate measures to secure the recovery of maintenance for the child from the parents of other persons having financial responsibility for the child, both within the State Party and from abroad. In particular, where the person having financial responsibility for the child lives in a State different from that of the child, States Parties shall promote the accession to international agreements of the conclusion of such agreements, as well as the making of other appropriate arrangements.

Article 28

1. States Parties recognise the right of the child to education, and with a view to achieving this right progressively and on the basis of equal opportunity, they shall, in particular:

   a) Make primary education compulsory and available free to all;

   b) Encourage the development of different forms of secondary education, including general and vocational education, make them available and accessible to every child, and take appropriate measures such as the introduction of free education and offering financial assistance in case of need;

   c) Make higher education accessible to all on the basis of capacity by every appropriate means;

   d) Make educational and vocational information and guidance available and accessible to all children;

   e) Take measures to encourage regular attendance at schools and the reduction of dropout rates.

2. States Parties shall take all appropriate measures to ensure that school discipline is administered in a manner consistent with the child's human dignity and in conformity with the present Convention.

3. States Parties shall promote and encourage international cooperation in matters relating to education, in particular with a view to contributing to the elimination of ignorance and illiteracy throughout the world and facilitating access to scientific and technical knowledge and modern

teaching methods. In this regard, particular account shall be taken of the needs of developing countries.

Article 29

1. States Parties agree that the education on the child shall be directed to:

   a) The development of the child's personality, talents and mental and physical abilities to their fullest potential;

   b) The development of respect for human rights and fundamental freedoms, and for the principles enshrined in the Charter of the United Nations.

   c) The development of respect for the child's parents, his or her own cultural identity, language and values, for the national values of the country in which the child is living, the country from which he or she may originate, and for civilisations different from his or her own;

   d) The preparation of the child for responsible life in a free society, in the spirit of understanding, peace tolerance equality of sexes, and friendship among all peoples, ethnic, national and religious groups and persons of indigenous origin;

   e) The development of respect for the natural environment.

2. No part of the present Article or article 28 shall be construed so as to interfere with the liberty of individuals and bodies to establish and direct educational institutions, subject always to the observance of the principle set forth in paragraph 1 of the present article and to the requirements that the

education given in such institutions shall confirm to such minimum standards as may be laid down by the State.

Article 30

In those States in which ethnic, religious or linguistic minorities or persons of indigenous origin exist, a child belonging to such a minority or who is indigenous shall not be denied the right, in community with other members of his or her group, to enjoy his or her own culture, to profess and practise his or her own religion, or to use his or her own language.

Article 31

1. States Parties recognise the right of the child to rest and leisure, to engage in play and recreational activities appropriate to the age of the child and to participate freely in cultural life and the arts.
2. States Parties shall respect and promote the right of the child to participate fully in cultural and artistic life and shall encourage the provision of appropriate and equal opportunities for cultural, artistic, recreational and leisure activity.

Article 32

1. States Parties recognise the right of the child to be protected from economic exploitation and from performing any work that is likely to be hazardous or to interfere with the child's education, or to be harmful to the child's health or physical, mental, spiritual, moral or social development.

2. States Parties shall take legislative, administrative, social and educational measures to ensure the implementation of the present article. To this end, and having regard to the relevant provisions of other international instruments, States Parties shall in particular:
   a) Provide for a minimum age or minimum ages for admission to employment;
   b) Provide for appropriate regulation of the hours and conditions of employment; and
   c) Provide for appropriate penalties or other sanctions to ensure the effective enforcement of the present article.

Article 33

States Parties shall take all appropriate measures, including legislative, administrative, social and educational measures, to protect children from the illicit use of narcotic drugs and psychotropic substances as defined in the relevant international treaties, and to prevent the use of children in the illicit production and trafficking of such substances.

Article 34

States Parties undertake to protect the child from all forms of sexual exploitation and sexual abuse. For these purposes, States Parties shall in particular take all appropriate national, bilateral and multilateral measures to prevent:

a) The inducement or coercion of a child to engage in any unlawful sexual activity;

b) The exploitative use of children in prostitution or other unlawful sexual practices; and

c) The exploitative use of children in pornographic performances and materials.

Article 35

States Parties shall take all appropriate national, bilateral and multilateral measures to prevent the abduction of the sale of or traffic in children for any purpose or in any form.

Article 36

States Parties shall protect the child against all other forms of exploitation prejudicial to any aspects of the child's welfare.

Article 37

States Parties shall ensure that:

a) No child shall be subjected to torture or other cruel, inhuman or degrading treatment or punishment. Neither capital punishment nor life imprisonment without possibility of release shall be imposed for offences committed by persons below eighteen years of age;

b) No child shall be deprived of his or her liberty unlawfully or arbitrarily. The arrest, detention or imprisonment of a child shall be in conformity with the law and shall be used only as a measure of last resort and for the shortest appropriate period of time;

c) Every child deprived of liberty shall be treated with humanity and respect for the inherent dignity of the human person, and in a manner which takes into account the needs of persons of his or her age. In particular, every child deprived of liberty shall be separated from adults unless it is considered in the child's best interest not to do so and shall have the right to maintain contact with his or her family through correspondence and visits, save in exceptional circumstances; and

d) Every child deprived of his or her liberty shall have the right to prompt access to legal and other appropriate assistance, as well as the right to challenge the legality of the deprivation of his or her liberty before a court or other competent, independent and impartial authority, and to a prompt decision on any such action.

Article 38

1. States Parties undertake to respect and to ensure respect for rules of international humanitarian law applicable to them in armed conflicts which are relevant to the child.
2. States Parties shall take all feasible measures to ensure that persons who have not attained the age of fifteen years do not take a direct part in hostilities.
3. States Parties shall refrain from recruiting any person who has not attained the age of fifteen years into their armed forces. In recruiting among those persons who have attained the age of fifteen years but who have not attained the age of eighteen years, States Parties shall endeavour to give priority to those who are oldest.

4. In accordance with their obligations under international humanitarian law to protect the civilian population in armed conflicts, States Parties shall take all feasible measures to ensure protection and care of children who are affected by an armed conflict.

Article 39

States Parties shall take all appropriate measures to promote physical and psychological recovery and social reintegration of a child victim of: any form of neglect, exploitation, or abuse; torture or any other form of cruel, inhuman or degrading treatment or punishment; or armed conflicts. Such recovery and reintegration shall take place in an environment which fosters the health, self-respect and dignity of the child.

Article 40

1. States Parties recognise the right of every child alleged as, accused of, or recognised as having infringed the penal law to be treated in a manner consistent with the promotion of the child's sense of dignity and worth, which reinforces the child's respect for the human rights and fundamental freedoms of others and which takes into account the child's age and the desirability of promoting the child's reintegration and the child's assuming a constructive role in society.
2. To this end, and having regard to the relevant provisions of international instruments, States Parties shall, in particular, ensure that:

a) No child shall be alleged as, be accused of, or recognised as having infringed the penal law by reason of acts or omissions that were not prohibited by national or international law at the time they were committed;

b) Every child alleged as or accused of having infringed the penal law has at least the following guarantees:

   i) To be presumed innocent until proven guilty according to law;

   ii) To be informed promptly and directly of the charges against him or her, and, if appropriate, through his or her parents of legal guardians, and to have legal or other appropriate assistance in the preparation and presentation of his or her defence;

   iii) To have the matter determined without delay by a competent, independent and impartial authority or judicial body in a fair hearing according to law, in the presence of legal or other appropriate assistance and, unless it is considered not to be in the best interest of the child, in particular, taking into account his or her age or situation, his or her parents or legal guardians;

   iv) Not to be compelled to give testimony or to confess guilt; to examine or have examined adverse witnesses and to obtain the participation and examination of witnesses on his or her behalf under conditions of equality;

v) If considered to have infringed the penal law to have this decision and any measures imposed in consequence thereof reviewed by a higher competent, independent and impartial authority or judicial body according to law;

vi) To have the free assistance of an interpreter if the child cannot understand or speak the language used; and

vii) To have his or her privacy fully respected at all stages of the proceedings.

3. States Parties shall seek to promote the establishment of laws, procedures, authorities and institutions specifically applicable to children alleged as, accused of or recognised as having infringed the penal law, and, in particular:

a) The establishment of a minimum age below which children shall be presumed not to have the capacity to infringe the penal law; and

b) Whenever appropriate and desirable measures for dealing with such children without resorting to judicial proceedings, providing that human rights and legal safeguards are fully respected.

4. A variety of dispositions, such as care, guidance and supervision orders; counselling; probation; foster care; education and vocational training programmes and other alternatives to institutional care shall be available to ensure that children are dealt with in a manner appropriate to their well being and proportionate both to their circumstances and the offence.

Article 41

Nothing in the present Convention shall affect any provisions which are more conducive to the realisation of the rights of the child and which may be contained in:

a) The law of a State Party; or

b) International law in force for that State.

Part II

Article 42

States Parties undertake to make the principles and provisions of the Convention widely known, by appropriate and active means, to adults and children alike.

Article 43

1. For the purpose of examining the progress made by States Parties in achieving the realisation of the obligations undertaken in the present Convention, there shall be established a Committee in the Rights of the Child, which shall carry out the functions hereinafter provided.

2. The Committee shall consist of ten experts of high moral standing and recognised competence in the field covered by this Convention. The members of the Committee shall be elected by States Parties from among their nationals and shall serve in their personal capacity, consideration being given to equitable geographical distribution, as well as to the principal legal systems.

3. The members of the Committee shall be elected by secret ballot from a list of persons nominated by States Parties. Each State Party may nominate one person from among its own nationals.

4. The initial election to the Committee shall be held no later than six months after the date of the entry into force of the present Convention and thereafter every second year. At least four months before the date of each election, the Secretary-General of the United Nations shall address a letter to States Parties inviting them to submit their nominations within two months. The Secretary-General shall subsequently prepare a list in alphabetical order of all persons thus nominated, indicating States Parties which have nominated them, and shall submit it to the States Parties to the present Convention.

5. The elections shall be held at meetings of States Parties convened by the Secretary-General at United Nations Headquarters. At those meetings, for which two thirds of States Parties shall constitute a quorum, the persons elected to the Committee shall be those who obtain the largest number of votes and an absolute majority of the votes of the representatives of States Parties present and voting.

6. The members of the Committee shall be elected for a term of four years. They shall be eligible for re-election if renominated. The term of five of the members elected at the first election, shall expire at the end of two years; immediately after the first election the names of these five members shall be chosen by lot by the Chairman of the meeting.

7. If a member of the Committee dies or resigns or declares that for any other cause he or she can no longer perform the duties of the Committee, the State Party which nominated the member shall appoint another expert from among its nationals to serve for the remainder of the term, subject to the approval of the Committee.
8. The Committee shall establish its own rules of procedure.
9. The Committee shall elect its officers for a period of two years.
10. The meetings of the Committee shall normally be held at United Nations Headquarters or at any other convenient place as determined by the Committee. The Committee shall normally meet annually. The duration of the meetings of the Committee shall be determined, and reviewed, subject to the approval of the General Assembly.
11. The Secretary-General of the United Nations shall provide the necessary staff and facilities for the United Nations shall provide the necessary staff and facilities for the effective performance of the functions of the Committee under the present Convention.
12. With the approval of the General Assembly, the members of the Committee established under the present Convention shall receive emoluments from United Nations resources on such terms and conditions as the Assembly may decide.

Article 44

1. States Parties undertake to submit to the Committee, through the Secretary-General of the United Nations, reports on the measures they have adopted which give effect to the rights recognised herein and on the progress made on the enjoyment of those rights:

   a) Within two years of the entry into force of the Convention for the State Party concerned; and

   b) Thereafter every five years.

2. Reports made under the present article shall indicate factors and difficulties, if any affecting the degree of fulfilment of the obligations under the present Convention. Reports shall also contain sufficient information to provide the Committee with a comprehensive understanding of the implementation of the Convention in the country concerned.

3. A State Party which has submitted a comprehensive initial report to the Committee need not, in its subsequent reports submitted in accordance with paragraph 1 (b) of the present article, repeat basic information previously provided.

4. The Committee may request from States Parties further information relevant to the implementation of the Convention.

5. The Committee shall submit to the General Assembly, through the Economic and Social Council, every two years, reports on its activities.

6. States Parties shall make their reports widely available to the public in their own countries.

Article 45

In order to foster the effective implementation of the Convention and to encourage international cooperation in the field covered by the Convention:

a) The specialised agencies, the United Nations Children's Fund, and other United Nations organs shall be entitled to be represented at the consideration of the implementation of such provisions of the present Convention as fall within the scope of their mandate. The Committee may invite the specialised agencies, the United Nations Children's Fund and other competent bodies as it may consider appropriate to provide expert advice on the implementation of the Convention in areas falling within the scope of their respective mandates. The Committee may invite the specialised agencies, the United Nations Children's Fund, and other United Nations organs to submit reports on the implementation of the Convention in areas falling within the scope of their activities;

b) The Committee shall transmit, as it may consider appropriate to the specialised agencies, the United Nations Children's Fund and other competent bodies, any reports from States Parties that contain a request, or indicate a need, for technical advice or assistance, along with the Committee's observations and suggestions, if any, on these requests or indications;

c) The Committee may recommend to the General Assembly to request the Secretary-General to undertake on its behalf studies on specific issues relating to the rights of the child;

d) The Committee may make suggestions and general recommendations based on information received pursuant to articles 44 and 45 of the present Convention. Such suggestions and general recommen-dations shall be transmitted to any State Party concerned and reported to the General Assembly, together with comments, if any, from States Parties.

Part III

Article 46

The present Convention shall be open for signature by all States.

Article 47

The present Convention is subject to ratification. Instruments of ratification shall be deposited with the Secretary-General of the United Nations.

Article 48

The present Convention shall remain open for accession by any State. The instruments of accession shall be deposited with the Secretary-General of the United Nations.

Article 49

1. The present Convention shall enter into force on the thirtieth day following the date of deposit with the Secretary-General of the United Nations of the twentieth instrument of ratification or accession.

2. For each State ratifying or acceding to the Convention after the deposit of the twentieth instrument of ratification or accession, the Convention shall enter into force on the thirtieth day after the deposit by such State of its instrument of ratification or accession.

Article 50

1. Any State Party may propose an amendment and file it with the Secretary-General of the United Nations. The Secretary-General shall thereupon communicate the proposed amendment to States Parties, with a request that they indicate whether they favour a conference of States Parties for the purpose of considering and voting upon the proposal. In the event that, within four months from the date of such communication, at least one third of the States Parties favour such a conference, the Secretary-General shall convene the conference under the auspices of the United Nations. Any amendment adopted by a majority of States Parties present and voting at the conference shall be submitted to the General Assembly for approval.
2. An amendment adopted in accordance with paragraph 1 of the present article shall enter into force when it has been approved by the General Assembly of the United Nations and accepted by a two-thirds majority of States Parties.
3. When an amendment enters into force, it shall be binding on those States Parties which have accepted it, other States Parties still being bound by the provisions of the present Convention and any earlier amendments which they have accepted.

Article 51

1. The Secretary-General of the United Nations shall receive and circulate to all States the text of reservations made by States at the time of ratification or accession.
2. A reservation incompatible with the object and purpose of the present Convention shall not be permitted.
3. Reservations may be withdrawn at any time by notification to that effect addressed to the Secretary-General of the United Nations, who shall then inform all states. Such notification shall take effect on the date on which it is received by the Secretary-General.

Article 52

A State Party may denounce the present Convention by written notification to the Secretary-General of the United Nations. Denunciation becomes effective one year after the date of receipt of the notification by the Secretary-General.

Article 53

The Secretary-General of the United Nations is designated as the depositary of the present Convention.

Article 54

The original of the present Convention, of which the Arabic, Chinese, English French, Russian and Spanish text are equally authentic, shall be deposited with the Secretary-General of the United Nations.

In Witness Whereof the undersigned plenipotentiaries, being duly authorised thereto by their respective Governments have signed the present Convention.

d) The Committee may make suggestions and general recommendations based on information received pursuant to articles 44 and 45 of the present Convention. Such suggestions and general recommen-dations shall be transmitted to any State Party concerned and reported to the General Assembly, together with comments, if any, from States Parties.

Part III

Article 46

The present Convention shall be open for signature by all States.

Article 47

The present Convention is subject to ratification. Instruments of ratification shall be deposited with the Secretary-General of the United Nations.

Article 48

The present Convention shall remain open for accession by any State. The instruments of accession shall be deposited with the Secretary-General of the United Nations.

Article 49

1. The present Convention shall enter into force on the thirtieth day following the date of deposit with the Secretary-General of the United Nations of the twentieth instrument of ratification or accession.

2. For each State ratifying or acceding to the Convention after the deposit of the twentieth instrument of ratification or accession, the Convention shall enter into force on the thirtieth day after the deposit by such State of its instrument of ratification or accession.

Article 50

1. Any State Party may propose an amendment and file it with the Secretary-General of the United Nations. The Secretary-General shall thereupon communicate the proposed amendment to States Parties, with a request that they indicate whether they favour a conference of States Parties for the purpose of considering and voting upon the proposal. In the event that, within four months from the date of such communication, at least one third of the States Parties favour such a conference, the Secretary-General shall convene the conference under the auspices of the United Nations. Any amendment adopted by a majority of States Parties present and voting at the conference shall be submitted to the General Assembly for approval.

2. An amendment adopted in accordance with paragraph 1 of the present article shall enter into force when it has been approved by the General Assembly of the United Nations and accepted by a two-thirds majority of States Parties.

3. When an amendment enters into force, it shall be binding on those States Parties which have accepted it, other States Parties still being bound by the provisions of the present Convention and any earlier amendments which they have accepted.

Article 51

1. The Secretary-General of the United Nations shall receive and circulate to all States the text of reservations made by States at the time of ratification or accession.
2. A reservation incompatible with the object and purpose of the present Convention shall not be permitted.
3. Reservations may be withdrawn at any time by notification to that effect addressed to the Secretary-General of the United Nations, who shall then inform all states. Such notification shall take effect on the date on which it is received by the Secretary-General.

Article 52

A State Party may denounce the present Convention by written notification to the Secretary-General of the United Nations. Denunciation becomes effective one year after the date of receipt of the notification by the Secretary-General.

Article 53

The Secretary-General of the United Nations is designated as the depositary of the present Convention.

Article 54

The original of the present Convention, of which the Arabic, Chinese, English French, Russian and Spanish text are equally authentic, shall be deposited with the Secretary-General of the United Nations.

In Witness Whereof the undersigned plenipotentiaries, being duly authorised thereto by their respective Governments have signed the present Convention.

Bibliography

Administrative Staff College of India (Child Labour Action and Support Project), Eliminating child labour through community mobilisation: A study on an NGO's efforts to eliminate child labour in the carpet industry in Mirzapur, India, New Delhi, ILO, 1996.

Ashagrie, K., "Statistics on child labour: A brief report", in Bulletin of Labour Statistics, Geneva, ILO Bureau of Statistics, No. 1993-3, 1993.

Boudhiba Abdelwahab, Exploitation of Child Labour: Final Report of the Special Rapporteur of the United Nations Sub-Commission on Prevention of Discrimination and Protection of Minorities, Geneva: UN, 1983.

Chhetri, Devendra, *Child Issues and Poverty in Nepal*, APROSC & IDRC, December 1996, Kathmandu.

David C. Pitt. "Child Labour and Health," in Usha S. Naidu and Kamini Kapadia (eds.). *Child Labour and Health: Problems and Prospects*, Bombay: Tata Institute of Social Sciences, 1985.

Department of Women and Child Development, Government of India., Child prostitution—In the twilight, Report of the Central Advisory, Committee on Child Prostitution, India, 1994.

Dingwaney, M., Bonded labour in India, New Delhi, Rural Labour Cell, 1987.

Elias Mendelievich, "Explosion of Child Exploitation in South Asia", SAARC Link, No. 2, 1993.

Hammarberg, Thomas, A School for Children with Rights: The significance of the United Nations Convention on the Rights of the Child for modern education policy, Innocenti Lectures, UNICEF International Child Development Centre, Florence, 1997.

Haq, Mahbub ul, and Khadija Haq, Human Development in South Asia 1998, The Human Development Centre, Karachi, April 1998.

Human Indian Social Institute, Freedom from Bondage: Citizens Commission Bonded and Child Labour, First National Convention, New Delhi, 1995.

Ministry of Labour, Report of the Committee on Child Labour, Nasik: Government of India Press, 1979.

Ministry of Women and Children Affairs, Poverty Reduction in South Asia: Promoting Participation by the Poor. Informal workshop cosponsored by the World Bank and the South Asia Association for Regional Cooperation (SAARC), 1991.

Pradhan, Gauri (ed.), *Misery Behind the Looms: Child Labourers in the Carpet Factories in Nepal*, CWIN. Kathmandu, 1993.

Sattaur, O., *Child labour in Nepal,* London, Anti-Slavery International, 1993.

Satyarthi, K., *Break the chains, save the childhood*, New Delhi, South Asian Coalition Child Servitude, 1994.

Teddy Arellano, "Child Labour in South Asia", *Asian Labour Update.* Issue 14, January-March, 1994.

UNICEF, *The State of the World's Children* 1997, UNICEF, New York, 1996.

Index